NUMBERS

PREACHING THE WORD
Edited by R. Kent Hughes

Genesis: Beginning and Blessing

Exodus: Saved for God's Glory
by Philip Graham Ryken

Leviticus: Holy God, Holy People
by Kenneth A. Mathews

Deuteronomy: Loving Obedience to a Loving God
by Ajith Fernando

1 Samuel: Looking for a Leader
by John Woodhouse

Proverbs: Wisdom that Works
by Raymond C. Ortlund Jr.

Ecclesiastes: Why Everything Matters
by Philip Graham Ryken

Isaiah: God Saves Sinners
by Raymond C. Ortlund Jr.

Jeremiah and Lamentations: From Sorrow to Hope
by Philip Graham Ryken

Daniel: The Triumph of God's Kingdom
by Rodney D. Stortz

Mark: Jesus, Servant and Savior, 2 vols

Luke: That You May Know the Truth, 2 vols

John: That You May Believe

Acts: The Church Afire

Romans: Righteousness from Heaven

2 Corinthians: Power in Weakness

Ephesians: The Mystery of the Body of Christ

Philippians: The Fellowship of the Gospel

Colossians and Philemon: The Supremacy of Christ

1 & 2 Thessalonians: The Hope of Salvation
by James H. Grant Jr.

1 & 2 Timothy and Titus: To Guard the Deposit
by R. Kent Hughes and Bryan Chapell

Hebrews: An Anchor for the Soul, 2 vols

James: Faith That Works

1 & 2 Peter and Jude: Sharing Christ's Sufferings
by David R. Helm

Revelation: The Spirit Speaks to the Churches
by James M. Hamilton Jr.

The Sermon on the Mount: The Message of the Kingdom

Unless otherwise indicated, all volumes are by R. Kent Hughes

(((PREACHING *the* WORD)))

NUMBERS

GOD'S PRESENCE *in* *the* WILDERNESS

IAIN M. DUGUID

R. Kent Hughes
Series Editor

WHEATON, ILLINOIS

Numbers

Copyright © 2006 by Iain M. Duguid

Published by Crossway
        1300 Crescent Street
        Wheaton, Illinois 60187

Cover design: Jon McGrath, Simplicated Studio

Cover image: Adam Greene, illustrator

First printing 2006

Reprinted with new cover 2012

Printed in the United States of America

ISBN-13: 978-1-4335-3548-2
ISBN-10: 1-4335-3548-3
PDF ISBN: 978-1-4335-1334-3
Mobipocket ISBN: 978-1-4335-0841-7
ePub ISBN: 978-1-4335-1860-7

Library of Congress Cataloging-in-Publication Data

Duguid, Iain M.
    Numbers : God's presence in the wilderness / Iain M. Duguid,
R. Kent Hughes, general editor.
      p.   cm.—(Preaching the word)
    Includes bibliographical references and indexe.
    ISBN-13: 978-1-58134-363-2
    ISBN-10: 1-58134-363-9 (hc : alk. paper)
    1. Bible. O.T. Numbers—Commentaries. I. Hughes, R. Kent. II. Title.
III. Series.
BS1265.53.D84   2006
222'.1407—dc22   2006000485

Crossway is a publishing ministry of Good News Publishers.

TS		22	21	20	19	18	17	16	15	14	13	12
15	14	13	12	11	10	9	8	7	6	5	4	3	2	1

To

Jack & Kay Dundas, Ken & Yoori Han, Paul & Cindy Keck,
Rick & Janny Ligtenberg, Gerry & Lori Marinucci,
and Ray & Bette Sammons

As godly elders and elders' wives,
you have been a gift of the Lord's grace to the ministry of
Grace Presbyterian Church, Fallbrook

Contents

"The LORD bless you and keep you;
the LORD make his face to shine upon you
and be gracious to you;
the LORD lift up his countenance upon you
and give you peace."

NUMBERS 6:24-26

A Word to Those Who Preach the Word

There are times when I am preaching that I have especially sensed the pleasure of God. I usually become aware of it through the unnatural silence. The ever-present coughing ceases, and the pews stop creaking, bringing an almost physical quiet to the sanctuary—through which my words sail like arrows. I experience a heightened eloquence, so that the cadence and volume of my voice intensify the truth I am preaching.

There is nothing quite like it—the Holy Spirit filling one's sails, the sense of his pleasure, and the awareness that something is happening among one's hearers. This experience is, of course, not unique, for thousands of preachers have similar experiences, even greater ones.

What has happened when this takes place? How do we account for this sense of his smile? The answer for me has come from the ancient rhetorical categories of *logos*, *ethos*, and *pathos*.

The first reason for his smile is the *logos*—in terms of preaching, God's Word. This means that as we stand before God's people to proclaim his Word, we have done our homework. We have exegeted the passage, mined the significance of its words in their context, and applied sound hermeneutical principles in interpreting the text so that we understand what its words meant to its hearers. And it means that we have labored long until we can express in a sentence what the theme of the text is—so that our outline springs from the text. Then our preparation will be such that as we preach, we will not be preaching our own thoughts about God's Word, but God's actual Word, his *logos*. This is fundamental to pleasing him in preaching.

The second element in knowing God's smile in preaching is *ethos*—what you are as a person. There is a danger endemic to preaching, which is having your hands and heart cauterized by holy things. Phillips Brooks illustrated it by the analogy of a train conductor who comes to believe that he has been to the places he announces because of his long and loud heralding of them. And that is why Brooks insisted that preaching must be "the bringing of truth through personality." Though we can never *perfectly* embody the truth we preach, we must be subject to it, long for it, and make it as much a part of our ethos as possible. As the Puritan William Ames said, "Next to the Scriptures, nothing makes a sermon more to pierce, than when it comes out of the inward affection of the heart without any affectation." When a preacher's *ethos* backs up his *logos*, there will be the pleasure of God.

Last, there is *pathos*—personal passion and conviction. David Hume, the Scottish philosopher and skeptic, was once challenged as he was seen going to hear George Whitefield preach: "I thought you do not believe in the gospel." Hume replied, "I don't, but *he does*." Just so! When a preacher believes what he preaches, there will be passion. And this belief and requisite passion will know the smile of God.

The pleasure of God is a matter of *logos* (the Word), *ethos* (what you are), and *pathos* (your passion). As you *preach the Word* may you experience his smile—the Holy Spirit in your sails!

R. Kent Hughes
Wheaton, Illinois

Preface

Before I began work on this volume, I had little exposure to the book of Numbers. I had never preached on a text from Numbers, nor, as far as I know, had I ever even heard a sermon on the book of Numbers. According to my anecdotal surveys of other pastors, I am far from being alone in that regard. When I told another Old Testament professor that I was currently preaching through the book, he expressed the opinion that it was scarcely meant to be preached. I'm sure he was simply saying out loud what many pastors have thought, and at times during the past eighteen months I have been tempted to sympathize with that opinion.

However, I hold firmly to another conviction that trumps any practical difficulties, the conviction that "All Scripture is breathed out by God and profitable for teaching, for reproof, for correction, and for training in righteousness, that the man of God may be competent, equipped for every good work" (2 Timothy 3:16, 17). In addition, I understand the central message of the Scriptures from beginning to end to be the sufferings of Christ and the glories that would follow (1 Peter 1:10, 11; see Luke 24:44-47). I believe that a Christ-centered approach to preaching, which seeks to explore the way in which Old Testament passages prepare for and foreshadow the gospel, makes its truths accessible again to God's people. This approach feeds the hearts and souls of believers, as well as challenging unbelievers, with the result that even less familiar passages can speak powerfully to our congregations.

What I found as I proceeded was that the book of Numbers confronted us week by week with the challenge to live faithfully as pilgrims and aliens in a wilderness world and the encouragement to look to the One who has gone through this wilderness world ahead of us. I would therefore like to thank Dr. Kent Hughes for the generous invitation to write this book and undertake the challenge of preaching through the book of Numbers. Thanks are due, too, to Ted Griffin and the staff at Crossway for their help in the production of the book.

I would also like to thank the people of Grace Presbyterian Church, Fallbrook for being such eager hearers of God's Word. Every preacher needs people who have the gift of listening, and it has been a delight to preach the unsearchable riches of God's Word to you and to see your evident love for Christ and his gospel week after week. As I leave this pastoral position and move to a college teaching ministry at Grove City College in Pennsylvania, I will miss you all. Special thanks are due to my co-pastor Ken Han, who has shared the ministry with me for the past two years and will continue to feed the flock there faithfully from God's Word.

Finally, the greatest thanks are due to my family. My wife, Barb, is my truest friend, constantly reminding me of my own desperate need of a Savior and pointing me to God's grace, while my children are a wonderful encouragement to me as they grow in their knowledge of and delight in God's Word. As a father, my greatest joy is to see my children walking in the truth.

Iain Duguid
January 2006

1

In the Wilderness

NUMBERS 1:1

SPORTS COME IN MANY DIFFERENT LEVELS OF COMPLEXITY. At the simplest level, some sports are easily understood by everyone. What is complex about the 100 meter dash? Someone shoots a gun, the athletes run as if the man was firing at them, and the one who breaks the tape first wins. The next level up is baseball. Once again, it is a fairly straightforward game to follow, at least in broad outline. You hit the ball, you run, and you try to get all the way around the diamond. The field positions are easily comprehensible from their names: right field, center field, left field, first, second, and third base, and so on. More complex still is American football. The first time I watched it, I had no clue what was going on. The players kept stopping and starting inexplicably, while the umpires were constantly throwing their handkerchiefs in the air. Why in the world did they do that? Why is a tight end called a tight end? What is the difference between a fullback and a halfback? I've been watching for years now, and I still don't know the answers to some of these questions.

However, when it comes to truly complex sports, there is nothing to match cricket. None of the fielding position names make any obvious sense: there is a third man, but no first man or second man, and the long leg may be only five feet, two inches in height. If you are batting on a sticky wicket and fail to distinguish between a googly and a leg-break, you may end up caught in the slips or at silly mid-on. Are you following me? What other sport could be played for five full days and still end in a draw because they ran out of time? The uninitiated novice certainly needs an experienced guide to comprehend the complexities of England's national summer pastime.

It is the same way with literature: it comes in differing levels of complexity. At one end of the range, you have the simplicity of a children's story, like *The Tale of Peter Rabbit*. At the other, there is the mammoth and sprawling canvas of books like The Lord of the Rings, which comes complete with interspersed songs about totally unrelated events from the fictional history of Middle-Earth and citations in several completely fabricated languages such as Dwarf and Elvish. It is a daunting step upward from Peter Rabbit to The Lord of the Rings, and still further to complex Russian novels like *War and Peace* or *Crime and Punishment*, where every character seems to have at least three different names and a deeply tortured relationship with his or her soul. When you read such books, there are often times when you wish for an accompanying wizard to shed a little light on what is going on.

The Book of Numbers—a Complex Book

The Bible too is made up of books of varying complexity or, perhaps, different kinds of profundity. Even the simplest tale in the Bible, such as the epic battle of David and Goliath, is actually far more profound on close reading than it at first appears. The Bible is, to paraphrase something Augustine once said, shallow enough for a child to paddle in and yet at the same time deep enough to drown an elephant. There are really no simple tales in the Bible. Yet even having said that, there are some books of the Bible where the elephant will disappear from view more easily and in which the child sees little benefit in splashing.

The Book of Numbers is certainly no Peter Rabbit story: it is a complex and involved tale that, like Tolkien's mines of Moria, seems likely to swallow up the unwary. At the same time, however, this too is the Word of God, all of which is inspired and profitable for reproof, correction, and training in righteousness (2 Timothy 3:16). There is a blessing attached to the reading and hearing of God's Word, and it is my prayer that over the course of these chapters, with the guiding of the Holy Spirit, we will unfold some of the riches of this book.

The Book of Numbers—a Christ-Centered Book

Nor is the book of Numbers simply a book about ancient Old Testament history. The gospel is not a New Testament invention; on the contrary, it is the center of the whole Bible. When Jesus caught up with the dispirited disciples on the road to Emmaus that first Easter Sunday, he rebuked them for being "foolish" and "slow of heart" because they had failed to recognize that fact (Luke 24:25). Then, taking them on a tour of the Old Testament, beginning with Moses (Genesis to Deuteronomy) and continuing through all the Prophets (Joshua to Malachi), he showed them how obvious it should have been that the Christ had to suffer death and then enter his glory (vv.

26, 27). Sometimes we may wish that we had been able to eavesdrop on that conversation, because it may not always be immediately obvious to us as we skim the book of Numbers exactly how this book points to the sufferings of Christ and the glories that will follow. Yet if we approach the book with an understanding of this apostolic hermeneutical key,[1] we will find that what seemed at first sight dusty and irrelevant antiquities open up their pages to us and yield rich food for our souls.

An Overview of the Book of Numbers

To begin our study, we need to get a perspective of the big picture of the book. This is one book of the Bible where it is extremely helpful to have a sense of the overall organization of the book before we plunge into the details. This is all the more important, paradoxically enough, precisely because the book at first sight doesn't seem to have much order to it. We look in vain for a developing plot line, with a beginning, a middle, and an end. This is a different kind of story from the ones with which we are familiar. It is a story that doesn't really have a beginning. Grammatically it starts in mid-sentence, as it were, with a Hebrew narrative form that usually links back to the preceding verb. That is because the book of Numbers wants you to know that it never existed as an independent narrative: it is itself a continuation of the story of God's dealings with his people already begun in Genesis, Exodus, and Leviticus.

Nor does the book of Numbers really have much of an ending: it seems to peter out with the story of the request by Zelophehad's daughters that they too might share in their father's inheritance, even though they had no brothers (36:1-13). We'll see later why that is, after all, a fitting ending to the book, but it is not exactly a resounding conclusion. Contrast that with the book of Genesis, which begins in the Garden of Eden and ends with a coffin in Egypt. There is movement there—a story. Or consider the book of Exodus, which begins with Israel enslaved in Egypt and ends with them set free to worship the Lord, who is present in their midst in the tabernacle, just as he promised. There's a story there.

Two Generations in the Wilderness

The book of Numbers, however, starts out in the wilderness and ends up in the wilderness. In fact, the Hebrew name for this biblical book, fittingly enough, is precisely that: "In the Wilderness." Israel started out the book of Numbers on the brink of the Promised Land, being counted for the holy war that would be required to enter, and they ended it still on the brink of the Promised Land, ready to have another chance to enter into the enjoyment of what God had promised. In between the beginning and the end are thirty-six chapters of wandering, chapters that cover some forty years and record the lives of a whole generation. Yet at the end of the book, even though geographically the Israelites had progressed in three stages from the sojourn at the wilderness of Sinai (Num. 1:1—10:10), by way of the journey to Kadesh-barnea (10:11—20:1), and then on to the plains of Moab (20:1—36:13), they had in some ways simply come full circle, back to where they started. They are still in the wilderness, waiting to enter the Promised Land. The essentially circular narrative structure, lacking in progress, is not an error or failure on the author's part but is a mark of his literary skill, a part of his message.

In fact, though, the end is not quite a complete return to the beginning. The book of Numbers is essentially the story of two generations.[2] Each generation undergoes a census in the book: the first generation at the beginning of the book, and the second generation in Numbers 26. Numbers 1—25 is the story of the first generation—a story of unbelief, rebellion, despair, and death. It shows us what happens to the generation that refuses to place their trust in the Lord in spite of his manifest trustworthiness: they are unable to enter his rest, and their bodies are scattered over the wilderness. Numbers 27—36, though, starts the story of the next generation, a story that begins and ends with Zelophehad's daughters, whose appeal for an inheritance is the first issue to be addressed in the beginning of that story in Numbers 27 and the last to be covered as the book concludes in Numbers 36. These women of faith are emblematic of the new generation because they were deeply concerned about ensuring that their descendants would have an inheritance in the Promised Land—even though not one inch of it had yet been won by Israel at the time when they first raised the issue in Numbers 27. Zelophehad's daughters believed firmly in the promises of God, and so they acted in faith on those promises, claiming a share in the future inheritance of God's people for themselves and for their children too. So, in broad terms we may say that the story of the book of Numbers is the story of two consecutive generations, a generation of unbelief that leads to death and a generation of faith that will lead to life.[3]

A People Living Between Salvation Accomplished and Salvation Consummated

We're going to explore all of this in much more detail in the chapters ahead, but for now I just want to pick out a couple of fundamental observations that follow from the opening verse of the book and its overall structure. The first verse runs like this:

> The LORD spoke to Moses in the wilderness of Sinai, in the tent of meeting, on the first day of the second month, in the second year after they had come out of the land of Egypt.

The story of the book of Numbers is written to a people whose lives are lived between the accomplishing of their redemption and its consummation, between the exodus and the Promised Land. The book starts by identifying this people as those who came out of Egypt. The story of the book of Numbers essentially picks up where the books of Genesis and Exodus left off. God chose for himself the family of Abraham and redeemed them from their bondage in Egypt. He then brought them into the wilderness to Mount Sinai where he graciously entered into a covenant with them. They were to be his people, and he would be their God. As a token of that promise, he gave them the tabernacle, a tent in which he would dwell in their midst. The Lord has done what he promised Abraham in bringing his descendants out of their bondage—but he has not yet brought them into the Promised Land. They live in between the times, and their present experience is not one of the fullness of their salvation but rather of the wilderness along the way.

This should all sound familiar to us. We live as they did—between salvation accomplished and salvation completed. We live between the work of God in accomplishing our salvation at the cross and the time when that salvation will be brought to its consummation when Christ returns. We too live between the times. What is more, our experience of this world is likewise one of wilderness rather than fullness. Jesus promised his disciples one sure thing in this world—tribulation (John 16:33), and he has been faithful to his promise. Wars, sickness, sin, broken relationships, misunderstandings, pain, tears—all of these are part of our experience in this world. We should surely therefore be able to identify with the experiences and temptations of the first wilderness generation.

However, as we journey toward the consummation of our salvation when Christ returns, there is one other certainty that Jesus promised his disciples, isn't there? Jesus promised us his presence with us in the wilderness: "Behold, I am with you always, to the end of the age" (Matthew 28:20). This too matches Israel's experience in the wilderness, for God did not bring them out of Egypt and then abandon them to make their own way through the wilderness. The provision he made for them in the tabernacle in the wilderness should therefore speak to us also, for we have God's presence with us through his Holy Spirit.

The Temptation to Lose the Plot

What are the chief temptations of life in the wilderness? The first temptation is surely the danger of losing the plot. The people of Israel were constantly tempted to doubt that there really was a Promised Land ahead. All they could see with their eyes was the barrenness of the wilderness. All they could hear with their ears was the howling wasteland around them. All they could taste on their tongues was the hunger and thirst of the wilderness. The wilderness was very real, and the obstacles in terms of opposition and lack of resources were very visible, while the Promised Land seemed very remote. Life must often have seemed to be a succession of completely unrelated and random events that were getting them nowhere. They surely felt as if their whole lives were slipping away from them in one meaningless round of unsatisfying experiences.

Isn't that somewhat like our lives? The surface structure of our lives often appears chaotic and random, just one frustration after another, like the surface narrative of the book of Numbers. You wake up, you go to work, you go home, you go to bed. There is never enough time to get everything done, never enough money to meet all your commitments, never enough of you left for yourself or to give to others. Events that God could so easily have orchestrated to make your life more straightforward regularly become tangled and twisted. This life is often a chaotic wilderness.

So what is life all about? Sometimes we are tempted to believe that the wilderness we see is really all there is: that when all is said and done, there is no guiding purpose or meaning to this world. Our lives appear as meaningless as the game of cricket is to the uninitiated: days full of incomprehensible activity that at the end of them accomplish exactly nothing. Yet the deeper structure of the book of Numbers points us in a different direction. On the surface our lives may seem to wander from one place to the next, driven apparently off-course by our grumbling and sin and the vicissitudes of fate. Yet under and through and behind it all, there is a guiding hand, a divine author, who holds the whole grand narrative in his hand and brings it around to the ending he himself has written for us. There is a story line to our personal stories, an intricate plot that will, after all of life's twists and turns, end up with him bringing us into the place he has prepared for us. That is the reality to which we need to firmly hold.

The Need to Live by Faith

That is what it means to live by faith: to affirm the reality of God's plot for our lives even when we cannot see it with our eyes. The first generation did not live by that faith; they believed their eyes and distrusted and abandoned God and so experienced the bitterness of death in the wilderness. The second generation, however, had a new opportunity to begin again on that journey and start afresh to live by faith. The story of the next generation has just begun at the end of the book of Numbers. The end of their story is left open because the writer is not simply interested in recording the faith or folly of ancient generations. He is far more concerned to challenge us as to our faith in God's promises. As Paul put it in 1 Corinthians 10:6, after summarizing the wilderness experience, "Now these things took place as examples for us, that we might not desire evil as they did." The question for us, therefore, is: "Do we believe the Word of God, and are we consistently willing to act upon it, whether or not it makes sense to those around us?" The lives of faithful pilgrims show the indelible marks of their faith. Their lives are utterly inexplicable unless the Word of God is true and Heaven is their ultimate destination. Everyone around them can see that they have staked everything on the faithfulness of God to do what he has promised. In contrast, others live as if their lives are simply tied to eking out the best existence they can in the wilderness, as if this really is all there is.

It is profoundly challenging to ask ourselves how our lives would be different on Monday morning if there were no Heaven. I suspect that for most of us the answer would be, "Not much." That's why we grumble so much about the food and the accommodations along the way, as if this temporary way station were really our home. That's why our lives are not radically different from the non-Christians all around us. We've lost the plot of our story and have forgotten that we are in the middle of an incredible exodus from death to life, a journey from the city of destruction to our heavenly home.

Keeping Faith Alive: the Presence of the Lord

How do we keep faith alive in the wilderness? How do we hang on to the plot? The answer is surely that we must remember and respect the presence of our holy God in our midst.[4] It is therefore no coincidence that having identified the people as those who have come out of Egypt, the other item that Numbers 1:1 mentions is the presence of God, who speaks to Moses in the Tent of Meeting. The Tent of Meeting is another name for the tabernacle, a name that focuses our attention on its function as the place of communication from God to man. We follow a God who speaks, who orders the existence of his people. The Lord is the one who orders their lives; he is the one who commands their worship. That is why blocks of law are regularly interspersed with narrative throughout the book of Numbers, to remind us that the God who is with us is our covenant overlord who demands our obedience. The God who dwells in the midst of his people is holy.

To keep your life in this present wilderness on track, you need to orient it constantly around the presence of God. You need to seek his face daily, reading his Word, the place where he promises to meet with us and communicate to us by his Spirit, just as the Israelites went individually to the Tent of Meeting to seek the Lord (Exodus 33:7). However, the primary focus of the tabernacle was not as an individual meeting place with God. The tabernacle was the place of corporate worship, where the tribes of Israel worshiped together. There is no place for becoming isolated in the wilderness: isolated believers will die alone in the desert. We need each other and the encouragement and challenge that comes from the church gathered together.

In order to keep a firm hold on the plot of life, we therefore need to come together as God's people weekly to celebrate his redemption, to remember the exodus that Jesus accomplished for us through his incarnation, perfect obedience, crucifixion, resurrection, and ascension, and to remind ourselves of the place he has gone to prepare for us. Our hearts need to be constantly refreshed by his gospel announced in the preaching of the Word and tasted in the Lord's Supper. Our lives need to be re-submitted to his ordering, as his Word challenges us week after week to live a life worthy of the calling we have received (Ephesians 4:1). In the wilderness, we desperately need the blessings that flow to us through the means of grace that God has established in the church.

The Centrality of the Gospel

Do you ever get tired of hearing the gospel? Is it possible to focus on it too much in church? If you think that, you are in desperate danger of losing the plot and starving to death in the desert. For the amazing truth of the gospel is that God himself has shared our wilderness wanderings with us, first in the Old Testament tabernacle and then in the person of Jesus Christ. The Word became flesh and tabernacled in our midst (John 1:14). He came from the undisturbed glories of Heaven and took on himself the frustrations and temptations of wilderness life. In fact, at the beginning of his earthly ministry, after his baptism in the Jordan, Jesus went out into the wilderness just as Israel had done for a forty-day fast (Matthew 4:1-11). In that way, he shared fully in the experiences and sufferings of his people. He went into the wilderness, where he faced exactly the same temptations that his Old Testament people had faced, but he remained faithful to the end. This was a picture of his earthly ministry in microcosm: voluntarily facing the same temptations that his people face and passing the tests that we fail. Where we grumble constantly, he never grumbled. Where we doubt God's goodness and question his provision, he never doubted or questioned.

Jesus has thus gone through the wilderness for us, as the author and perfecter of our faith (Hebrews 12:2), the one who himself accomplished our salvation. He journeyed through the wilderness not simply to show us that it could be done and that it was possible for a human being to live a life of obedience there. That would simply have added to our condemnation and sense of guilt because we have not obeyed as he did. No, the gospel is not that Jesus survived the wilderness and so can you. It is that Jesus went through the wilderness faithfully in our place, establishing the perfect righteousness that he now gives to us. His obedience credited to us as a free gift is what enables us to stand in God's presence.

What is more, having passed through the wilderness, Jesus has now ascended into Heaven to prepare a place for us. This wilderness will eventually end, to be replaced by the promised land of rest. How can you know that for sure? You can be certain of Heaven because Jesus has already reached it, and he has promised that where he is, we too shall be one day. If you are united to Christ by faith, then his destiny is yours: where he is, so shall you also be. That is the ultimate plot structure of your life. That certain assurance for the future is what then stirs our faith in the present to become like Zelophehad's daughters. We too should be those who in the midst of our present wanderings are so sure of our future inheritance that we become unbelievably bold in what we ask for by faith and incredibly eager to reach that place where our inheritance will finally be received. We should have the boldness and eagerness that comes from true faith. We should cry out, "Come, Lord Jesus, and feed our hungry hearts with your presence now. Come back, Lord Jesus, and slake our thirst for your presence with us in a communion that will never end!" This is what the book of Numbers should do for us as we study it: it should stir us up to present faith in Christ and thanksgiving to his name, along with a hunger for the end of the wilderness and the beginning of our final rest.

2

Stand Up and Be Counted

NUMBERS 1:1-46

I RECENTLY WENT TO A LARGE ONLINE BOOKSTORE to see if I could find a book entitled *The Joy of Accounting*. I didn't find it. I found *The Joy of Cooking*, *The Joy of Photography*, even *The Joy of Juicing*. But there was no book called *The Joy of Accounting*. Why in the world would that be? I wonder. The answer is, perhaps, that for most people accounting—organizing endless columns of numbers—doesn't seem like all that much fun. Now before some of you besiege me with protestations that accounting is really far more complicated than that and that accountants are profoundly interesting people with hearts and souls as well, let me hasten to agree with you. My own sister and brother-in-law are accountants. Accountants are wonderful people who are immensely useful in society. But admit the point: not many schoolchildren fantasize about growing up to be accountants. They want to be teachers and nurses, firemen and astronauts, sports heroes and presidents . . . but not accountants. For all its strong points as a career path, there is not much glamour and glitz in that profession.

That is one reason why our eyes instantly glaze over at the sight of lists of names and numbers such as we find in Numbers 1. It looks like a runaway accounting file. What spiritual truths could possibly be lurking in this passage, or even in a book that contains such passages? This certainly does not seem at first sight to be a promising text in which to spend our time. Some of us are perhaps thinking that we should have chosen to study the book of Romans instead. In reality, though, our first response to this passage is profoundly wrong. Our society actually loves lists of names and numbers every bit as complex and apparently obscure as this one. All we need to make the list jump to life are keys to understanding what the list is all about and why it is relevant to our situation.

The Joy of Numbers

Let me begin by showing that each one of us has some area of life where we obsess about names and numbers. We could start with the daily newspaper. Turn to the sports pages, and what else is there but names and numbers? Baseball is all about RBIs, ERAs, and slugging percentages. Football is rushing yards, third down completions, and interceptions. Next turn to the business section. There you will encounter the Dow Jones Index and the S&P 500. There is the Price/Earnings data and year on year growth. Perhaps, though, we are not investors or sports fans. Consider the advertisements section. There we find yet more lists of items and numbers. Some of those numbers describe performance data (256 gigabytes, 172 horsepower, 72-inch screens, 1 carat diamonds, 24 cubic feet capacity, and so on); some of it is price data (50 percent off; buy one, get one free). The newspapers wouldn't fill their pages with lists of names and numbers if everyone's eyes glazed over whenever they saw such lists. They publish them precisely because they know that in certain areas that are of personal interest to us we are intensely fascinated by lists.

Let me add one more example for those (like my wife) who still think that I haven't included them. Let me rehearse a fairly typical domestic conversation for you. Myself: "Honey, I just got a call from Brian to say that Julie had her baby." My wife: "Tell me all about it." Myself: "She had a boy." My wife: "When was he born? What's his name? How long is he? What was his weight? How long was the labor?" Myself: "Ummm . . ." Believe me, we all have some area of life in which names and numbers mean a great deal to us—the exact same statistics that to an "outsider" may seem to be boring and irrelevant details.

The Message in the Numbers

The problem with this text is therefore not that it consists of a list of names and numbers. Rather, it is simply that we come to the text like non-sports fans to the baseball pages, clueless about the vital meaning of the numbers contained there. Once we learn what the numbers are about and what these stats tell us, then it will all make sense and come to life. So what is this set of names and numbers all about?

First, this set of names and numbers is about commitment. In the United States, the government takes a census every ten years. There are two main reasons for doing this: they want to know how many resources they have and how many resources they need. A census tells us how many people should pay taxes and could theoretically be drafted to fight in our armed forces, and also how many roads and schools and senators each town and state should have.[1] By means of a census, we find out how many citizens we have in our country, how many people are willing to "stand up and be counted," as we say. Those are the people who contribute resources to the community and who we need to ensure have resources available to them.

It was basically the same in the ancient world. The primary reasons to take a census in the ancient world were for taxation and for military planning. You wanted to know how many people you could call up to fight for you in case of need and how much money you could raise from them. Think of some well-known censuses from Biblical times. Why did Caesar Augustus order a census throughout the Roman Empire when Quirinius was governor of Syria, at the time when Jesus was born (Luke 2:1, 2)? It was because the Romans wanted to check their tax records. Why did King David want to count the people in the book of Samuel? It was because he wanted to know how many fighting men he had (2 Samuel 24:2). What then does it mean for Israel to be numbered here in the book of Numbers? It was an opportunity and obligation for them to say, "I'm here. If there are taxes to be paid, you know where to find me. If there is a war to fight, I'm on your list. You can count on me."

Of course, that kind of commitment is not always willingly given. That's why censuses have often been unpopular, both then and now. Not everyone wants to be counted in and counted on. People try to dodge being tallied one way or another, precisely because they don't want to have to be committed to their community. But we read of no census dodgers in Numbers 1: everyone was on board; everyone was willing to stand up and be counted. They were willing to be identified by name as part of the community and to pay the cost that went with being a member of the people of God.

Edge-Bounded Groups

Sociologists tell us that there are essentially two ways in which people come together into groups. There are edge-bounded groups and center-focused groups. Center-focused groups are organizations in which the glue that holds the group together is a common interest or center, around which the group comes together. So the Audubon Society comes together because everyone there is excited about birds, while those in an operatic society meet because they share a common love of opera. In a center-focused group, everyone can tell you what holds the group together, but they can't necessarily put an exact count on who is in the group and who is outside. The edge of the group may well be rather fuzzy, with people moving in and out around the fringes.

An edge-bounded group, on the other hand, has a clearly defined boundary. Everyone in the group knows who is in and who is out, though they may not be equally clear on what this particular group has in common. The family is an edge-bounded group: you either are part of the family or you are not. There are no fuzzy boundaries. Yet it is not always clear what this disparate mass of individuals have in common, particularly once you get up to the level of extended family. We are so different in our interests, in our beliefs, in our concerns, and yet we are all part of the same family. People can come into the family through birth or marriage, and they can leave the family through death, divorce, or being disinherited, but there is no fuzzy middle. With an edge-bounded group, you are either in or out.

So what kind of group is the people of God? Numbers 1 shows us that the people of God is an edge-bounded group. It is a family. You are either in or you are out. Nowhere is that clearer than when there is a census among the people of God. A census presses the question, "Are you in or are you out? Do you want to be counted in or do you want to be excommunicated? What's it going to be?" We will see in the next chapter that the people of God make up an edge-bounded group that is also center-focused, but here in Numbers 1 the focus is on the people of God as an edge-bounded group. To be counted means being identified as part of the people of God, with all of its responsibilities and privileges.

This is true just as much for the present-day people of God as it was for Old Testament Israel. The church, which Paul calls "the Israel of God," is God's family or household (Galatians 6:16). It is a flock, a fellowship of people who are bonded together in covenant with God and with one another. It is a group with defined limits, and you are either inside or outside. Otherwise the book of Acts could hardly have talked about specific numbers of people being added to the church (e.g., 2:41).

Responsibilities and Privileges

So what responsibilities and privileges go with being part of the people of God? The first responsibility that came with being part of God's people was giving. There is mention in Exodus 38:21-31 of a similar census[2] that took place during the previous year in the wilderness wanderings, a census that provided many of the materials for the construction of the tabernacle. Everyone who was counted had to contribute exactly the same amount to the Lord's work: one half shekel. If you were to be part of the community, anticipating the blessings of the inheritance that would come to you as part of God's people, you had to contribute financially to support the work of the ministry. There are responsibilities that go with being part of the people of God.

The purpose of this new census in Numbers 1, though, was not to raise money. It was to get organized for war, which is the second responsibility that comes with being part of God's people. That purpose is prominent throughout the listing: Moses was not to count everyone but only those men twenty years and older, who would serve in the army (1:3, 22, 24, etc.). Unlike some similar census lists in the ancient world, there was no upper age limit to those who were to be counted.[3] This was one war in which there was no exemption for senior citizens. All those who could fight, should fight, and the census was a means of finding out who they were and how many they were.

Total Commitment

The idea of the kind of total commitment that this census embodies is not a popular one in the modern world, not even in the modern Christian world. We live in a world where advertisers promise us "Nothing more to buy" or "No annual contract." People don't stay with the same employer for life or live in the same town in which they grew up. In many cases they don't even remain with the same partner for life. In our modern world we live very disconnected lives in which it is easy for us to become fragmented individuals, only loosely connected to other people.

You see exactly the same problem in the church: people float from one fellowship to the next, loosely connecting with those who attend there, hanging around on the fringes, but never really coming in and being committed. Many today don't want to stand up and be counted as part of any particular church, with the obligations and benefits that come with it. One of the attractions of worshiping at a mega-church is that you can be anonymous, slipping in and out unobserved. The vision of the counted people of God in Numbers 1 challenges this aspect of modern society. The church's motto is not, "Brethren, hang loose." We are to be a family of insiders, people who have made a commitment to one another and a commitment to this particular expression of God's people, with all of its faults and foibles and quirks. That's what being family is.

That is not to say there are never legitimate reasons for leaving one church and joining another. Certainly not! We may need to leave a church if we discover that it is built on significantly flawed theological foundations, or that the gospel is not being faithfully preached in a way that feeds our souls, or that we cannot trust those in leadership to shepherd our souls faithfully. But we should only leave in order to find a place where we can truly cleave. Our goal must always be to find an expression of the family of God where we can fit and commit. The inheritance of the saints toward which we press is not a vision of myself and Jesus sitting down at a table for two: it is a vision of the people of God gathered together to feast with him. That is our equivalent of the inheritance in the Promised Land that God's Old Testament people were pressing toward. What we press toward is not an individual heavenly cottage in a clearing in the forest but rather a place in the midst of the city of God, surrounded by his people, worshiping together at his throne. Now if this is what Heaven is, and if we are truly excited about that prospect, then its realization must also be something for which we strive constantly while we are here on earth.

That is why church membership is an important step to take. It is the equivalent of standing up to be counted in the census. When you become a member of a local fellowship, you are saying to them, "You can count me in. You can count on my contributing my resources to this community of believers, and I'd like you to count me when you think about the flock you are watching over." You are saying that you are going to contribute as much as you are able to the work of ministry in that place, both in terms of financial support and using your own personal spiritual gifts to edify and build up that particular expression of Christ's body. You are saying that you are joining up with that battalion of Christ's army in the spiritual warfare that engages all of us, young and old, men and women. You are saying, "I'm going to fight alongside this family, wrestling together in prayer, reaching out together with the good news, tending the wounded with love and care, sounding the trumpet of God's greatness together with you in worship." God's people still need to stand up and be counted.

The Privilege of Belonging

However, this census in the book of Numbers is not just a call to commitment. It is not simply a paraphrase of John F. Kennedy's famous challenge: "Ask not what your God can do for you; ask what you can do for your God." In fact, it is quite the reverse. The first privilege of being counted is precisely that of belonging to a family. The people of God were not counted as 600,000 disparate individuals, essentially disconnected from one another. The individuals were counted family by family, clan by clan, tribe by tribe. To be in the people of God was to fit somewhere in this order that God had set up, with other members of the family of God around you. The only way to be part of Israel was to be part of a family network.

What makes this striking is that not all of these family members necessarily came into Israel's family by birth. When Israel came out of Egypt, a multitude of others came with them (Exodus 12:38). Many who had seen the Lord's power wanted out of the bondage of Egypt. Others also sought to join them on their pilgrimage for a variety of personal reasons. Even at the very first Passover, there were outsiders who wanted to join them; so there needed to be regulations about how they could participate in the feast (Exodus 12:48). Yet Moses was not instructed to create a thirteenth tribe, a kind of Israelite Foreign Legion, for the ragtag assortment of strays and immigrants who wanted to be part of what God was doing. On the contrary, in order to be part of Israel, you not only had to be part of one of the twelve tribes but part of a family and clan as well. These strays who joined Israel, who were circumcised and came by faith to Israel's God, had to be welcomed into the family structure, where they fully became a part of the people of God.

The second privilege that came with being part of the people of God was having a share in the division of the Promised Land. This was the greatest blessing of being in God's people. To be counted in the census meant that when your tribe and your family and your clan received an assignment in the Promised Land, you would be listed there too. Even those who had been adopted into the family structure of Israel would receive an inheritance along with their adoptive family. Being counted as part of Israel thus meant the prospect of an inheritance among the Lord's people when they reached the land of Canaan. This was, after all, the goal of the whole exodus, the end for which they had begun their journey. Being counted in as one of the Lord's people was therefore an act of faith that what God had promised would one day be theirs, even though in the present they could not yet see it with their eyes.

The Foundation of God's Faithfulness

However, the act of faith was not a complete leap in the dark. It was a leap based on God's past faithfulness. God's faithfulness was the foundation for this census. The most prominent feature of the numbers that are returned from the accounting is their huge size![4] This was an enormous people! From the family of seventy or so that went down to Egypt in the time of Jacob and Joseph, the people of God had swelled to become an enormous nation, more than 600,000 men of fighting age, plus women and children. This is a vast host, a dramatic fulfillment of God's promises to Abraham. God had said to Abraham in Genesis 12:2, "I will make you a great nation," and he did. He had said to Abraham in Genesis 15:5, "Look toward heaven, and number the stars, if you are able to number them. . . . So shall your offspring be." In answer to that promise, here now was the host of Israel, as abundant as the stars of the sky. The Lord had said to Abraham in Genesis 17:4, "you shall be the father of a multitude of nations," and now he was.

The census was thus a tangible, physical reminder that God had been faithful to the promises he had made to multiply his people and to bring them out of Egypt (see 1:1). God had been faithful to his Word: the numbers don't lie. This should have been a source of great encouragement to God's people as they headed into battle to take the Promised Land. They certainly didn't lack the resources to do the task that God had assigned them. Since God had been faithful to his promises in the past, he could be counted on also in the future.

A Greater Fulfillment to Come

Yet even while the census figures show us God's faithfulness to his promises in the form of a concrete head count, they also leave us looking for more.

God didn't just tell Abraham he would become many, but specifically that he would become innumerable, like the stars in the sky. Paradoxically, the same counting process that shows us God's faithfulness in the past leaves us looking for a greater fulfillment in the future: Israel was huge, to be sure, but she could still be counted. Israel had come out of Egypt, just as God promised, but she had not yet received the land of promise. She had tangible tokens of God's faithfulness to do what he had promised, while at the same time being reminded that there was still more for God to do.[5] The wilderness is not Heaven; this world is not our home. However, the God who has brought us safely thus far can be trusted faithfully to complete everything that he has committed himself to do.

This is an important aspect of church membership as well. When we stand up and make vows to join the church, we do not simply commit ourselves to do our part in the spiritual battle. We first affirm our testimony that God has done his part thus far and our faith that he will continue to be faithful to his promises until our redemption is complete. We confess that when it comes to standing up and being counted, God has already done that for us. The army with which he accomplished our salvation consisted not of 600,000 men but of one single God-man, Jesus Christ. Jesus entered the wilderness of this world in our place and persevered faithfully through all of its trials and tribulations. He became part of a human family and then committed himself to twelve disciples, into whose life he poured his own. He gave everything he had to his mission—all of his financial resources and all of his personal resources. Everything he was and everything he possessed were poured out without reserve on behalf of his people.

There was nothing fringe about Jesus' involvement in the world either. On the contrary, he came into this world to fight for our lives. He entered into a spiritual battle for our souls, a battle that on the cross took the ultimate commitment on his part: "Greater love has no one than this, that someone lays down his life for his friends" (John 15:13). On the cross Jesus not only called us his family—he called us his friends. He laid down his life for us, so that we who by nature were not part of his family could be brought in. The result of his death is that those who were once strangers and aliens have now become naturalized citizens of the kingdom. Those who were once the enemies of God have become his friends and now experience the peace and blessing that flow from a living relationship with him.

It is because Jesus has committed himself to us in that extreme way that he calls us to take the extreme and countercultural step of belonging, of standing up today and being counted as part of his people in our local communities. Jesus calls us to belong to his church and to be one of his counted ones. Have we each received the gift of life from Jesus? If we have, then we can praise God for the family he has given us in our churches. With all of our faults and failings, we are God's gift to one another. We should let others know that we appreciate their presence and involvement in our churches.

If we are part of Christ's people but not yet connected with a particular local church, we should find a family that we can fight alongside. Membership in Christ's church is not restricted to those who were born insiders or to those who can pass some complicated theological entrance test. Membership in the church is open to all who simply confess their faith in Christ, to those who believe that his victory in the battle with sin is also their victory and that by faith they are insiders with God through Christ. If that is you, stand up and be counted! Be committed to a local group of believers, a fellowship where you can give your resources generously and cheerfully. Find a place where you can support the work of ministry with your financial and spiritual gifts, that the promise of God that he would establish a family without number may be fulfilled.

God will fulfill his purposes either way—with or without our help. God is going to establish his church and make it an innumerable host from all nations, tribes, and languages, a family brought together in his Son and bonded together into local fellowships. He will build his people and give them their inheritance, with or without our involvement. Yet he invites us in his grace to be counted, and thus to count: to have a part in his cosmic plan of blessing for his people and the world. Make sure your name is recorded on his list today, added to the number of those who are enrolled in his service and to the fellowship of those who are ready and eager to serve him right here in their own community and to the ends of the earth.

3

A Place for Everyone and Everyone in His Place

NUMBERS 1:47—2:34

ONE OF MY DAUGHTER'S FAVORITE TELEVISION PROGRAMS is called *Clean Sweep*. On that show a group of professionals come into an incredibly messy room and transform it into an ordered paradise, with storage places for everything and everything in those storage places. Our family, for one, could certainly use some help in that department. Perhaps some of you would be eager to volunteer for that program as well. It seems to me that the writer of the book of Numbers would have been well-qualified to work on that show. He had a mind for order and structure, an eye for a world in which everything and everyone had their place. In that appreciation for order, of course, he was simply following the lead of God himself, the one who first took formless chaos and rendered it into an ordered cosmos in Genesis 1. The creation of this universe was the original clean sweep.

The key to order, though, is not just having a place in which to put things. It is having the *right* place in which to put things. If we don't understand the writer's concern for locating everything in the right place, we may miss what is going on in this chapter. As I write this, we have just completed a sleepover for one of my sons, with a dozen or so of his friends. At bedtime we piled them all into a big bedroom and told them to find a place for their sleeping bags. We knew there was enough floor space for everyone and weren't too concerned which child occupied which piece of carpet. This chapter of the book of Numbers, however, is not content simply with everybody having a place to pitch their tent somewhere in the camp. Rather, the writer wants everyone to be in the right place, the place assigned to him by God. That is the driving vision behind this particular set of names and numbers and locations: it is designed to put people in their proper place. Essentially, what we will see in this chapter is this: first, *that* the people of God are arranged around God; second, *how* the people of God are arranged around God; and third, that the Levites were assigned the key task of standing between the people and God.

Arranged Around God

First, then, the passage shows us that the people of God are arranged around God. Sometimes important elements of a story may be so obvious that we can completely overlook them. That is the case here. The Lord instructed Moses and Aaron: "The Israelites are to camp around the Tent of Meeting" (2:2, NIV). At the very center of this vast and complicated arrangement of an enormous people was a simple reality: the presence of God was to be at the heart of everything they did. After all, the presence of God with his people was the goal of the covenant that the Lord made with Israel, in which he promised, "I will be your God, and you will be my people."

That promise was far more important to Moses than the Lord's promise of land or blessing for his people. He wanted the presence of God with them more than anything else in the whole world. Thus in Exodus 33, when the people had broken covenant with God through their sin with the golden calf, and the Lord threatened not to go with his people on their journey to Canaan lest he destroy them along the way, Moses pleaded that he would indeed be with them. God offered to send an angel to make sure they received the land he had promised them, but that offer was not enough for Moses. He responded, "If your presence will not go with me, do not bring us up from here. For how shall it be known that I have found favor in your sight, I and your people? Is it not in your going with us, so that we are distinct, I and your people, from every other people on the face of the earth?" (vv. 15, 16). Moses was saying, "Who cares about the Promised Land, or about abundant food and drink, if you are not with us, Lord? Other nations have wonderful lands in which to live, with palm trees and blue skies and abundant food. But only we are the Lord's people. The only truly distinctive thing about us as a people is your presence in our midst, Lord." God heard his prayer and answered it with an assurance that his presence would indeed be with the people. The Tent of Meeting in the center of the camp was the answer to Moses' request.

A Center-Focused Group

What this means is that the people of God is not only an edge-bounded group, an entity defined by its outer limits. It is that, as we saw in the last chapter, but it is also a center-focused group, an entity held together by a common center. The people of God, both in its Old Testament manifestation and in the church, is a fellowship focused on the reality of God's presence in our midst. Both elements that define the church—the boundary and the center—are important. The boundary line reminds us that the church is a community, and you are either inside or you are outside. There is a clear line around the perimeter of the people of God, and you need to make sure you are on the right side of it. You need to repent of your sins, trust in Christ for your salvation, and stand up and be counted as part of the fellowship of faith. Yet some churches and individuals spend so much time patrolling the boundaries of the faith that they run the risk of losing sight of the center, the guiding reality that calls us all together.

This loss of focus can happen in a variety of ways. Some people confuse crossing the physical line into the community of faith with crossing the finish line in the race of faith. They will tell you that they made a decision for Christ at a particular event or church service or that they were baptized into the church, and they think that is all they need to do. Yet Jesus did not tell us to go out into all the world to seek professions of faith but to make disciples. All of his followers, no matter how young or how old, need to be looking toward the center, pressing toward the mark, moving on in discipleship. We need to grow constantly in our knowledge of the truth, our love for all the saints, our obedience to God's Word, and our desire for our heavenly home. In fact, we can say it more strongly than that: if you are genuinely inside the community of faith, you will inevitably press on toward the goal of holy living. This is certain because Christ not only dwells in the midst of his church, he also dwells in the hearts of all of his people by his Holy Spirit. If there is no fruit of that indwelling, no movement of your heart toward Christ as the center of your life, then there is good reason to doubt whether you are genuinely on the right side of the line. Crossing the line physically into the church is the beginning of the adventure of faith, not the end of it.

Another way in which we can lose sight of the center in our zeal for the boundaries is to form a doctrinal or behavioral correctness patrol. This is not for a moment to undervalue doctrinal correctness. There is a boundary, an edge to the camp, and it is important to discern where it is. It is as ridiculous to say, "Let's all love Jesus and forget about theology" as it would be for a husband to say to his wife, "Honey, let's not talk about who we are, or the story of our lives before we met and since we came together, or what we like and what we dislike, or what our deepest hopes and dreams and aspirations are—let's not talk about any of that stuff. Let's just love each other." Such a proclamation would lead you to suspect that the man had a very shallow understanding of what a true loving relationship looks like. Doctrine and theology are our food and drink as believers, because they are the foundation for healthy growth in our relationship with God. They are the means by which we grow in a true and accurate knowledge of the God whom we profess to love. Likewise, living in accordance with God's Word will be a matter of passionate desire and great delight to the believer. Yet just as some people become overly obsessed with the food they eat, so too it is possible to become overly obsessed with minor theological details or minor lifestyle concerns to the point that we lose the big picture. We can become like the Pharisees, meticulously tithing the herbs that grow in small quantities in our gardens, while ignoring the weightier matters of our relationship with God. In our constant search for boundary transgressions, it is possible for us to lose sight of the center of the camp, God himself.

The Importance of Worship

That is why worship is so important to our hearts and souls. Worship is not just a warm-up exercise that we do on Sundays before we plunge into the rigors of the sermon, lest we pull a spiritual muscle when we attempt some theological heavy lifting. Worship is a reorientation of our souls toward the center of the camp—a reminder that God is at the heart of everything that we do and are. He is the one for whom and by whom we exist: he is our Creator, our Redeemer, and our Sustainer. The Lord is our Rock and our Refuge, our Shepherd and our Savior. Daily we need to refresh our vision of who he is, opening up the Scriptures on our own so that our hearts can be reoriented toward him. Weekly we come together with others to sing God's praises and turn our eyes toward him once more. That is why it is so important that we make the content of our songs of praise, and indeed of our whole worship service, as fundamentally God-centered and Scriptural as possible. We don't simply want to sing about our commitment to love God or to spend our time looking at one another looking at him; we want instead to look directly at him as he has revealed himself in his Word. In worship we turn our hearts away from ourselves and our preoccupations and toward our true center, God himself, experiencing and enjoying his presence in our midst.

That worship, the enjoyment of who God is and his favor toward us in Christ, is to be what we seek above all things. It is the one thing that is truly distinctive about us as God's people. If the church does not provide political commentary and social action, others may step into the gap. But if the church doesn't worship God, no one else will give him the glory he deserves. What is more, just as Moses didn't want the Promised Land if it came without God's presence, so too we are not to seek God because of the blessings that may come to us when we do, but simply for himself. Heaven itself should be desirable to us not just because it offers a preferable lifestyle option to the alternative destination, Hell, but because there we will truly be able to know and appreciate God as we ought. There we will be able to worship him without the sin and distractions that hinder our relationship here. That is why for the true believer the prospect of Heaven is far more desirable even than the very best this world could ever offer.

The God-Centered Life

How can we know if that is really our attitude? Let me suggest a couple of simple tests. First, what is our reason for going to church? Some people go to church to see their friends. Some go because it is entertaining and intellectually stimulating. Some go to be seen as respectable members of the community. Others, however, go to church to meet with God. These people assess the worship service by the answer to these questions: "Did I meet with God today? Was his Word proclaimed in a way that showed me clearly the glory of Christ and the gospel? Did the songs remind me afresh who God is? Did the prayers help me enter his presence, confess my sin and unworthiness, and bring my petitions and praise to him?" As a pastor, I long for all of my people to come to church with those concerns on their hearts—and I pray for myself and the others who assist in leading worship that God would help us lead them toward that goal.

The second test is this: what are we living our life for? If the goal of our whole life is to glorify God and enjoy him, then our heart's desire will be to become oriented more and more toward the center, to be increasingly submitted to God's plan for our life. God's tent was in the midst of the camp not just because he is the center of our devotion, but because the center of the camp in the ancient world was the location of the king's tent.[1] God is our King. This is not unrelated to the previous point, of course: we worship God, among other reasons, because he is our King. Yet it is worth making the point explicitly that for God to be at the center of our lives must mean obedience to his commands. Following God is not simply a matter of emotional attachment and warm fuzzy feelings in church on Sundays: it must also result in transformed lives of obedience. We have not become true disciples of our Lord until we have gone beyond learning information about his ways to putting them into practice. God is not really at the center of our lives unless his truth finds expression in every corner of them.

Such a radically God-centered focus for our existence is far more of a commitment than what most modern people want from their religion. Edmund Clowney describes the normal preference today in these terms:

> [Many people] do not want to lose all contact with God, but prefer that their relations with him be handled by a professional. Let a clergyman do the praying. It is as well to have God available at no great distance. We might need his help—in a counseling center perhaps, or as a national deity who could restrain the Kremlin. But to have God at the center of our lives—that is decidedly too close. His presence would be most inconvenient for some of our business deals, our entertainment, or our grabbing a little of the gusto that the TV commercials advertise.[2]

Do we really want God at the center of our lives? That is a challenging test. If God were to call me to leave my comfortable home and life and go somewhere else to serve him, would I really be willing? I used to be willing to drop every-thing and go anywhere at God's call when I was younger. Of course, it was a whole lot easier then: there was so much less to leave behind. It is so easy now, however, to think that I couldn't possibly do without all of the comforts and securities to which I've grown accustomed and step out in faith. Or what if God were to take my life through pathways of suffering and pain—either my own suffering or the suffering of someone I love? Would I be willing in the midst of that harsh and bitter reality to say, "Lord, I have no clue why this is happening to me, but I know you are both good and all-powerful. You are my King, and I accept this assignment from your hand as designed to glorify you and to sanctify me"? Am I ready for that? Is my whole life so camped around the presence of God as my King that I can say, "Lord, so long as I have you, there is nothing else that I need. My life is yours to command, for sickness or health, for prosperity or poverty, for useful service or an apparently wasted life, given up for you"? That is a profound test, isn't it?

The Arrangement of the Camp

The most fundamental reality expressed in Numbers 2, then, is that the camp of Israel was to be arranged around the central presence of the Lord. However, the camp was also to be *arranged* around the central presence of the Lord, and this is what takes up most of the detail of the chapter. It only takes one verse to tell us *that* the camp is arranged around the Lord; it takes another thirty-two verses to tell us exactly *how* they are arranged. Once again the extensive details may look at first sight as useless as a page of football trivia to those who hate sports. Look again, though, and let me show you what is being accomplished here.

First of all, you need to understand that the people are arranged by their tribes in a square shape around the tabernacle. In the old English legend, King Arthur is said to have had a round table constructed for his knights to prevent any of them from claiming that he held a higher position than the others. This, though, is the opposite. Israel's tribes are not placed in a circle, in which every position is equally significant and valuable, but rather in a square, with three tribes on each side. In the order in which we meet them, there are three tribes to the east, three to the south, three to the west, and three to the north. That order itself is significant because in the orientation of the Bible, east is forward, the most important direction.[3] The prime position in the camp is to the east, and then (in clockwise direction) to the south, the west, and the north.[4]

So who receives the prime assignment in the camp of Israel? Judah. To see clearly the fact that this is not simply a random assignment, it is worth noting that this is the third different order given for the twelve tribes in the book of Numbers. The first order of the tribes is in Numbers 1:5-15, where the princes of the tribes who will assist Moses are named. This was the order of natural precedence. It starts with the firstborn, Reuben, and proceeds through the children of Leah (omitting Levi who is not to be counted). That takes us down to Zebulun. Then we have the children of Rachel, who were born after Zebulun: Joseph has a double share, Ephraim and Manasseh, to keep the number of tribes at twelve even though Levi is removed, and then comes Benjamin. Only after we have heard all of the names of the children of Leah and Rachel do we get the names of the four sons born to their maid-servants: Dan, Asher, Gad, and Naphtali. Although they were born before Issachar, Zebulun, Joseph, and Benjamin, these brothers rate behind them. Their names are also given without reference to their mother or their order of birth, another way of putting them in a lower place.

The second order in which the tribes are given is the order of the census itself. Here there is the same order of natural precedence, with one exception: Gad is moved up to third place. Why this sudden promotion for Gad? The answer is that the census is already preparing the tribes in groups of three for the march. Gad needs to be where he is in the census, in company with Reuben and Simeon, to get the whole people organized for the place they will have in the camp.

That background then prepares us to look at the order in the camp. On the east side, the prime location, we have Judah, Issachar, and Zebulun, who were the second threesome in the census list. On the south, we have Reuben, Simeon, and Gad, the first threesome. To the west, we have Ephraim, Manasseh, and Benjamin, while to the least favored north we have Dan, Asher, and Naphtali. So the tribes are arranged like this:

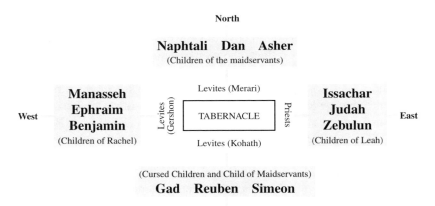

The Arrangement of the Twelve Tribes

Notice the crucial exchange of the first and second threesome from the census order when it comes time to order the camp. Natural precedence is not decisive for your place in the kingdom. Reuben was born first, but he lost his privileged place as firstborn through sexual sin: he slept with his father's concubine, Bilhah (Genesis 35:22). For that reason, when his father Jacob blessed his sons at the end of his life, his words for Reuben were a mixed "blessing":

> Reuben, you are my firstborn, my might, and the firstfruits of my strength, preeminent in dignity and preeminent in power. Unstable as water, you shall not have preeminence, because you went up to your father's bed; then you defiled it—he went up to my couch! (Genesis 49:3, 4)

Simeon and Levi, who would normally have been next in line, likewise lost their position through sin. When Dinah was raped by Shechem as recorded in Genesis 34, they tricked the inhabitants of his city into thinking they could incorporate Jacob's family into their community if only they would agree to be circumcised. Then, once they had gained their trust, Simeon and Levi slaughtered them all. Their father's blessing on them too was more of a curse:

> Simeon and Levi are brothers; weapons of violence are their swords. Let my soul come not into their council; O my glory, be not joined to their company. For in their anger they killed men, and in their willfulness they hamstrung oxen. Cursed be their anger, for it is fierce, and their wrath, for it is cruel! I will divide them in Jacob and scatter them in Israel. (Genesis 49:5-7)

Jacob's blessing on Judah, however, was a true blessing, assigning him the place of leadership and ultimately of kingship. The ordering of the tribes in the book of Numbers reflects the words of Jacob. Reuben and Simeon have lost their position of natural precedence and are placed on the south side, alongside the son of one of the maidservants, facing the other three sons of the maidservants. Meanwhile, Judah and the other brothers of Leah are on the favored east, facing the three tribes descended from Rachel—Ephraim, Manasseh, and Benjamin. The arrangement of the camp shows us that the words of the old blessing were being fulfilled.

Yet the point being made here is not quite the one you might think at first. You might assume that since Reuben and Simeon lost their primary positions due to their sexual sin and violent disposition respectively, the message is simply a warning against illegitimate sex and meaningless violence. Certainly that is part of it: the writer is showing us that sin has consequences, and those consequences may affect our children as well as ourselves. It was not just Reuben and Simeon personally who suffered because of their sin: 400 years later their tribes were still feeling the effects of their actions. That should caution us against ever taking sin lightly. Satan wants us to think we can sin without it hurting anyone, but the camp of Israel shows that sin has serious and lasting consequences.

Curse Transformed

Yet if the main point is that sin has lasting consequences, then it is hard to explain the present layout of the camp. After all, Judah was not exactly blameless on the sexual integrity front. In Genesis 38 we read of his liaison with Tamar, whom he mistook for a Canaanite prostitute. Meanwhile, all of the brothers together, including Judah, plotted to bring Joseph's life to a violent end in Genesis 37. Judah, however, learned through his experiences and came to a greater understanding of God's grace. The result of that learning process was evident when the brothers went down to Egypt a second time in search of food to sustain the family. Judah was the one who volunteered to take the punishment in his younger brother's place, after Joseph had accused Benjamin of stealing a silver cup. Judah's thoughts were now solely of the sorrow that the loss of Benjamin would cause his father. He was willing personally to pay any cost to save his father from that pain. Thus the life of Judah shows us a different lesson. It shows us that even though sin may have its consequences, the experience of grace can have lasting consequences of its own: it can take and transform the results of our sin. Because of Judah's willingness to substitute himself for his brother and bear the living death that had been assessed on his brother, he was now a fit ancestor for the line from whom Jesus would come.

The same point, that curse may be transformed into blessing, is seen also in the fate of the tribe of Levi. Jacob's "blessing" on Levi condemned him, along with his brother Simeon, to be scattered throughout Israel for their massacre of Shechem. Yet when the people of God went astray and worshiped the golden calf while Moses was on Mount Sinai, the tribe of Levi's moment of transformation came. There the Levites joined with Moses in bringing judgment on those who were rebelling against the Lord and had their own curse transformed into a blessing (Exodus 32:27-29). Their confrontational temperament, under the direction of the Lord, had now been harnessed as an asset in their service of him rather than a liability. They would still be scattered among Israel, just as Jacob had prophesied, but now their scattering would be a blessing to them and to Israel, not a curse. The tribe of Simeon was scattered and ultimately disappeared, mainly absorbed by the tribe of Judah. However, the tribe of Levi was scattered and prospered, in numbers if not materially, as they brought the Law of Moses to all of the towns and communities of God's people. Their radical commitment to protect God's holiness at Sinai earned them the privilege and responsibility of camping immediately around the tabernacle.

Do you see the principles, then, that God is making clear by the way he arranged the tribes around the camp? On the one hand, the people are being reminded that sin has consequences. Sometimes our sin has long-term results that affect our children as well. Whether divorce or adultery, alcoholism or eating disorders, even gossip or pride, our sins can be a negative legacy that has a lasting impact on our children. From my own family I learned the art of making sarcastic remarks, dismissive words that cleverly cut someone else down to size. As a result I have spent my whole lifetime trying to unlearn that "skill" and retrieve situations damaged by my tongue. Learning how to sin was easy; unlearning it is much harder. Learn this, then, from the arrangement of Israel's camp: our sins have consequences that are real and may be lasting.

Yet at the same time God's grace is greater than our sin or the sins of our parents. God will in some cases reverse or modify those consequences, and even turn them to his own glory. Sometimes God takes the damage we have done and turns it around in our own lives, as he did with Judah, or in the lives of our children, as he did with the Levites. We all come to God as intensely damaged people, damaged by our own sin and the sins of our parents; yet God in his grace and mercy can restore what sin has torn asunder. Sometimes God demonstrates his power by delivering us dramatically from our patterns of sin. At other times our pain and ongoing personal struggle is precisely what equips us to minister God's grace to others in the midst of their pain. At all times, awareness of the depths of our sin is what drives our appreciation of the enormity of God's mercy toward us.

We certainly cannot presume on God's grace, however. Reuben lost his place of primacy forever, and Simeon was irretrievably scattered, lost as a separate tribe. Not every effect of our sin can be waved away with a wish and a pinch of pixie dust. Yet it is worth noting that for all of the ongoing effects of their sin, Simeon and Reuben were still there within the camp of Israel around the Lord's Tent. For all of its consequences, even their flagrant and deep sin couldn't remove them from the circle of God's care. God had chosen all of the sons of Jacob to be his people, and not even their transgressions could prevent God from achieving his purposes. God's grace will win the final victory, not our sins.

The Role of the Levites

Finally, though, the third thing to notice about the arrangement of the camp is that the Levites were assigned the key role of camping between the Lord and the people. We will address this role more fully in the chapters that follow, but for now we will simply note the fact that they needed to be there. There was a reason why God was reluctant to go with his people on the journey up to Canaan: it was because of the risk that he would get angry with their sin and destroy them along the way. The Lord is a holy God, so it is a dangerous thing to have him present in the midst of the camp. There needs to be a separation between him and the unholy, lest that which is unholy be vaporized by his holiness.

It is this role of acting as a human safety cordon around the tabernacle that the Levites filled within the camp. They were to camp between the Israelites and the tabernacle and to take care of all of the responsibilities associated with it "so that there may be no wrath on the congregation of the people of Israel" (1:53). All who stepped out of their appointed place in God's order risked bringing judgment upon themselves and upon the whole community of God's people: the Levites were to do all of the work associated with the tabernacle and to keep the rest of the people away, or those who transgressed would be put to death (see 3:10, 38). That this warning is no empty threat will become clear when we get to Numbers 16, 17, the rebellion of Korah along with Dathan and Abiram. These chapters show what happens when the order set up by God is violated: the result is death. The Lord is not a tame God: to be in his presence is not safe, and the warlike Levites were there to protect against precisely such tragic incursions.

This is a profound picture of our dilemma in the world in which we live. In Eden it was safe for man to be in God's presence because Adam and Eve were created holy. In the garden they could walk and talk with God in the cool of the day. But then Adam and Eve fell and sinned against God: they were cast out of the garden, and a barrier was placed between them and the life-giving presence of God (Genesis 3:24). The cherubim and a flaming sword kept them at a distance, a kind of heavenly equivalent of the Levites. Yet herein lies our dilemma. In order for our life to have meaning, it needs to be centered around the Lord, our Creator and God; at the same time, though, his holy presence means certain death to sinners such as us. His presence in the midst of his people, while surrounded and protected by fierce guards to keep people at a safe distance, can only be an interim solution. It is better than not having him present in the midst of his people, but it is rather less than a return to Eden.

A Return to God's Presence

The final solution to our problem comes in the person of Christ. In him, the Word became flesh and tabernacled in our midst (John 1:14). God took on safe human form in Jesus, so that we could look upon his glory and experience his presence among us. Our King came to live with us on our wilderness journey, sharing our hardships and trials. Yet Jesus came to do more than simply show us God. He came to bring us into God's presence by equipping us with his perfect righteousness, imputed to us by grace. That is what effectually bridges the gap between God's holiness and our sin: Christ gave us his holiness that enables us to be welcomed in. The guards are waved aside, and we can enter into God's presence, clothed in his righteousness.

At the same time, our sin had to go somewhere. It couldn't just be ignored; it had to be paid for. The wages of death had to be deposited into someone's account. So Jesus took into himself the death that unclean sinners deserve for the sins that separate them from God. He placed himself under the flaming sword that separated us from God and paid in full for Adam's sin and ours as well. Through his death, he made a way through the Levites into the very presence of God for you and me, so that in him we can approach with boldness the throne of God's grace.

God dwelling in the midst of his Old Testament people was remarkable grace, given their track record of rebellion and sin. What, then, shall we say of our own experience of God? There are now no barriers and no second-class citizens in our camp. Descendants of Judah and of Reuben, Jew and Gentile, male and female, black and white, slave and free—all are one in Christ Jesus, and all are welcome to come in and abide with God forever. He has prepared a place for us and has given us the promise that where he is, there we shall be also. There is a place for us, and at the end of all things we shall find ourselves in our place forever.

Will you be there? When they call the roll in Heaven, will your name be on the list? Then give thanks for that assurance, and center your life here and now around the presence of your awesome, almighty, and holy King. Celebrate his goodness and his grace. Magnify his holiness, and delight in his love and favor to you. Rejoice that in Christ you too have been found worthy to stand in his presence.

4

Do or Die!

NUMBERS 3

MOST JOBS ARE NOT EXACTLY LIFE OR DEATH. For most of us, a simple error in the way we carry out our tasks will not kill anyone. This is true not simply for relatively unskilled occupations like hamburger flipping and garbage collecting but even for more highly skilled professions like lawyers and teachers. The cashier who rings up your purchase wrongly may cost you or the company some money, but nobody dies. The teacher who gets mixed up on the names of the different kinds of cloud formations or who misrepresents the true causes and effects of the Russian revolution may contribute to the ignorance of the next generation, but nobody will have to be buried as an immediate result of the error. There are some jobs, however, where each day people take their own lives and the lives of others into their hands. Airline pilots and air traffic controllers, anesthetists and surgeons, parachute packers and bomb disposal experts—these people have a job that must be done right or someone may die.

Do or Die Ministry

Into which of these categories do religious professionals fit? Surprisingly enough, the focus of Numbers 3 is that in the economy of God the ministry of the priests and Levites is literally "do or die," a life or death service on behalf of the community. If they do not carry out their job correctly, it will lead straight to the morgue. Moreover, this message is not just ancient history. God has not changed in the time between then and now, and so we still need someone to perform that "do or die" ministry on our behalf. As the chapter unfolds, we will see exactly what this ministry of the priests and Levites is, who it is that undertakes this role for us, and the lessons that communicates to us in our situation.

The theme of a ministry that leads to life or death is introduced right at the outset of the chapter. It begins with the words, "These are the generations of Aaron and Moses" (v. 1). This is actually a standard formula in the book of Genesis that marks the transition into a new section of the book, with a focus on a new group of people. Invariably, the center of attention in the new section is on the offspring of the people named in the opening formula. So the words "Now these are the generations of Terah" in Genesis 11:27 introduces the story of Terah's son, Abram, while "These are the generations of Isaac" in Genesis 25:19 launches the story of Jacob and Esau. So too here in the book of Numbers the account draws our attention immediately to the next generation, the four sons of Aaron: Nadab, Abihu, Eleazar, and Ithamar (3:2).

What we learn about these young men, in very brief terms, is that in carrying out their "do or die" ministry, two of them "did," and two of them "died." Nadab and Abihu, the older pair, offered unauthorized fire before the Lord, a story that is recorded in more detail in Leviticus 10. Instead of using "kosher" coals from the altar to burn their incense (see Leviticus 16:12), they used coals from another source. These coals had not been authorized by God for such use. As a result, fire came out from the presence of the Lord and burned them up (Leviticus 10:2). The message to be gleaned from their fate is not hard to discern: carelessness in serving a holy God can be fatal. Not only were they themselves killed—their lines in the family tree came to an abrupt halt, for they had no children (Numbers 3:4). Just as in parachute packing and brain surgery, in ministering before the Lord there is no room for error.

Their brothers Eleazar and Ithamar learned that lesson. As a result, they served the Lord safely as priests alongside their father Aaron (v. 4). Those who were careless died, but those who honored and respected the Lord's holiness served him faithfully throughout their lives. Air Force pilots have a saying: "There are old pilots and there are bold pilots, but there are no old, bold pilots." In that profession, if you cut corners and take risks, your chances of living to retirement age are slim. It was the same way with serving the Lord: it had to be done right, in accordance with his commands, or the priests might well die. There were no old, bold priests in the service of the Lord.

The Levites

The family of Aaron could not carry out that life or death ministry of caring for the tabernacle alone, however, and so God assigned the tribe of Levi to help them in their work (v. 5). This one tribe out of Israel was to be completely devoted to looking after the tabernacle, working on behalf of Aaron and on behalf of the whole community (v. 9). Other tribes could pursue their own interests and desires, but the Levites were to be entirely dedicated to the Lord from birth. As a result, it was not simply the Levites who were old enough to fight, those twenty years and older who were to be counted, as was the case for the other tribes. Rather, *all* of the Levites one month old and older were to be counted. From their earliest days, they belonged completely to the Lord.

The job assigned to the Levites by God had two main parts.[1] The first task of the Levites was that of guard duty around the tabernacle whenever the people were settled in their camp. The Hebrew phrase that is translated "perform duties" in Numbers 3:7 (NIV) always has the sense of guard duty in the Old Testament, and this passage is no exception.[2] The second task of the Levites was doing the miscellaneous work of the tabernacle, especially that of carrying and caring for the tabernacle and all of its furnishings while the people were on the march (v. 8). The carrying function of the Levites will be the particular focus of Numbers 4, while their guarding function is more prominent here in chapter 3. It was the Levites' job to put to death anyone other than Aaron and his sons who sought to encroach on the holy ground of the tabernacle (v. 10). Only those whom God had chosen and appointed could serve as priests: anyone else who tried to approach God was subject to the death penalty. If unauthorized people approached the Lord, the Levites were to execute them, just as divine fire had consumed Nadab and Abihu when they tried to offer unauthorized fire.

The Call to Ministry

It is worth noting at this point two basic principles of ministry that may be seen in this assignment. First, those who are leaders in ministry do not appoint themselves to those positions; they are called by God to serve him and his people. Prophets were called individually by God to serve him, while the priests and Levites were set apart by God as a tribe. In both cases, though, God was the one who called them. It is the same way in the church. Those who are ministers, elders, and deacons in the church do not appoint themselves to their task, nor is it merely a matter of a democratic vote of the members of the church. God is the one who calls people to those offices.

Since God is the one who calls people to these offices, he is the one who determines which classes of people are eligible for those offices. In God's Old Testament people, if you were not a male Levite from the family of Aaron, between thirty and fifty years old, you could not serve as a priest. It didn't matter what gifts you had or what the culture around you might think of such apparently outdated and repressive restrictions, God's Word had to be followed. God is the King, the one before whom the priests and Levites would serve, and it is therefore his prerogative to make the rules.

If you know anything about the history of Israel, you won't be surprised to hear that these rules, as others, weren't always kept. When the kingdom of Israel was divided into north and south, the northern kingdom set up its own temples at Dan and Bethel to keep people from going down to Jerusalem. These northern temples had a much more flexible and less restrictive view of worship than the temple in Jerusalem. They each had golden calves, idols, to represent the Lord to people who found the worship at the Jerusalem temple too austere (1 Kings 12:28). These temples offered a more popular way of worshiping Israel's God, more in keeping with the sensibilities of the religious seekers around them. Moreover, King Jeroboam appointed priests to these temples "from all sorts of people, even though they were not Levites" (1 Kings 12:31, NIV). It was thus all around a kinder, gentler, more inclusive version of the Lord's worship. Yet the prophets that the Lord sent repeatedly denounced these temples as idolatrous abominations (e.g., 1 Kings 13). Every subsequent king of the northern kingdom was evaluated on the basis of his attitude to Jeroboam's golden calf idols. God makes the rules about how he is to be worshiped, and he expects those rules to be followed scrupulously.

In the same way God has ordained certain qualifications for ministers, elders, and deacons in his church in the New Testament. Paul instructs the church as to what those qualifications are in his letters to Timothy and Titus: ministers, elders, and deacons must be men who fit the description of 1 Timothy 3 and Titus 1. To many people in our society that standard seems hopelessly restrictive and old-fashioned. They want the church to "move with the times" and open up these offices to women as well as to men, and they cannot understand why evangelical churches are not willing to do so. The answer is simple. We want to follow God's ways, not the ways of the age in which we live. We serve a God who is very precise about those who are to serve him.

Now to be sure, that does not mean that women in the church should lack opportunity for ministry. Women have gifts of spiritual leadership that should certainly be exercised among us, just as Titus 2:3-5 anticipates. There is no Biblical warrant for patting intelligent women on the head and consigning them to the kitchen to make tea. Rather, as Paul told Titus, the older women have a calling to train the younger women in godliness and love for Christ, a calling that must be pursued diligently. This is a profound and vital ministry of training and discipleship that requires all of the gifts of mature, godly women in our churches.[3] However, we cannot and must not ordain women to the Biblical offices of elder or deacon, whatever the cultural pressures, because it is God who chooses those who serve him, not our culture.

Varieties of Ministries

The second basic principle of ministry here is that different people are called to different ministries within the people of God. The priests served before the Lord in their particular calling and ministry, while the Levites had a different calling, one that involved serving the priests and the people. In the eyes of the world, that was perhaps not the most glorious and exciting ministry. Standing guard outside the tabernacle or carrying its heavy furniture through the wilderness for days on end was not the most thrilling assignment. Nevertheless, that was the ministry that they had been called to do by God, and that calling gave their service a glory all of its own. Any service offered to the King, however humble, has its own glory and requires our total commitment. Whether it is setting out the Bibles for church or washing up after a potluck lunch, serving in the nursery or teaching Sunday school, if it is labor done for the King, it is glorious. It is not only so-called spiritual work that is glorious. One of the rediscoveries of the Reformation was that every person has been called by God to his or her particular position in life. That means that all of life has a sacredness, a glory of its own because it is service to the King.

In the New Testament church there is a similar division of labor. At first in the early church the apostles did everything. However, already by Acts 6, they were finding the workload overwhelming. There was a daily program of food distribution to widows that was becoming far too much for them to do. So the apostles told the congregation to choose men filled with the Holy Spirit and turned over the responsibility for the food distribution to them, so the apostles could devote themselves to the ministry of the Word of God and to prayer (Acts 6:4). The apostles had their task in the kingdom of God, and rather than be distracted from it, they appointed "super-deacons" to assist them by undertaking the care for the poor.

The reason for this division of labor is twofold. On the one hand, everyone has some spiritual gifts, and on the other hand, no one has all of the spiritual gifts. If a few people try to do all of the work of ministry, they will burn themselves out and also deprive others of the opportunity to minister. It is not the job of the minister and the elders to do all of the ministry of the church. We have a particular task assigned to us: we are to be committed to the ministry of the Word and prayer, along with watching over the spiritual needs of the flock. We dare not become too busy with other things to the point where those obligations get squeezed out. That's where the ministry of the whole body of Christ comes in though. Every single Christian should be involved in helping the ministry of the church in some way or another, large or small, according to his or her gifts. It may be helping to set up or take down; it could be helping in the nursery or with the music ministry. It may be cleaning up the kitchen after a church dinner or getting out the church calendar. It may be following up new visitors and welcoming strangers. If all members of the body use their own gifts and do their part, then no part of the body gets overloaded with an excessive burden and burned out.

The Levites and the Firstborn

What gives God the right to assign the Levites to these menial jobs around the tabernacle? The answer is that the Levites belonged to God in a unique way. They belonged to God as the substitutes for the firstborn sons of Israel (v. 12). All Israel belongs to God, of course, but the firstborn sons of that first generation belonged to God in a special way. Why? Because when God sent the destroying angel to go through Egypt and kill all of the firstborn sons in the land, he passed over the firstborn sons of Israel. The firstborn of Egypt were struck down, while God spared the firstborn of Israel from death. As a result, the firstborn in Israel belonged to God. And God chose the Levites to take the place of the firstborn sons of Israel and be especially dedicated to his service.

Having chosen the Levites, they too needed to be numbered and arranged, just like all the rest of the tribes. They weren't counted along with the rest of the Israelites as a preparation for war, but they still needed to be counted. They totaled 22,000 men and boys, nearly the same number as the total number of the firstborn of Israel, which was 22,273. Close is not enough in God's service, however. Every single one of those firstborn sons who had been spared had to be personally and particularly redeemed. The Levites did not just generally substitute for all of the firstborn as a crowd. They particularly substituted for them one by one. Each firstborn who was to be redeemed needed to have a corresponding Levite to take his place. Those firstborn who were left over at the end needed to have their redemption paid for one by one at the rate of five shekels per head.

The Arrangement of the Levites

Once they were counted, the Levites too were arranged in a square around the tabernacle, inside the square formed by the other tribes. In the prime place to the east of the tabernacle, Moses camped along with Aaron and his family, the priests. To the south, in the second most important place, was the clan of Kohath. Their importance is seen not only in where they camped but in what they were to carry: they were assigned the ark and table on which the bread was placed before the Lord, along with the rest of the furniture from the inner sanctuary, the holy of holies (v. 31). The clan of Gershon, which is named first in the list because Gershon was older than Kohath, received the next spot in importance, camping to the west of the tabernacle and carrying the tabernacle itself along with the curtains and so on (vv. 25, 26). The third and youngest clan, the Merarites, were assigned the least important north side to camp on and were given the frames, crossbars, and posts of the tabernacle to carry—all of the less important equipment (vv. 36, 37).

What is striking about this arrangement is that once again natural precedence is not decisive for position in God's kingdom. Just as in the arrangement of the tribes in the outer square, so too with the Levites; the clan descended from the firstborn son did not merit the most important place. Rather, the clan of the second son, Kohath, was given that lead role. In this case, though, no reason is given for the switch in order. It is not because of any particular sin on the part of Gershon or his clan, nor because of any special righteousness on the part of Kohath and his clan. It is God's prerogative to choose the younger ahead of the older, as he does so often in Scripture, to demonstrate that standing in his kingdom is a matter of grace and not of works. The sovereign King can choose not simply which of the tribes of Israel is to serve as his bodyguards but even which clans of that tribe are to be assigned to which tasks. They belong to God, and they are therefore his to command as he pleases.

It is the same way in our service of God. God assigns us our place in his kingdom and gives us the gifts he sees fit. To some he gives large gifts and responsible places of service, ministering to thousands. To others, he gives smaller gifts and smaller places of service. Much frustration in ministry flows out of the desire for a larger place than God has assigned us. The world around us rates our ministries on the basis of the number of people who attend our churches and the magnificence of our buildings and programs. As Jesus' Parable of the Talents reminds us, however, God rates us on the basis of faithfulness to him and diligent use of the gifts he has given us in the context in which he has placed us (Matthew 25:14-30). The man who used his two talents faithfully received exactly the same commendation from the Lord as the man who was faithful with five. God doesn't evaluate ministry in the same way that the world does.

Throughout this chapter we read that Moses did exactly "as the LORD commanded him" (vv. 16, 39, 42, 51). He counted all of the Levites one month old and upward and arranged them in the order God had laid down. He counted all of the firstborn male Israelites and made sure that the redemption money for the extra 273 firstborn males was duly paid. The Levites were installed as the substitutes for the firstborn Israelites in God's service, taking on themselves the risks of standing guard over the tabernacle, so that the whole community might be kept safe from any outbreak of wrath from God if an unfit person encroached on his holy presence.

Learning from the Levites

However, all of that is old history. To be sure, we have derived some general principles from this account, but what specifically may we learn from the role of the Levites? We don't have a tabernacle in our situation, nor do we have to assign elders or deacons to guard duty, for fear that someone might accidentally get too close to God. What does this aspect of the camp of Israel have to say to us as New Testament believers?

First, it is important to see how seriously God takes his worship. Coming into God's presence is a "do or die" matter, then and now. It is not something to be taken lightly, as if it were a day trip to the beach. When we come to worship, we stand in the presence of the King of kings, the Lord of the universe. God calls us to worship him at the outset of the worship service, and we in response ask him to be present in our opening prayer of invocation. Jesus promised that wherever two or three of his people are gathered together, there he will be in the midst of them (Matthew 18:20), just as he was in the midst of the camp of Israel. This promise certainly includes our worship services. God is in our midst by his Spirit. We stand on holy ground whenever we assemble as God's people. That should inspire awe and reverence in our worship, not flippancy and a casual attitude.

Do we take worship that seriously? If so, then we will arrive in plenty of time for the service rather than straggling in whenever we get there. Yes, there are times when life conspires to make it hard to get to church on time, but we should be as careful about being at church on time as we are at work. Taking worship seriously also means coming with hearts prepared to meet with God, eagerly longing to hear his Word. That's not a natural state for our hearts to be in. If you are like me, you will need to prepare your heart to approach God. Listening to Christian music while you are getting ready may help. It may mean getting up a few minutes earlier so that the whole morning is not quite so rushed. Isn't God worth that effort? One of the things I have noticed, of myself as well as others, is that we tend to put a great deal more effort into preparing to meet our spouse before we marry them than we do after we are married. Isn't it the same way in our relationship with God? The pagans who are lost and confused about the truth of God are often more diligent in their efforts to meet God than we who have already been found by him. How shameful it is that we whose redemption was so costly should take the celebrating of it so lightly.

Nor has God left it up to us to decide how we should worship. In his Word he has commanded us what things we are to do in the worship of him: prayer; the reading and preaching of his Word; the singing of psalms, hymns, and spiritual songs, testifying to his goodness and grace; administering the sacraments of baptism and the Lord's Supper; receiving his blessing in the benediction. We are not free to add our own innovations to the commands of Scripture or to incorporate all manner of additional elements into our worship services. Anything not commanded by God for use in his worship is not permitted. Ministers and elders who oversee the worship of God are to guard it as carefully as the Levites guarded the tabernacle. We are responsible before him to see that in worship everything is done in accordance with his Word.

The Grace of Redemption

Yet in the midst of the seriousness and reverence of our worship there also has to be a note of joy. Serious worship that lacks joy is as much of an abomination as joyful worship that lacks any reverence. The Levites were not simply a symbol of the solemnity of God's Law but also a constant reminder of the grace Israel received in redemption. By their very existence they were a perpetual pointer to the fact that God rescued his people out of Egypt and that they did not experience there the judgment plagues that descended on the Egyptians. They are a reminder that when God rescued his people, he did so with a price. Someone had to substitute for the Israelite firstborn if they were not to die. In fact, in the plan of God there were two aspects to this redemption. In the first place, someone had to pay the price of the death that Israel deserved in their place, which was the role of the Passover lamb. Second, though, someone also had to pay the price of the life of obedience that Israel owed, by being completely given over to God in their place. That was the part that the Levites had to play in all of this. In the redemption of the firstborn, it was not so much a matter of "do *or* die" but "do *and* die." The job of the Passover lamb was to die; the job of the Levites was to live, completely devoted to God.

Do you see how all of this provided a picture of the gospel ahead of time? Jesus Christ, the Son of God, came to execute a similar "do and die" ministry on behalf of Israel, God's firstborn. Jesus had to live a perfect life, wholly devoted to God, just like the one the Levites were called to live. Then, as our Passover Lamb (1 Corinthians 5:7), he had to lay down that perfect life and die the death that we deserved. His ministry of redemption, however, was not so much about keeping unqualified people out of God's presence as it was about providing the holiness necessary to bring sinners in. Jesus came to turn unqualified, unholy people into those who were now qualified to stand in the presence of a holy God because they came clothed in his righteousness. To be sure, the unqualified are still shut out from God's presence. God's holiness cannot and will not be compromised: nothing and no one impure can ever enter into the new Jerusalem, our heavenly home (Revelation 21:27). Without perfect righteousness, no one can see God. The heavenly equivalent of the Levites still stand on guard to bar the door to anyone who comes in their own goodness, no matter how stellar their performance by human standards. Yet they stand aside whenever we approach God in the name of Jesus and bid us welcome to come. Christ has substituted for us.

Nor has Christ simply substituted for humanity as a mass, making it possible for some undefined number of human beings potentially to be saved. Like the Levites, who substituted for the firstborn of Israel on a one for one basis, redeeming each particularly, so that those who remained over had to be purchased one by one, so also Christ's perfect life and death atoned particularly for all of his elect. He did not simply write a blank check that was sufficient for humanity. On the cross he wrote a check that specifically provided the payment for each and every one of his elect people, not just making their salvation potentially possible but actually purchasing them. He therefore now owns each one of us, just as God purchased the Levites, obliging us to live lives that are wholly devoted to him. We have been bought with a price, which in our case was not five shekels of silver or even ten talents of gold, but the precious blood of Christ, our spotless Passover Lamb (1 Peter 1:18, 19). We are therefore no longer our own but are called to live now in his service. We are called to defend his honor and reputation, to guard his holiness and the holiness of his people, to serve his people with all of the gifts he has given us.

Like the Levites, then, you and I are engaged to be servants of the Great King throughout our lives. We have a task to do, a mission to be undertaken. We are to glorify and enjoy the holy and majestic God who has redeemed us and to bring the news of his glory to those who have not yet heard. Because Christ has come, our job is not to tell the unholy and unqualified, "Keep out, lest you die." It is to tell them come to Christ, for *he* has died. He has died and has risen again and now stands as the open doorway into God's presence. There is no other safe way into the presence of God. All other roads to God lead to a fiery death. Yet if you are one of his people, one of those for whom he paid the price on the cross, you will most certainly come. His sheep hear his voice and come running. Come to God through Christ today, whether you are coming for the first time or you have been coming to the Father through Christ for seventy or eighty years now. Come into God's presence afresh today. Revel in his holiness, his glory, and his grace. Lift up your hearts to him in worship, and hear him direct you outward again to serve his people and to glorify his name.

5

Danger! Levites at Work

NUMBERS 4

HAVE YOU EVER HAD THE EXPERIENCE of putting together something that came in a box? It can be a challenging task, and it is often one that takes far longer than you expected. One Christmas we bought a dollhouse for our daughters that had on the box the three most feared words in the English language: "Some assembly required." The instructions claimed that it was a thirty-minute project. I don't know what set of space-time coordinates they were operating within, but two days later I was still working on it!

One of the challenges of this kind of construction project is that the instructions often seem to be written by someone whose first language is not English. As a result, many steps in the process are hard to follow, and crucial instructions are often completely omitted. All of this leads to much frustration on the part of the construction engineer and those who are eager to play with the finished product. What you may not know, though, is that this experience is not confined to toy assembly. The commissioning procedure for the newly constructed oil terminal at Nigg Bay in Scotland in which I participated in my first job after graduation as an engineer was distressingly similar. The construction drawings frequently didn't match what was actually there on the ground, instruction manuals were vague and sketchy, and we had to figure out many aspects of the operation as we went along. What made this rather more serious than constructing a child's dollhouse was that very soon we were expecting the first oil tanker to dock and unload a cargo of crude oil! If the pieces were hooked up in the wrong way, the consequences for the surrounding environment would be catastrophic. In a situation where mistakes carried such serious potential consequences, what you longed for was a clear, incredibly detailed manual to follow.

In the light of that example, it is perhaps easier to understand why the detailed instructions of Numbers 4 were necessary. Moving the holy objects in the tabernacle from place to place was a delicate job, as fraught with risk as commissioning a nuclear reactor. One false step, one wrong move, and someone could die (vv. 18-20). The ministry of the Levites was always a labor of life or death, as we mentioned in the previous chapter, a ministry that could not be undertaken too carefully. Whereas the previous chapter focused on their first task of guarding the sanctuary and gave the rationale for why the Levites were assigned to assist Aaron and the priests, this chapter focuses in great detail on their second responsibility, that of moving the sacred objects of the tabernacle from one campsite to the next.

The Ordering of the Levites

Essentially the chapter breaks down into four parts. The first three assign to each of the Levite clans their respective responsibilities as part of the moving crew, while the fourth sums up the chapter and the entire unit that runs from chapter 1 to chapter 4 by recording the numbering of the three clans. The order of the clans in Numbers 4 matches the location each was assigned to camp around the tabernacle in the previous chapter. The clan of Kohath came first and carried the most important objects. They were to camp on the south side of the tabernacle, the position second only in rank to the priests, who camped on the east. Next came the clan of Gershon, who camped on the west and carried the middle-rank sacred objects. Finally, the clan of Merari was introduced, who camped on the least important north side and carried the odds and ends of the tabernacle.

We noted previously that this ordering is not the order of natural precedence. Gershon was the older brother of Kohath, and you would therefore normally have expected his clan to have the more important place. However, it was God's prerogative to choose the younger over the older and to reverse the natural order, just as he did with Jacob and Esau and with Ephraim and Manasseh. God is sovereign, and he assigns us to the places he chooses for us. In this case there is no obvious reason why God chose the clan of Kohath ahead of the clan of Gershon. They are not the most numerous clan of the Levites, nor do they have any particular distinguishing virtues. God simply chose them out of his mercy and grace.

This is an important point to grasp because we are often far too impressed by the attributes that the world values. We look at the external features a person possesses: if a man is rich and famous or is a naturally gifted speaker and leader, he will often be pressed to use those natural gifts and abilities in the church. It seems that whenever a Hollywood celebrity, a pop singer, or a movie star becomes a Christian, he or she is instantly thrust into the limelight and paraded around the Christian speaking circuit, whether or not he or she knows anything about theology. Like the prophet Samuel, sent to interview the sons of Jesse for the job of Israel's king, we too are struck by impressive features and natural giftedness. God, however, looks on the heart (1 Samuel 16:7). Sometimes the people God chooses to use are not those with impressive presence and strong resumés. On the contrary, he often chooses the weak things in this world to shame the strong and the foolish things in the world's eyes to shame the wise (1 Corinthians 1:27). God's chosen instruments are not necessarily the ones we would have picked.

Graded Holiness

Thus it was the clan of the middle brother, Kohath, that was charged with the task of carrying the most sacred objects rather than that of the elder brother Gershon. The sacred objects to be carried are listed in decreasing order of sacredness, with the first objects requiring special care and attention. First and foremost comes the ark of the covenant. This was the footstool of God's throne and the box that contained the sacred documents of the covenant, the two tablets of stone that God gave Moses on Mount Sinai. Covenant treaty documents such as these were often buried at the feet of the respective gods of the nations in their temples. In Israel, however, there was only one God, and his footstool was mobile; so both copies of his covenant with Israel were contained in the ark. The ark was to be covered by the curtain that separated the Holy of Holies from the rest of the tabernacle. This curtain was made of cloth containing all three of the sacred colors: blue, purple, and scarlet (Exodus 26:31). The package was then to be further wrapped in a protective covering probably made of goatskin dyed yellow-orange.[1] An outer layer of the most sacred color, blue, completed the covering process.

The second most precious object, the table on which the bread of the presence was laid out before the Lord, was covered with only two of the sacred colors, blue and scarlet, before it was wrapped in the protective layer. The lampstand and the gold altar and their associated articles received a single covering of the most sacred color, blue, while the bronze altar was also wrapped in a single layer, but of the less sacred color, purple. This was because the bronze altar was located outside the tabernacle proper in the courtyard and was therefore less sacred than the objects within the tabernacle.

In this passage, therefore, as in all of the texts dealing with the tabernacle, you can see visually depicted a theology of graded holiness.[2] The objects that are at a distance from the Lord can be made of ordinary materials, such as bronze. However, the closer you come to the presence of God, the higher the standard of materials and workmanship required. Within the Holy of Holies itself, only pure gold may be used. The same graded standard that applies to the construction materials and to the packaging process applies to the people who approach God as well. Even common people could enter the outer courtyard to bring their offerings, but only the High Priest could enter the Holy of Holies, and that only once a year. In the camp of Israel, the ordinary tribes were encamped around the ark in the outer square, while the more holy Levites and priests formed the inner ring. The consistent message being communicated to God's people by these diverse means was that only the very best and purest that we have is sufficient for the presence of the King of kings and that the closer we get to God, the greater the degree of holiness required.

Because of this principle of graded holiness, the Kohathites were not permitted to touch the sacred objects themselves. They had to carry them once they were safely packed up, but only the priests could do the packing. In fact, the Kohathites were not even allowed to look at the sacred objects lest they die (v. 20). Even though they were themselves wholly devoted to the Lord and were seeking to serve him faithfully, if they made one wrong move or stole one wrong glance, they would be struck dead. Only the priests possessed the holiness required to pack up the sacred things.

After the Kohathites had been charged with their responsibilities for the journey, the Gershonites and Merarites were assigned theirs. Because they were to carry the less holy, and therefore less dangerous, objects, the instructions given to them could be briefer. Whereas the Kohathites received twenty verses of instructions, the Gershonites only needed eight verses and the Merarites a mere four. Their ministry was less critical and therefore needed less attention. For all of the clans of the Levites, though, the ministry of porterage was only to be assigned to men aged from thirty to fifty years old. All of the Levites of whatever age were eligible for guard duty, but the duty of carrying the sacred things required men in the prime of their life, exercising all of their powers in the service of God. For the Levites, life really did begin at thirty!

Every aspect of the Levites' work was to be done under the oversight and direction of the priests. God assigned the general duties to the clans, but the more specific assignments of who carried which piece of furniture, or even which tent peg, were not to be left to chance. Aaron and his sons were instructed to regulate every detail of the transportation process, ensuring that every aspect of the process was done in an appropriate manner. Finally, the account concludes with the details of the counting of the Levites, which sums up and draws together both this chapter and the whole first section of the book, Numbers 1—4. The conclusion emphasizes once again the point that we have seen throughout this section: everyone was counted and arranged exactly as the Lord commanded Moses, with each assigned to his own particular station and task.

Transcendence and Immanence

What, then, may we learn from this passage of Scripture? First, we need to see that this section of the book of Numbers presents a view of God that runs entirely counter to our culture and indeed perhaps every culture that ever lived. Every other culture or religion worships a god who is either transcendent or immanent. Their god is either transcendent—utterly distant and uninvolved with us—or he is immanent, present with us. Transcendent gods are completely unlike us, while immanent gods are a lot like us. In Islam, for example, Allah is transcendent—the high and holy one—but he is not immanent. He does not dwell with his people; he is completely Other. He cannot easily be approached by ordinary people, nor does he really involve himself personally and intimately with the lives of human beings. On the other hand, Norse gods like Thor and Wodin were utterly immanent: they were just like human beings, feasting and fighting, marrying and committing adultery. Apart from their raw power, there was nothing transcendent about them at all.

The Bible presents a far more profound and far more sophisticated understanding of God than any other religion. In the Scriptures we meet a God who is utterly transcendent and yet at the same time utterly immanent. Our God lives in a high and holy place (transcendence), yet also with him who is contrite and lowly in spirit (immanence) (Isaiah 57:15). His ways are not our ways, and his thoughts are not ours; yet he has created us in his image, and so we are able to know something of who he is. Both his transcendence and his immanence are prominently present as aspects of God's character in Numbers 4. He pitched his tent in the midst of the camp of Israel, a radical act of immanence; yet at the same time his tent was surrounded by mystery and danger. It was not to be approached by ordinary people, or even by ordinary Levites, lest they die. The God who dwelt with Israel is a holy God, and all of his things are holy. The principle of graded holiness stressed the "otherness" and transcendence of God, that he is not like his people. At one and the same time, therefore, this God is thoroughly immanent, present with his people, and also utterly transcendent, completely Other.

What is your view of God? The profundity of the Scriptures always confronts the shallowness of our natural cultural and religious views. The Bible challenges those who worship a purely transcendent god, like the God of Islam or medieval Catholicism. Such a God can only be approached in a foreign language, through mystery, as in the Mass. In contrast, the Bible invites us to meet the God who is with us, the God who is not simply our exalted master and King but also our Father. On the other hand, though, the Bible also challenges the very immanent view of God that is present in American culture. God is usually perceived as being just like us on our better days, only with a little more power. Anyone can approach God anytime, anywhere without any special preparation or holiness. He is our buddy, our "copilot," whose angels are friendly neighbors who are constantly using their supernatural powers to touch our lives and make them run a little more smoothly. According to our culture, he is a very safe, even tame God, who of course has a wonderful plan for our lives and the lives of everyone else in this world he has created. Songs of praise to such an immanent deity can sometimes barely be distinguished from poems of love for another human being. The Bible confronts those who believe in such a domesticated God with the reality that our God is a holy God, of purer eyes than to look upon evil, whose wrath is continually extended toward the wicked.

The God of the Bible is thus radically different from the God of our culture or of our imaginations. He is not tame, nor even necessarily "safe," if by "safe" we mean that he will always work things out in ways that make sense to our wisdom. Though he dwells in the midst of his people, his holiness is always threatening to break out and consume the unholy people who are all around him. Nor is this merely an empty threat. As the rest of the book of Numbers will show us, the threat of death from God's holiness is a clear and present danger throughout the wilderness wandering. The warnings that are presented in Numbers 3, 4 are found to be true in the rest of the book. An entire generation suffered the ultimate sanction for their unholiness and disobedience, being put to death in the wilderness. The God of the Bible is radically different from the way we tend to conceive of him.

To Live and Not Die

Yet the tragedy of those deaths in the book of Numbers is that every one of them was preventable. They were warned of the dangers, but they ignored the warnings. God is not an arbitrary tyrant who lashes out unpredictably and liquidates innocent bystanders. On the contrary, he gave detailed and clearly comprehensible instructions to his people as to how they should behave and what they should do, written in plain Hebrew so that all might understand their significance. The purpose of all of these detailed instructions for the Levites was declared in Numbers 4:19: "that they may live and not die when they come near to the most holy things." In fact, this was the purpose behind all of the extensive ordering of the camp of Israel in Numbers 1—4. The people were being carefully arranged so that God could dwell in their midst as a blessing to them and not as a curse. As long as Moses and the people followed these instructions carefully, the result would be blessing and life.

God has not changed in his commitment to holiness. He has given us, too, detailed instructions in his Word as to how we should live, instructions that are not merely suggestions but commandments. I remember once when our children were little hearing a young mother tell us that she never said no to her children because that word was too negative. Rather, she would tell them, "Please don't." My response was that if I meant "Please don't" I would say that, but often precisely what I wanted to communicate to my children was "No!" There are times when our children's lives may literally depend on their obedience to our word. Perhaps they are about to run out into the road in front of an oncoming truck. At times like that, "Please don't" isn't enough! Our children need to hear and heed the word *no*.

So also God in his Word has given us an abundance of detailed commandments. Some of them are "No!" while others are "Yes!" Don't commit adultery or murder. Do honor your father and mother. Don't take advantage of the poor and helpless. Do speak the truth in love. Why has God given us such a myriad of commandments, and why should we obey them? Is he simply trying to spoil our fun? On the contrary, he gives his law to us for the same reason that good fathers give their children a myriad of instructions to obey. These instructions are the way to life and joy, to spiritual health and peace. Out of his kindness and mercy, God has not left us to construct lives and families with a few vague and confusing instructions that are barely English, like the dollhouse manufacturer. Instead, in his Word he has given us an abundance of guidance that is clear, straightforward, and direct.

Loving God's Law

Do we appreciate the magnitude of that gift? The psalmist said, "Oh how I love your law! It is my meditation all the day. Your commandment makes me wiser than my enemies, for it is ever with me. I have more understanding than all my teachers, for your testimonies are my meditation. . . . How sweet are your words to my taste, sweeter than honey to my mouth! Through your precepts I get understanding; therefore I hate every false way" (Psalm 119:97-99, 103, 104). Is that the attitude you and I have toward God's Law? Do we love it and give him thanks that he has given us such an abundance of detailed instruction? Or do we think to ourselves that we know what to do in our situation better than he does?

One reason why we don't love God's Law is because we have forgotten God's transcendence. Why is it that teenagers in particular have a hard time obeying their parents' instructions? It is because they are at an age when they don't really believe their parents are smarter than they are. At five years old you think your parents know everything; at fifteen you think they know nothing at all. Then you are amazed at how rapid their learning curve is as you enter your twenties and thirties! You once again start to respect their wisdom and seek out their insight. In the same way, if we truly grasp the fact that God is vastly higher, holier, and wiser than we are, we will love his law and cherish his detailed instructions for life. His wisdom is so profound; how could I ever imagine that I know better than he does? How could I second-guess his providence and the paths he leads me down? They are not necessarily the paths I would have chosen, but is that surprising? On the contrary, if I remember that his thoughts are as high above mine as the heavens are above the earth, I would expect that to be the case. It would have been easy for the Gershonites to resent the privilege given to the clan of Kohath to carry the most holy things, unless they remembered who it was who gave the orders. Why should Kohath have top place and not Gershon? God knows the reason, and that is enough: we don't necessarily need to know.

At the same time, though, to love God's Law you not only need to remember his transcendence, you also need to remember his immanence. There is another reason why teenagers find it hard to obey their parents' instructions, isn't there? It is because they think their parents cannot identify with them in their situation. To a teenager, their parents naturally seem old and out-of-touch. "You just don't understand" comes the cry, along with the expressive rolling of eyeballs. So too, if we only remember God's transcendence, we may be tempted to think that he is out-of-touch with our situation. "He doesn't understand what I'm going through," we say to ourselves, excusing our sin. The God of the Bible, though, is not merely transcendent, he is immanent. He is with us in the midst of our situation. He knows what we wrestle with and sees our struggles. His law is not imposed upon us arbitrarily from a great height but is shaped to meet the needs of the creatures whom he made and whom he loves. There is therefore no cause for you to roll your eyes at God and think that he is out-of-touch with you. On the contrary, he knows your sorrows and your griefs. His law is wise and good not just for mankind in general but for you in particular. In some profound way, each clan's burden was right for them, whether it was large or small. So too the personal burdens that you carry through life come to you by God's assignment, and they are therefore in a profound way "right" for you. These are the good works that God has prepared in advance for you to do (Ephesians 2:10).

Dealing with the Curse

There is a problem, though, with the arrangement of the camp of Israel, with a holy God dwelling in the midst of his people. The problem is that as long as it rests on human obedience, the result will always be a curse. If God's favor toward me rests on my personal ability to keep God's strict and detailed injunctions, then I am necessarily under a curse, because the fact is, I am a lawbreaker. Galatians 3:10 puts it like this: "For all who rely on works of the law are under a curse; for it is written, 'Cursed be everyone who does not abide by all things written in the Book of the Law, and do them.'" If your ability to approach God is a function of your own obedience, then you will find him to be a consuming fire, for your obedience is always less than perfect. The God whom we see in the book of Numbers does not grade on a curve. He doesn't say, "The last ninety-nine times you packed up this furniture you didn't sneak an illegitimate peek at the holy things, so I'll let you off this time." No; one single error, one single glance in the wrong direction, was enough to kill. In fact, the surprising part of the book of Numbers is not that so many of the Israelites died but that any of them survived! You might ask, "Who would want to be a Levite, serving this close to the all-holy God?" Yet are we any safer than they were, since Jesus himself commanded us, "You therefore must be perfect, as your heavenly Father is perfect" (Matthew 5:48)? Any lack of perfection in us is enough to condemn us not merely to physical death but to eternity in Hell.

So how then can God ever dwell in our midst without his holy, transcendent presence becoming a curse to us? How can he live in the center of our community without destroying us? The answer lies in the ultimate fusion of transcendence and immanence that took place in the Incarnation. There in the person of Jesus, the high and holy God took on flesh and dwelt in our midst. The disciples beheld his glory day by day as he walked on this earth and in heightened form on the Mount of Transfiguration, and yet they were not struck down for gazing at the face of God in Christ. Why not? Certainly it is not because they were free from sin. Rather, it is because in Jesus the transcendent, holy God took into himself the death that we deserved for our sins. Christ's purpose in coming was so that we too might live and not die when we approach the most holy things.

This safety is not the result of our following the example of Christ and meriting approaching God in our own righteousness. Not at all. We could never match up to his standard of perfection. That requirement would crush us. No; Jesus came to live the life of perfect holiness that we could never live. He died the death our sins deserved. The result of his perfect life and sacrificial death is that the Old Testament gradations of holiness are eliminated. In the new Jerusalem depicted in the book of Revelation, there is no inner ring of Levites around the throne whose task is to keep us at the distance from God that our lives merit. On the contrary, the whole new Jerusalem has now become a gigantic Holy of Holies, completely covered in pure gold. It is a Holy of Holies where God himself has his throne, yet to which the doors stand constantly open. All those who are in Christ share his holiness and are therefore welcomed into the very center.

This means, on the one hand, that there is no place for despair. Do your sins mount up to Heaven and cry out your unfitness to enter there? So do mine! Yet the blood of Jesus shouts still louder, "This one is mine. I died to make him holy. I bled for these sins of hers. They are welcome to come in, for my sake." No matter how slow the progress of your sanctification, you can never despair as long as Jesus stands there interceding for you, inviting you in. His good work begun in you will one day be brought to completion (Philippians 1:6).

On the other hand, it also means there is no room for complacency. If God took his holiness so seriously in the Old Testament and judged severely those who took it lightly, how can we treat it as a light thing whether or not we obey him? If God took the identity of the person who carried the tent pegs of his tabernacle through the wilderness so seriously, how can we be casual about breaking any of God's laws? How can we trample the Ten Commandments underfoot and think that it doesn't matter? We more easily recognize the sins of others in this regard, but we need to search our own hearts as well. We have not really delighted in God's laws, meditating upon them day and night. We have not pondered deeply not only how to avoid breaking the letter of the Law but also how to fulfill wholeheartedly its spirit. In Christ, God not only eliminates the barriers that prevent access to him—he also raises the bar of holiness for all of his people. We are called to be a royal priesthood, a holy nation in his service (1 Peter 2:9). Every single one of us is to take our duty in God's service as seriously as the Levites had to in the book of Numbers.

God has bought us with a price and has commissioned us for his service. We too are therefore to bear the emblems of his presence wherever we go. It is our privilege and responsibility to pick up the cross and carry its message everywhere we go day by day. For some, the good news of the gospel will be a welcome message, the aroma of life in a dark world. For others, it will be unwelcome, the stench of death because of their unwillingness to bow before the truth. But the calling to share Christ's burden is a matter of great joy for us. We are ambassadors of the one holy and transcendent God who has dwelt among us in Christ and even now fills us with his Spirit. What a blessing it is to know this God and have the ministry of making him known to others!

6

Dealing with Disorder

NUMBERS 5

ALMOST EVERYONE IS FAMILIAR WITH the Second Law of Thermo-dynamics. In scientific terms, it says, "Entropy tends to increase." Or, to put it in more popular language, "Chaos happens." I see the law at work in my house every day. The dust molecules never decide to organize them-selves neatly in a pile in a corner. Left to their own devices, they distribute themselves evenly across the floor, the desk, and every other object in the room. I've noticed that entropy increases particularly swiftly in my chil-dren's bedrooms. The toys distribute themselves all across the floor, almost without perceptible human involvement. However, they never reorganize themselves tidily into the closet without extensive and disciplined human intervention. Chaos is natural; order needs to be worked at.

It is the same way in the camp of Israel. The order that God has set up in Numbers 1—4 is not naturally self-sustaining. Chaos happens. Disorder and sin are part of our normal experience in this fallen world. It is normal, yet at the same time it is also dangerous, threatening the presence of God in the midst of his people. This fact of life needs to be accounted for if God is to dwell in the tabernacle at the heart of the camp. Order will not always exist naturally in Israel's camp. The people therefore need to be instructed about disorder and sin—especially how to deal with it properly—just as much as they need guidance on the way things ought to be. Nor are we in a different situation from them. Although in our culture we would like to be able to talk about happy things all the time, the reality is that we too are sinners who need to know how to deal with that fact. Numbers 5 will help provide us with the answers we need.

Narrative and Law

As we mentioned in the very first chapter, the whole structure of the book of Numbers is an alternating series of stories and laws that fit together in a complex structure. Why is that? Why is the story line of the journey through the wilderness constantly being interrupted by a sequence of laws? Charles Dickens and Emily Brontë didn't do that with their novels. Even J.R.R. Tolkien's Lord of the Rings, which encompasses almost every conceivable genre of literature within its vast scope, doesn't contain law codes. So why does the book of Numbers? The answer is that the heart of the book of Numbers is the dwelling of a holy God in the midst of his people, first of all in the pilgrim camp in the wilderness and ultimately looking forward to the day when he will dwell in their midst in the Promised Land. Since Israel's God is holy, therefore his people must be holy also. An unholy people who come in contact with a holy God will be consumed by his wrath. If they continue to be unholy, he must either abandon them or destroy them altogether. The way to life, therefore, is necessarily the way of obedience to God's laws. These are not arbitrary, meaningless regulations, busywork assigned to his people by an overcontrolling deity who has nothing better to do with his time. These laws are the way to life and blessing, the wisdom of a sovereign God unfolded for the benefit of the people with whom he has entered a covenant relationship. Life in all its fullness means life lived in the presence of God, according to his Law.

Yet that still doesn't answer the question why these particular laws are given at this particular point in the story. They are not a comprehensive treatment of the laws connected with any particular issue. Some of these laws were given in more expanded form in Leviticus. Many key questions of jurisprudence are left unanswered. Yet for some reason these particular laws were inserted at this particular point in the story. We cannot therefore treat these laws in isolation from the narrative; they go together with it. What is the precise focus of the legislation in this chapter? Having organized the camp, God here gives his people some case studies in dealing with potential disorder, so that they may learn how to resolve the entropy issues that were bound to arise and threaten the presence of God in the midst of his people. After four chapters about holiness, this chapter is all about sin and how to deal with it.

There are three case studies in this chapter, each of which deals with a different issue and in turn shows us a different perspective on sin. In the first case, the issue is unintentional ritual defilement (vv. 1-4). The second situation deals with a deliberate sin that has been repented of (vv. 5-10), while the third case study deals with the complex issue of an accusation of adultery that lacks formal evidence (vv. 11-31). Each of these cases is addressed in a different way, but in each of them sin is recognized and dealt with. It is these ways of dealing with sin and counteracting its danger to the camp of God's people that form the message of the chapter.

Case Study 1: Sin as Defilement

The first case study is very straightforward. It was possible for a person to contract ritual defilement in a number of ways in ancient Israel. The rules are spelled out in far greater detail in Leviticus 13—15; all we have here is a thumbnail summary. In essence, these ritual impurities focused on three elements that brought a person into contact with the realm of death: the loss or discharge of blood or semen, various wasting skin diseases, and contact with dead bodies.[1] Contact with dead bodies self-evidently brought you into contact with the realm of death. Equally, blood and semen were associated with life, so their loss or emission moved you away from the realm of life into the realm of death. Finally, skin diseases of the kind that withered or ate away the flesh were a kind of living death, in which the body was literally dying in front of your eyes. All such contact with the realm of death in the Old Testament unfitted you for the presence of the true and living God. Therefore those who had contracted such ritual defilement were to be sent outside the camp. The laws were not concerned with public health or the potential infection of others with contagious diseases; the concern was simply that such defilement would make it impossible for the living God to dwell in their midst.

As we read the Biblical passages about ritual defilement, our instinctive reaction is perhaps to see this concern as superficial and unfair, even offensive. Why were these things regarded as important? To modern people, these laws may well seem like a primitive taboo that has no relevance to us. Why should someone be excluded from the presence of God simply because he suffers from a particular medical condition? Why does preparing a father's body for burial make someone unfit to stand in God's presence? Why should faithful married sexual intercourse keep anyone away from worship? At first sight, these regulations seem rather arbitrary and unjust to us.

Yet these laws were intended as a mirror to reveal to us the profound depths of our problem as human beings. The significance of this defilement picturing our alienation from God is enormous. Far from the Biblical perspective being shallow, on the contrary it is our culture's view of sin and alienation that is shallow. In our society, people generally think that the only problem standing between them and God is their behavior. *If I'm a good person, God will surely accept me; if I am a bad person, then God will reject me.* The Bible, however, shows us that this analysis is superficial and thoughtless. Sin is not just about what you do; it is about your very nature as a human being in this world.

Our Root Problem: Death

Do you see the implications of this? If the issue that makes us unfit to stand in God's presence is not simply an outward, behavioral one, then our problem isn't simply saying bad words and hanging with the wrong crowd at school. It isn't simply those who cheat on their wives and rob banks who are alienated from God. Our human problem, at its deepest root, is the principle of death that is consuming our souls just as surely as leprosy devours the flesh. We are dead men walking, surrounded on all sides by a community of the dead. Even while physically we continue to live, our souls atrophy and waste away from the inside out in the absence of God.

The prophet Isaiah put it eloquently in his own day when he said, "Woe is me! For I am lost; for I am a man of unclean lips, and I dwell in the midst of a people of unclean lips; for my eyes have seen the King, the LORD of hosts!" (Isaiah 6:5). He understood that mutual contact in the midst of a society of sinners continually defiles us all. Left to myself, even the highest and holiest of human acts does not move me nearer to God but keeps me away from him. As the prophet goes on to say, "We have all become like one who is unclean, and all our righteous deeds are like a polluted garment. We all fade like a leaf, and our iniquities, like the wind, take us away" (64:6). Even my righteous deeds, such as being kind to my neighbor and loving my children, defile me and everyone with whom I have contact.

If that is true, then there is absolutely nothing I can do to present myself as acceptable to God. I inherited this body of death from my first forefather, Adam. His sinful nature, transmitted to me, turned even God's high and holy law into an instrument of death in my life (Romans 7:7-13). I am by nature defiled and unclean, and therefore I defile everything I touch. This natural depravity and darkness comprehensively unfits me for God's presence. Of course, my natural depravity proceeds to work itself out in all manner of particular sins for which I am also accountable, but my fundamental problem is deeper than that: it lies in the fact that I am a sinner. In the penetrating analysis of the human condition that the Bible presents, I am born unfit for God's presence, only deserving permanent exclusion from the camp of God.

What is more, in order to be admitted into God's presence, the root problem had to be dealt with. If the problem was an emission, the person needed to be washed clean before he or she could reenter the camp. If the problem was a skin disease, his or her flesh needed to be made whole before he or she could come back in. Wholeness and cleanliness were needed before you could enter into God's presence. If you were a leper, you might well stand outside the camp crying out what the Apostle Paul cries in Romans 7:24: "Who will deliver me from this body of death?" If you had a permanent flow of blood, you might cry out, "Who will wash me and render me clean?" That cleansing and cure was not in your own power to accomplish. You couldn't simply decide to follow God and then you could come in. On the contrary, your inclusion required a miraculous act of God if it was to be achieved.

The Answer for Our Alienation

Yet if the Old Testament picture shows us the depth of our alienation from God, the New Testament shows us the glorious answer to that alienated condition. We too are alienated from God, dead in transgressions and sins. But the answer to the leper's cry, "Who will deliver me from this body of death?" is "Thanks be to God through Jesus Christ our Lord!" (Romans 7:25). Jesus is the one who has come to deliver us from death and wash us clean. That is why we see Jesus in his earthly ministry bringing into the covenant community those who under the old covenant had been excluded. The woman who had had an emission of blood for many years and had tried in vain to find medical relief for her condition came to Jesus and touched him (Luke 8:43-48). From the perspective of the book of Numbers, that was an extremely dangerous act! An unclean woman was deliberately bringing herself into physical contact with the Holy One of Israel. No wonder that when Jesus stopped and demanded to know who had touched him, she came forward trembling. But in Jesus she found physical and spiritual wholeness, rest for her body and peace for her soul. She who was once an outsider, alienated from God and his people, was now brought in through the touch of Jesus.

The lepers too came to Jesus, and he touched them (Luke 5:12-15). He healed them from their living death and told them to go and show themselves to a priest, just as the Law required, so that they would be able to return to the worship of God. Notice that in neither case did Jesus say, "That law is silly and outdated. I hereby abolish it." Rather, in each situation he dealt with the person's need for cleansing so they could enter God's presence. The profound picture of separation from God that was set up in the Old Testament found its answer in Jesus Christ. He came to deal with the living death in our souls by washing our hearts clean. He came to take us from death and bring us into life. Indeed, he did so by taking upon himself the very exclusion from the presence of God that we deserved. He was himself taken outside the holy city of Jerusalem to be crucified, "outside the camp" as Hebrews 13:11-13 puts it. He was cut off from fellowship with his Father on the cross, in a black night of agony in his soul that far outweighed the physical sufferings of crucifixion. That is how he enabled our alienation from God to be dealt with, so that we might no longer be outsiders, condemned to eternity away from the presence of God. Now we are God's children, welcome into his presence for Jesus' sake.

Case Study 2: Sin as Transgression

The second case study in dealing with sin in Numbers 5:5-10 is quite different from the first. Instead of addressing the conditions that are largely outside our control that unfit us for God's presence, it addresses a variety of potential sins that are quite deliberate. Our sin problem is much more than our wrong thoughts and actions, but it is certainly not less than them. The exact nature of these sins is not explained in detail. The parallel passage in Leviticus 6 suggests that the most common issues that these provisions related to involved theft by deception or misrepresentation, but here the offense is left deliberately vague, perhaps because the focus is not so much on how to *define* the sin as it is on how to *deal with* the sin. In contrast to the previous case study, which showed us sin as *defilement*, this study shows us sin as *transgression*.

In focusing our attention on sin as transgression, this passage reminds us that sin often has two dimensions: it is an offense against God and against man. Therefore, dealing with the sin involves addressing the offense that has occurred in both directions. The first step in dealing with such sin is always confession—recognizing publicly that a wrong has been committed (v. 7). Taking responsibility for one's actions and agreeing with God that they were wrong is an important part of the process of dealing with sin. As long as we are still excusing our actions, we have not come to recognize their true nature. Confession by itself was not enough, however. It was also to be accompanied by restitution of the full amount misappropriated, plus 20 percent (v. 7). The persons who had committed the sin not only had to say they were sorry but also had to do what was in their power to put it right. If the damaged party was no longer alive, restitution could be paid to a close relative. If there was no relative, it was to be given to the Lord instead (v. 8). In any event, justice would be seen to be done.

Thus far we have simply been dealing with the horizontal aspect of sin, putting right the damage that transgression does to those whom we have offended. But sin is not only, or even primarily, an offense against other human beings. It is far more profoundly an offense against God. That is why after David committed adultery with Bathsheba and had her husband Uriah exposed on the front lines of battle and left to die, he cried out, "Against you, you only, have I sinned" (Psalm 51:4). David didn't mean that his sin had no impact on other people—far from it! People had died as a result of his actions. Yet the most fundamental aspect of sin as transgression is the offense that we cause to a holy God. For that reason in Numbers 5, after confession and restitution, the sinner was required to offer a ram to make atonement for him (v. 8). In this way, the fact that the offense was committed against the Lord was recognized publicly. If the sinner were not himself to die, something or someone must die in his place.

The Answer for Transgression

The perspective of sin as transgression reminds us that even after there has been confession and restitution, there still needs to be a sacrifice. The wages of sin are death, and those wages have to be paid, either by the sinner or by someone else. This perspective too points us forward to Christ, the Lamb of God who makes atonement for his people in his death on the cross. Why did Jesus have to die such a brutal death? He is the atoning sacrifice for our sins (1 John 2:2). He had to die to pay the penalty for my sin and your sin, and that penalty is death itself. He took our place in death to satisfy the justice of God, to cover the offense that our sin causes to a holy God.

The sacrifice of Christ certainly doesn't give us a free pass to sin all we want. On the contrary, when we sin, we too are to confess our sin, as 1 John 1:9 reminds us. Where appropriate, we too are to make restitution to the ones hurt by our actions. When the tax collector Zacchaeus became a believer, he offered restitution to the tune of four times the amount to anyone he had defrauded (Luke 19:8). The effect of grace on our lives is to make our hearts eager to do what is right. Yet ultimately it is not our confession or our restitution that saves us but Christ's death in our place.

Case Study 3: Sin as Unfaithfulness

So then, in Numbers 5 we first of all see sin as defilement and transgression. Most of the chapter, however, is taken up with the third case study: the woman who is suspected of marital unfaithfulness. There was no proof of her guilt or innocence, only the suspicion that she had been unfaithful. To deal with this situation, she was subjected to what may seem to us to be a bizarre and primitive ritual. What is going on here? Why does this particular offense attract such extensive description at this point in the book of Numbers?

The answer is, I think, to see that here we have a third picture of sin: sin as *unfaithfulness*. Since marriage is the key metaphor for the relationship between God and Israel, it is not surprising that adultery is the key metaphor for breaches in that relationship. Whenever Israel went after idols, they were at the same time being untrue to their Husband, the Lord.

So how was Israel to deal with the situation where a wife was suspected of such a serious breach in the relationship, yet there was no conclusive proof? The answer is that they were to take it to the Lord and leave judgment in his hands. When he brought the charge against his wife, the husband was also to bring a grain offering (v. 15). The word for grain offering (*minḥâ*) was elsewhere used of gifts given as a mark of submission to a superior. So to bring a grain offering was an act of submission to the Lord. This grain offering, however, was devoid of the usual markers of joy that would be offered with it—oil and incense (v. 15). There was no joy in this matter.

Meanwhile, the priest was to prepare a cup containing a mixture of holy water and sacred dust from the floor of the tabernacle (v. 17). The woman stood before the Lord with her hair down, a symbol of the potentially broken covenant of marriage, and the priest was then to charge the woman on oath with a self-imprecatory curse. He said in essence, "If you have not been unfaithful, then let this water not cause you harm; but if you have been unfaithful, then may you become barren." The woman was then to respond with the words, "Amen. So be it" (vv. 19-22). The written curses would then be washed off into the water, which the woman would have to drink, emphasizing the fact that these were words that she would literally have to eat (vv. 23, 24). The cup itself is said to be a cup of bitter water, not so much in terms of the taste (though that probably wasn't particularly pleasant either) but the potential outcome. If she were guilty, the Lord would impose the curse that she called down upon herself, and her abdomen would swell and her thigh waste away—most probably a reference to the disordering of her reproductive organs so that she was unable to bear children. If she were innocent, however, the curse would have no effect, and she would continue to live a normal, fruitful life.

Calling it a cup of bitter water (*mey hammārim*) recalls the water that the people of Israel could not drink at Marah because it was bitter (*mārîm*; Exodus 15:23). On that occasion, immediately after they crossed the Red Sea, God enabled Moses to transform the water to make it sweet by adding a piece of wood. This was, the Lord said, a test: If they obeyed his laws and did what was right in his eyes, then they would not suffer the curses that came upon the Egyptians but would experience God as their healer (Exodus 15:26). The similarities are striking, especially in the light of the fact that barrenness and a miscarrying womb was a standard curse for covenant unfaithfulness (see Exodus 23:26).[2] God the healer can transform bitter water and make it sweet, removing its power to harm. Yet he is also God the Judge, who has the power to bring a curse on covenant-breakers. Her obedience, or lack of obedience, would determine the outcome of this test on the woman.

This parallel shows us that the test was not thought of as magic. There was nothing intrinsic in the water or dust or ink that would harm her if she were an adulteress. Only God could bring about the curse upon her. It was an act of faith on the part of the woman and the community, placing judgment in the hands of God, who sees the unseen, rather than in the hands of man. We should also note that it was not an unfair procedure. Unlike many apparently similar rituals that existed in the ancient world, it didn't presume the woman's guilt or innocence. She wasn't thrown into the river to see whether or not she would drown. The procedure protected the innocent against unfounded charges as much as it brought the guilty to the bar of justice. The adulterous wife would experience God's covenant curse for her unfaithfulness, while the innocent wife would emerge vindicated.

The Answer for Spiritual Adultery

Yet if adulterous wives were certain to receive God's covenant curse, even in the absence of compelling human testimony, what will God do with his own adulterous wife, Israel? In her case, there was no doubt as to her guilt. The prophets repeatedly document her long history of whoredom, which is a metaphor for the people's spiritual unfaithfulness to God (see Hosea 1—3; Ezekiel 16, 23). No tribunal in the land would declare the charge against her unproven. So what would happen to her before the bar of the heavenly tribunal? The answer is that God himself, the jealous husband (Numbers 5:14), will bring her to trial and make her drink the cup of God's wrath. In Isaiah 51:17, 22 and Ezekiel 23:30-34 we see God giving his unfaithful bride a bitter cup to swallow, a cup full of lamentation and woe. Since she is self-evidently as guilty as sin, how will she escape when she drinks the cup? Will she not feel the full force of God's curse upon her? Will her reproductive power not be cut off, so that she bears no more children?

The answer is yes—and no. Yes, Israel was forced to drain the bitter cup to its dregs at the time of the exile. She faced the punishment of exile and the death of a whole generation away from the Promised Land, the ultimate sanction of the covenant for her long history of unfaithfulness. Yet that was not the end of the story for Israel. God rescued her from the wilderness of the nations and brought her back to her own land. He went after his unfaithful wife and wooed her back.

How can that be? Does God have a double standard—hard on human adultery but soft on spiritual adultery? By no means. God was able to go after his errant wife and bring her back because Jesus Christ would himself take up the bitter cup and drain it in the place of his bride, the church. At the last supper he lifted up the cup and said, "This cup . . . is the new covenant in my blood; drink it in remembrance of me" (Luke 22:20). We are so familiar with those words that we repeat at every Communion service that they have lost their power to shock us. "This cup is . . . *my blood*," said Jesus. It wasn't literally his blood, of course, any more than the cup that we drink at the Lord's Table is literally changed into something different than wine. It remained the same substance. Yet for the cup we share to be a cup of blessing for us, it had to become a cup of suffering and woe for him, a bitter cup. In order for us who are covenant-breakers to be invited to the covenant meal, he himself had to drink the cup of our suffering in our place, shedding his blood for us on the cross. His curse for my blessing—his death for my life. Jesus is the answer to the plight of the guilty adulterous wife, who is each of us: we are all by nature idolatrous, following the desires and fancies of our own hearts and not God.

Isaiah 53 draws all three of these pictures of the remedies for sin together in the experience of the Suffering Servant. He was cut off from the land of the living for our sake (v. 8); his life was our guilt offering (v. 10); and who can speak of his descendants (v. 8)? He was pierced for our transgressions and crushed for our iniquities; yet the result of his bearing the curse is that he will see his offspring and prolong his days (v. 10). Jesus is the one who has dealt with our sin in such a way that we are able to come just as we are to a holy God, there to find mercy and grace sufficient for our needs. It doesn't matter who we are or what we have done. Whether our problem is defilement, transgression, or spiritual adultery, Christ has paid the price for us and has enabled us to draw near to receive God's blessing. He therefore invites us to come to his table and participate by faith in his feast, looking forward to the final covenant meal at which the cup we will share together will be completely free from suffering and pain, filled to overflowing with joy and adoration.

7

All for Jesus

NUMBERS 6:1-21

IN THE 1960S there was a radical countercultural movement that found expression in changed hairstyles among young people. As a sign of freedom, or of rebellion against authority, almost everyone started growing their hair long, both men and women. At first sight this may look like something similar to what we see in Numbers 6, a kind of early "Hippies for Jesus" movement. On closer examination, however, the two trends can't exactly be the same, not least because the hippies were not exactly known for abstaining from wine, or any other intoxicating substance for that matter. Alternatively, if the Nazirites were not early hippies, is this chapter a kind of precursor of the monastic movement of the Middle Ages, in which people took upon themselves a voluntary vow of poverty, celibacy, and obedience in order to devote their lives to the service of God through asceticism? This analogy is perhaps closer to the mark; yet the differences between a monk and a Nazirite are as striking as the similarities. Both the monk and the Nazirite were devoted to God, but the Nazirite was no ascetic. Apart from wine and grape products, he could eat or drink whatever he wanted. He or she could live in a fine house and sleep in a comfortable bed and enjoy normal marital relations with a husband or a wife. In addition, the Nazirite vow was normally only a temporary commitment, not a lifelong vow. So the Nazirite was not exactly committed to the ascetic lifestyle as the way to a higher, more spiritual life in the way the monastic movement was.

If a Nazirite was neither a hippie nor a monk, what was he? In essence the Nazirite vow was a temporary separation from normal life to be devoted to God in a special way. In so doing, the Nazirite provided a mirror in which Israel was to look and be reminded of who she ought to be permanently as a holy nation. The Nazirite was a person who was consecrated to the Lord, just as Israel as a nation was to be consecrated to the Lord. Every time the Israelites saw a Nazirite, therefore, they would have been reminded of their own calling to serve the Lord.

The Nazirite Vow

To see this, we need to begin by looking at the nature of the Nazirite vow. A Nazirite was a man or a woman whose vow was a temporary personal commitment to avoid three things: he (or she) would abstain from grapes and alcoholic beverages, let his hair grow and not cut it, and stay well away from dead bodies. Each of these commitments were to be carried through to radical lengths. The Nazirite was not just to abstain from wine and strong drink but also from vinegar, grape juice, grapes, and raisins. Even the seeds and skins of grapes were off-limits (v. 4). It wasn't simply a matter of avoiding the intoxicating effects of alcohol, therefore, but of doing without everything associated with the grape. Since wine was the primary symbol of joy in the ancient world, to do without grape products was a vivid commitment voluntarily to turn away from life's normal pleasures.

Similarly, the Nazirites were not simply to let their hair grow—they were to grow it long, without cutting it at all, throughout the length of their vow. Because the hair is a living part of the body, it was a natural symbol for the life of a person.[1] To let your hair grow without human restriction represented giving your life over completely to God's control. It was a vivid symbol of giving God the reins of your life.

Finally, the Nazirites were not simply to stay away from corpses in general, as all Israelites were required to do. Corpses had defiling power, as we saw in Numbers 5, and therefore the people of the living God were not to come in contact with them. Yet in normal life there were exceptions permitted to this general rule. Somebody had to prepare the bodies of the dead for burial, and normally this would be the task of a close relative. The Nazirites, however, were to stay away even from the bodies of their closest family members if they should die (6:7). This was a vivid symbol of their extreme separation from the realm of death to serve the living God. These vows were thus not random commitments, as if the Nazirite could equally well have promised to exercise for sixty minutes every day and to stay away from carbohydrates and sugar. The Nazirite made an extreme, radical commitment to serve the Lord through maintaining ritual holiness, a commitment far more radical than anything devised in the sixties.

Each of the areas of commitment—alcohol, hair control, and corpse contact—were also regulated for the priests of Israel, though in a less extreme way. The priests too were required to abstain from alcohol, but only while they were on duty (Leviticus 10:9). Wine was a good gift of God intended to bring joy and gladness. Yet there was a time to abstain from that gladness when they were employed in the service of the Lord. The priests also had to be careful with their hair, and they were forbidden to shave it (Leviticus 21:5). The high priest in particular was not allowed to disarrange his hair as a sign of mourning (Leviticus 21:10). Priests generally were also required to be careful to avoid contact with dead bodies, because such contact with the realm of death made one unclean (Leviticus 21:1-4); but the high priest, like the Nazirite, had particular obligations. He could not come in contact with a corpse even to mourn his own father and mother (Leviticus 21:11). When you put these obligations side by side, it is possible to observe that the Nazirite was a kind of temporary lay priest—someone who for a period of time lived according to the special level of ritual purity demanded of those whose lives were lived constantly in the Lord's presence.

A Picture of Israel

This, of course, as we said earlier, made the Nazirite a perfect picture of what Israel was intended to be. They were to be "a kingdom of priests and a holy nation" (Exodus 19:6). God had chosen them uniquely out of all of the nations of the earth to be his people in order that he might dwell in their midst. In consequence, they were to be separate and distinct from the other nations. The existence of the Nazirites in their midst would constantly have reminded them of that necessity to be different and to be holy.

The prophet Samuel is a good example of this. He was born at a time of great spiritual decline in Israel. The priests of the day, Hophni and Phinehas, the two sons of Eli, were bringing religion into disrepute by running the temple for their own personal profit and sleeping with the women who served there (1 Samuel 2:22). Samuel entered that dark picture as a child, dedicated by his mother at birth to be a lifelong Nazirite (1 Samuel 1:11). His devotion to the Lord stood in constant contrast with the corruption of Hophni and Phinehas. In fact, the narrator highlights that contrast by switching the spotlight back and forth from Samuel to Hophni and Phinehas and back again, as if to invite you to set them side by side and draw your own conclusions. Samuel the Nazirite was a living picture in his own day of who Israel ought to be as the people of God.

Of course, simply taking a vow of holiness does not necessarily transform a person internally, as the story of another Nazirite from birth, Samson, demonstrates. Like Samuel, he too was dedicated to the Lord as a Nazirite before he was born, according to the instructions given to his mother by the angel of the Lord (Judges 13:3-5). Yet a less dedicated Nazirite than Samson would be hard to find. The first episode recorded in Samson's adult life relates his desire to marry a Philistine woman (14:1-3). Far from keeping himself separate from the uncircumcised enemies of the Lord, he wanted to climb into bed with one. On his way to marry her, Samson turned aside to see a lion's corpse where bees had made their nest (14:8). As a Nazirite, he should have stayed well clear of all corpses, but Samson was motivated more by his appetite than by his calling. Instead of keeping his distance, he went over and scooped some honey out from the dead body.

When he arrived at the home of his future in-laws, Samson celebrated a feast there (14:10). The Hebrew word for feast, *mišteh*, comes from the verb "to drink," and I doubt very much that Samson was there as the designated driver. The second vow, abstaining from alcoholic beverages, thus apparently went by the board as well. Finally, he revealed to Delilah the source of his strength, and she shaved his head, thereby breaking his third Nazirite vow (Judges 16). Instead of being a mirror to Israel of who she ought to be, a people distinct from the surrounding nations and consecrated to the Lord from birth, Samson was a model depicting who she really was, a people untrue in every respect to her calling to be holy.

Broken Vows

In the light of this function of the Nazirite as a mirror to Israel, it is fascinating to note where Numbers 6 focuses its interest. As with the laws of Numbers 5, it is not a comprehensive review of the legislation surrounding the Nazirite vow. It doesn't tell us how or why people would take the Nazirite oath. Instead, once we have been reminded of the nature of the Nazirite vow, the attention of the passage turns immediately to two related matters: what happens if the vow is inadvertently broken, and what happens at the end of the time of the Nazirite vow. In fact, the passage spends almost as much time on each of these two matters as it does on the nature of the vow itself.

First, then, what should someone do if his Nazirite vow was inadvertently broken? Suppose he was quietly minding his own business when someone dropped dead in his presence (6:9). Now what should he do? It wasn't his fault that his vow to keep separate from corpses was broken, but nonetheless it was broken. His consecration to the Lord had been defiled, and even such an inadvertent sin required substantive atonement. He had to bring two birds as a sin offering and a burnt offering, shave his head, and then start the period of his vow all over again (vv. 9, 10). Birds were required because they were the least expensive offering that involved the shedding of blood. A grain offering wouldn't have been sufficient because blood had to be shed to atone even for unintentional sin. As well as the sin offering and burnt offering, reparation had to be paid through the offering of a one-year-old lamb as a guilt offering. After that, the period of the vow could be restarted (v. 12). Even though the breach of the vow had been entirely unintentional, blood had to be shed to atone for it, and the vow had to be completed exactly as promised. The message is clear: sin, even of the unintentional variety, requires costly blood payment, and nothing short of perfect fulfillment of what was promised is sufficient. God is a holy God whose standards are high indeed.

Second, though, what happened when the period of the vow was completed? A person couldn't just walk away from his life of complete devotion to God and return to ordinary life. He had to offer a smorgasbord of offerings, covering all the basic kinds of sacrifice. At the end of his vow he had to complete symbolically all of the covenant obligations in miniature. He had to offer a whole burnt offering, which symbolized total consecration and general atonement for sin. Along with it, he offered a grain offering, or tribute offering, which served as a mark of submission to the Lord as master and king (vv. 14, 15). After that, he was required to offer a sin offering, symbolizing the forgiveness that was required for particular sins (v. 16). There were also the offerings of unleavened bread—unleavened because leaven represents change and decay and therefore sin—and the associated drink offerings (v. 17).

Finally and climactically, the Nazirite would offer a fellowship offering, symbolizing communion with God around a common table (v. 17). The fellowship offering was a symbolic meal with God: part was offered on the altar along with the Nazirite's hair, which had finally been shaved off, symbolizing his life offered up to God. Meanwhile, the remainder was consumed by the worshiper and his family. The end of the vow was thus a celebration of joy, of life in God's presence, after which the worshiper returned to his normal life once more. The Nazirite was now freed from his vow and was once again able to drink wine and cut his hair.

Called to Be Holy

So what is the point of this passage? Is the goal of this passage the recruiting of new Nazirites, encouraging people to devote themselves to God in this extreme way? If that was its purpose, it is hard to explain why so much of the attention is focused on the (unintentional) failure of the vow or the intended goal of completion of the vow. Rather, the very existence of the Nazirite vow shows us the weakness and inability of the Old Testament people of God to meet God's standard of perfect holiness. The Nazirites were some Israelites who took a vow of special holiness for a limited time. Even out of these people, there were some who were not able to complete their period of sanctification without sacrifices and starting over. What is more, almost all of those who did take this vow eventually reverted to a normal way of life. Yet if all Israel had been truly and permanently set apart to God, what need would there have been for Nazirites? The Nazirites were called to be holy because Israel wasn't holy. They were called for a while to be a miniature kingdom of priests because the larger people were not fully and perpetually devoted to the Lord.

The same is true of us. We should all have the same level of committed devotion to God that the Nazirites did. We should all be wholly dedicated to the service of God. Yet if you are like me, the reality is that we don't even keep the resolutions we make to serve the Lord, let alone the resolutions that we ought to be making. Our sins and broken promises to God are not merely inadvertent but deliberate and repeated. We do and say the things we ought not to do and say, and we fail to do and say the things we ought to do and say. Even if we turn over a new leaf for a while, sooner or later we always seem to fall back into our old ways of doing things. For the most part, we are not personally committed to giving up the joy that might legitimately be ours for the sake of the kingdom. Few of us are easily content to give the control of our lives into the hands of God, nor are we ready and eager to separate ourselves from the realm of sin and death. Can we really claim that we are ready right now to give our all for Jesus? The law of the Nazirite exposes our hearts as well as those of ancient Israel.

The Final Nazirite

Even the best Nazirites needed more than their own personal best efforts, though. After they had successfully competed the period of their vow, they couldn't simply waltz into God's presence and say, "Here I am. What a wonderful asset to your kingdom I have been." On the contrary, even after they had completed the vow faithfully, they still needed to offer a sin offering before they could share a covenant meal with the Lord. Even our very best acts of obedience always fall short of God's perfect standard.

What Israel needed, and what we need, therefore, is someone who would come and permanently and finally and perfectly fulfill the role of the Nazirites on their behalf. They needed someone who would give up the joy that might otherwise legitimately be his and who would give control of his life into the hands of others while keeping himself permanently pure on their behalf. They needed someone who at the end would offer up his very life in order to enable them to enter the feast. The answer to this need is certainly not Samson, and not even Samuel. They were not able to bring about lasting rest and peace for God's people. Rather, the one who has come as our perfect Nazirite is Jesus Christ.

He was truly separated to God from birth, not by outward symbols but by the inner reality of a holiness that pervaded every aspect of his life. He was not a Nazirite in terms of the outward marks of being separated from wine or having uncut hair or complete separation from the dead. On the contrary, he himself transformed the water into wine at the wedding at Cana in Galilee in his first miracle (John 2:1-11), and he regularly touched corpses, bringing them back to life (e.g., Luke 8:54, 55). His consecration was thus not in the outward forms but in the inner reality to which these forms pointed.

Do you want to see someone who set aside the joy and comfort that might otherwise legitimately have been his? Look at Jesus, who left the glories of Heaven and came down to live in our midst. Do you want to see someone who gave up complete control of his own life, giving it over into the hands of his heavenly Father? Look at Jesus, who seeing the reality of the cross in front of him cried out in the Garden of Gethsemane, "not as I will, but as you will" (Matthew 26:39). Do you want to see someone separated from sin and death? Look at Jesus whose life of perfection was such that he was completely without blemish or flaw. He had no sin, deliberate or involuntary, that needed to be atoned for. He needed no sin offering or guilt offering made on his behalf in order to enter the presence of his heavenly Father. On the contrary, Jesus himself was the spotless atonement offering whose blood enables you and me to draw near to the presence of the holy God and experience his blessing. He gave his life to enable you to share in God's feast.

Complete Commitment

So what is your response to his complete commitment? If Israel was supposed to be reminded of their own need to be holy every time they saw a Nazirite, how much more should you and I be convicted of our need to be holy every time we contemplate the commitment of Jesus. Let me suggest three areas that match the areas of the commitment of the Nazirite in which we may need to hear this convicting voice.

First, are you willing to give up earthly means of joy for Christ? The Nazirite made the radical commitment to give up all grape products as part of his vow; Jesus gave up the glories of Heaven to win your salvation. So to what are you clinging? What is there that you say you must have if you are to be happy here? Perhaps it is a habit that you are unwilling to break, or a pleasure that you are unwilling to forego, or a dream that you desperately want to see fulfilled. Whatever it is, it is not necessarily sinful in itself, but it has come to be more precious to you than it ought to be. Remember that you are called to be part of a holy nation, a kingdom of priests, wholly devoted to your God.

Second, are you willing to give up control of your life? The irony here, of course, is that we don't really have control of our lives to begin with. We cannot even make our own hair grow, as the burgeoning market for baldness products continues to demonstrate. Yet we like to maintain the illusion that we really do have the power to direct our own lives. Thus, when God directs our lives in a way that we would not have chosen, we often go along kicking and screaming. That was not the way of the Nazirite, nor was it the way of Jesus. Instead we too need to learn to say to God, "not as I will, but as you will," even when we foresee the thorniness of the road that his will has chosen for us. God has the right to direct your life according to his wisdom, in whatever way he sees fit.

Third, are you willing to be separate from the realm of death and sin? In his second epistle, Peter appeals to his readers that in view of the prospect of the return of the Lord they should "be diligent to be found by him without spot or blemish, and at peace" (3:14). John reminds us, "God is light, and in him is no darkness at all. If we say we have fellowship with him while we walk in darkness, we lie and do not practice the truth. But if we walk in the light, as he is in the light, we have fellowship with one another, and the blood of Jesus his Son cleanses us from all sin" (1 John 1:5-7). There must be a difference between your lifestyle and that of the world around you. Your heart should long to be separate from the spiritual death and corruption that surrounds you on every side.

One way to stir up our hearts to renewed commitment is to read the biographies of those who have gone before us, who gave up much for the sake of the kingdom. As we read of pioneer missionaries who left everything for the expectation of a short and painful life in the wilds of Africa or of the martyrs who suffered prison and torture for the sake of Christ, it is almost impossible for our hearts to remain unmoved at the contrast between the sacrifice of these believers and our own self-protective attitudes. There is little doubt which of these two approaches to life is more in line with the gospel we have received. Our bodies are to be offered to our Lord as living sacrifices, wholly committed to his service.

There is one more thing to observe, however. The Nazirite vow was generally not forever. A Nazirite did not give up these things because the spiritual life is automatically enhanced by a life of giving things up. He or she was not an ascetic. Rather, he or she gave these things up temporarily, knowing that at the end of the time he or she would sit down in the presence of the Lord for a covenant meal. So too, whatever you and I may give up in this life, it is only a temporary loss. There is an end coming. There is a time ahead of us when all of the separation and tears and pain will be over, and we will sit down in the presence of our covenant Lord for a grand feast. At that feast there will be wine in abundance and fullness of joy in a celebration that will never come to an end.

This glorious feast is paid for by Jesus' perfect life in our place and his death on the cross, and it is sure because his time for giving things up is already over. Jesus has now completed his period of suffering obedience and has returned to his Father's side. He is seated there even now, planning the menu for you and me and preparing the table for our arrival. Eye has not seen, nor has ear heard, nor has the mind imagined what that celebration will be like when it finally happens (see 1 Corinthians 2:9). No one there on that day will ever think that they gave up too much for God. On the contrary, all of our earthly trials and sufferings will then seem like "slight momentary affliction" (2 Corinthians 4:17) in comparison to the glories that have been prepared for us. Remembering that such a glorious feast awaits us will surely help us faithfully endure the hunger and sorrow of the journey that God has plotted out for us and to remain faithfully committed to following the path of holiness.

8

I Am So Blessed!

NUMBERS 6:22-27

I AM A BIG FAN OF COUNTRY MUSIC. That comes as a surprise to many people who know me. After all, as a Scot who works daily with ancient Hebrew texts, I do not exactly fit the stereotype. However, the reason I like country music is because many of the songs seem true to life. They describe the feelings of ordinary people who live down-to-earth lives. Because of that fact, I often feel that I can relate to these songs and that the writer is someone like me. Take, for example, the song by Martina McBride, "Blessed." In the song she describes the simple things in life that bring her pleasure, such as the feel of a hardwood floor under her feet or hearing the sound of her children at play, and she concludes "I am so blessed." That surely is a universally desired feeling. We all want to be able to say of our lives, "I am so blessed." Yet how do we find that life of blessing? In this often troubled world, where is true blessing to be found? That is what this passage in the book of Numbers is about: the life of blessing and how we may receive it. This brief portion of Scripture gives us three foundational truths about blessing: where blessing comes from, what blessing is, and how we can receive it.

Blessing Comes from the Lord

The first truth of the passage is where blessing comes from: it comes from the Lord. It doesn't come from having hardwood floors—speaking from experience I can tell you that they can be a mixed blessing, unless like Martina you have a maid to keep them spotless! It doesn't even come from having happy children. Blessing comes from the Lord. That notion is central to the passage. Three times the Lord reiterates it: "The LORD bless you and keep you; the LORD make his face to shine upon you and be gracious to you; the LORD lift up his countenance upon you and give you peace." The Lord, Jehovah, the personal name of God, is identified three times as the one from whom blessing comes. Then, at the very end of the passage, just in case you somehow missed it earlier, the Lord sums it up by saying to Moses "I myself"—literal translation, the Hebrew is emphatic here—"I myself will bless them" (v. 27).[1]

Why is there so much emphasis here on where our blessing comes from? Surely it is because of our natural tendency to look for blessing in all the wrong places. In Jeremiah 2:13 the Lord laments this tendency on the part of his people: "my people have committed two evils: they have forsaken me, the fountain of living waters, and hewed out cisterns for themselves, broken cisterns that can hold no water." Instead of going to seek blessing from God, the one from whom all blessings flow, they tried to find their own blessings in places where there was no true blessing to be found. Instead of the fresh springs of the living water of blessing that flow from the Lord, they scratched around in stagnant, muddy pools of their own making. For Israel that often meant looking to other countries like Egypt and Assyria to protect them from their enemies instead of going to the Lord. It meant worshiping the idols of the nations instead of the true and living God. It meant making golden calves out of the plunder of Egypt instead of devoting it to the worship of God in the tabernacle.

We too have tried to dig our own cisterns and to find blessing in all the wrong places. We have our own muddy pools from which we drink. Some of us have tried to find blessing in possessions: we have tried to find significance by acquiring everything on our want list. Perhaps your list included a beautiful house, a luxury car, fine clothes and fur coats, or possibly the latest computer and electronic toys. You felt that if you just had those things, then you would be blessed. Or perhaps you sought blessing in relationships: you wanted to have a wife or a husband (or perhaps a *better* husband or wife); you longed for a son or a daughter. If you just had those relationships, you thought, then you would be blessed. Or maybe you sought blessing in being respected by your colleagues at work or admired by your friends at home or at school. When you have these things, then you will feel blessed, you think.

Identifying Our Idols

How do we know where we are finding our hope of blessing? The answer is to follow our feelings back to their source. Tracing back the smoke of our strong desires will lead us to the smoldering fire of the altar we have erected to our idol. Examining carefully our anger and our despair, along with our daydreams and our anxious fears, will provide a map for us that will uncover where we are finding our hope of blessing. For example, if our hope of blessing lies in possessions, then we will feel greatly blessed when we get new things, yet we will also be extremely anxious about losing them. We will be excessively elated when we get a new car—and overly deflated when it acquires its first scratch. If a woman's hope of blessing lies in relationships, she will daydream about the day when her prince will arrive and sweep her off her feet, or she will fear that perhaps she will never have the perfect family sitting around the table. We get angry when the object of our blessing seems threatened and are overjoyed when it seems to be within our grasp. Our strong emotions will show us the inner recesses of our heart, if we take the time to study them.

What we will invariably find, if we study our strong emotions carefully, is that we've been seeking blessing in all the wrong places. For me, one of the places that I seek blessing is in respect. I desperately need the approval of people, and so I am driven to work hard to show everyone around me what a great person I am. Because of my idolatry, I get extremely anxious if I have to confront someone. I fear that if I confront them, they won't respect me, and my idol will curse me. My idolatry shows up in what I fear most, which is being useless: what if I were disabled and couldn't walk, or talk, or even write? Who would respect me then? I grew up reading the Thomas the Tank Engine stories, in which the ultimate accolade the engines could receive from the controller of the railway was to hear him say, "You are a Really Useful Engine." My heart cries out for someone to say that to me— and as it does so, my strong emotions uncover my idolatry. They show me where I have been seeking my blessings instead of seeking them from the Lord.

What Is Blessing?

What is blessing though? If blessing does not lie in having it all—not in having abundant possessions or wonderful relationships or even being judged "really useful"—what is it? The priestly benediction tells us. It is very simple: blessing lies in a face-to-face relationship with the Lord, experiencing his protection and favor. First, the benediction simply states, "The LORD bless you and keep you." In other words, may the Lord provide us with what we need and protect us from harm. The Lord knows that we need food and drink to sustain our body. He knows that we need clothes to wear and a house to live in. He knows what our future holds, and he has crafted it to fit the work he is doing in our hearts and through us in the lives of others. The Lord's blessing includes and encompasses all of those things, given to us in exactly the right measure with fatherly wisdom. There is nothing wrong with desiring all of these things and asking him to give them to us. The Lord's protection and keeping of his people is a wonderful and reassuring truth.

However, God's blessing on his people is so much more than having enough in our cupboards to eat and nothing to cause us to worry. Otherwise many of us would have to conclude that in reality we are not so very blessed right now. There must be more to God's blessing than that—and there is. The priestly benediction unpacks the deeper aspects of the Lord's blessing in two vivid and related images: "The LORD make his face to shine upon you"—"the LORD lift up his countenance upon you." True blessing is knowing God face-to-face. The idea of having God's face shine when he looks at us is a wonderful image. Have you ever seen anyone's face shine? Perhaps you have watched children on Christmas morning as they open their presents. Or you watch young lovers as they walk together in the park and look at each other: they glow with the delight of being together. This is the heart of blessing: to have the Lord delight in us so much that it is as if his face shines whenever he sees us. Blessing is not just that our faces shine when we look at the beauties of God, but that he delights to turn his face toward us and look at us. Blessing is our heavenly Father's face beaming as he looks upon us. Can you imagine God delighting in you in this way?

This is what every child longs for from his or her father. Children want above all things to know that their father delights in them. They need to know that they are important to their father, that their father lights up whenever they walk into the room. Some of us never got that from our earthly fathers. We wanted so desperately to know that we mattered to them, but we never felt it. We never felt their faces shine when they turned toward us. But God wants you to feel his blessing today: he wants you to feel his pleasure, to feel that his face shines when he looks upon you. In the movie *Chariots of Fire*, Eric Liddell justifies the importance of his running in the Olympics by saying, "God has made me for a purpose—he made me for China. But he also made me fast, and when I run, I feel his pleasure." In the same way, the Lord wants you to know that his face is turned toward you in grace and in peace.[2] He wants you too to "feel his pleasure."

God thus wants our relationship with him to be one where we not only know his protection and his keeping, but also where we know his presence. This is blessing indeed, to know that the Lord's face is turned toward us and that we know his favor. We have no claim on that favor, as if it were ours by rights. Otherwise it wouldn't be a matter of grace. But the Lord commanded the priests to remind the people daily that by his grace they could know that he delighted in them. Do we know the blessing of that kind of relationship with our heavenly Father?

How to Receive Blessing

The third aspect of the passage, though, is how we receive this blessing. The answer is that the Lord gives it to his people freely, out of his grace and mercy. That's not how most people back in ancient times thought about the gods. They thought you had to twist the arm of their deity to get his blessing. They had to manipulate good things for themselves from the gods. That was usually why they went to the priest, because the priest was the person who had the connections and knowledge that would enable them to get what they wanted.

In other words, the ancients often viewed dealing with the gods the way we view dealing with the government. The government has enormous ability to help us and to make our lives run smoothly on the one hand or to make our lives miserable on the other. However, it is often very difficult to get the government to give us what we need, as I discovered for myself when I tried to get a Resident Alien card. You go to one office, and there is a long line. Five hours later, when you reach the front of the line, you discover that no one there is able help you. You have to go to another office on another day and speak to another person. Perhaps they will decide to help you—or perhaps not. It is hard to get a blessing from the government because all too often it seems that the government doesn't really care about our little issues. What we really need when dealing with the government is someone who knows how to work the system. We need an immigration lawyer who can get us around the line and into the system through the back door so we can get our blessing.

That is how people thought of the gods. You went to the priest because he was the expert who could get you in through the back door, bypassing the line and perhaps getting a blessing for you. This perspective leads to the attitude of someone like Jacob. God had promised him a blessing before he was even born (Genesis 25:23). Yet he spent his whole life trying to steal the blessing that he had been promised. Jacob wrestled, so to speak, with his brother for the birthright (25:29-34; 27:1-29); he wrestled with Laban for his daughters and his sheep (29—30); yet all the time God was the one he really needed to wrestle with. Finally, in that climactic wrestling match at the fords of the Jabbok, Jacob received the blessing he had been seeking all his life when he was too wounded to wrestle any longer (32:22-31). When all he could do was to cling on to God, he was finally ready to receive God's blessing! That was when he met God face-to-face and saw that what really counted was the Lord's favor.

We are so like Jacob. We think we need to steal a blessing from the Lord. So we seek to wrestle a blessing from his reluctant grasp or to twist God's arm into giving us his blessing. We are sure that he doesn't really approve of us at all, but maybe, just maybe, if I am a "really useful person," he will smile on my efforts. But what do we see in this passage? God is the one who initiates the blessing. Aaron doesn't first ask the Lord, "How do I bless this people?" Moses doesn't file a request in triplicate to initiate a blessing for the people. God comes to Moses and Aaron and says, "I want you to place my blessing on this people: here is how you do it." There is no magic or trickery or wrestling with God in the priestly benediction: the Lord initiates it because he wants to bless his people and give them his peace.

Undeserved Blessing

What makes God's desire to bless us so truly amazing is that we don't deserve his blessing at all. In the two chapters before this blessing in the book of Numbers, there are a whole series of laws for two very different kinds of people. Numbers 5 records the laws that cover the test for a wife who is accused of unfaithfulness. Numbers 6 gives us the laws for the person who takes a Nazirite vow—a vow to live for a period of time as someone especially devoted to the Lord. In these chapters, two completely opposite situations are presented: a faithless wife and someone who is completely devoted to the Lord. Now which of these two people is more like Israel—the completely devoted person or the faithless wife? Israel was certainly supposed to be completely devoted to the Lord. The Nazirite was supposed to be a picture to Israel representing the kind of devotion she was to show to the Lord. But in practice throughout her history, and perhaps particularly during the book of Numbers, Israel was often the faithless wife, going after other gods, complaining against the Lord, grumbling and rebelling.

Which of these people is more like you? Are you more Nazirite or faithless wife? For myself, I don't have to think hard to decide. By nature I am completely faithless. Before God found me and brought me to himself, I was dead in my transgressions and sins, as Paul says in Ephesians 2. Even after God found me and saved me, showing his great love for me, my heart still wanders and complains and grumbles. Far too often I still look for my blessing in other places and in other things. I am the faithless wife, not the Nazirite.

Yet God is nonetheless determined to bless me! The Lord wants his blessing and his name placed on me. The people that Jesus came to seek and to save are not the Nazirites but the sinners, for we all fall short of God's perfect standard. That is why Jesus came to the Samaritan woman at the well, who was a faithless woman if ever there was one—she had had five husbands and was then living with yet another man (John 4:18). Yet Jesus told her about his Father who sought worshipers among people like her (v. 23). The Lord's blessing is poured out on faithless ones like us.

Blessing Through Curse

God is able to bless faithless people like me because he sent his Son to be completely devoted to him in my place. Jesus Christ came and lived a life of perfect devotion to God. He was the true embodiment of the Nazirite ideal of separation from evil and death, the one who kept God's Law in every detail. His heart was constantly filled with loving obedience to God, and so he truly earned the Lord's blessing. It was not surprising that at his baptism his Father said, "You are my beloved Son; with you I am well pleased" (Luke 3:22). On the Mount of Transfiguration, when his glory was revealed to his closest disciples, those disciples heard the Father say of Jesus, "This is my beloved Son, with whom I am well pleased" (Matthew 17:5). On the mountain, Jesus was physically illuminated with the reflected glory of his Father's favor. He knew his Father's face turned toward him in blessing.

But then came the week of Jesus' passion, when obedience to his Father's will took Jesus into the darkness for us. It wasn't just the weight of the heavy cross on his flayed back that drove him to his knees; it was carrying the burden of my unfaithfulness, and yours as well. He paid for the sin of my faithless hands and wandering feet in the nails that transfixed his obedient hands and feet. He atoned for the sin of my idolatrous heart as his faithful heart was pierced by the Roman soldier's spear. As God the Father made him who knew no sin to be sin for me, Jesus took upon himself my curse. The Scriptures of the Old Testament declared solemnly that anyone hung on a tree was cursed of God (Deuteronomy 21:23). On the cross, Jesus didn't simply withstand the cursings of men, therefore, but took onto himself the very curse of God. It wasn't just the crowd that cried out, "Let him be crucified!" It wasn't just the Roman soldiers who mocked him and the chief priests who said, "let him come down now from the cross, and we will believe in him" (Matthew 27:23, 29, 42). There on the cross Jesus felt the Father's curse.

In fact, the cross is the very antithesis of the priestly benediction. Did God the Father bless Jesus and keep him when he was on the cross? No, he handed him over into the power of those who hated him and wanted to kill him. Did God the Father make his face shine upon Jesus on the cross? No, he poured out his wrath and his crushing anger against sin upon him. Did God the Father turn his face toward Jesus on the cross and give him peace? No, he turned his face away from him, so that Jesus cried out in agony, "My God, my God, why have you forsaken me?" As Jesus lifted his eyes toward Heaven, for the first time in all eternity there was no answering light from the Father's face. Even the sun turned away its countenance from Jesus, as if the universe itself could no longer bear to look upon him. At that moment for Jesus there was no peace. He was bruised for our iniquity; he was broken for our sin; he was abandoned for our faithlessness; he was cursed for our blessing.

Jesus Our Peace

But he himself is our peace. In Jesus we now receive God's blessing. Now my sin and faithlessness has been fully paid for. Now Jesus has been raised up from the dead and exalted to the right hand of the Father. He has returned once again to the Father's favor and has been given the name above every name, never again to be separated from his blessing. What is more, where he is, there shall I also be. Now the Father of our Lord Jesus Christ will certainly bless me and keep me, for his sake. Now I know that nothing in all creation can separate me from the love of God (Romans 8:38, 39). Now I know that the Father looks on me with pleasure, and his face lights up every time he sees me because he sees me through Jesus. The Father sees me in his Son whom he loves. As a Christian, I have the name of Jesus written indelibly on my soul, and so the Father delights to bless me in Christ with every spiritual blessing, for his sake (Ephesians 1:3). God's face is turned toward me in Christ, and no matter what I encounter in life, it can never, ever be turned away from me.

Some have never experienced this blessing of God. They have never felt his favor, for they have never given their life to Christ. They have never submitted their heart to him. The Father's favor is not given indiscriminately to all humanity, just as the Aaronic blessing was not to be administered to all peoples: it is only given to those whom he calls his own people in Christ. If you have never done so, you need to come to Christ today and thus receive the blessing of a new life under the smile of God. Confess your sins. Repent of all of the ways in which you have sought to manufacture your own life of blessing, and bow down today to God's only way to blessing. Receive God's favor in Jesus Christ. It is the only way to true blessing and peace, a blessing that will last for all eternity.

Forgetting Your Blessing

Or perhaps you are a believer, but you have forgotten where your blessing is to be found. That is why you are so concerned about the worries and cares of life, uncertain that the Father will protect you. That is why you are so consumed with anger and fear, unsure of your Father's love. That is why you are so tied in knots about your future, devoid of the Father's gift of peace. You have forgotten your Father's sure favor and the cost with which it was bought. Fortunately, the Lord knows your weakness and mine. That is why Aaron was instructed to repeat this blessing to the Israelites often, because the Lord knows that we so easily forget and seek our blessing in all the wrong places. That is why we conclude our church services week after week with a benediction, God's authoritative statement of his favor toward us in Christ.

Christian, you and I need to repent of the other places that we have looked for satisfaction and blessing apart from the Lord. We must repent, and look again at the cross. We must marvel again that God loves us this much. We can rejoice that his favor is still extended to us in Jesus, unfaithful and unprofitable servants though we are. Every day the Father's face lights up to behold us because he sees us clothed in the sacrifice of his Son. Every day he looks on us, turns his face toward us, and says to each of us, "This too is my son whom I love; this too is my daughter with whom I am well-pleased. Receive my peace, beloved of the Lord, upon whom his favor rests."

> The LORD bless you and keep you;
> the LORD make his face to shine upon you and be gracious to you;
> the LORD lift up his countenance upon you and give you peace.

9

"And a Partridge in a Pear Tree . . ."

NUMBERS 7

"ON THE FIRST DAY OF CHRISTMAS my true love sent to me a partridge in a pear tree." So runs the traditional Christmas carol. The song then proceeds to detail the gifts sent to the beloved, which increase incrementally day after day, until we reach the climactic twelfth day. At this point you may well be wondering where she was supposed to put the vast array of wildlife, servants, and entertainers she had by now accumulated.[1] Here is a gift giver who certainly does not believe that "More is less!"

When More Is Not Less

There are certain similarities between the Christmas carol and Numbers 7. It is not only the common motif of the number twelve; it is also the repetitious description of the same gifts given over and over. Why does the writer take no fewer than eighty-nine verses to describe these gifts? It is not so much that he is adding new information each time around; on the contrary, the gifts given by each tribe are identical. Rather, he wants you to understand that here was an overwhelming outpouring of love on the part of each and every one of the tribes of Israel that cannot be captured in a few words or phrases. Only a full rendition of the details will give an adequate sense of what is transpiring here. If it is true in giving that sometimes "More is indeed more," then it is also true in describing giving that "More is more."

Although the chapter itself is extremely long due to the repetition, it is really only seeking to convey two essential pieces of information. The message of this chapter of the book of Numbers is contained in what the people gave to the Lord and the attitude with which they gave it. As we study these things, we will be challenged in terms of our own giving to the Lord.

What Can You Give God?

First, what did the people give God? What can *we* give God? What could we possibly buy for the deity who not only already has everything but actually made everything? In my experience there are some people for whom it is very difficult to purchase presents because they already have everything they want. My father is like that. He doesn't have a great array of hobbies or interests, and he has enough money to buy the limited range of things that he needs and wants. That makes Christmas shopping on his behalf a challenging proposition. You might think that it would be even more difficult to procure something suitable for the Lord, the God of the entire universe. In this case, though, the Lord was about to move into his newly completed and consecrated house, the tabernacle. As a result, housewarming gifts were highly appropriate.

What are the best housewarming gifts? They are the gifts given to us by people who know us well enough to know what will be useful and appreciated. There is no point giving a corkscrew to a teetotaler or a pound of fine coffee beans to someone without a coffee grinder. The best gifts are those that exhibit a personal knowledge of the recipient, and the gifts given by Israel to God were no exception to that rule. Every single tribe brought exactly the same housewarming gifts to God's tabernacle not because they lacked imagination and flair but because they understood the nature and function of the tabernacle. They brought items that reflected the needs of the tabernacle. The gifts that each tribe brought were designed to accomplish three things: they provided means of transport, means of sacrifice, and means of ministry for the tabernacle.

Means of Transport

The first set of gifts that they brought were six carts or wagons and twelve oxen (v. 3). The people knew that the tabernacle was intended as a mobile sanctuary that would move around with the people. At the same time, the tabernacle contained many heavy items, made of gold and silver and bronze. These carts would ease the task of the Levites, whose job it was to transport the tabernacle from place to place. In response, the Lord instructed Moses to receive these gifts and apportion them out as required (v. 5). The carts were not evenly distributed or given preferentially to those with the highest status, but rather were to be given to those with the greatest need for them. Thus four carts went to the Merarites, the least significant group of Levites, but the group who had the greatest amount of heavy lifting to do. They were responsible for the frames, posts, and bases of the tabernacle (4:31, 32). Meanwhile, two carts went to the Gershonites, who had to carry the various curtains of the tabernacle (4:24-26). The Kohathites, on the other hand, received no carts at all because theirs was the most precious cargo: the ark of the covenant and the contents of the Holy of Holies itself (7:9). These special burdens were to be hand-carried.

These carts were gifts that showed thoughtfulness as well as care. The Lord did not command Israel to bring carts, but as they considered the tabernacle and the needs of caring for it, they realized the blessing that such gifts could be to those charged with its transportation. That should challenge us in our giving, shouldn't it? It is one thing to write a weekly or monthly check and drop it in the offering plate. It is another to look around at the ministry needs of the church and, without being asked, find a need that we can meet, then meet it. What a blessing it is to have such people in a congregation.

However, we do need to be careful that our proposed gifts are kosher ways of meeting needs. Carts for the Kohathites might have looked like a great gift on the surface of things—but that was not God's way of doing things. We may think it would be a wonderful ministry to endow a troupe of liturgical dancers or fund a life-size statue of Jesus in our church sanctuary, but such a gift doesn't fit with the scriptural depiction of how we should worship God. That's why it is a good idea to bring our gifts to those whom God has placed in spiritual oversight of the church and allow them to use their spiritual maturity and insight to put our gifts to work in accord with God's plan and purpose for the church.

Means of Sacrifice

In addition to carts to provide for the transportation needs of the tabernacle, the princes of the tribes also brought resources for the regular sacrifices and ministry of the tabernacle. These are the gifts that are enumerated twelve times over: utensils and supplies for the grain offering and incense offering, along with various animals to be offered as burnt offerings, sin offerings, and fellowship offerings. These gifts demonstrate that they understood the purpose of the tabernacle. It wasn't just a glorious building to attract tourists and serve as a cultural center for the community. The tabernacle was to be a place where various kinds of sacrifices would be offered.

These sacrifices served a number of different purposes in Old Testament Israel. Some sacrifices had as their primary purpose atoning for sin in general.[2] When whole burnt offerings were presented, their smoke would ascend to God and appease his wrath against sin (Leviticus 1:9). The animal paid the wages of sin, which is death. To use a different metaphor, these atoning sacrifices paid the ransom that sin had incurred, enabling the broken relationship between the people and their God to be put right. Similarly, sin offerings served the purpose of purifying the sanctuary from the toxic effects of accumulated sin that would otherwise prevent the presence of a holy God from remaining in the midst of his people (see Leviticus 4).

Other sacrifices, such as the grain offerings, were tribute offered to God as a mark of submission to him (see Leviticus 2). Just as every citizen of our country is required to pay taxes to the government, so they were required to offer these grain offerings as a sign of obedience to the Lord. Still other sacrifices, such as the fellowship offerings or peace offerings (Leviticus 3), were ceremonial meals to be eaten in the Lord's presence. These sacrifices symbolized the enjoyment of the relationship with him that God graciously offers his people. For that reason, only part of the animal was offered on the altar to the Lord in these sacrifices; part of the remainder went to the priest for his family, while the worshiper and his family ate the rest of the animal. The incense, meanwhile, ascended to God, not merely providing a pleasant fragrance, mixed in with the aroma of burning flesh, but representing the prayers and praises of God's people rising up before the Lord (see Psalm 141:2). Since part of each of these sacrifices was given to the priests, this system also provided an important aspect of funding the ministry that the priests provided in Israel.

Means of Ministry

The gifts given by the twelve tribes thus provided the resources for these regular daily sacrifices to be begun.[3] These daily sacrifices were the sacrifices that were routinely offered in the tabernacle, rather than those offered on special occasions of repentance or thanksgiving, such as the guilt offering or freewill offerings. The altar of the tabernacle had been anointed and set apart for holy use (7:10), but now the regular daily routine of sacrifice had to be initiated. This chapter shows us that the twelve tribes all eagerly played their part in providing the resources for a program of worship and fellowship with God. All of God's people came together to fund the ministry of the tabernacle and those who served in it.

What is more, the tribes did so freely, generously, and unitedly. The point of the passage is not simply the large amounts that were given to the Lord but the equal and united way in which those gifts were given. Everyone had an equal part to play. The larger tribes did not dominate the giving, leaving the smaller tribes feeling like second-rate contributors. Nor did the smaller tribes use their size as an excuse for giving less. Each tribe contributed exactly the same amount, for all shared in this ministry. Each tribe gave generously, without compulsion, yet with an eagerness that came from a sense of gratitude and expectation about the presence of the tabernacle in their midst. No guilt-driven appeals were launched to fund the ministry of the tabernacle: the people saw what needed to be done and gave generously and unitedly to meet those needs.

What is more, the end result of this generous giving was that the tabernacle functioned exactly as it was intended to do. That is the point of the final note of the chapter:

> And when Moses went into the tent of meeting to speak with the LORD, he heard the voice speaking to him from above the mercy seat that was on the ark of the testimony, from between the two cherubim; and it spoke to him. (v. 89)

Many scholars see this verse as an irrelevant insertion, but it is not. It shows what happened when God's people gave: God dwelt in their midst and spoke to Moses from the Holy of Holies in the tabernacle. There was fellowship between God and his people, accomplishing the goal of the covenant in every age and generation.

Giving Flows from Grace

This chapter is intended to provide a pattern for us in our giving as well. To be sure, we don't have a tabernacle that needs to be carried about, nor do we have a regular sequence of animals to offer; yet ministry continues to have financial needs and costs associated with it. There is much that we can learn from their model of giving.

In the first place, notice that their giving was not an attempt to buy God's favor but rather flowed out of the experience of God's favor. It is not coincidental that this chapter comes after Numbers 6:22-27 and not before. The Israelites did not give generously to God so that they could hear him say in response, "I will surely bless you." On the contrary, God blessed his people first, and then they gave. This perspective is fundamental to all true Christian giving. Just as we love because God loved us first, so too we give because God gave to us first. God doesn't need our money. He owns the cattle on a thousand hills and can direct the hearts of millionaires as he pleases. He therefore certainly doesn't need your check or mine to accomplish his ministry goals. Let me put it more strongly: if it is God's ministry, he will provide the funds to support it. It is that conviction that frees us from trying to induce people to give out of guilt. Pragmatically speaking, guilt may be a very successful fund-raising tool, as many people have discovered. However, it is not a Biblical fund-raising tool. Biblical giving does not flow out of a sense of guilt or a desire to win God's favor; it flows out of a sense of God's grace.

That's why Paul can say in 2 Corinthians 9:7: "God loves a cheerful giver." Guilt-driven givers are never cheerful givers: you need to squeeze every last penny from them, and they give it as if it really was their last penny. I know such guilt-driven giving when I see it because that is my own natural mode. Perhaps it is my ethnic heritage: we Scots are notoriously (though not always fairly) noted for our tightfistedness. However, it is far more likely that is simply a convenient excuse for my sinful heart. I am not naturally a grace-driven giver. My tendency is always to give the minimum necessary to assuage my guilt, forgetting the God from whom I have received so much. But if God owns everything, he doesn't need my gifts. If God gives his blessing to me freely, I don't need to give to try to buy that favor. It is already mine. If our vision for ministry comes from the Lord, he will certainly supply the resources necessary to carry it out. Knowing this leads us to an attitude of prayerfulness and patience while we wait for God to provide for our needs.

Yet, on the other side of the coin, the God who owns the cattle on a thousand hills does not choose to oversee them personally. He is not the great cowboy in the sky. Instead, the cattle that he owns are assigned into the care and stewardship of his people, from whom he receives them again when he has need of them. God didn't need the gifts of the princes of Israel, nor did he promise them additional favor in response to their giving; but nonetheless they lined up one after another to give sacrificially to his ministry. Perhaps they recognized that they could afford to be generous because they remembered where they got all of these riches in the first place. God gave this wealth to them by enabling them to plunder the Egyptians on their way out of Egypt (Exodus 12:35, 36). This was not gold for which they had personally labored: God had given it to them in the first place, and now they simply gave it back to him.

The way in which God meets the needs of his ministry is by moving the hearts of his people to remember who gave them everything they have. In this way he prompts in us an eagerness to give back. He reminds his people once again of the blessing and favor that he has shown toward them, and as the reality of his grace lays hold of their hearts afresh, they ask, "What can I give? How can I contribute something back to the Lord for the salvation that he has given me? What do I have that I can contribute to his cause?" Grace lays hold of our hearts and makes us cheerful givers, not just of our money but of our time and gifts as well.

Joyful Giving

That raises a question for each of us, doesn't it? When there is an opportunity to give, as there is Sunday by Sunday and in between, what is our attitude? When there is work of ministry to be done, are we eager to volunteer? It is not simply a matter of "How big is your check?" or "How many ministries do you serve in?" Those are different questions. For some, giving generously and joyfully may not have many zeros on the end of it, while others may give millions and yet have hearts that are entirely untouched by grace. Jesus pointed that out when he told the story of the widow's offering. Surrounded by wealthy givers, she only gave two copper coins. Yet Jesus affirmed that her gift was greater than their larger ones because they gave out of their abundance, while she gave everything she had to live on (Luke 21:1-4).

Similarly, some people may pour their hearts joyfully into a single ministry, while others may wear themselves out for the church, grumbling inside all the time. The Israelites gave freely and joyfully because they knew themselves to be so blessed by the Lord. You and I need to join them in giving generously out of a heart that is conscious of great blessing.

The Shape of Our Giving

So far we've been addressing the fact that the *how* of our giving needs to reflect a similar attitude to that of ancient Israel. How about the *what* of our giving, though? In what ways does their giving provide us with direction in the shape of the ministry toward which we should be giving? I think there are several suggestive aspects to that. The carts that they provided to transport the tabernacle remind us that the place of their worship was constantly mobile. So, too, we are pilgrims and strangers in this world, constantly on the move (Hebrews 13:14). The temptation for us is always to try to settle down and put down roots, as if this world is our home. Yet here in this world we have no settled city, and the shape of our ministry should reflect that.

One temptation that faces us is to transfer our trust from God to a building. There are certainly advantages to having a settled building in which to worship; yet how easily a building can become an idol. One mark of that may be the fact that we can be more heavily invested in beautifying the building than we are in meeting with God. Those congregations, like ours, that meet in rented facilities are freed from that temptation, and from a great deal of expense. This freedom ought to release us to be able to pour more resources into ministry. If we don't have a building, we should be able to provide the resources necessary for a variety of ministries, even as a relatively small fellowship of God's people. Larger churches face the challenge of keeping their budget focused on ministry as their resources grow, not merely focused on maintaining ever-expanding facilities.

In addition, the giving in Numbers 7 was focused on providing for the sacrifices, with their multidimensional presentation of worship. So, too, our giving should be the expression and means of reaching the same goals. We don't ask people to bring along a goat or two to church each Sunday. This is not simply because there are zoning laws in our community against slaughtering animals in church buildings, but because what these sacrifices pointed toward has already been fulfilled in Christ. So our giving enables us to meet together Sunday by Sunday to focus our hearts afresh on the gospel. It enables us to gather around the Word and hear God speak in our midst as its truths are proclaimed afresh to us. We meet around the Lord's Table and feast together on Christ, our Passover lamb, just as the Israelites feasted together on the body of the fellowship offering in God's presence. We lift up our prayers and petitions before God, just as the incense ascended before God from the tabernacle.

However, it is not simply that our giving enables us to come together in a local church. More than that, what we do when we come together is itself in a fundamental sense an offering of ourselves in God's service. Our sacrifice is a sacrifice of praise (Hebrews 13:15), a laying of our own bodies on the altar as living sacrifices (Romans 12:1). We are called cheerfully to lay down our lives at the feet of Christ week after week and to commit ourselves afresh to take up our cross and follow him.

Living Sacrifices

When I was seventeen years old, the Lord called me to serve him with my life, and I began (through a convoluted route) to prepare for a career of ministry. Perhaps someone reading these words will likewise sense God's call to turn aside from other labors and watch over his sheep. Yet as I get older, I realize increasingly that serving the Lord with my life is not a single decision but a daily commitment. As someone once said, the problem with living sacrifices is that they have a habit of crawling off the altar. Day by day we need to make the commitment afresh to serve the Lord wholeheartedly in whatever his calling is for us.

We make that commitment because, like God's Old Testament people, we know how much we have been blessed. They had the shadows of redemption and were nonetheless richly blessed. What then shall we say of ourselves since we experience the fullness toward which the shadows pointed? We know and experience the Lord's blessing and love in a whole new way in Christ. In Christ, God himself took on flesh and tabernacled in our midst (John 1:14), pursuing his own pilgrim journey in our midst. He is the reality toward which the Old Testament tabernacle pointed, the glory of God dwelling in the midst of his people.

Yet when Jesus came to his own people, they did not receive him (John 1:11). Instead of joyfully bringing him abundant gifts and laying down their lives in his service, they stripped him and beat him and nailed him to a cross. There Jesus himself became the reality toward which the whole Old Testament system of sacrifices pointed. He offered himself completely to God, an atoning ransom for our sins. Throughout his earthly pilgrimage he gave the homage of complete obedience to God, even to the point of death on the cross. Through that death and resurrection, Jesus ushered us into the reality of fellowship with God forever. In the Garden of Gethsemane, his pleas and petitions to be spared the cup of suffering and death came before the Father; yet they were not answered in the affirmative, so that God could say "Yes!" to us and welcome us into his family. As a result, it is in Christ that you and I have been blessed with every spiritual blessing in the heavenly realms (Ephesians 1:3). You and I have been invited to his great feast. How could God have blessed us any more than he already has?

Do you know the reality and scale of the blessing you have received in Christ? If so, no one will have to beg you to give or beat you into giving. You will have a heart that longs to give, that delights to give as much as you possibly can, so that the name of Christ can be lifted up and his grace magnified. You will eagerly and joyfully pour out your life in his service, so that the wonder of his mercy can be known more widely. If God's kingdom and the deserved fame of Jesus' name can be extended, then my life will truly have been worthwhile. Nothing else in Heaven or earth could be more worth living for or giving to than that.

10

The Light of the World

NUMBERS 8:1-4

THE RELATIONSHIP BETWEEN FORM AND FUNCTION has been a classic debate in architecture for most of the last century.[1] Which is more important—the shape of a building or the function that it has to serve? Is architecture "art for art's sake"? Or is architecture constructing the best possible structure to achieve a given purpose? In fact, choosing either extreme ends up in architectural disaster. If architecture is simply "art for art's sake," you end up with architecturally striking buildings that are incredibly impractical. Woody Allen once parodied this kind of approach by imagining what would happen if your dentist were to take a similar view of reality: you would end up not with the orthodontic work you needed but with the shape of teeth that he thought best expressed his art![2] On the other extreme, though, if architecture is simply about function, you end up with boxlike, soulless structures of the kind that characterize the worst modern housing developments. It turns out that in architecture you cannot simply choose either form or function to the detriment of the other: both need to be taken into account.

Form and Function in the Tabernacle

The same is true of God's perfectly designed building, the tabernacle. Everything in the tabernacle had a practical reason for existence; everything had a function. At the same time, however, every piece of furniture also contributed in some distinct way to the larger message that the tabernacle was intended to convey; it had a particular form. If you focus entirely on the function of the furniture, you may miss the significance of its form and the message it was intended to convey. On one level, for example, the table in the Outer Sanctuary was simply a table: it functioned as somewhere to put the twelve loaves that were set before the Lord each day. It was never just a table, though. The twelve loaves it held in front of the Lord also represented the daily offerings of each of the tribes of Israel. Equally though, if you focus entirely on the form of the furniture, it is possible to read too much into every little detail of the tabernacle's construction and furnishing. To see an example of this, listen to what one ancient commentator said about the table of showbread in the Outer Sanctuary:

> The table made from acacia wood is the Holy Scripture composed out of the bold words and deeds of the holy fathers. In showing us what the joys of eternal blessedness might be and how they might be attained, it surely supplies us with the food of salvation and life. This [table] has length, because it suggests to us perseverance in religious undertakings; width, because it suggests the amplitude of charity; height, because it suggests the hope of everlasting reward.[3]

Actually, it seems to me, the table has length and breadth and height in order to serve its function as a table, somewhere to put the bread. Yet at the same time, the table has its own place within the symbolism of the tabernacle. It is not simply a practical accessory. It has both form and function.

Form and Function in the Lampstand

In the same way, the lampstand of the tabernacle, which is the focus of this passage, had both form and function. It had a practical purpose: to give light in the Outer Sanctuary. There were no windows in the Outer Sanctuary, and there were thick, heavy curtains all around it. The priests who ministered day by day at the altar of incense and the table of the showbread needed to have some light to work by, and the lampstand provided that light. Yet the lampstand was never just a utilitarian light: they couldn't simply have replaced it with a bank of fluorescent tubes. It had a form that conveyed a message of its own, a message that comes to expression in the opening verses of Numbers 8.

Numbers 7 ended with Moses meeting with the Lord in the tabernacle. God conversed with Moses from his invisible throne above the cherubim on the ark of the covenant, and Moses responded (v. 89). God was dwelling in the midst of his people, and the tabernacle had been inaugurated, and its operation was beginning exactly as God had commanded. As part of that inaugural instruction, God commanded Aaron to set up the seven lamps on the lampstand in such a way that they faced forward and threw their light in front of the lampstand. The design for the lampstand had been given to Moses back in Exodus 25. However, now that it was time for the lampstand to be put into action, God was insistent that the lamps should face forward and shed their light forward. Why is that small detail important enough to require its own passage? To understand that, we have to understand what the lampstand symbolized and what stood in front of it and was to receive its light.

What did the lampstand symbolize? It symbolized God himself. That is why this piece of furniture was made out of pure gold, hammered into shape (8:4), unlike all the other objects in the Outer Sanctuary, which were made of wood and merely plated with gold. It had seven lamps on it, symbolizing the completeness and perfection of God's presence. This symbolism is confirmed by the description of the function of the lampstand. It was to "give light," exactly the same Hebrew word that the priestly blessing used of God's face shining upon his people (6:25). The light of the lampstand thus represented God's favor or blessing shining out into the darkness.

Where, though, does this light shine in Numbers 8? It is to shine forward, on the area "in front of the lampstand," upon the place where the table of the showbread stood. Again, this table had on it twelve loaves representing the offerings of the twelve tribes of Israel. That is surely why this note about the lampstand follows Numbers 7, where all twelve of the tribes presented their offerings to the Lord, and the Lord accepted them. What we see in Numbers 8:1-4 is a visual metaphor. What the priests declared in the words of their benediction, the lampstand of the tabernacle proclaimed as a daily reality: the light of the Lord's blessing rested upon all of the tribes of his people, making their offerings acceptable in his sight. God's love and acceptance of those who were his was depicted at the very heart of the tabernacle.

The Light of God's Blessing

So what though? It is all very well to say that the Lord's blessing rested on all of his people in the days of Moses, but all these years later we don't have either a tabernacle or a lampstand. What are the implications of this passage for us as New Testament believers? The answer is that we have the reality toward which the tabernacle lampstand pointed. Jesus Christ is himself the one in whom the light of God's blessing shines upon all. He embodies in himself the visual depiction of God's favor resting upon his people. That's the point that John makes in the opening words of his Gospel: "In him [Jesus] was life, and the life was the light of men" (John 1:4). That's why the angels told the shepherds at his birth, "Glory to God in the highest, and on earth peace among those with whom he is pleased!" (Luke 2:14). Or as Jesus himself says later on in John's Gospel, "I am the light of the world. Whoever follows me will never walk in darkness, but will have the light of life" (John 8:12). Jesus is the light of God's favor shining in the world.

Right away we need to notice two things about the fulfillment of the Old Testament image in Jesus. On the one hand, the fulfillment is more extensive than the image. In the Old Testament image, the light only shone on the twelve loaves of bread, representing the twelve tribes of Israel. God's favor and blessing was limited in the Old Testament era, primarily directed to the children of Abraham, just as he promised Abraham in Genesis 12. Others could come and join them and be incorporated into Abraham's family, even in the Old Testament era, but these were relatively few and far between. With the coming of Christ in the New Testament, however, the boundaries upon which the light shines have expanded. Jesus is not simply the light of his own people, but the light of the world! In Christ, the blessing of God extends more broadly than ever before, including those who in the past were not part of God's people. This too was anticipated in the Old Testament. The Lord said through the prophet Isaiah, "It is too light a thing that you should be my servant to raise up the tribes of Jacob and to bring back the preserved of Israel; I will make you as a light for the nations, that my salvation may reach to the end of the earth" (Isaiah 49:6). In Christ, that "light for the nations" has appeared.

Yet at the same time as the fulfillment in Christ is wider than the Old Testament image, it is also narrower. In Christ, blessing comes to the nations; yet at the same time many of his own people rejected him and missed the blessing. As John put it, "He came to his own, and his own people did not receive him" (John 1:11). Nor was it only his own people who rejected him. Jesus tells us, "And this is the judgment: the light has come into the world, and people loved the darkness rather than the light because their deeds were evil" (John 3:19). God's blessing is not automatic: it has not only to be given, it also has to be received.

The Divisiveness of the Light

What that means is that the coming of Christ into the world is necessarily a divisive thing. Light has a way of revealing the truth in all of its beauty or ugliness. For the weary traveler lost in a blizzard, a light up ahead is a welcome sign of hope that draws him toward it and the life it represents. For the cockroach, however, light is an unwelcome reality. Cockroaches much prefer darkness to light because of the nature of their nefarious activities.

So which are you—weary traveler or cockroach? Your true nature is exposed by your response to the light, to Jesus. If Jesus draws you irresistibly and if you find in him life and hope and peace, then you are shown by that response to be a weary traveler. But if you will have nothing to do with Jesus, if you regard him as an irrelevance at best and a positive danger at worst, then your cockroach nature is on full display. Don't be surprised by that reality. The truth is that each one of us is by nature a cockroach at heart! We all once loved darkness rather than light. Only the transforming power of the Holy Spirit moves us to faith in Christ and gives us a new heart that delights in the light. The glory of the gospel is that God has taken us out of our natural darkness into light. As 1 Peter 2:9 says, "You are a chosen race, a royal priesthood, a holy nation, a people for his own possession, that you may pro-claim the excellencies of him who called you out of darkness into his marvel-ous light." It is God's transforming grace alone that enables you to delight in the light by dealing with the sin that makes you want to hide. Cockroaches are rightly afraid of being stepped on, and until their nature is changed they will always be afraid of the light. God's transforming grace calls you to come out of your dark corner into God's wonderful light. Lay down your inner dark-ness and the sinful actions and thoughts and attitudes that have marked your life, and come into his wonderful light. Abandon your efforts to please God in your own strength, and receive the free gift of life that God offers you in Christ. Those who are indeed God's people come into his light.

The Transforming Power of the Light

Yet God is not done with us when he brings us out of darkness. He also wants to transform our darkness into light and set us on fire with his glory, making us lights to the world around us. In the book of Revelation, Jesus Christ stands in all his burning glory in the midst of the seven churches of Asia Minor, which themselves are represented by lampstands. Do you see how amazing that image is? The lampstand was the representation of the glory of God shining out in blessing on his people. In the Old Testament it became an image for the temple, the place from which God's glorious blessing flowed out to his people (see, for example, Zechariah 4). Yet now in this New Testament era, the places from which God's glory flows out to the world are the very real, very flawed churches. We are the lampstands. Christ stands in the midst of the churches, and so they shine out his glory to the watching world. Our task as the church is thus to be the images of Jesus, showing forth his glory to the community around us.

That is why in addition to saying, "I am the light of the world," Jesus also said, "You are the light of the world" (Matthew 5:14). To whom was he talking when he said that in the Sermon on the Mount? We tend to read his words individualistically, as if I personally am to be the light of the world. So the old children's song runs: "Jesus bids us shine with a pure clear light / like a little candle burning in the night. / In this world of dark-ness, Jesus bids us shine / you in your small corner and I in mine." That is not what Jesus is saying though. What he actually said was, "You [plural] are the light of the world. A city set on a hill cannot be hidden." I can no more individually be the light of the world than I can individually be a city on a hill. Both images are corporate: it is as the church that we are the light of the world, shining out God's glory together. As Jesus comes into our midst as his people and inhabits our church, his glory shines out from us to those around us.

Living Lampstands

So how does the church, as a living lampstand, shine God's light to the world around us? The first aspect of being a lampstand for our world is being a channel of God's blessing to those around us. That is the point of Jesus' analogy: as the light of the world, or the city on the hill, we are to let our light shine before men so that they may see our good deeds and praise our Father in Heaven. Are we that kind of channel of blessing to the community around us? Do people see our good deeds and praise God? Or do we instead have our light hidden away under a bucket where no one can see us? Are we a lampstand whose light shines forward and out, communicating God's blessing toward where people are? If God were to remove our church from the community, would anyone notice? If our churches no longer existed, would anyone mourn our disappearance? If not, then we have to ask ourselves to what extent we are shining out the light of God's blessing to our community.

Second, though, the church as a lampstand is to challenge our community. Light and darkness can never peacefully coexist. They are always in competition, always seeking to drive one another out. You cannot have light and darkness comfortably side by side. So if we are faithfully to be a lampstand in a dark world, we are going to be an annoyance to some people. Do we as the church bother anyone because our light gets in their way? Would anyone in the community actually celebrate our disappearance because it gives them more room for their darkness?

These are pretty challenging questions, aren't they? In many cases the church has very little impact on the community, either for blessing or as a challenge. For the most part the community is pretty well able to ignore us and pretend that we don't exist. They drive past church signs on Sundays, but those are rather easy to overlook. For the rest of the week, perhaps nothing that we do catches their attention. Could our churches really be called the lights of our community, lampstands that impact the wider area?

Perhaps we can't yet be called "the light of our city," but nonetheless that is what Jesus is calling us to become. Perhaps we are numerically weak, short on resources, with little in ourselves to offer our community. That doesn't excuse evading our calling, however. In fact, it's not a bad thing to recognize how weak we are, provided at the same time that we recognize God's power to take weak people like us and set us on fire for the gospel. It is not a bad thing to recognize that we have nothing to bring to this task of reaching our community if at the same time we also recognize that God has all of the necessary power. His glory is always made perfect in weakness; his richness is made clear in the midst of our evident poverty.

The Source of Our Light

It is thus good to look around you and see that God does not have much to work with here, so long as we remember the power of this God who is at work in and through us. As Paul reminded the Corinthians, the God whom we serve is the same one who first called the light to shine out of the darkness at the beginning of creation (2 Corinthians 4). If God can make a world like this without any raw material, he can surely build a church out of miscellaneous sinners that his grace has called together to impact our community. He can take our corporate chaos and turn it into light and life. It is not just creation that evidences this truth either. His vast power has also been made clear in our own spiritual journey as he called us personally out of the darkness into "the light of the knowledge of the glory of God in the face of Jesus Christ" (2 Corinthians 4:6). If God is able to create a universe out of nothing and to rescue and regenerate dead sinners, he can surely work through nothing people like us to accomplish his purposes of impacting the world around us.

God promises to supply the power for us to be what he calls us to be as we wait upon him in prayer and supplication. The more we are aware of our own weakness and neediness, therefore, the more we will be inclined to throw ourselves down and beg for his strength. The people were commanded to bring the loaves to place on the table. Aaron was called to set up the lamps just as God had commanded him. However, the reality to which those lamps and loaves pointed—the blessing of God shining upon his people—was not in Aaron's power to kindle. Only God could do that. So as you and I look outward at the vastness of the task that faces us if we are to be God's lampstands in our communities, we are not to be overwhelmed by its size. We are not called to be God: God himself will do that. However, we are called to do what he has commanded us to: taking out the light of God's blessing to our friends and neighbors, sharing the love of Christ with them, and pointing them repeatedly to the grace of God.

We are therefore to be communities where God's grace is most evident and welcoming, inviting strangers to God to become his friends. We are to be communities that are impossible to ignore, where an inexplicable light beams out, constantly confronting people with changed lives through the gospel. As we do what God has commanded, we can be confident that we will see him do what he has promised—opening up closed hearts, breaking down stubborn defenses, and enabling dead sinners to emerge from the darkness and become part of his people. Some will celebrate the light of blessing that we bring; others will reject us and the One who sent us. If we are faithful, however, no one will be able to say on the last day that they knew nothing of God's light. The light of Christ will shine forward into the darkness, and the darkness will not overcome it.

11

The Substitute

NUMBERS 8:5-26

WE LIVE IN AN AGE OF SPECIALIZATION. In the olden days people did almost everything for themselves. They cut their own hair, baked their own bread, took care of their own gardens, washed their own cars, and cleaned their own houses. Increasingly, though, we now employ others to undertake these chores on our behalf. There are a variety of reasons why we employ substitutes for these roles. In some cases we have others do these responsibilities for us because they do them better than we could. I could cut my own hair, but I probably wouldn't want to be seen in public for a while afterwards. The local barbershop simply does it better. In other situations we employ substitutes because we would rather not do these jobs ourselves or because we are simply too busy and don't have the time to do them. I'm quite happy in the heat of summer to pay someone else to mow my lawn for me so I can devote my time to more fulfilling pursuits. Specialist substitutes are useful for a variety of different reasons.

Specialist Substitutes

The Levites were specialist substitutes in ancient Israel. They were called by God to be set apart to his service, taking the place of the rest of Israel in ministry before the Lord. Why were they called to that task? Was it because the rest of Israel was too lazy or too incompetent to carry out their own responsibilities in serving the Lord? Or was it because the Levites had a special preparation and calling that enabled them to perform their unique ministry in a special way? This passage in Numbers 8 opens up key aspects of the ministry of the Levites for us, and through understanding their ministry it opens a window on the way ministry in general works in God's kingdom.

First, this passage reminds us once again that God chose the Levites and called them to be his servants as substitutes for the people (v. 6). God didn't ask for volunteers for this ministry. He didn't put a sign-up sheet on the welcome table for those who had a special sense of calling to this task. As the sovereign God, he chose the Levites out from the rest of Israel and called them to be devoted to his service. He didn't ask their opinion or seek their permission, any more than he asked Israel's permission when he first chose them out of all the nations around them. God didn't need their permission to choose them—or indeed to choose us! He is the sovereign King, and it is his prerogative to choose whomever he will to serve him. By the same token, it is his prerogative to pass over whomever he will.

There was a rationale behind God's choice of the Levites to serve him, however. Just because God's choice is sovereign doesn't mean that it is arbitrary and capricious. In their service of the Lord, the Levites acted as representatives of the whole people of Israel. More precisely, they were substitutes for the firstborn sons of Israel (vv. 16, 17). These firstborn sons of Israel belonged to God in a special way because when he brought judgment on Egypt in the tenth and final plague, he passed over the Israelite houses that were marked with the blood of the Passover lamb and spared their firstborn. The firstborn sons of the Egyptians were struck down by the destroying angel, but the firstborn of Israel were spared, protected by the blood at the entrance to their homes.

Set Apart for Service

In place of all of these firstborn sons of Israel, God claimed the Levites. We saw earlier in the book of Numbers that when the census was taken, the totals for the firstborn and for the Levites were very similar, and the difference was made up by a payment of redemption money for each and every one of the extra firstborn sons (3:40-50). Now, though, in a graphic ceremony, the Levites were publicly to be set apart to take the place of Israel in this ministry. The Israelites were to bring the Levites before the Lord and lay their hands on them (8:10). The significance of this gesture becomes clearer a few verses later on when the Levites themselves were instructed to lay their hands on the heads of the bulls that would be used as a sin offering and as a guilt offering to make atonement for the Levites (v. 12). This was a routine practice in the offering of a sacrifice. The person offering the bull would place or, more precisely "press," their hands on the sacrifice. They weren't just to touch the animal but to lean on it.[1] This act of laying on of hands identified the animal as belonging to the worshiper and therefore as taking his place.[2]

So when the Israelites laid hands on the Levites, or "leaned" on them, they were identifying them as a kind of sacrificial offering, presented to the

Lord in their place. In fact, verse 13 makes this explicit: the Levites were to be presented as a "wave offering" (or better, "dedication offering")[3] before the Lord. They were thereby set apart as belonging to the Lord. They were to "make atonement" for the Israelites (v. 19), just as the bull of the burnt offering earlier "made atonement" for the Levites (v. 12). In other words, just as that sacrifice was a ransom that took the place of the Levites, so too they were a living sacrifice that took the place of Israel in the work of serving God.[4] The Levites were God's chosen substitutes to take the place of the people as a whole in being consecrated to the Lord.

Purified for Service

Second, this passage shows us that those who serve the Lord must first be purified. That is the focus of the first section of the chapter. Before they were offered to the Lord, the Levites had to be purified in two ways—by cleansing and by sacrifice. They were to be sprinkled with the water of cleansing, to be shaved all over,[5] and to wash their clothes (vv. 6, 7). The general meaning of this ceremony is not hard to discern: those who present themselves to serve the Lord must be free from all defilement, spiritually clean.

Yet even this outward cleansing was not enough. The Levites also had to offer sacrifices for their sin: a burnt offering and a sin offering were needed to make atonement for them (v. 8). These two offerings had different functions. The focus of the burnt offering was to serve as a ransom, healing general breaches in the relationship between God and man. The smoke ascended to God, effecting a change in his relationship to the person or community offering the sacrifice. The purpose of the sin offering, however, was to deal specifically with the defilement brought upon the community and the sanctuary by actual sins. It was not to purge the individual who brought the sacrifice but rather to deal with the wider polluting effects of his sin on the community and the sanctuary.[6] Washing could deal with minor impurities, but only sacrifice could take away substantial impurities and neutralize sin's polluting power. Only the pure could stand in the presence of God.

The Work of the Sanctuary

In addition to being chosen by the Lord and cleansed, the Levites had a task assigned to them: they were to do the work of the Tent of Meeting on behalf of the Israelites (v. 15). As we have seen in our earlier studies, that duty involved guarding the sanctuary against profane intruders, carrying the sanctuary from place to place, and assisting with the sacrificial offerings. All of these aspects were necessary if the people were to serve God and see his blessing instead of his curse unleashed on the community. By guarding the sanctuary and transporting its parts carefully, the Levites acted like the sin offering, protecting the sanctuary against the kind of defilement that would inevitably have brought judgment on the community. By assisting in the regular offerings at the altar, they themselves acted like the burnt offering, effecting a change in God's attitude to his people through their own total self-commitment. If there had been no Levites, the presence of the tabernacle of God in the midst of the community would inevitably have brought plague upon Israel rather than prosperity, because there would have been no one to protect the sanctuary from defilement or to restore the covenant relationship when it was breached. The Levites' faithful service protected the community against God's curse.

Moreover, the Levites' task was a work that demanded the very peak of their powers. Only those at the height of their strength, those aged between twenty-five and fifty, could serve the Lord in this ministry (v. 24). Strength was needed to lift and carry the items of the tabernacle, as well as to guard and protect. Sacred objects could not be assigned to those who might drop them or faint under the load. Older men could certainly still assist the younger men in the work (v. 26): there was no formal retirement age for the Levites at which they were sent off to play golf! However, the work of guarding and keeping the sanctuary was so demanding that only men in the prime of life were qualified to do it.

The Levites and the Work of Ministry

So much for the description of the work of the Levites. We said earlier, though, that this chapter opens up a window onto the nature of Christian ministry more generally. What is that window?

In the first place, the ministry of the Levites points us forward to the ministry of Christ. They were substitutes for the firstborn of Israel who were to be dedicated to the Lord through personal cleansing and a symbolic sacrifice, given over to a lifetime of service in God's house. The result of their ministry was to be that the remainder of the Israelites would be able to approach God without receiving a covenant curse. Every single one of these aspects points us forward to Jesus. He is the ultimate firstborn, not only the firstborn of Israel but of all creation (Colossians 1:15). What is more, he began his public ministry with a public cleansing, being baptized in the Jordan River by John the Baptist (Matthew 3:13-17). Why should Jesus be baptized? Baptism was for sinners, for repentance and cleansing. John himself said to Jesus in essence, "I don't understand. I should rather be baptized by you. Why should the sinless one be baptized along with the sinners?" The answer was that Jesus must identify with his people, and so he joined them in the symbolic cleansing of water baptism. After his baptism Jesus began his formal ministry, a brief but full lifetime of perfect service and obedience to God. He himself was the tabernacle of God, the glory of God in flesh, and he guarded that tabernacle carefully against sin, remaining utterly without spot and blemish.

In this active obedience, keeping the Law and guarding God's holiness, Jesus is our substitute. He kept the Law's demands in our place, making a renewed relationship with God possible and the dwelling of God in our midst once again a reality. Yet Jesus was never more clearly our substitute, our ransom, than when in his passive obedience he suffered and laid his life down in our place. As Jesus himself said in Mark 10:45: "the Son of Man came not to be served but to serve, and to give his life as a ransom for many." This too was foreshadowed in his baptism, for baptism is a sign not only of cleansing but of judgment. The water of cleansing is a token not only of the purifying Holy Spirit but also of the floodwaters of judgment. Jesus referred to this in Luke 12:49, 50: "I came to cast fire on the earth, and would that it were already kindled! I have a baptism to be baptized with, and how great is my distress until it is accomplished!" Jesus was talking here about the reality of cosmic judgment that would be poured out upon him on the cross, where he would become the ransom, the final sacrifice of atonement, for his people. By taking on himself our plagues, he made it safe for us to draw near to God. The fire of God's wrath is removed from us because it was poured out on him. The water that cleanses us is safe because it has washed over him and drowned him. Jesus identified with his people in the symbolic judgment of water baptism because he knew that he would bear for them the reality that it represented. Jesus has thus fulfilled the ministry of the pure Levites, a ransom for God's people.

The Levitehood of All Believers

Now since we as Christians are united to Christ by faith, we share in this same ministry. In our own baptism we were baptized into Christ's death and resurrection. Our fate is inextricably tied up with his, and so too is our calling in this world. We speak of the priesthood of all believers, since we are all joined to Christ, the great High Priest. So too we can speak of the Levitehood of all believers because we are joined to the one who has fulfilled their ministry. What, though, does that mean?

First, it means that we are all called to be pure servants of the Lord. Week by week as we come together in our local churches we enter into the very presence of God. There are no "Keep back" signs posted around the perimeter of the building, no armed guards to keep us at a safe distance. Yet the God into whose presence we come is the same all-holy Lord of the universe. This means that our access is only safe insofar as we are covered by the blood of the Lamb, slain in our place. At the same time, it means that we should in a growing way exhibit faithfully the obedience that God requires. If we have been baptized, we have been marked out as belonging to a pure and holy God. How then can we take what God has made clean and drag it through the gutter? How can we persist in pride or gossip or lust or pornography or selfishness or hard-heartedness toward our neighbors? We are called to live pure and holy lives in service to God and are marked with a seal, showing that we belong to God. We must live as what we are!

Second, it means that we are to guard the presence of God in our midst in such a way that those around us receive a blessing from God and not a curse. If the natural state of Israel was to incur God's judgment unless the Levites intervened, how much more will that be the case for our neighbors and our society? People all around us are theologically and ethically confused, offending a holy God moment by moment; yet they are often totally unaware of that fact. Our calling is to protect that which is sacred, so that our friends and our neighbors are guarded from God's wrath.

That is a complex task in the society in which we live. We are called to speak the truth to our neighbors, yet at the same time to speak that truth in love. We have a calling as God's people to stand up and speak against the evils of our day, yet in a way that points people again and again to our true ransom in Christ. For some that will mean taking a public stand against abortion or homosexual marriage, using the legitimate freedoms we have in this country to address the hearts and minds of our hearers. For others it will mean a less visible but nonetheless equally vital role of counseling pregnant teens or ministering to AIDS patients. In both situations, the balance of truth and love needs to be maintained. It is possible to denounce evil without love, just as James and John were eager to summon down fire on the Samaritan village that refused to receive Jesus (Luke 9:54). Furthermore, it is possible to give practical help while at the same time neglecting the equally desperate needs of the human heart because we are afraid of confrontation. Further complicating matters, it is possible to be so paralyzed by the dangers on both sides that we do nothing at all and hide ourselves away in a safe refuge, far away from the action.

God calls all of us to give our best in service to him. In Jesus Christ he has made atonement at the cross for our community. He doesn't call us to re-create that foundational act. Yet he calls us, like the Levites, to bring that atonement to bear on our society. This is one task that we cannot delegate to others. Pastors and elders have their place in the church, but their calling is to equip the saints for the works of ministry, not to do those works of ministry for them (Ephesians 4:12). The calling to purify ourselves and to serve our community in Christ's name and in the power of his Spirit rests on all of us. May it be said of us, just as it was of Israel in Numbers 8:20, "According to all that the LORD commanded Moses concerning the Levites, the people of Israel did to them."

12

The God of the
Second Chance

NUMBERS 9:1-14

LAW. IT HAS A VERY NEGATIVE RING TO IT, DOESN'T IT? It sounds like rules and regulations, which we naturally hate. We instinctively respond, "Don't tie me down! Don't tell me what to do or who to be!" We want to define ourselves and do whatever we wish. Mercy and forgiveness, on the other hand, are very popular. Everyone wants to be allowed to fail, to escape the negative consequences of our actions, and to be given a second chance. Nowhere are these diverse attitudes more apparent than in the spiritual realm. As soon as you talk to people about God and God's Law, the questions and opinions flow. Do you want to start a heated discussion at your place of work or school? Just ask the question, "Is God a God of rules and regulations, or is he a God of grace and mercy and love?" and sit back and watch the results. That's a question about which everyone has an opinion. Even those who don't believe God exists have ideas about what kind of God he ought to be if he did.

Many of those ideas revolve around the relationship between law and grace, obligation and mercy, regulation and forgiveness. Some people describe their understanding of a God who is almost all justice and obligation, with very little mercy and grace. Others (a much larger group) urge a view of an easygoing God whose obligations and regulations are fairly negotiable, swamped by his general beneficence toward mankind. Many would depict the Old Testament view of God as the former, an unbending, harsh, legalistic God, while suggesting that the New Testament shows us a kind, loving, and merciful God. That's not a new idea. It goes all the way back to the second-century heretic Marcion, who wanted to separate "modern" New

Testament Christianity from its "old-fashioned" Old Testament roots. Whatever your view, though, clearly the relationship between law and grace, between God's justice and God's mercy is an important one, and one that this passage in Numbers 9 is going to clarify for us in some remarkable ways.

The God of Rules and Regulations

The first thing this passage confirms for us is that God is indeed a God of rules and regulations, a God who is concerned about precise obedience. God spoke to Moses and commanded the Israelites to celebrate the Passover (v. 2). It was not simply an invitation to join him at the temple of their choice if they felt like it. God *commanded* them to celebrate the Passover. This was the first month of the second year of the exodus; so it would have been the first time that the Israelites celebrated the Passover after the original historic event of the Passover meal. God was reminding them that this meal had not been instituted simply as a unique event but as an annual celebration, a lasting commemoration for the generations to come (see Exodus 12:14).

Nor were the Israelites free to improvise and innovate when it came to the manner in which they celebrated the Passover. God had told them when and how they were to celebrate the Passover: in the first month from the evening of the fourteenth day until the evening of the twenty-first day, they were to eat bread with no yeast. At the end of that time, each family was to take its own Passover lamb and slaughter it, collecting the blood. They were to smear the blood on the top and sides of the entrance to their house (Exodus 12:22), and then to eat the body of the lamb inside their safely marked houses. They were not to break any of its bones (Exodus 12:46). Nor was this simply a mime show. Unlike circumcision, which demanded no comprehension from those taking part, the children participating in this ceremony were expected to ask questions and to understand the answers. They would ask, "What does this ceremony mean?" and receive the answer, explaining the significance of the Passover as a reenactment of the great act of deliverance by which God's people were redeemed out of Egypt (Exodus 12:26, 27).

The proper and precise celebration of the Passover is thus very much the focus of the opening section of Numbers 9. God told the people not simply to celebrate the Passover but to celebrate it at the appointed time, in accordance with all of its rules and regulations (vv. 2, 3). The Israelites could not celebrate the Passover however they felt led—for example, with lox and bagels rather than lamb and matzos, or on the night of the fifteenth rather than the fourteenth because the fourteenth was always their night for going bowling. It was not enough to do what God had asked in some vague way. Precise, detailed obedience was necessary on the part of Israel, and precise, detailed obedience was what they delivered. We are told, "according to all that the LORD commanded Moses, so the people of Israel did" (v. 5). The same concern for rules and regulations emerges again at the end of our passage (v. 14): the resident alien who lived among Israel could also celebrate the Passover (if he had been circumcised; see Exodus 12:48), but he too must follow all of its rules and regulations.

The Principle of Precise Obedience

Here, then, is our first principle from this passage: in serving God, precise obedience to all of his rules and regulations is necessary. This is true in all of life: in every area we are to be governed by God's rules and regulations, by the richness of God's revelation of his will for our lives in his Word, the Bible. I am to obey God in everything—in the words that I say, in my conduct, even in the thoughts that I think. Even brushing my teeth or choosing whether to buy a new car or one that is used are acts that are governed by his Word in a general way.

However, it is particularly true that our worship of God is to be governed by his Word. After all, God has a lot more to say in his Word on the subject of worship than he does about tooth brushing and car buying. One of the principles that is to govern the church in our worship, just as for their Passover, is that we are always and only to do what God has commanded in his Word. He has not simply commanded us to worship him and left it up to us to decide how that worship is to be offered. On the contrary, when we worship him we do so according to all of the rules and regulations in his Word, seeking carefully to do not only *what* he has commanded but to do it *in the way* that he has commanded. This is the principle that is often called "the regulative principle of worship."[1] We don't do anything in worship simply because it appeals to our emotions or to our culture or because it is traditional. We need to have a good Biblical reason for why we do everything that we do in worship.

Now, of course, just believing in the regulative principle of worship doesn't solve all worship issues, any more than agreeing with your daughter that she should dress in accord with Biblical guidelines tells you exactly which outfit she should wear today. Some forms of attire are obviously clearly excluded by the Biblical requirement of modesty. It is not hard to reach agreement that extremely revealing necklines and ultrashort skirts do not meet the Biblical test. Other outfits will be more debatable. Biblical modesty does not mean, at least in my judgment, that girls need to dress like transplants from the last century. Different families will sometimes come up with different guidelines and different judgment calls. The important thing, though, is that having agreed on the basic principle with your daughter, you have a basis on which to have good discussions and reach godly conclusions.

It is the same way with worship.[2] Some churches that affirm the regulative principle of worship may do things in worship that make me uncomfortable, while others may interpret the Bible in ways that are more restrictive than my understanding. Yet if we agree on the principle that in worship we only do what God has commanded and absolutely nothing else, no matter how well-intentioned, then we have a basis to sit down and talk and seek to reach a fuller awareness of what the Word of God actually says.

That is the principle that governs the worship at the church I pastor: we will only do what God has actually commanded us in his Word. Because of this commitment, we don't do some things that you will find in many other evangelical churches. At the same time, our worship is not necessarily the same as every other Reformed church: the regulative principle of worship does not necessarily lead to cookie cutter conformity. Whatever we do in worship—or don't do—we believe we have a Biblical reason for it. Behind all of the specifics is the bigger principle that in worship we only do what God has commanded us. The God of the Bible is a God to whom specifics matter, a God who is concerned about rules and regulations, about precise obedience to his commands.

The God of Second Chances

Yet the focus of the passage as a whole is not simply on the fact that God is a God of specifics who expects his rules and regulations to be observed precisely. It also shows us a second principle—namely, that God is a God of second chances. The center of the chapter addresses the situation of a number of Israelites who were unable to take part in the regular Passover meal because they were ceremonially unclean. That was a severe problem since taking part in the Passover was not an optional activity. You couldn't just say, "Oh well, I'll catch the fun next year." On the contrary, anyone who did not partake in the Passover was to be excluded from the community (Exodus 12:19, 47). It was not that this group of people had willfully ignored the Passover command or even carelessly neglected their duties. They had come in contact with a dead body, either accidentally or as a matter of necessity, and so were unable to partake at the regular time (9:7). What were they to do? Must they be excommunicated from the Lord's people?

That was the issue that these men brought to Moses, which he in turn took to the Lord (v. 8). In response to their inquiry, the Lord gave an additional commandment that addressed not only this situation but others that were like it. The question they had asked concerned only those who were ceremonially unclean through contact with a dead body (v. 7). The answer was broader, however, addressing also those who might be unable to keep the Passover because they were on a long journey (v. 10). In other words, God used this specific incident to address a wider issue in worship.

What was the Lord's response? In the first place, notice that the solution to their problem was not to pretend there was no problem. God didn't say to them that exact obedience doesn't really matter, provided their heart was in the right place. The Lord didn't permit these men to participate in the Passover in an unclean state, nor did he let them celebrate it at whatever time they may wish. Yet at the same time, he recognized that precise obedience is not always possible in a fallen world, and so he provided for a second-chance Passover, an "irregular" celebration. This second-chance Passover was to be celebrated exactly one month after the first and was to be observed in accordance with all the same rules and regulations (v. 11). It was the same precisely observed Passover, simply one month later. What is more, this second-chance Passover was only for those with a valid reason for not observing the Passover at the proper time. Those who had no excuse and simply failed to observe the Passover at the time when they ought to were still to be cut off from the community (v. 13).

The Irregular Principle

This irregular principle of worship (and, more broadly, of life) is very important to our thinking as Christians because in a fallen world we often find ourselves in situations where precise obedience to God's Word is simply impossible. Sometimes our past sin places us in a situation where there seems no way to get from where we are to where we ought to be. Perhaps a man married someone who is not a Christian, even though he knew it was wrong to do so. Now he finds himself stuck in an awkward situation, unable to do everything God's Word requires. Or perhaps a wife finds spiritual leadership in her home thrust upon her because she's married to an unbeliever (what the Bible calls "an unequal yoke"). If God were simply a God of rules and regulations, such persons would be without hope. Yet because God is the God of second chances, there is hope for them. They can repent of their sin and find a way back to an obedience that is as close as possible to what it ought to be. God's grace is sufficient for all of us.

Perhaps you find yourself on the horns of a dilemma because of the general fallenness of the world and the complexities of life. Starting a new church involves all kinds of irregularities. Biblically, churches ought to be governed by a plurality of elders (see Titus 1:5). That is undoubtedly the right way to do things, and wherever possible it is the best way to plant a church as well. Yet in a new church you cannot always have multiple elders present from the outset. Sometimes the church planter is effectively alone in spiritual oversight, a kind of local pope. Is that the right way of doing things? No. However, if you only ever did things the "right" way, many ministry opportunities would be lost! Is it wrong to sometimes have a church under the oversight of a single church planter? No, it is not wrong, but it is irregular.

Sometimes a tribe of polygamists comes to faith in Christ. It is not

Biblical for a man to have more than one wife. Yet if the husbands put away their multiple wives, these women may be left facing shame, poverty, and isolation. One solution is to recognize this as an irregular situation: those who have married multiple wives in the past can keep them and continue to provide for all of their needs, but no more polygamous marriages are permitted within the church. Over the course of time the situation gradually moves from irregular to regular.[3]

The irregular category bridges the gap between right and wrong by recognizing that there are some situations where pursuing one Biblical principle and meeting people's needs necessarily brings you into conflict with another Biblical principle. The solution is neither to declare the Biblical principles irrelevant, as liberals would, nor to declare people's needs disposable, like the Pharisees. It is rather to seek God's direction and to do the best you can in the present circumstances, while moving as quickly as possible toward fulfilling all of the Biblical principles. As this passage shows us, God is not just the God of rules and regulations, but the God who extends grace and mercy into the messy world of reality.

Grace to the Aliens and Strangers

Further, God's grace is not simply extended to his own people, to the descendants of Abraham. That brings us to the third principle in this passage: God's grace reaches out to include the aliens and strangers among his people in the Passover meal (v. 14). Think about the profound symbolism of that inclusion. The Passover meal was the celebration of God's redemption of his people out of Egypt, in faithfulness to his promise to Abraham. God had obligated himself to deliver this people and to give them a land in which to live. Yet he had no obligation to anyone beyond the boundaries of that family. He had made no promises to these aliens and strangers of the kind he had made to Abraham. Yet even those who by birth were outsiders to the covenant could be included in his people and celebrate the Passover. All they had to do was to come by faith and receive the covenant sign of circumcision in order to be received into the covenant community. Then they too could eat the Passover meal, with all of its symbolism.

This is a principle that we saw graphically depicted for us recently in my church through the baptisms of three children adopted from other countries. By nature these children were outsiders to God's promises. They weren't born into the homes of believing families. Left to themselves, they might each have grown up as outsiders to the gospel, never even hearing about faith in Jesus Christ. Yet by God's grace they have been brought into the covenant community, just as our natural-born children are. When they are able to understand and profess the reality of that redemption for themselves, they too can partake in the new-covenant meal of the Lord's Supper. Indeed,

God's gracious inclusion of aliens and strangers into his people covers most of us. Hardly any of us are by birth children of Abraham. Yet God in his mercy and grace has reached out more widely than simply to Israel with the gospel. He has brought those who were once far from him into his kingdom as his sons and daughters.

Law and Grace

How can this be though? How can one God be a God of rules and regulations, a God who insists that we worship him in strict accord with the principles laid down in his Word, and at the same time also be the God of mercy and grace who gives second chances and includes aliens and strangers? Is God schizophrenic, unable to make up his mind whether to be strict or to be merciful? Certainly not! Nor is this a contrast between a rule-making God of the Old Testament and the gracious God revealed in the New Testament. Both aspects of God's character are here in the Old Testament. The Passover itself shows us how God can be both the God of absolute obedience and of grace and mercy. At the first Passover, one life was substituted for the life of another. The Passover lamb took the place of the firstborn son and enabled him to live through its death. Nor was it an even exchange. You couldn't just take a mangy and worthless lamb and offer it as your Passover lamb. It had to be a lamb without any spot or blemish, perfect in every way, without a broken bone even in death. Yet your firstborn son didn't have to be perfect at all: whether he was a little angel on the one hand, or a rambunctious, self-absorbed hellion on the other, his personal holiness had nothing to do with his life being spared. All he needed was the faith to be inside the house that was daubed with the blood of the perfect lamb.

No wonder Paul calls Jesus Christ "our Passover lamb" (1 Corinthians 5:7). For Jesus Christ is the reality to which that Passover lamb pointed year after year. The Passover lamb testified to a salvation that came by grace through simple faith to sinners. It pointed them to God's commitment to save a people for himself by the perfection of a substitute, someone who would fulfill all of God's rules and regulations in their place, enabling God to extend his grace and mercy to them. It spoke of a cosmic second chance for unclean humanity—that even though in our first parent, Adam, we all sinned and therefore deserve God's rejection and his wrath, in Christ we receive his mercy and his blessing. All we have to do to receive forgiveness is place our faith in Christ.

Does that mean, then, that it doesn't matter how we live because Christ has done it all for us? By no means. Those who received a second-chance Passover were not to be emboldened to sin by that opportunity. On the contrary, as they sat down to eat the body of their Passover one month after everyone else, their hearts should have been stirred to such thankfulness for the Lord's mercy and grace that they resolved to live lives of new obedience to all of his rules and regulations. It is no coincidence that the Passover feast combined the sacrifice of the spotless lamb with a period of abstention from anything containing leaven. Leaven, with its association with change and decay, was a natural symbol for sin, corruption, and death. Those who are redeemed from death by the lamb should be eager to flee from sin and death. This is the connection that Paul makes in 1 Corinthians 5:7, 8: "For Christ, our Passover lamb, has been sacrificed. Let us therefore celebrate the festival, not with the old leaven, the leaven of malice and evil, but with the unleavened bread of sincerity and truth."

God's rules and regulations are nothing less than his wisdom written down to guide and guard our hearts and lives. There is therefore no conflict in the end between God's precise demands and his loving-kindness. He has fulfilled the Law's demands for us in Christ and thereby enables us to come to him with reverence and delight and profound wonder. We who once were aliens and strangers, completely separated from his people, have by his grace and mercy been grafted into his people. We who are God's second-chance people by grace should as a result be eager to worship and serve this God according to all of his revealed will, so that he might receive the praise and glory that is due him.

13

Setting Out

NUMBERS 9:15—10:10

STARTING SOMETHING NEW CAN BE a nerve-racking experience. Whether it is stepping out on the first day of a new school or a new job or trying to make a new set of friends when you move into a new community, that which is new often makes us afraid. Our children sometimes find these occasions especially daunting. Many a parent's heartstrings have been tugged as their prospective kindergartner sobs, "Come with me, Mom . . ." As we grow up, we realize that Mom and Dad can't always be there to help us over the hurdles of life, but that doesn't keep us from sometimes secretly wishing that they could be. How comforting it would be to have the constant presence of someone who really knows what they are doing with us as we launch out into a particularly challenging new venture!

A New Start

Israel was on the verge of a new start here at the end of Numbers 9. They were about to set out from Mount Sinai where they had been camping for almost a year. It was there at Mount Sinai that God gave them his Law and the instructions for building the tabernacle, as we see in the book of Exodus. It was there that he taught them about his sacrifices and the priesthood, as recorded in the book of Leviticus. It was there that he arranged the camp and prepared them to set out on this journey, as we have seen already in the book of Numbers. Now it was time for the talking and preparing to end and for the action to start. It was time for the Israelites to put their feet into motion and begin the journey into the wilderness, marching toward the Promised Land. That was a challenging prospect for Israel. There was so much that was unknown. Where would they camp? What would they eat and drink? When

129

would they get there? Would their mission be a success? There must have been quite a few uneasy hearts in the camp.

God with Them

There was one thing that was not to be an unknown, however. They wouldn't have to go into the wilderness alone: God was going to go with them. The central focus of the second half of Numbers 9 is to underline the connection between the cloud and the tabernacle. The tabernacle was the visible symbol of God's presence in the midst of his people, the tent of their heavenly King at the center of the camp. It was not just an empty symbol, however: it was inhabited by the cloud of God's glory that descended onto it on the very day it was first set up (v. 15). This descent of God's glory demonstrated that God would indeed dwell in the midst of his people. What is more, the book of Exodus ended with the recounting of the same event (40:34-38). By repeating it here, the narrator is linking this new journey into the wilderness with the journey in the book of Exodus that took them to Sinai in the first place. Just as God had accompanied them out of Egypt on the way to Mount Sinai by means of the pillar of cloud and fire, so now the same pillar would rest on the tabernacle. God was indeed present with his people. Here was comfort for uneasy hearts.

God Leading Them

God was not just present with his people as an observer, however. He was not just along for the ride, or even sitting in the copilot's chair. God was going to lead them into the Promised Land. By means of the cloud, the Lord would tell Israel when they were to set out and when they were to camp. He would decide how long they were to remain in a particular place, whether one night or two days or a month or a year (9:22). The Lord would guide them and direct them on every leg of their journey. In fact, to make sure that you don't miss this point, the narrator labors it somewhat in 9:17-22. Essentially, all he is saying in these verses is, "When the cloud moved on, the people would set out, and when the cloud stopped they would camp"— yet he takes six verses to say it, utilizing almost every possible permutation. By means of this repetition, he stresses the fact that on this march there was no room for creativity and individualism on the part of God's people. There was no place for fussing and crying out, "Are we there yet?" What they had to do was watch the cloud and follow carefully wherever it went. It is not coincidental that the phrase "at the command of the Lord" occurs seven times in verses 18-23.[1] The narrator wants us to be aware that this journey is at the will of the Lord himself and under his direction every step of the way.

Now it might seem as if such an obvious marker of the Lord's leading as a fiery cloud would be evident enough that all could follow it directly, but that was not the case. Getting such a large number of people ready for the march was no easy undertaking. This should not come as a surprise to those of us who are parents. I find it a major challenge to get five children up and out of the door to school in the morning, let alone an enormous nation. What is more, as we saw in the earlier chapters, the people were not to progress forward as a disorganized rabble but as a disciplined body, an army arranged by tribes and families (see Numbers 2). Achieving this kind of order would have required significant coordination. For that reason God commanded that the actual instructions for the people to move out were to be mediated through the priests by means of the silver trumpets (10:1-7). These special trumpets were not employed as musical instruments but as signaling devices, just as the military used to employ bugle calls to direct the actions of troops on the battlefield. The priestly trumpet calls were the signal for the various sections of the camp to set out on their journey, so that everything could be done in good order, exactly as God had commanded them.

The Silver Trumpets

At the same time, we need to notice that the use of these trumpets was not simply a convenient signaling device, one that could equally well have been replaced by an alternative method of getting the word out, such as semaphore flags or carrier pigeons. The second part of the passage about the trumpets reminds us that these trumpets would continue to have an ongoing use in Israel: this was to be "a perpetual statute throughout your generations" (10:8). After the journey through the wilderness was over and the people had entered the Promised Land, these trumpets were still regularly to be used for two events: warfare and worship. They were to be sounded whenever the people went into battle (10:9) and whenever they gathered for their festivals (10:10). At the sound of the trumpet, the community would gather together either to fight or to fellowship in praise. The trumpets would issue a continuing call to exercise obedience to God's demands.

The sound of the priestly trumpets was not simply a rallying cry to bring the people of God together either. The sound of the trumpets also brought them to the Lord's remembrance (10:10). As well as being a call for the people to come together and act as one, it was a cry to God to come and act on their behalf. Whenever the Israelites faced their enemies, they could sound the trumpet and know that God would remember them and come to their aid (10:9). Whenever the people brought their offerings at the great festivals, the priests could sound the trumpet and know that God would hear from Heaven and pay attention to their offerings (10:10). Their sins would be forgiven, and their acts of worship would be received and accepted.

So the trumpets not only called the people together to renew their obedience but reminded them and assured them of God's continuing presence and favor toward them. It is not coincidental that these themes of presence and obedience are the same themes that we saw highlighted at the end of Numbers 9.

The note about the continuing function of the trumpets thus says something profound and enduring about the nature of the journey on which Israel was embarking: the wandering people of God were about to begin a pilgrimage that would revolve around the twin themes of warfare and worship. That pilgrimage would continue even after they had entered the land. What is more, God's presence and their obedience were absolutely necessary if these tasks were to be carried out successfully.

The Wandering People of God

This observation points us toward the way in which this passage addresses us in our contemporary setting. For we too are the wandering people of God, as the book of Hebrews reminds us, located between our exodus from the bondage of sin and death and our entry into the promised land of Heaven. We too face a daunting journey through the wilderness, surrounded by hostile terrain and many enemies. We may not literally travel through a land without water and food as they did or face the prospect of fierce battles against well-equipped enemies, but we too have many struggles in this world. We should have no illusions about the difficulty of our pilgrimage. This world is not our home, and it is frequently not a hospitable environment for believers. Jesus puts it this way in John 15:18-20:

> If the world hates you, know that it has hated me before it hated you. If you were of the world, the world would love you as its own; but because you are not of the world, but I chose you out of the world, therefore the world hates you. Remember the word that I said to you: "A servant is not greater than his master." If they persecuted me, they will also persecute you.

Since this is the case, what is needed if you are to survive the pilgrimage and make it to the other side of the wilderness? You need exactly the same two things they needed: you need the presence and favor of God with you, and you need to obey his directions.

God with Us

The first thing you need to endure this wilderness is to know God's presence and favor with you. This presupposes, of course, the fact that God is not equally present and favorable toward everyone in this world. The

Canaanites were religious people, many of whom doubtless sincerely believed in their gods. Yet the decisive difference between the two nations was ultimately this: God had chosen Israel and called them to be his people, while he did not choose and call the Canaanites. God certainly didn't choose the Israelites because they were better than the Canaanites—that becomes clear enough as the book of Numbers unfolds. Nor were the Canaanites innocent bystanders, good people who wished they too could be included in God's people but were excluded by a harsh decree. On the contrary, they were sinners whose sin had now reached its full measure (see Genesis 15:16). God had good reason for bringing judgment upon the Canaanites. What is more, those Canaanites who wished to switch sides and abandon their idols in favor of the true and living God could do so at any time, and by God's grace and mercy some did. However, as long as the Canaanites remained faithful to their gods and were strangers to the Lord, they would receive no favor from God. For them, his presence was something to be feared, not something to be sought.

So too in our context God's presence and favor is not equally bestowed on all. It is true that none of us deserve God's presence or his favor. By nature we are all just like the Canaanites: aliens and strangers to the true God whose whole lives are committed to serving something or someone other than him. Yet in his mercy and grace God promises both his presence and his favor to those who come to him by faith in Christ. As Paul puts it in Romans 5:1, 2, "since we have been justified by faith, we have peace with God through our Lord Jesus Christ. Through him we have also obtained access by faith into this grace in which we stand." What Paul is saying is that we didn't always have peace with God or access to his presence, but now we have both of those things through Jesus Christ. As he goes on to say three chapters later, "There is therefore now no condemnation for those who are in Christ Jesus" (Romans 8:1). God's wrath remains on those who are alienated from him, but there is no condemnation for those who are in Jesus Christ. On the contrary, they now experience peace and fellowship with God.

Do we know God's presence and favor? If God's presence and favor are vital for life and if they are not for everyone, then that is a crucial question for which to know the answer. When we stand before God, are we trusting in whatever goodness and righteousness we can muster? There is no peace in that affirmation. Peace, the absence of condemnation, the experience of God's favor—these things are only to be found by pleading the righteousness of Jesus Christ in our place. If our hope is resting on the righteousness of Christ, then we have the favor of God and the presence of God with us right now.

Jesus promised his disciples his presence and favor when he said, "And behold, I am with you always, to the end of the age" (Matthew 28:20). We often look to that verse as encouragement in the work of missions and evangelism, and appropriately so. It is the assurance that as we go and share the good news with those around us, God will go ahead of us, touching hearts and lives by his Spirit before we even open our mouths to speak. However, there is more to the verse than that. When we trudge through some of the weariest valleys of life, this verse assures us that Jesus is there with us. When we face uncertainty in relationships and are not sure if we can trust someone, Jesus is there with us. When we feel ready to faint and give up because of the painful difficulty of life, Jesus is there with us. The one in whom the glorious presence of God took flesh and dwelt on earth has promised that he will constantly be with us by his Spirit: he will never leave us or forsake us, no matter what life may throw at us.

Obedient Living

The second thing you need in order to endure this wilderness is obedience to the Lord's directions. The Israelites were to take their cue from the cloud and follow its leading. So, too, you and I are to take our cue from God's Word, the Scriptures, and to follow its directions. Which directions? All of them! There are no commands in God's Word that are irrelevant or negotiable; there are no proposals or suggestions, only commands. However, let me highlight two particular areas where we need to obey God's Word that are particularly relevant to this passage. First, we need to hear the trumpet call to come together for spiritual warfare instead of fighting as individuals. I'm not talking about declaring some kind of evangelical jihad on the non-Christian world around us. I'm talking particularly about the spiritual struggles that each of us faces individually and together as a society. Often we try to face our struggles on our own. We live after all in a culture that cherishes individualism. Yet we are to be a community of believers, a family of God's people, a military unit that fights together and is committed to the policy, "No man left behind." When one person hurts, we all hurt; when one person rejoices, we all rejoice.

In order for that policy to be a reality, though, we need to be involved with other believers outside the setting of church on Sunday morning. There are a variety of ways to build those connections. It could be an evening Bible study or singing in the choir or participating in the youth group. We all need to find a context in which we come together with other believers to build deep and strong relationships. We need to make a space in our life where we encourage them and they are able to encourage us in our daily warfare.

We also need to work together if we are to make an impact on the society in which we live. We are called to be salt and light in our community, acting as a preservative against rottenness, as well as communicating the gospel (Matthew 5:13-16). If we only act as individuals, our influence is limited; but when we come together, we can have a bigger impact for good. Once again there are a variety of ways in which we can have that impact on the surrounding culture. But in order to maximize our impact we need to be called together to fight as a unit, not as a disorganized group of individuals.

Worship and Fellowship

In addition to coming together to serve one another and to fight together, we also need to hear the trumpet call to come together for worship and fellowship. Perhaps the most important thing we do as God's people is to come together to worship God. The world certainly doesn't think so. The world thinks we are wasting our time when we come together to praise and exalt the Lord, and it asks us when we are going to get busy doing something useful. In reality, though, there is nothing more useful in all of the world than singing God's praises and studying his Word. This is what reorients our thoughts in the right direction and empowers us for renewed service by filling us with an accurate understanding of who God is and what he is doing in this world. Activity is good, but it has to be activity that accomplishes something real. It is not enough simply to start marching and to determine the destination later: you have to know where you are heading before you get underway. Scripture is both where we receive our marching orders and where we are reminded what we are marching toward.

When Wandering Days Are Done

The third point we need to be reminded of, though, is that our wandering is not forever. Israel would one day hang up their marching boots and enter the Promised Land. It would take them a long time to get there because of their sin, but eventually they would reach the goal that God had set for them. One day, too, Israel would be able to hang up their swords and their spears, at least temporarily, when God gave them rest from their enemies all around during the reign of King David (2 Samuel 7:1). However, even when their wandering was done and their warfare was finished, they would never leave worship behind.

So too for us, the trumpets that we now hear summoning us to spiritual warfare and spiritual worship are not the only trumpets there will be. One day the final trumpet will sound, announcing the definitive arrival of God's presence on earth (1 Corinthians 15:52). This time it will not be in the form of a fiery pillar or as a baby at Bethlehem, but in the triumphant return of Jesus Christ to establish the new heavens and the new earth. The final trumpet will sound, and the dead in Christ will rise, and those believers who are still alive will be caught up into his presence (1 Thessalonians 4:16, 17). Then our wandering and our warfare will finally be over, replaced forever by worship. But for all those who do not belong to Christ, that day of God's presence will be a day of great fear and anguish. They will hear the dreaded words, "Depart from me, you cursed" and will be sent out of the presence of God into the blackest darkness forever (Matthew 25:41).

Now is the time to bow the knee to Jesus. Now is the time to hear and heed the trumpet call to worship him joyfully, trusting in his righteousness and rejoicing in his grace. Now is the time to celebrate his mercy, that he would choose a foul sinner like me and call me to serve him and fellowship with him forever. Now is the time to delight in the words of forgiveness and acceptance: "There is no condemnation; you have peace with God through Jesus Christ!" Now is the time to revel in his presence with us, and to recommit ourselves to full obedience to his leading and direction. Don't wait until you hear the final trumpet: the trumpet sounds for you today to summon you to enter into his presence and bow down.

14

A Good Beginning

NUMBERS 10:11-36

IN LIFE WE CAN LEARN MANY EXTREMELY VALUABLE LESSONS from the successes and failures of others. Over the course of my wandering years I have been part of many churches around the world. Each of them had its own distinctive strengths and weaknesses, and I would say that I have learned something from each church. The most valuable lessons, however, came from the churches at the extremes of the spectrum of health: I have learned most from the churches that were the healthiest and from those that were the most dysfunctional, while I learned rather less from the churches in between. In the healthy churches, I observed the shape of the faithful and skilled practice of ministry, while from those at the other end I discovered the painful consequences that ensue when ministry is not done well. Both lessons have been immensely useful to me in my own ministry!

First Impressions

In this passage in Numbers 10 we receive our first impression of Israel on the march, and what we see is entirely positive. They began the journey so well. In fact, if they had continued in the same way that they started out, they would have been in the Promised Land within a few short weeks. First impressions can be deceptive, though. As we will see, things began to unravel in short order as the journey continued. Nonetheless, it is important to notice the fact that Israel began well. This shows that the problems that subsequently developed were not due to ignorance on Israel's part or a lack of clarity on the Lord's part. God was faithful to do what he had promised, and the Israelites knew exactly what they ought to do. The problems that would soon emerge were thus entirely their own fault.

As we follow the wanderings of the Israelites over the next few chapters, we will encounter both positive and negative lessons. We will see their faithfulness and their unfaithfulness, and the consequences that flow from both attitudes. The first lessons we will see, though—the ones we will look at in this chapter—are the ones that result from the good beginning that they made. These lessons provide a positive paradigm for us to follow in our own wilderness journeys.

A Life of God-Centered Pilgrimage

The first point to observe is that at the outset Israel understood that the wilderness life is to be a life of God-centered pilgrimage. It is camping out, not coming home. This is perhaps an obvious point, but we should never overlook the obvious in the Bible. The Israelites were on the march from Mount Sinai to the Promised Land. The Lord had brought them out of Egypt, but they had not yet received their inheritance in the place that God had promised to give them (v. 29). In the meantime they were not to settle down while they were in the wilderness, nor were they to expect to enjoy all the comforts of home there: they were simply camping.

Now, I have to confess that I am personally not much of a camper. My idea of enjoying the great outdoors is throwing open the window of my comfortable hotel room and taking in the stunning view and fresh country air. I find it difficult to understand why anyone would voluntarily give up a comfortable bed, properly cooked food, and easy access to drinking water. The whole idea is rather a mystery to me—unless, of course, you are going somewhere special and this painful inconvenience is the only possible way to get there.

So too the Christian life is rather a mystery to many people. Why would anyone endure the things that many Christians voluntarily endure? Some go on missions trips, paying good money to work hard for the sake of others in a hot and humid climate instead of lazing on the beach with a good novel. Many Christians spend their free time meeting with other believers to discuss the finer points of the Bible and theology instead of watching television or talking about sports. They give generously of their time and money to support the work of their church instead of using it to create a more comfortable lifestyle for themselves. In some countries Christians even endure time in prison and lay down their lives for the sake of the name of Jesus. Why would anyone do these things? Isn't that a waste of your life? The whole idea is rather a mystery—unless, of course, we are going somewhere special and this is the only possible way to get there. We need constantly to remember that the Christian life is a journey, a pilgrimage, which necessarily involves discomfort and suffering. It is a journey whose sacrifices only make sense in the light of the outcome.

On that journey the people were arranged around the symbol of God's presence, the tabernacle of the testimony (v. 11). The tabernacle was the tent of their heavenly King, the Lord, a King who was not merely present with his people when they camped but also while they were on the march. Whether in camp or on the march, the tabernacle and its holy objects remained at the center of the community, carried by the Levites between the tribal groupings (vv. 17, 21). Calling it "the tabernacle of the testimony" reminded Israel that inside the tent were the most sacred objects from Israel's sojourn at Mount Sinai, the two tablets of stone containing the Ten Commandments, the official treaty documents that ratified the covenant between God and his people. It drew their attention to the promises that they had made to God at Mount Sinai, as well as those that the Lord had made to them.

Nor were the people simply gathered around the tabernacle in an unruly mass. On the contrary, they were arrayed exactly as God had instructed them back in Numbers 2. The arrangement by which the Israelites camped was the same arrangement by which they marched, according to the Lord's commandment. At the beginning of the journey no one among the Israelites said, "Why do you have to spend so much effort in telling us exactly where we should stand? Let's just love the Lord and march however we like." They understood that there is no conflict between love and careful obedience. If they loved the Lord, they would be eager to do exactly what he had said. Nor is this perspective simply an Old Testament view of what God expects from his people. Jesus himself said, "If you love me, you will keep my commandments" (John 14:15). Obedience in the Christian life is never an option for the exceptionally spiritual: it has always been a mark of the believer's true love for the Lord. At this initial stage of the journey, this attitude also marked out the Israelites.

A Life of Constant Warfare

Second, the Israelites also understood that wilderness life is a life of constant warfare that can only be won in God's strength. This is evident even in the ordering of the march: the Israelites were arranged by military divisions under their various tribal standards, as if marching out to war (vv. 12-28). Leading them from the front on the initial three-day leg of the journey was the ark of the covenant, which represented not only God's throne but his chariot as well (v. 33). God was going to be their advance guard in the forthcoming conflict.

As a reminder of the true nature of their wilderness life, every time they broke camp, Moses would say, "Arise, O LORD, and let your enemies be scattered, and let those who hate you flee before you" (v. 35). "Arise" here isn't just a request to God to get up and get going, as you or I might shout,

"Rise and shine" to our children in the morning. The Jewish commentator Baruch Levine translates it, "Attack, O Lord!" It is a word that is sometimes used in military contexts as a summons to begin the assault (see Judges 5:12).[1] Moses is thus invoking the Lord's warrior presence with them in the conflict with their enemies.

The same theme reemerges in the words that Moses would say whenever the ark came to rest because the cloud had stopped moving: "Return, O LORD, to the ten thousand thousands of Israel" (10:36). The New Jewish Publication Society translation renders the Hebrew more literally, "Return, O Lord, you who are Israel's myriads of thousands."[2] When it came to fighting, the Lord himself was the countless thousands of Israel, the decisive contributor to their victories. As long as the Lord was fighting for them, Israel's victory was assured, no matter how heavily outnumbered the Israelites were by the opposition.

This is a truth to which many of God's people have testified. In the nineteenth century, the pioneer missionary Mary Slessor went undaunted through the dangers of the African jungle to bring the gospel to unreached tribes in the Calabar area of Nigeria. Many of those to whom she went had had little or no contact with white people. Some were cannibals, while on other occasions she physically stood between two warring tribes to keep them apart. When asked how a single woman, once described as "wee and thin and not very strong," could go where she went, she simply replied, "God and one are always a majority."[3] It doesn't matter who is against you if God is on your side—or, more precisely, if you are on his side.

The same principle also operates in the opposite direction, however. If God is not with you, then it doesn't matter how many people you have fighting for you, defeat is inevitable. The psalmist stated this clearly: "Unless the LORD builds the house, those who build it labor in vain. Unless the LORD watches over the city, the watchman stays awake in vain" (Psalm 127:1).

A Truth to Be Repeated

This truth is not exactly a profound and obscure Biblical insight that can only be discerned after years of intricate research in the original languages. It is a central Biblical teaching. So why did Moses feel the need to repeat the formula in the people's hearing so often? It is certainly not because otherwise God might forget to go with them on their journey! Rather, Moses asked God to go and fight for the Israelites every time they set out as a reminder to himself and to his people. He knew that God's people constantly need to be reminded of this reality. Is the same not true of us as well? I know that it often is for me. I constantly forget that my pilgrimage is a fight in which, unless the Lord wins the victory for me, all of my best efforts are in vain. How many things in my life would be different if I remembered that truth!

If I remembered this reality, I would pray more and be more constant in invoking God's aid in my struggles. I would awaken every morning crying out, "Rise up, O Lord! Protect me against my enemies and against temptation. Walk with me throughout this day!" I would go to sleep at night asking the Lord to remain with me, thanking him for his sustaining presence and power throughout that day. Moment by moment, in between rising and resting, my thoughts would return repeatedly to the Lord to invoke his presence and his power with me.

If I remembered this reality, I would be less puffed up with pride when life goes well. On the Sundays when my ministry is a blessing to people, I would recall that it is the work of the Lord's Spirit that changes hearts and lives, not my carefully crafted words. When my life is relatively free from dramatic sin, I would be aware that this faithfulness is not the product of my matchless devotion to the Lord but his gracious preservation of my wandering soul.

If I remembered this reality, I would panic less when the struggles of life become intense and I feel myself to be utterly out of my depth. The truth is that I am constantly out of my depth in life and ministry, even when it comes to the tasks that are most familiar. I can easily put together a series of words that will fill up half an hour on Sunday morning, but in my own strength I am unable to write a sermon that will break the stony hearts of unbelievers and touch afresh the lives of the saints. Only God can do that. The same is true of my parenting. I can discipline my children and assure a certain level of outward conformity to polite moral codes, but in my own strength I can never show them the depth and gravity of their sinfulness and their desperate need of Christ. Only God can do that. Whenever I feel competent to cope on my own in this life, it is a delusion. Indeed, God in his mercy often chooses to take us through those deep waters where our lack of capability becomes most evident to our naturally blind eyes, in order that we may recognize what is always true: unless the Lord goes ahead of us and fights for us, we are utterly defeated. Like the Israelites, I need to be reminded constantly that this wilderness life is a conflict that only God can win.

Divine Sovereignty and Human Responsibility

At the same time, this truth does not mean that we simply sit back and wait for God to do everything. Sometimes people fear that a focus on the need for God's work in our lives will lead to passivity on our part. If we believe in the sovereignty of God in all things, won't that lead us to neglect outreach to unbelievers and the pursuit of holiness in our own lives? Nothing could be farther from a Biblical position. There is no conflict between absolute trust in God's work and responsible human activity on our part, a theme that finds expression in this passage in the invitation to Hobab to accompany the Israelites (vv. 29-32). Commentators are divided over this little incident. Some see it as evidence of a lack of faith on Moses' part. Why should he invite Hobab to be the eyes of the community, finding good camping spots for them in the wilderness, if the Lord had promised to do that for them?[4] Isn't that a sign of unbelief?

The text itself, however, doesn't seem to place a negative light on the request of Moses. Rather, I think the commentators' problems flow from the fact that they are placing a false dichotomy between divine guidance and human responsibility.[5] Biblically, these things belong together. Trust in the Lord as divine builder and guard does not exempt the laborer from building or the watchman from keeping his eyes open (Psalm 127:1). In the same way, the request for Hobab's assistance is not a mark of a lack of faith in God's guidance on the part of Moses but simply the wise use of the gifts and abilities of another in service of the Lord's people. Moses recognized that Hobab might be the means by which God's provision for their needs would come to expression. In this life of warfare, even though victory can only be won in the Lord's strength, sometimes his strength is ministered to us through the very ordinary means of the people he has placed around us with exactly the combination of gifts and abilities that we need.

Finding Rest

The third truth that Israel needed to remember on their march is that even though the wilderness life is a pilgrimage and a war, the goal of the pilgrimage is neither constant traveling nor constant conflict, but rest in the land God had promised. The reason the ark went ahead of them on their travels was not simply to protect Israel from dangers and enemies but to find for them "a resting place" (v. 33). This was the goal of the whole pilgrimage, to find a place of rest in the land that God had promised to give them.

This loss of perspective is what so often discourages us in life, isn't it? We forget that we are only camping here, only passing through on our way to eternal glory. We start to believe that this world really is all there is, and so we grumble about our accommodations and our food here. The conversation between Moses and Hobab shows us what it means to keep our eyes fixed on the goal. Moses didn't invite Hobab to join him on a miserable trek through the apparently endless wasteland that stretched out before them. No, he invited Hobab to look beyond the wilderness and join Israel in coming to the land where the Lord had promised good things for his people. What is more, when Hobab initially declined, saying that he would rather return home to his own land and his own people, Moses continued to press him, affirming that Israel would share with him whatever good things the Lord gave them (v. 32). In effect, he invited Hobab to join the spiritual descendants of Abraham, who left his home and his people by faith, seeking a city with foundations that God had promised him.

Is that where our eyes are fixed? When someone asks us why we are followers of Jesus, what is our response? The answer is certainly not because since the time we became Christians our lives have begun to work out more successfully. I cannot say that God always gives me everything I want or think that I need, nor does he always make my life run smoothly and easily. What I can say, though, is this: God has promised me eternal life in his presence, a place where I shall stand before him forever and do what I was created to do, which is to worship him. God has promised us that in view of the glory set before us, this is the very best life we can experience in this world. Eternal life will make worthwhile whatever losses we have to suffer in the present. What is more, the Lord has promised his presence with us in the midst of all of the present difficulties of life. Eternal life in Christ has already begun, but only in part. Even for the most fortunate, rest is only partially tasted in this world: the best is always yet to come.

Inviting Others to Share God's Rest

This should not only be where our eyes are presently fixed but also where we endeavor to get others to fix their gaze. Moses really cared about what was best for Hobab, and so he boldly invited Hobab to join the covenant community on their journey. Hobab was not an Israelite. Moses could simply have said, "You go your way, and I'll go mine," especially when Hobab initially declined his invitation. Hobab did not respond to Moses' words by immediately pleading for the opportunity to come along with Israel. He was certainly no Ruth, crying out, "Where you go I will go. . . . Your people shall be my people and your God my God" (Ruth 1:16). In fact, we never do find out for certain whether Hobab came along with the Israelites or not.[6] What we do see, though, is Moses' passionate desire that the Gentile next door should be included in the family of faith.

We need to have the same passion for our "outsider" neighbors. Moses knew that to be in the wilderness with God's people was better than enjoying the comforts of home and family because of the rest that God had promised to his people. We should be able to say the same to our family and friends. We must have a passionate desire for them to come to know God and walk with his people, a desire that keeps on inviting them to become part of God's people. We should long for them too to join us on our pilgrimage. If we do not, it is most likely because we have lost the conviction that God's rest is the only true good in this world. If God's rest is indeed the best this life has to offer, then even though it may be costly for someone to acquire it, it is worth the price. That is the point of Jesus' parable in which he compares the kingdom of heaven to a pearl of great price. Whatever it costs, the pearl is worth the price (Matthew 13:45, 46). So too, if you and I believe passionately with all of our hearts that God is the only good in this world, and if to be in his presence for all eternity is our supreme desire, then that belief will spill out of us into all of our conversations and our relationships. Friends, neighbors, family—yes, even our in-laws—all will know what is most important to us, and by the grace of God some may be added to the pilgrim people of God.

The Trailblazer

Yet there is a problem with this picture, isn't there? The people of Israel began well, but they couldn't keep it up. Moses himself began well, but even he did not make it all the way to the Promised Land. So what good is holding up the ideal beginning of the Israelites and saying, "Be like this" if even they couldn't carry it off? If they sinned and grumbled, led as they were by the ark of the covenant and the fiery cloud of God's presence, what hope is there for us? If the lesson of this chapter is, "Be like the Israelites," that simply leaves us depressed and condemned by our own inability to do what we ought. A perfect model is of no use to radically imperfect people like you and me.

What we need is someone to journey through the wilderness on our behalf and to be faithful throughout the journey. That, according to the book of Hebrews, is exactly what we have in Jesus. He is "the trailblazer[7] and perfecter" of our faith (12:2). As God, we could truly say that it was Jesus who led Israel on their journey through the wilderness.[8] However, it is in becoming man that Jesus has most profoundly traveled the road through the wilderness before us as the ultimate pilgrim and warrior. After his baptism, Jesus went out into the wilderness, where he bore all of Satan's temptations in full force—a force we have never known because we always give in long before the real test comes (Matthew 4). In his humanity, Jesus faced the wilderness test and passed it by faith. He confessed his dependence upon his heavenly Father moment by moment, even though he was himself God in human flesh. He kept his eyes fixed on the rest that was set before him, the joy that would arrive through bearing the cross. Jesus sought constantly to bring others too into this rest, crying out, "Come to me, all who labor and are heavy laden, and I will give you rest" (Matthew 11:28). He has demonstrated and accomplished the life of faith in this fallen world, all the way to an obedient death on the cross. He didn't just begin well; he ended well, seated in triumphant victory at the Father's right hand.

The result of his obedience is that now my rest is won. He blazed the trail and lived the perfect life of faith in my place. Now when God looks at me, he sees the perfect obedience of Jesus, not my flawed efforts. If my salvation depended on my own best obedience, then I would be utterly lost.

I might start well, but I would never carry it through. It wasn't enough for God to bring Israel out of Egypt, give them his Law, point them in the right direction, and say, "Now go, capture the Promised Land." They might begin well, but they would never carry it through. A trailblazer alone would not be enough. More still is necessary: God needed to do everything required for my salvation, and that is exactly what he has done in Jesus.

What is more, Jesus took on the wilderness "for the joy that was set before him," the writer to the Hebrews tells us (12:2). Think about what love that demonstrates! What was "the joy that was set before him"? It was the prospect of our salvation! It was the glory that would redound to God himself—Father, Son and Holy Spirit—through redeeming lost humanity. God loved you enough that he sent his Son into this wilderness world, into the realm of temptation and sin, into the arena of sickness and death. That thought was what sustained Jesus through his darkest hours of suffering—the knowledge that his suffering would mean your salvation. How awesome is God's grace!

Fixing our eyes on the rest that God has promised thus means nothing more and nothing less than fixing our eyes on Jesus. He is the beginning of our faith and its end. He is the one who has accomplished our salvation and the one who now applies it to us by his Spirit. He is the one who promises to go with us on our journey and the one who has already gone ahead of us, scouting out the next steps in our lives. He is the one who fights our battles for us and assures the victory of all those who are in him. He is the one to whom we are to point our neighbors and our friends and say, "Here is rest for your soul. Come with me and meet this glorious Savior. Come and share the good things he has promised to all those who belong to him." He himself is the joy that is set before us, the joy into which we will finally enter in fullness and completeness when our wandering days are done.

15

Surprised by Grumbling

NUMBERS 11

GRUMBLING NEVER GETS MUCH ATTENTION AS A PROBLEM. Grumbling is not one of the traditional seven deadly sins. In fact, it probably wouldn't make it onto the list even if the list were expanded to include the fifty deadly sins. Nobody ever goes to see a counselor and says, "Help me! I'm addicted to grumbling." There are no meetings of Grumblers Anonymous or twelve-step programs designed to cure the condition. This is certainly not because of a lack of people who suffer from the problem. Which of us has never grumbled about something in this life? We grumble about our politicians and car mechanics, our jobs and our homes, our spouses and children.

Perhaps we assume that since we all do it so often, grumbling can't really be so bad. It is virtually our national pastime, so engrained that it has even been described as a "God-given right."[1] Only rarely is grumbling recognized in its true seriousness. In this study we will see the power of grumbling, the deadly consequences of grumbling, and God's true remedy for grumbling. Grumbling is here exposed in all of its destructiveness; yet the good news of the Bible is that grumbling's complaint will not be the last word.

Scene One: A Cameo Picture

The story unfolds in Numbers 11 in two related incidents. There is a brief cameo scene in verses 1-3, recounting the events that took place at Taberah ("burning"), followed by a much longer and more complex scene in verses 4-35, recounting what transpired at nearby Kibroth-Hattaavah[2] ("graves of craving"). These two scenes work in tandem, with the second scene providing a contrast to the paradigm laid out in the first.[3] As a paradigm, the first scene is stripped down to its most basic elements. First, the people grumbled against the Lord (v. 1), and he responded with anger and fiery judgment. There we see grumbling and its deadly consequences. Yet when the people cried out to Moses, he interceded with the Lord on their behalf and the judgment ceased (v. 2). Only the outskirts of the camp were consumed. There we see the remedy for grumbling: the effective intercession of the mediator God has appointed. In other words, the first scene shows us that grumbling is a sin that has potentially serious consequences, but those consequences could be averted by the intercession of Moses.

This cameo scene shows us that what is at stake in this chapter is not just the sin of grumbling. It is also the role of Moses as a prophet. An important part of the work of a prophet in Old Testament times was to intercede for the people. On the day when the Lord's judgment was about to be poured out on his people, it was the prophet's calling to stand between the people and their God, averting God's wrath by intercessory prayer. This was hard and dangerous work, a task compared to standing in the breached wall of a besieged city, the most dangerous position in an assault (see Ezekiel 13:5; 22:30). Yet without faithful prophets, the people's future would be bleak indeed. As the archetypal prophet, the pattern after whom all other prophets were framed (see Deuteronomy 18:15), Moses had both the ability and obligation to approach God and intercede for the people. This is exactly what he did at Taberah.

Scene Two: Grumbling in Full Flower

With that information as background, we are now ready to look at the second and much more complicated scene in the latter half of Numbers 11. Once again the story begins with grumbling. In this second scene, the power of grumbling becomes much clearer. The grumbling started with "the rabble," the riff-raff (*hāsapsup*),[4] who lived on the fringe of the camp (v. 4). This is the mixed multitude of all nationalities who came out of Egypt with God's people but had never fully assimilated and taken on Israel's values and standards. The grumbling then spread from the riff-raff to infect the rest of the Israelites (v. 4). Soon everyone joined in. The content of the grumbling also becomes clear in this episode: it is no longer simply the difficulty or "misfortunes" (literally, "evil," *rā*) of the wilderness (v. 1), but rather the recollection of the supposed goodness of Egypt. In the imagination of the people, Egypt was now transformed into the land flowing with milk and honey—or at least the land of free fish and varied vegetables—cucumbers, melons, leeks, onions, and garlic (v. 5). Meanwhile, the people complained that in the wilderness all they had to taste and look at was boring old manna (v. 6).

The Contagious Nature of Grumbling

Their complaint exposes a pair of important lessons about the sin of grumbling. In the first place, grumbling is extremely contagious. It is an infectious disease that is easily passed from one person to the next. It typically originates among those with little or no spiritual insight, but it can easily be passed on from them to the whole community and draw in those who ought to know better. This is true in our setting just as much as it was for them. Grumbling is a sin you can catch from others, which means that you need to be careful who you spend your time with and how you spend your time with them. I'm certainly not suggesting that you should cut yourself off from everyone who lacks spiritual maturity, but in such relationships you should certainly be aware of who is influencing whom.

The contagious power of sin means that ministry is always a messy business. One of the challenges that Israel faced constantly was balancing on the one hand their calling to incorporate Gentiles into the community of faith (as with Hobab in Numbers 10:29-32) with the danger on the other hand that such people would bring into the community their flawed worldviews and perspectives and end up leading Israel astray. That remains a challenge for the church, doesn't it? We are certainly not free to cut ourselves off from those who most need the gospel—after all, Jesus came to call the sick, not the healthy (Matthew 9:12). Our calling as the church is to be a spiritual emergency room, not a spiritual health spa. Yet at the same time we need to recognize the dangers that come with our calling and be on our guard against the spiritual diseases that can so easily infiltrate and infect our community. In particular, we need to watch out for the communicable disease of grumbling.

Grumbling and Unbelief

The reason why grumbling typically starts with those who have little or no spiritual insight, those on the edge of the community, is because the root of grumbling is unbelief. The vision of the grumblers was fatally flawed. Their perspective on both the past and the present was distorted. The past suddenly became a golden age in which everything had been wonderful: "Egypt! The old country! That glorious place of fish suppers and great salads! How green was the grass in the Nile valley!" Now one might well ask, "If it was really such a wonderful place, why were they so eager to leave it? What about the harsh taskmasters of Egypt, the endless making of bricks without straw?" (Exodus 5:6-21). Their memory of the past had become strangely forgetful, developing strategic holes.

Not only was their memory of the past selective and flawed, so was their perspective on the present. We might paraphrase their grumbling like this: "If I see one more piece of manna, I think I'm going to be sick. Manna, manna, manna—that's all we ever eat anymore. Manna is boring, unattractive, and tasteless. We want some other kind of food." That was their skewed perspective on God's provision, and lest we be deceived into having some sympathy for them, the narrator takes the time to challenge each of their assertions in turn.

First, he points out the fact that the manna was not unattractive; on the contrary, it looked like bdellium (v. 7), a prized substance that was one of the products of the area immediately surrounding the Garden of Eden (Genesis 2:12). The Israelites didn't have to pay for the manna either: it came down free every night, along with the dew (v. 9). Nor was it boring: it could be prepared in a variety of tasty ways—ground or boiled or baked (v. 8). Given the opportunity, an ancient cooking magazine could surely have produced an issue entitled "365 Ways to Cook Manna!" Finally, far from being tasteless, it was extremely appetizing (v. 8). The NIV's description, "like something made with olive oil," or even that in the ESV, "the taste of cakes baked with oil," doesn't sound nearly as mouth-watering as it should. Much better is the translation, "it tasted like a pastry cooked with the finest oil" (HCSB). It may have looked somewhat like porridge, but it actually tasted more like the most delicious donuts. It was indeed "the bread of heaven," as Psalm 78:24 (NKJV) calls it, the original angel food cake! This is the food that was not good enough for them!

Isn't this what grumbling always does? Grumbling distorts your vision. It reimagines the past as a golden land, it despises the good gifts that God has surrounded you with in the present, and it completely ignores God's promises for the future. That's why I say that the root of grumbling is unbelief. Grumbling is an unbelief that robs you of your joy. It is the exact opposite of faith, which sees the past and present with clear eyes but has its gaze joyfully fixed on God's promises for the future. Faith believes God's promises to be certain, no matter what difficulties the present may hold.

This also explains why grumbling is so contagious: when we talk to people of faith, we find that strengthens our faith, for we begin to see the world through their eyes. However, when we sit with people caught in unbelief, it is very easy to have our own perspective skewed. We too can start to think more highly than we should of the past and more critically than is accurate of the present. We too can start to say, "Before I became a Christian, how easy my life was. I didn't have to get up on Sunday mornings or give my money to the church or get along with all these people. But now—oh, how awful it is! My life is more than anyone should have to bear." Or we may say, "Before I got married or had children or moved to my present town, my situation was so much easier and better than it is now. How miserable my life has become!" Or perhaps, "When I was in such and such a church, what a wonderful place it was. We had none of the problems there that we see with this church." In reality, though, your past was almost certainly not as rosy as you remember it, nor is your present quite as bleak as you may think it to be.

Grumbling and Faith

But what if it we are in dire difficulties right now? Let us suppose, just for a moment, that the past really was better than life is now and that our present is truly miserable in comparison. What then? The eye of faith is fixed not in the past, nor in the present, but in the future, on the glorious things that God has promised his people. That is where solid and lasting joy comes from, unaffected by the circumstances in which we find ourselves. Imagine that Egypt was indeed a fine place to live and that the manna in the wilderness was truly miserable fare. So what? The Israelites needed to remember that they were only camping out there on the way to the land God had promised to give them. The wilderness was not their home.

This is how faith conquers the temptation to grumble. Faith laughs over short rations and hardships because it remembers that the present is not all there is. These present difficulties will only make the final rest all the sweeter. The tougher the climb, the sweeter is the rest at the top of the mountain. The more limited the food at the campsite, the better the steak tastes when we finally return to civilization. When we flew home after two years in Liberia, we stopped overnight in Amsterdam. What I remember vividly is the breakfast buffet the next morning, stuffed with all kinds of food that we hadn't tasted for two years. Even ordinary things like fresh milk tasted so sweet because it had been so long since we had enjoyed them. Faith remembers how to look forward to the buffet! When your eyes are fixed on future glories, present trials become not only bearable but ultimately inconsequential. Faith is what conquers grumbling and leads to a life of joy.

The Grumbling of Moses

Yet grumbling is such a powerfully contagious sin that in the wilderness it even infected Moses. Faced with a weeping people, Moses himself was caught up in the spirit of grumbling. He didn't grumble about the food but about the people: they were an evil[5] and a burden to him (v. 11). He said to God in essence, "What did I do to deserve this? Why should I be weighed down with them? Am I their mother or their nurse? Where can I get meat for them all? I cannot carry such a burden, so you might as well put me to death right now" (vv. 11-15).

In the Hebrew original, in these five verses of complaint Moses refers to himself no fewer than twenty times. This is not coincidental. Whereas faith looks to God, unbelief turns in on ourselves and our inability. Moses' thinking had become just as skewed as that of the riff-raff, completely focused on his present pain and oblivious to the Lord's promise of protection and provision. Instead of taking his burden to God and asking for strength, he grumbled about it. Instead of trusting God to do the good things for his people he had so confidently asserted in the previous chapter (10:29-32), Moses questioned God's ability to do what he had promised and to provide the meat that the people craved (11:21, 22). How could even God provide meat for such a vast army? Moses was caught up in unbelief.

The result of Moses' unbelief was that instead of interceding for his lost and straying people, he joined them in their sin of grumbling. This is a common temptation for all those in leadership over God's flock. When the sheep are unwilling to be led in the way they should go, it is easy for us to become frustrated with them and grumble about them. However, when we grumble about our flock, we are merely revealing the unbelief in our own hearts. We have failed to believe that God will sanctify our sheep in his time. Often it is our pride that has been challenged, for we are used to taking the credit for whatever progress our flock is making. If we have faith in the efficacy of God's sanctification program, however, and remember that it is his work through and through, we will intercede for our errant sheep instead of grumbling about them. Instead of fuming over our assignment, we will pray for our people patiently, confident that God will work in their hearts in due time to accomplish all of his purposes for them and for us.

Moses' failure to intercede for his people posed a serious problem for Israel. In the paradigm scene, the Lord became angry and judged the people, but Moses interceded on their behalf. This time, though, there was no intercession, no one to turn away the Lord's anger. What would happen to the grumblers if there was no one to intercede for them? Would Moses and the people all have to die for their sin?

Judgment and Grace

What happened was a unique combination of judgment and grace, both for Moses and for the people. On the one hand, God gave the grumblers exactly what they wanted. Moses got the help he asked for, and the people got their meat. Yet the apparent similarity highlights the ultimate difference. Moses got what he sought in a way that combined judgment and blessing, while the people's answer was entirely judgment.

Let's look first at the way God dealt with the grumbling Israelites. They wanted meat? God gave them meat, more than they could ever have believed possible. Moses might not have been able to imagine where enough meat could be found to feed such a multitude, but God's power was not limited by Moses' lack of faith. The Lord simply sent a powerful wind that drove in vast flocks of quail that rained down all around the people (v. 31).[6] Even those who gathered least collected ten homers (roughly sixty bushels, or more than enough to fill a pair of fifty-five-gallon drums). God never does things by half measures. The people got exactly what they asked for. Yet at the same time this demonstration of God's power was a curse, not a blessing. Even while they were taking the first bites of their longed-for meat, the Lord's anger burned against his people and struck down those who had had the craving for meat. They saw the demonstration of God's power but did not live to enjoy it.

Is it too strong to say that God deals with some people in the same way today? He apparently gives to some people everything they ask of him: fame, wealth, health, and a life of ease. The psalmist saw wicked people in his day who were prospering and thriving, and it almost caused his faith to stumble (Psalm 73:2-14). But then he came to understand that though the present might seem to hold everything these people wanted, God had placed them in a slippery location, and their final destiny was death (vv. 18, 19). One of God's most profound judgments on lost sinners is to give them everything they ask for. They are on a smooth road to destruction, with nothing to turn them around.

Yet God didn't deal with Moses in that way. Even though Moses sinned by grumbling and though his sin would have ongoing repercussions, God dealt with him graciously. He was not struck down for his sin. Why did God deal with Moses differently from the riff-raff? They all grumbled, and they all doubted God's Word and his goodness; yet God's answer to the request of Moses was ultimately a blessing both to him and to the people, whereas in the case of the others the answer to their request led simply to death. The answer is that God's grace was shown to the one he had chosen. It is not that Moses was better than the others, but rather that God's purposes were better for him. God had chosen Moses and was gracious and merciful to him, but he showed no mercy to the others, to the outsiders. That is God's prerogative. *None* of them deserved God's mercy. Yet God is sovereign: he has mercy on whom he will have mercy and hardens those whom he will harden.

What that means is that you and I, as believers, do not have to fear that if we sinfully grumble and demand the wrong thing from God, it will lead to our destruction. If we have trusted in Christ, then we have been chosen by God for good purposes—for blessing, not curse. God is at work in us to make us holy and to present us before him blameless; having begun that good work, he will not abandon it, even though we sin (Philippians 1:6).

The Sharing of Leadership

Yet we still cannot take the sin of grumbling lightly. Both judgment and blessing are evident in the way that God dealt with Moses. Moses wanted someone with whom to share the burden of leading the people. God gave him what he requested in greater abundance than he could have imagined. God took from the Spirit he had placed on Moses and transferred part of it to the seventy elders (vv. 17, 24, 25). When they received the Spirit, they prophesied briefly, demonstrating that they had been empowered for leadership alongside Moses.[7] Nor was the Spirit shared merely with those who were present with Moses at the time. It also fell on two other elders, Eldad and Medad, who were nowhere near Moses but were in the camp (v. 26). They too prophesied, showing that the work of the Spirit could bypass Moses altogether. God could pour out his Spirit on anyone, whenever and wherever he chose.

No wonder Joshua was concerned by this turn of events. He understood clearly the implications of this: if the Spirit could descend on anyone anywhere, then Moses' unique role as prophetic mediator in the community might be compromised. Such a sharing of the Spirit that was in Moses necessarily diminished Moses. It is no coincidence that from this moment forward in the book of Numbers, the question of Moses' leadership of the people became an issue. Recognizing what was at stake, Joshua urged Moses to take action immediately to stop this turn of events (v. 28). Moses, however, responded to God's dealings with him with greater spiritual maturity than Joshua. He was not concerned about his own status, and instead of worrying about the judgment aspect he focused rather on the blessing that God was bringing. He said in essence, "Joshua, don't worry about my reputation. Even if God bypasses my leadership altogether and gives all of God's people gifts of leadership, that would be a wonderful thing" (v. 29). Moses had started thinking like a believer again: instead of grumbling, he was content to believe that God would work all of this together for his good.

Needed: A Better Prophet

If even a godly leader like Moses gets angry and upset with God and grumbles, requiring God's mercy and grace, then we need someone better than Moses to intercede for us. We need a better prophet—someone who will not only intercede for us consistently when we sin but who himself will take the wrath of God in our place. We need someone who can bear the burden of the leadership of his people on his own without growing weary and frustrated. We need someone who can stand in the gap and take the punishment we deserve. We need Jesus.

Jesus is indeed a better mediator than Moses. He does not give up on us after the first incidence of grumbling. He does not need seventy helpers to share in the ministry of intercession, for he possesses the Spirit in full measure. He is never too tired or cranky to intercede for us but, on the contrary, always intercedes on our behalf (Hebrews 7:25). This is illustrated by the events of his final night on earth. As he looked around the table at the last supper, he was surrounded by men who would either betray him or abandon him in the hours ahead. Instead of supporting him in prayer, they would fall asleep in the Garden of Gethsemane. Had I been in his position, I would surely have grumbled about the disciples I had chosen. Yet even when Peter cockily asserted that he would never deny Jesus, Jesus did not grumble. Instead he simply said to Peter, "I have interceded for you." His High-Priestly prayer of John 17 is an extended intercession for these soon-to-be-unfaithful followers—and for us as well, who are no more reliable than they. Where Moses grumbled, Jesus interceded: he is indeed a better mediator than Moses.

What is more, Jesus himself bore the judgment curse that we deserved because of our grumbling and unbelief, and in exchange he gave us the blessing that was his by rights. Are you a grumbling unbeliever? I know that I often am. Because of my grumbling unbelief, Jesus went to the cross where he experienced the full weight of the Father's wrath against sin. Through his uncomplaining and faithful obedience in draining the cup of undeserved suffering, Jesus earned the Father's favor on my behalf. It is his sacrifice that enables a just and holy God to show me undeserved mercy and grace instead of the eternal death that I deserve by nature. Jesus earned that grace on my behalf, and in him I receive it free of charge.

If that is so, how can I grumble any longer? If my God has loved me that much and has paid that price to redeem me from my lostness, how can I complain about the rations he has provided along the way? How can I moan about the company and the conditions of service when Jesus has gone through the valley of death and separation from God on my behalf? God has been so faithful and so good! Keeping your eyes fixed on the cross will surely inoculate you against the temptation to grumble.

The Answer to Moses' Prayer

What is more, in Christ the prayer of Moses has finally been granted. Moses longed to see all of God's people filled with the Spirit, and on the Day of Pentecost that dream came finally true (Acts 2:14-41). Since Christ's ascension into Heaven, the Spirit is shared not only with seventy elders but with all believers, Jews and Gentiles alike, as many as the Lord God calls to himself. That means that if you are a believer today, you have received the gift of the Holy Spirit.

The gift of the Spirit empowers us for witness. When the Holy Spirit came on the elders, they prophesied, bringing God's truth to bear on those around them. For them it was only a partial, temporary experience, a sign to the community of the Lord's presence and work. For us, the Spirit's work is permanent, an ongoing sign of the Lord's presence and activity in our hearts.

The Holy Spirit gives each of us power to witness to him, enabling us to speak to those around us about their need of a Savior and God's provision in Christ. Grumbling and its root, unbelief, are not the only contagious things in Scripture. Faith is also contagious, and we are called to be carriers of faith, passing on the truth to everyone with whom we have contact. Whom do we plan to infect with the gospel this week? Like the common cold, the gospel is not passed on from a distance but through personal contact and close relationships. We must pray and plan, therefore, for opportunities to spread our faith to all those with whom we come into contact.

The gift of the Spirit also means that we have all been empowered to intercede for one another. One of the great works of the Spirit in the New Testament is teaching us how and for what we should pray (Romans 8:26). The Spirit takes our ill-formed requests and makes them presentable before the presence of God himself. Moses couldn't carry the burden of intercession alone. It was too great a task for him. So, too, the work of interceding for one another in prayer is not simply a task for the pastors and elders of the church. It is a work in which we can all join. Young people are not too young to pray for their friends and for others in their church. Some older believers may be physically unable to perform other ministries, but they are never too old to intercede. Why don't you make a list of five people for whom you will commit yourself to pray regularly? If you change the list every month, then every year you will pray for sixty people. Imagine the impact that such prayers will have, both in your church and around the world.

Unbelief works itself out in grumbling, which leads to judgment and death. Faith works itself out in thanksgiving and intercession, which leads to blessing and hope. Praise God for the gift of his Son, whose death frees us from the consequences of our unbelief. Give thanks for the gift of the Spirit, whose ministry enables us to be intercessors. Live with faith in God, looking to his promises, crying out to him on the basis of them, and grumbling will find no soil in which to take root in your heart.

16

Grumbling and Envy

NUMBERS 12

IN THE LAST STUDY we looked at an outbreak of grumbling in the midst of God's people—a sin that we said would never be included as one of the Seven Deadly Sins, but one that nonetheless had deadly consequences. Many of those who grumbled lost their lives as God judged them for their sin and as Moses, who was himself caught up in their sin, failed to intercede for them. You might think that a series of events like that would have such a sobering effect on the community at large that no one would dream of grumbling about anything, at least for a while. Unfortunately, that was not the case. As the philosopher Hegel once astutely observed, "The only thing we learn from history is that we learn nothing from history." He could have been writing the epitaph of Old Testament Israel—and perhaps our epitaph as well. The reality for us is that we too often fail to apply the life lessons with which the Scripture presents us, only recognizing our mistakes after we have made them yet again.

Grumbling Driven by Envy

What more do we need to learn about the sin of grumbling? Here in Numbers 12, though the sin is the same, the dynamics of grumbling are different. The occasion for the grumbling in chapter 11 was the difficulty of life in the desert. When life was hard for Israel, the temptation was to idealize the "good old days" of the past and then to complain about the present. The root of their grumbling at those times was unbelief that doubted the reality of the future promises of God and despised the goodness of the present provision of God. In this case, however, Miriam and Aaron grumbled not because they compared their present to an imagined golden past but because they compared their situation to that of someone else, in this case Moses. The root of their sin was not so much unbelief as it was envy.

Like grumbling, envy is an underrated sin today. Grumbling is perhaps our national pastime, but envy is the motor that drives our economy. Many television commercials work because they stir up envy in our hearts. We are encouraged to envy our neighbors' car, our neighbors' house, even things as trivial as the fluffiness of our neighbors' towels—which is, of course, due to their using the right fabric softener. We are constantly urged to envy anything our neighbor has that we don't. In our culture the commandment is no longer "Thou shalt not covet anything that belongs to thy neighbor" but rather "Thou shalt covet everything thy neighbor has, and thou shalt acquire as much of it as thy credit cards will permit." Envy is no longer viewed as a sin but as a civic virtue.

Miriam and Aaron were sucked into grumbling through the path of envy. They set themselves and their situation side by side with that of Moses and found cause for complaint. Miriam was the chief instigator in this sin. Her name is listed first, and the Hebrew verb used at the beginning of Numbers 12 is feminine. Once again, though, grumbling proved to be contagious. Aaron too was caught up in the sin of grumbling along with his sister.

The Ground of Grumbling #1: Moses' Marriage

The first ground for their grumbling was that Moses had married a non-Israelite, a Cushite (v. 1). Cush in the Old Testament describes two separate locations: Ethiopia and Midian. Therefore, this could potentially be a reference to Zipporah, the Midianite girl whom Moses married before his return to Egypt (Exodus 2:21). However, the fact that the narrator takes the time to confirm the accuracy of their charge that Moses had indeed married a Cushite suggests that Moses had taken another wife more recently, either after the death of Zipporah or in addition to Zipporah.[1] Clearly, though, the issue was the fact that Moses' wife was not an Israelite and that Miriam and Aaron started speaking against Moses because of it.

Notice that Miriam and Aaron didn't talk to Moses about the problem. Nor did they talk to God about the problem. Instead they simply grumbled about it, complaining to anyone who would listen about Moses' unfitness to be the sole leader of the people. In that way they began to feel superior to Moses. This is a classic pattern, for us as much as for them. When there is an issue between us and someone else, it is much easier simply to grumble about the other person instead of going to him or her and seeking to resolve the issue. Biblically, though, the right thing to do when you see your brother or sister caught in a behavior that seems to you to be sinful is to go to him or her and raise it with him or her privately (see Matthew 18:15). Such persons may not know that their behavior is wrong or that you find it offensive.

Much of our grumbling about others would be choked off at the source if we just committed ourselves to solving interpersonal problems in a Biblical manner, going first to the offending party and seeking to resolve the issue with him or her.

When we bring our concerns to another person, though, we need to be aware that sometimes the problem is with our conscience and not with that individual's behavior. In this case there was no dispute as to the facts: Moses had indeed married a Cushite woman. The dispute was whether that was a problem. Miriam and Aaron thought Moses' behavior was wrong, while Moses thought his behavior was appropriate. Which of them was right? In terms of the Law of God, marrying a Cushite was not a sin. At this point in the Bible there was no explicit prohibition in God's Word against marrying outside of Israel. Yet, equally, there were plausible grounds for Miriam and Aaron's concern. Israel had already been warned of the danger of intermarrying with the Canaanites when they came to live in the Promised Land because of the danger of being drawn away from worshiping the true God to follow idols (Exodus 34:14-16; Deuteronomy 7:3, 4). Marriage outside the covenant community was not forbidden (except for marriage to the tribes that occupied the land of Canaan); yet it was potentially risky behavior. There was the inherent danger of marrying someone who might not share your spiritual values. The key point is that it was not forbidden by God per se. Perhaps Miriam and Aaron would have claimed simply to be concerned for Moses' spiritual welfare, but the fact is that they sought to safeguard it in the wrong way, by expanding the scope of the Law beyond what God had decreed.

Danger: Legalism at Work

This kind of legalism continues to be a problem for the church. Out of our zeal to keep and protect God's Law, we can easily surround it with all kinds of human traditions and regulations that may in the end choke out the intent of the Law in the first place. In our zeal to protect ourselves and others against the flood of sex and violence that the entertainment industry churns out, some would impose a complete ban on watching movies and reading novels where the Scripture does not. In an attempt to keep the Sabbath a special day for the Lord, we can surround it with so many restrictions that it becomes a day more reminiscent of the emptiness of Hell than the joys of Heaven.

What is more, we can easily confuse our personal interpretations of God's Law with the Law itself, so that we look down on anyone who seeks to obey God's Law in any way other than the way we deem "correct." If we have the power to do so, we may then bind the consciences of others to do as we say. If we don't have the power to compel others to follow us, we may look down on them as "unspiritual" and may then gossip and grumble to others about these people's "deviant" behavior. In either case we have set ourselves up as masters and judges of others in a realm of which God alone is Lord and Judge.[2] Christian liberty—the freedom to apply God's Law in good conscience, untrammeled by the traditions and teachings of men, however well-intentioned—is an important Biblical principle.

How can you tell if you have fallen into this kind of legalism? The classic fruit of legalism is a judgmental attitude that feels proud of our law-keeping and looks down on others who don't do things in the same way that we do. Miriam and Aaron didn't simply think that marrying a Cushite was unwise—they felt they were better than Moses because they had more "kosher" relationships. If you think more highly of yourself than others because you don't drink or smoke or watch certain forms of entertainment, then you are likely in the grip of this kind of legalism. Ironically, even the law of Christian liberty can become its own legalism, so that some believers look down on those who don't exercise as much freedom as they do!

A true love for God's Law, however, seeks to find the best way to obey God's Word in our own lives and to help others discern for themselves what obedience would look like in their situation. True love for God's Law never leads to pride because the more we understand the searching depths of God's Law and its thoroughgoing claims on our hearts, the more we see the depths of our own sinfulness. And the more we recognize our own sinfulness, the more grateful we are for the good news that the perfect righteousness of Christ has satisfied the claims of God's Law upon us. We stand before God accepted on the basis of his obedience, not our own. So where is there any room for pride?

The Ground of Grumbling #2: Leadership Envy

The second ground for Miriam and Aaron's grumbling exposed the real issue in their hearts, however. The fact that the Cushite marriage was a smoke screen for their real concerns can be seen from the fact that God didn't even address it in his response to them. The primary issue was the question, "Has the LORD indeed spoken only through Moses? Has he not spoken through us also?" (v. 2). Here the note of envy comes out clearly. Moses had a unique place of leadership in God's people (in spite of Miriam's and Aaron's thinking of his marriage as dubious), but they felt they should share that place because they too had received God's revelation.

Perhaps this complaint was triggered by the events in the previous chapter: Moses had grumbled about his unique leadership role, and the Lord had responded by empowering the seventy elders with the gift of the Spirit (11:25). In a sense, then, the Lord had himself demonstrated that Moses was not entirely unique, and therefore Miriam and Aaron felt the time was ripe for a little more recognition for themselves. Perhaps what really chafed was that in response to that issue the Lord had chosen the seventy elders to assist Moses, and not Miriam and Aaron! In any case, the heart of their grumbling was envy: God had dealt with someone else (Moses) in a way that they felt was better than the way he had dealt with them—even though they had not married outsiders, as he had.

Envy is a potent source of grumbling in our lives as well. We too grumble because our lives aren't as good as we imagine someone else's to be. In envy-driven grumbling, the same two steps pertain in our case as in the case of Miriam and Aaron: we first compare ourselves to others and declare ourselves better than them, and then we compare our situation to theirs and complain because our situation is not as attractive as theirs is.

As in the case of unbelief, our perception may be a long way from reality. In the first place, our claim to be better than the other person may be based on false standards, on legalism rather than on a true assessment of God's Law. In addition, though, our assessment that someone else's situation is better than ours may also be flawed. In the last chapter Moses would probably quite happily have given Miriam and Aaron not only a share of his authority but all of it! He might well have said to them, "Take these people, please! Be my guest! You lead them, and I'll go back to taking care of a few sheep. That is a much easier calling." In fact, we might be surprised how often the very people whom we envy would actually envy us as well. That is because envy downplays everything that is positive about our situation and emphasizes the negative, while doing the opposite about the other person's situation. Married people may envy the freedom of single people, while those who are single envy the connectedness of families. Those with important and demanding jobs may envy the lighter load of those with a simpler schedule, while those who feel stuck in a rut may envy the significance of doing a job that really seems to matter. Envy rarely sees things as they really are.

The Cure for Envy-Driven Grumbling

If the cure for grumbling rooted in unbelief is faith, then the antidote for grumbling rooted in envy is contentment. Contentment is not a naive closing of the eyes to the difficulties that face you in your situation. Rather it is a solid assessment of who you are in Jesus Christ and a sure confidence that, no matter how difficult your life may be, it comes to you personally from the hand of your sovereign heavenly Father.

The first step toward contentment is knowing who you are in Jesus Christ. Who are you? You are an unprofitable servant, deserving eternal judgment, saved by God's grace and mercy alone. The great saint John Newton, author of the hymn "Amazing Grace," certainly understood who he was. He had inscribed on his tombstone: "John Newton, Clerk, once an infidel and libertine, a servant of slaves in Africa, was, by the rich mercy of our Lord and Saviour Jesus Christ, preserved, restored, pardoned, and appointed to preach the faith he had long labored to destroy." The knowledge of who he was gave him the humility and godly contentment that breathe through all of his writings.

The Apostle Paul knew the path to contentment through accurate self-knowledge. That is why he declared to the Corinthians, "what we proclaim is not ourselves, but Jesus Christ as Lord, with ourselves as your servants for Jesus' sake" (2 Corinthians 4:5). The first half of the verse doesn't strike us as too bad: we surely want to proclaim the lordship of Christ over all things. However, the second half hits us where it hurts: "we proclaim . . . ourselves as your servants for Jesus' sake." We would typically much rather proclaim ourselves "your leaders for Jesus' sake" and take center stage in the church. However, that is not Paul's approach. He understood that in Christ's kingdom, leadership means service.

If we truly understand that we too are simply unprofitable servants in God's kingdom, how can we think of ourselves as better than those around us? Are we free from certain sins that embroil others in their grip? It is only because God in his grace has kept us out of the grip of those sins or has released us from them. It is not us; it is all his work. Are we more accepted by God because of our law-keeping than they are? Certainly not. If we are able to come into the presence of God, it is on the basis of Christ's merits alone, not ours. So why do we think we are better than they? If we are not better than they are, though, what basis do we have to envy their situation? If we recognize that we truly deserve eternal judgment, how can we be discontented with our present circumstances? Is our present life really hellish? Or is it, in fact, the perfect program of sanctification for our souls, designed personally for us by the God who is working all things together for our good? If that is true, then everything we face—good or bad—must be part of that sovereign plan. Why would we long to exchange our perfect plan for someone else's plan of sanctification? Their plan may look easier to us, but even if it is (and remember, appearances can be deceptive), it wouldn't meet our needs. Godly contentment cures envy-driven grumbling.

Moses and the Prophets

The grumbling of Miriam and Aaron was not answered by Moses. His behavior in this chapter is a living affirmation of the narrator's description of him as more humble than anyone else on the face of the earth (v. 3). Moses knew who he was before God; so he didn't feel the need to stand up for his own rights and status. A servant doesn't feel the need to fight for the right to bear a towel. It is only when we misconceive Christian leadership as being like the world's model that we start to defend our turf. Instead, it was the Lord who heard the words of Miriam and Aaron and responded to them, just as he heard the earlier grumbling of the Israelites and responded in judgment

(v. 2; see 11:1). The Lord summoned all three of them to the entrance of the tent of meeting, where he separated out Aaron and Miriam, summoning them forward to hear his words. Don't miss the irony in the Lord's way of dealing with them here. They had claimed to hear God's words just as Moses did: now they would indeed hear the Lord's words, but only words of judgment.

The Lord's words to them first of all affirmed the fundamental difference between the revelation that he gave by Moses and that which came through all of the other prophetic mediators. To the prophets, God's word came in visions and dreams (v. 6), in riddles rather than in clear speech (v. 8). But the Lord spoke to Moses clearly, face to face (literally, "mouth to mouth," as in the ESV), not in such obscure forms. Such clear revelation by God through his servant Moses demanded their submissive respect rather than any arrogant claim of equality (v. 8).

This passage is very important for our understanding of the Scriptures as a whole. It teaches us that not all Scripture is equally clear, nor is it all to be interpreted in the same way. Sometimes you will hear people insist that prophetic books like Daniel and Revelation must be interpreted exactly like the rest of the Bible, by means of "plain, literal interpretation."[3] Thus whenever the prophets speak of Israel, these people say, they can only mean literal physical Israel, not the church. When they speak of a final battle with participants from particular named countries, that must mean a literal battle with precisely those nations. There isn't space here to explore fully this issue, but it is important to see that this passage in Numbers teaches us that this is explicitly not the way the Bible teaches us to read the prophets. On the contrary, we should expect the prophets to contain much that is difficult and obscure (visions and dreams), in contrast to the clear and straightforward manner in which we read the writings of Moses in the Pentateuch.[4]

Moses and Jesus

There is another even more important implication of this passage, though. If it is true that the revelation that came by Moses demands our reverent submission, how much more must that be the case now that we have the whole of God's revelation in the Scriptures? The writer to the Hebrews reminds us, "Long ago, at many times and in many ways, God spoke to our fathers by the prophets, but in these last days he has spoken to us by his Son" (1:1, 2). In other words, the revelation that we have available to us in the Scriptures is even greater than that which came by Moses, because it includes God's Word to us through his Son, Jesus Christ. Moses was a faithful servant of God, but Jesus is the Son, and he speaks with all of the authority of the Father (Hebrews 3:5, 6). So how shall we escape God's judgment if we rebel and speak against Jesus Christ since he is so much greater than Moses? We have the full and final revelation of God in the completed Scripture, which demands our submission. Our hearts must be content to bow before it, accepting whatever it teaches as the undoubted revelation of God's nature and his will for our lives. To speak against the Scripture is to speak against the authority that God himself has instituted.

Judgment and Mercy

Such acts of rebellious grumbling against the Lord lead to judgment. They certainly did in the case of Miriam and Aaron. Miriam, as instigator, was struck with a skin disease so that her skin became like snow—white and flaky (12:10). The punishment fitted the crime. She grumbled against Moses because he had married a Cushite, a woman who would likely have had darker skin than the Israelites, whether she was from Ethiopia or Midian, and God turned her skin as white as snow. In addition, her complaint was that she and Aaron too had equal access to God as channels of revelation: her punishment was a disease that excluded her permanently not merely from God's presence but from the community of God's people.[5] Now there was certainly no chance of her ever being regarded as the equal of Moses in appearing before the Lord.

The folly of Aaron's claim to equality with Moses was similarly exposed by the Lord. Faced with this judgment on his sister, Aaron could not go directly to God to seek its removal by himself. Instead he went to Moses to ask him to intercede for her (v. 11). Miriam's fate depended on the intercession of the one they had wronged. So Aaron went to Moses and requested that this state of living death, like that of a stillborn child,[6] might be removed from her.

The Intercession of Moses

How would you have responded to Aaron's request? How do you respond when someone who has wronged you and gossiped against you comes to you to confess his or her sin? Many of us might have been tempted to rub in the appropriateness of the judgment that Miriam was facing. Not so Moses. Instead he did exactly as Aaron had requested, bringing Miriam's need before the Lord. Notice how this confirms the reality of what the Lord had earlier told Miriam and Aaron: God not only spoke to Moses—he listened to him as well. They had a face-to-face relationship (see v. 8).

Yet in this case Moses' intercession was only partially granted. Miriam was healed of the disease immediately, yet still had to remain outside the camp for seven days, the normal period of shameful quarantine that defilement through skin disease carried with it. Her sentence was reduced but not entirely removed. The parallel that the Lord makes between her state and that of a woman disgraced by her father shows that the issue here is not cleansing as such but bearing shame. She had to bear the disgrace of her actions for a limited time; after that she could be brought back into the camp, her sin fully atoned for. Meanwhile, the entire community put their lives on hold until Miriam was restored (v. 15).

Grace Shown to Grumblers

Miriam received mercy from the Lord: she didn't have to bear the full consequences of her actions, which would have left her permanently in the realm of death. However, she didn't receive the same level of grace that you and I have received from the Lord. She bore her own disgrace outside the camp, but our disgrace has been fully taken from us in Jesus Christ. Our grumbling, whether flowing from unbelief or from envy, deserves nothing less than permanent death. We too should be shut out of the camp of God's people, for our souls are defiled by the reality that skin diseases pictured for Israel. We are stillborn creatures, spiritually speaking, our wholeness eaten away by the cancer of our sin from the moment we are born. How can a holy and pure God welcome such horribly disfigured and malformed creatures into his presence?

The answer is that he has taken our disfigurement into himself in the person of his Son, Jesus Christ. His perfect, pure wholeness was taken and dragged outside the camp, there to be maltreated. They disfigured his appearance with whips and with thorns; they pierced his flesh with nails and a spear. None of that awful abuse could match the experience of being disfigured with the load of our sin that he bore, however. Was he not the one with whom God spoke face to face from all eternity? Was he not the one who saw the Lord more clearly than any created being? Yet on the cross he became the one abandoned by God, the one spat upon by his own father. All of this was because he was bearing the solemn burden of our sin. He endured the pangs of death in the grave three days before he was brought back in triumph, before he emerged from the tomb victorious, interceding for those who grumbled against him and wronged him.

What is the cure for the grumbling that flows from envy? It is the cross. There God paid the price for your unworthy soul and for mine. There he purchased us back to be his servants, weak and feeble though we are. When we contemplate the greatness of his grace to us in the cross, we cannot doubt that he has our best interests at heart in the way he has brought our circumstances together, even though they are different from the circumstances of others around us. If God did not spare his own Son but freely gave him up for us, then what do we really think he is holding back from us (see Romans 8:32)? If you have been grumbling against others, come before God and freely confess your sin. Ask Jesus Christ to intercede for you with the Father. He will bring your case before the throne of God himself, and God will hear him and answer his pleas for you. Remember God's grace to you at the cross. Let that remembrance transform your perspective on your situation into a fresh contentment with God's plan for your life and a new determination to submit yourself to the direction of his Word, fully and completely.

17

Snatching Defeat from the Jaws of Victory

NUMBERS 13, 14

THE COURSE OF HISTORY IS LITTERED with "almost" victories. These are battles that could probably have been won, yet some small failure changed the direction of events. The Battle of Gettysburg would have been a very different affair if the Confederate forces had pressed on and occupied the high ground of Little Round Top at the end of the first day, when it was still open. The Battle of Waterloo could easily have gone the other way if the French had succeeded in capturing the crossroads of Quatre Bras. One small misstep for man, but a giant leap in the direction of history.

Contenders and Dead-Enders

The same may be true in the lives of individuals as well. In the movie *On the Waterfront*, Marlon Brando played a promising boxer who bowed to Mob pressure and intentionally lost an important bout in return for a small payoff. Years later he was still wracked by the effect that loss had on his life, cutting short his boxing career. Now instead of being a sports superstar he was just another dock laborer, condemned to a dead-end job. His whole existence was summed up in one immortal line, "I could have been a contender." Having lost his opportunity through one bad decision, could he ever recover it? His once-hopeful life seemed destined for emptiness.

Perhaps that is where we find ourselves. We may be wrestling with a decision that still has to be made, the consequences of which will be lasting. Or maybe we have to decide whether or not to resist the pressures that the forces of evil are exerting on us; it has yet to be determined whether or not we will be a contender. Or we may be struggling with the ongoing effects of a bad decision we made many years ago, the fruit of which is still very much in evidence in our lives. In our case the question is rather, what hope is there for failed contenders? The answers to these questions are addressed in the narrative of Israel's wanderings in Numbers 13, 14. When the end of their journey seemed to be in sight, the Israelites snatched defeat from the jaws of victory through their unbelief, going from contenders to dead-enders without a blow being struck.

Scouting the Land

At this point in the story, Israel stood on the brink of entering the Promised Land. The Lord had faithfully brought her out of Egypt and through the wilderness, and now the land of Canaan lay in front of them. He then commanded them to send out a task force to examine the land, made up of representatives from each of the twelve tribes (13:2). Unlike the two men Joshua would later send to Jericho, these men were not really spies in the technical sense of the word. There was no attempt at concealment on their part, which would in any event have been difficult with such a large party. Rather, they were scouts sent out to gather data on the land to be taken, prior to the anticipated military campaign.[1] They were to report on the nature of the land and its inhabitants and to bring back a sample of its fruit (13:17-20). The goal of their mission was not to decide whether entering the land was possible or desirable: the Lord had already reminded Israel that this was the land he was giving to them (13:1). All they had to do was receive it as a gift. Nonetheless, any major military undertaking requires good intelligence so that the best strategy can be evaluated. God's promise did not eliminate the need for responsible action.

In many respects their trip was a success. The scouts were able to roam the whole land from the southern end, where they entered it, all the way up to the northern border at Lebo-hamath (13:21). The main focus of their time was spent around Hebron (13:22), an area that resonated with memories of historical events that should have stimulated their faith. This was the place where the patriarchs were buried, a place as central to the history of their nation as Plymouth Rock or Fort McHenry are for the history of the United States. There they should have been reminded once again of God's promise to give this land to Abraham and his descendants and of God's faithfulness in fulfilling his promises thus far. He had brought them out of Egypt and made them into a great nation, just as he had promised Abraham (Genesis 15:5, 13-15). Certainly the scouts saw for themselves the abundant fruitfulness of the land, in the shape of a single bunch of grapes that was so large it took two people to carry it, along with pomegranates and figs (Numbers 13:23). For forty days they traversed the land safely, scouting it out without opposition or apparent danger.

Two Reports

At the end of that time the tribal representatives brought their conclusions to Moses and the people. Like many committees, they couldn't reach a consensus and so returned with a majority and a minority report. The facts were not at issue between the two sides. Everyone agreed, on the one hand, that the land was fertile and prosperous and, on the other, that its inhabitants were a powerful force to be reckoned with. The key difference between the majority and the minority was where to put the "but" in their report. For the ten-man majority, the defining "but" was the people who inhabited the land. Every part of the land was occupied; all four of the major geographical regions—the Negeb, the hill country, the area beside the sea, and the Jordan valley—had inhabitants who were powerful and lived in large, fortified cities (13:28, 29). There was no uninhabited portion where they might comfortably occupy the land without opposition. They saw the fortifications of the cities, which were indeed substantial. Archaeological explorations suggest that the walls of these cities were thirty to fifty feet high and fifteen feet thick.[2] What is more, the men who lived in the land looked like giants to them, like the Nephilim of old, who were mighty and fearsome warriors (see Genesis 6:4). Who could hope to prevail against such opposition? In comparison to these enormous giants, the scouts felt like grasshoppers (13:33). Grasshoppers were the smallest edible creature in the ancient world.[3] So we could perhaps render their thoughts into a modern equivalent by translating it as, "We felt like shrimps!"

There was a minority report to be considered as well, however. Joshua and Caleb saw exactly the same sights as the other ten did but drew different conclusions. Caleb blurted out the summary conclusion of their assessment: "We should definitely go up and take possession of the land, for we are certainly able to do so" (13:30).[4] Joshua gave the expanded version of their report in chapter 14. He started out with the basic facts: the land they surveyed was not merely good but "exceedingly good" (14:7). He didn't contest the powerful nature of the inhabitants of the land; yet the defining "but" in his report was not the size of the opposition but the presence or absence of God's favor. If the Lord was pleased with them, he would lead them into the land and give it to them (14:8). Far from the Israelites being at risk of being turned into shrimp cocktail by the Anakites, it was the inhabitants of the land who were on the menu: they would be food (*lehem*) for the Israelites to consume (14:9). Their gods could not protect them against the Lord; their shelter was gone (14:9). So long as the Israelites did not rebel against the Lord, they had nothing to fear from the inhabitants of the land.

Why the Difference?

How could these two groups come up with such different assessments of the same facts? The answer is not hard to find. The majority completely left God out of the equation. They described the land they toured as "the land to which you [Moses] sent us" (13:27), not "the land the Lord is giving us" (compare 13:2). They saw the size and number of the inhabitants of its cities and concluded, very reasonably according to their presuppositions, that invading that land was impossible. With such adversaries and with their own limited resources, they felt they had no chance of being a contender. Like the Israelites who centuries later faced another giant foe, Goliath, they looked at the odds stacked against them and saw a task that was too great for ordinary humans to tackle. They forgot the Lord, and so they feared their enemies.

Joshua and Caleb, however, looked at precisely the same facts but from the perspective of faith, not unbelief. Joshua's very name expressed his faith in the Lord. His name at birth was Hoshea, "salvation," but Moses gave him the name Yehoshua or Joshua, "the Lord saves"—a small shift, yet a crucial one (13:16). It is one thing to have faith in salvation. That may simply represent the generic hope expressed in a thousand Hollywood movies that if you only believe strongly enough, something will turn up at the crucial moment. It may simply be faith in faith, belief in the power of believing. The name Yehoshua, however, expressed the specific hope that at the crucial moment *someone* would turn up. Joshua had faith in the saving presence of the Lord, Israel's God.

That specific faith in the Lord's presence and favor with his people was what drove Joshua and Caleb's interpretation of the facts in front of them. They saw the same warriors as the majority did, protected by the same city walls, and yet concluded that those pagan nations not only *could* be but *must* be defeated. Like David facing Goliath, they saw their opponents according to a true scale. The difference between the majority and the minority reports was simply that the minority included God in their calculation. David saw Goliath not as a giant to be tackled by a small and ill-equipped shepherd boy but as a wild animal who had reared up against the sovereign Lord and would inevitably face the deadly consequences. So too Joshua and Caleb saw the inhabitants of Canaan merely as mighty obstacles that God would inevitably overcome so his purposes could be fulfilled. The Lord who had parted the Red Sea in front of his people would not abandon them now. Giants may seem enormous from the perspective of the shrimps, but comparing them with the power of the Almighty tends to cut them down to size. If you fear the Lord, you will be free from the fear of your enemies; if you forget God, you will inevitably fear men.[5]

The Eye of Faith

The same is also true in our experience. If we simply consider the obstacles that face our churches or the difficulties that we face as individuals, it is easy to conclude that we are overmatched and must inevitably fall short and fail. Humanly speaking, that may be an accurate assessment of reality. We have all sometimes felt like grasshoppers surrounded by giants on all sides. Our lives are full of impossible challenges, humanly speaking. Do you or I have the power within us to bring our neighbor to faith in Christ or to persevere in a difficult relationship at home or at work or to conquer a personal besetting sin? Humanly speaking, none of us do.

However, the eye of faith recognizes that in this world, reality is not accurately measured whenever we are "humanly speaking." This is *God's* world, in which his Word and his promises must ultimately prevail. No matter how great the opposition, if the Lord is pleased with us, our future is assured. If God is calling a neighbor to himself, then even our weak and fumbling words can be the door to eternal life for him or her. If the Lord strengthens us, then not only can we endure a difficult relationship, but we can shine within it as beacons of godly, self-sacrificial love. If God is at work in our hearts, we have not only the hope but the assurance that one day we will be done even with our most pervasive besetting sins. This knowledge is the bedrock that has enabled the saints of the past to endure great persecution and to step out in radical acts of faith and obedience. Humanly speaking, Joshua and Caleb's actions may have looked utterly foolish; but God was pleased with them, and so they endured. They feared God, and so they were freed from the fear of men.

The Irrationality of Unbelief

Unfortunately, the response of the people of Israel was not faith in the Lord but grumbling and rebellion. Instead of being motivated to obey, they sought to stone Joshua and Caleb for their words of faith (14:10). They believed the assessment of the majority report and grumbled against Moses and Aaron. The Israelites said,

> Would that we had died in the land of Egypt! Or would that we had died in this wilderness! Why is the LORD bringing us into this land, to fall by the sword? Our wives and our little ones will become a prey. Would it not be better for us to go back to Egypt? (14:2, 3)

They were even ready to elect a new leader and go back to Egypt, reversing the whole course of the exodus. This entailed a complete rejection of the Lord and of Moses, a rejection of the salvation the Lord had promised them and the mediator he had chosen to lead them.

Notice, though, how fundamentally irrational their unbelief was. The majority report was logically flawed. Contradicting the good report about the nature of the land that the scouts gave Moses at first, the majority spread a bad report among the people, saying that the land devoured those living in it (13:32). Yet in the very next breath they went on to describe its inhabitants as giants! Think about that for a moment. How could a barren land produce such fearsomely well-nourished inhabitants? It doesn't add up. Nor does the complaint of the people make any more sense. How could it be better for them to have died in Egypt or in the wilderness than to face death at the hands of the Anakim? Is certain death sooner preferable to possible death later? Does it make sense to believe that the Lord poured out earth-shattering plagues on Egypt, parted the Red Sea in front of his people, and then fed them miraculously with manna in the wilderness only to have them fall at the hands of the inhabitants of the Promised Land? Does God do one dramatic series of miracles in the lives of his people only to fail at the last hurdle, leaving them tantalizingly short of what he promised? That doesn't make sense.

Isn't our unbelief equally irrational, though? We believe and proclaim that our God created the universe out of nothing; yet we find it hard to believe that the results of a particular medical test belong to him. We believe and proclaim that our God directs the courses of kings and nations and that he has transformed our own dead hearts into living, responsive flesh; yet we find it hard to believe that he can bring our stubborn friends and neighbors to faith in himself. We believe and proclaim that our God entered history as a baby in Bethlehem; yet we find it hard to believe that he is active in our own personal history, holding our hand through the events of this week and the next. We believe and proclaim that he suffered on the cross for our sins and rose again triumphant from the grave to free us from our sins; yet we find it hard to believe that this particular sin of ours could ever be forgiven or that the power of that sinful habit could ever be broken. Our unbelief is always fundamentally irrational, a sinful refusal to fear God, which results equally inevitably in a sinful fear of people and circumstances. It is as irrational for us to cling to our unbelief as it is for a drowning man to cling to a heavy stone.

God's Verdict on Israel

The decisive verdict in this story in the book of Numbers, though, was not Israel's verdict on their God but his verdict on them. Ultimately their fate rested not on what they thought of him so much as it did on what he thought of them. Just as there are two verdicts by the scouts on the land, so there were two verdicts by God on his people—an initial verdict of judgment and a final verdict of salvation.

The initial verdict of God was the threat of death upon the whole people and a new beginning for Israel through Moses. God declared in his wrath:

How long will this people despise me? And how long will they not believe
in me, in spite of all the signs that I have done among them? I will strike
them with the pestilence and disinherit them, and I will make of you a
nation greater and mightier than they. (14:11, 12)

This was not the first time that God had made such a threat. He said the
same thing to Moses in Exodus 32:9, 10 after the incident with the golden
calf. Had the Lord really intended to carry through such a judgment on his
people, he could easily have carried it through immediately. Given their
persistent infidelity, Israel would hardly have had grounds for complaint.
Yet in both places it is striking that God spoke the threat to Moses instead
of executing it at once. It is almost as if God was cuing Moses to intercede
on behalf of his people so that they might be spared.[6] In each case that is
exactly what Moses did, and the threat was then (partially) lifted. Through
the intercession of Moses, lives were spared—if not the lives of the adult
generation, at least those of their children, and their children's children who
were as yet unborn.

Intercession

The intersection of God's eternal sovereign will and our prayers of intercession is, on some levels, a profound mystery. The best theological minds
through the ages have had difficulty in expressing fully how a sovereign,
eternal God can listen and respond to the prayers of temporal human beings
while still carrying out all of his holy will exactly as he designed it from all
eternity. Yet the reality and effectiveness of intercession on behalf of others
is a constant Biblical theme, albeit one we are far more likely to confess with
our mouths than act on consistently. The Bible tells us that the non-Christian
world around us stands under God's judgment of death. They have earned
the verdict of eternal separation from God as the wages of their "God-free"
lifestyle. Yet it also states that by means of our intercession, we may see
some of those prisoners freed from condemnation. By the power of prayer,
sinners are brought from death to eternal life. If we really heeded the cues
that follow from that Scriptural truth, how much more time would we spend
on our knees daily, interceding for our friends and neighbors?

Moses' prayer of intercession was based on two equally fundamental Scriptural truths: the requirements of God's glory and God's merciful
nature. He pleaded for his fellow-Israelites first on the basis of the requirements of God's glory (14:13-16). If the Lord were to blot out the Israelites
at this point, the Gentile nations around them would misunderstand his reasons. They had heard that the Lord's name was linked with this people, that
he had brought them out of Egypt, and that he had gone through the wilderness with them. If God were to kill them now, the nations might think it was

because he was unable to bring his people into the land, and they would be confirmed in their unbelief. The Lord's glory might be tarnished.

Second, though, Moses pleaded for the people on the basis of God's mercy (14:17-19). He quoted the Lord's own description of himself from Exodus 34:6, 7: the Lord is slow to anger, abounding in love, and forgiving sin and rebellion, yet not leaving the guilty unpunished. He does not falsify the Scriptural record by only quoting the first half of God's self-description. On the contrary, Moses acknowledges that the Lord is a God of both justice and of mercy; yet he asks that in accordance with his great *hesed*, the Lord's covenantal faithfulness to his people, he would be reconciled with them in spite of their continuing record of sin.

Both of these motivations should feature prominently in our own prayers of intercession. Why do we ask God to respond to our prayers? It is "for your name's sake," so that he might receive the glory he deserves. Why do we ask him to change our neighbor's heart toward him? It is so that the Lord might be glorified by another soul captivated by his beauty. Why do we ask him to strengthen our churches and add new people to them? It is so that we might more adequately and fully declare his praises in those places. Why do we ask for victory over our sins? It is so that our hearts might be more free to glorify him and delight in his presence. Praying for the sake of God's glory will dramatically reshape what we pray for and the way we pray for ourselves and those around us.

What is more, if we ask, motivated by God's glory, we will also be comforted when he does not answer our prayers in the way we had hoped. If God is more glorified in my continuing weakness, suffering, or even failure, then my prayer has nonetheless been answered when I remain weak or suffering. If God is more glorified by enabling me to rejoice in him in spite of a door being closed in front of me or a deep longing in my heart going unfulfilled, then my prayer for his glory has been answered. If God is more glorified by my failure than he would be by my success, then my prayer has been answered even when my best endeavors to serve him have been shipwrecked. If God is my servant or my partner, then my failure means that God has let me down. However, if God is my Master who does all things for my good as well as for his glory, then I can know that he has a glorious purpose in even the most inglorious circumstances of my life. It would be perverse indeed for me to pray for something and then complain because God gave it to me wrapped in a different form from the one I had anticipated.

Justice and Mercy

We should also pray with awareness of God's nature as a God of both justice and mercy. Often we tend to reduce God down to our size in one direction or the other. Either we conceive in our minds a God who is all justice, ready to condemn us for the least infraction and uncaring about the fate of those whom he created, or conversely (and more commonly in our culture) we think of God as being all love and compassion, easily placated by a cursory nod from us in his direction while we continue to live our lives in rebellion against him. Neither of these pictures is Biblical. God is indeed slow to anger, compassionate, and gracious toward those who are his people. Yet he is also a God of flaming and uncompromised justice who cannot simply ignore rebellion and sin. We must recognize both aspects of God's character in our prayers: he is a God who has the right to condemn us to eternal judgment with perfect justice, yet has also promised to be a faithful and loving God to all who come to him through faith in Christ. He has promised to be our God and the God of our children after us and the God of all those whom he calls to himself (Acts 2:39). That is the basis for our bold and passionate intercession on behalf of the children of believers and for others around us who do not yet know him, asking God by his grace and mercy to call them too into a living relationship with himself.

God's mercy does not eliminate justice in his dealings with Israel. The Lord responded to Moses' intercession by agreeing to continue his relationship with this people, as Moses requested. Nonetheless, his passion for his glory meant that he could not overlook their sin. This generation that saw his glory in the exodus and yet still did not believe would end up given over to a fitting punishment (14:21-35). Would they rather die in the wilderness than enter the land? So be it; that would be their fate (14:29). Would they rather go back to Egypt than enter the Promised Land? So be it: the next leg of their journey would be back toward the Red Sea rather than onward to Canaan (14:25). The children whom the parents feared would become slaves would be the ones who would experience the freedom of life in the land, while the older generation would die out over forty years in the wilderness—one year for every day of the scouting party's journey (14:31-34). Out of the original generation, only Joshua and Caleb would live to see God's promise fulfilled. The remainder of the scouting party were immediately struck down with a plague, a kind of firstfruits of the larger judgment to come (14:37).

If God is a God of justice as well as mercy, though, how can any of us survive? The people of Israel were not radically transformed by their experience of the Lord's mercy. Even though they mourned bitterly, they were far from repentant in their hearts. They were sorry for the effects of their sin, but not for the sin itself. You can see that was the case from the fact that their very next act was a continuation of their unbelief. Instead of following the Lord's instructions and setting out back toward the Red Sea, they set out to try and take Canaan in their own strength (14:40). In spite of Moses' warning that they would not succeed, they set off presumptuously to try to reverse the judgment on themselves. Earlier they *refused* to enter the land because of unbelief; now they *tried* to enter the land out of unbelief. Unsurprisingly, they were frustrated and ended up beaten back by the inhabitants of the land (14:45). Without the Lord's help, they should indeed have been afraid to take on the giants who occupied the land.

Mercy and Faithfulness

What could God do with such a stubborn and rebellious people? How long would he continue to bear with a people who showed him such contempt? The answer is, however long it would take to accomplish his sovereign purposes and fulfill his promises. He would not abandon them but would instead do exactly what he had promised. This is good news for us too. We also daily fail to obey him, choosing to believe in the promises of our idols rather than in the word of the living God. We too daily fail to attempt the things he has commanded us because of unbelief. We too daily set out to try to accomplish all manner of good things, but in our own strength, without his presence, as if it didn't really matter whether we had God's blessing or not. We too daily seek to confront our sins, husband our wives, parent our children, pursue our careers, and build our homes on the world's terms, or in accordance with the Lord's terms but without the Lord's presence. We truly deserve nothing other than God's judgment and contempt.

The Triumph of God's Faithfulness

Yet such is not what God has shown us. God's mercy and faithfulness triumph even over our persistent sin. Instead of condemning us for our unbelief and putting us to death in the wilderness, he has taken our faithlessness and laid it on Jesus Christ. This sacrifice is how the Lord can be a God of both justice and mercy. At the cross, mercy and justice joined hands as God's glory was made manifest most fully. Jesus Christ, our faithful pioneer, walked through this sin-tangled world with perfect righteousness not for forty days but for thirty-three years. In so doing, he earned life through his faithfulness, not just for himself but for all those who are united to him by faith. In his perfect life, God's righteous demands on us are satisfied. In his substitutionary death, God's justice is satisfied, and at the same time his mercy is displayed to outcasts and rebels. Everyone who looks to him and cries out in the wilderness, "Lord Jesus, be merciful to me, a sinner" finds in him God's invitation to eternal rest. That offer is open to you, no matter who you are or what you have done. You don't need to strive in your own strength any longer or to lament the depth of your failure. You are indeed no contender in the fight for eternal significance and never could have been, but Jesus Christ has contended for you and has won the victory on your behalf.

If that is true, what opposition in this world shall we fear? If Christ has completed the pilgrimage on our behalf, what can successfully stand in our way as we follow in his footsteps? If the Lord is pleased with us, for Jesus' sake, then no giants can bar our passage to Heaven, no walls can keep us from our heavenly inheritance. Unbelief is the only thing that can bar our access into Heaven and our enjoyment of peace along our earthly pilgrimage. Yet if Christ walks with us every step of the way, we will have a firm foundation for bold living and faith-filled obedience. *Lord, we believe—help our unbelief! Ravish our hearts with such a grasp of your glory and goodness that we are overwhelmed by your presence.* In the words of John Bunyan, may it be said of us:

> Who would true valor see,
> Let him come hither;
> One here will constant be,
> Come wind, come weather;
> There's no discouragement
> Shall make him once relent
> To be a pilgrim.

> Whoso beset him round
> With dismal stories,
> Do but themselves confound—
> No lion can him fright;
> He'll with a giant fight,
> But he will have a right
> To be a pilgrim.

> Hobgoblin nor foul fiend
> Can daunt his spirit;
> He knows he at the end
> Shall life inherit.
> Then fancies fly away,
> He'll fear not what men say;
> He'll labor night and day
> To be a pilgrim.

18

Demanding Grace

NUMBERS 15:1-21

THE ESSENTIAL INGREDIENT of a good story is sequence: a plot in which one event follows another in an orderly way, and every element plays its part in advancing the story line. Ever since Aristotle, it has been generally accepted that a story must have a beginning, a middle, and an end, and that these elements should normally be closely connected to one another. To be sure, we are perhaps more plot-driven in our culture than at most times and places in history. We tend to be impatient with slow-moving novels, and we expect our stories to evidence a tight narrative structure. A book like Victor Hugo's *The Hunchback of Notre Dame*, which contains a whole chapter that simply describes the view over fifteenth-century Paris from the roof of the cathedral, quickly makes us seek out the abridged version. Yet even that chapter has a function within the larger narrative of *The Hunchback*, giving the book a gothic, overdecorated tone that matches the architecture of the cathedral itself.

What function does Numbers 15 play in its context though? Why does the writer suddenly switch from telling a story to recounting what seems at first sight to be a series of miscellaneous laws? Is this simply poor storytelling technique? Or is there a method to his apparent madness, a reason why these particular laws fit into this particular context and move the overall narrative forward? You may remember that we asked the same question back in our discussion of Numbers 7 and found there that the laws inserted in the narrative had a particular significance within their specific narrative. The same is true here.

Israel's Sacrifices

Numbers 15 is primarily about different kinds of sacrifices. The connection between the various sections of this chapter and what precedes this chapter becomes clear when you understand the purpose of these sacrifices. Israel's sacrifices served a number of different functions in their religious life. Some sacrifices provided atonement for sin, others paid tribute to their heavenly overlord, while still others were the means of enjoying table fellowship with their covenant King. In this chapter, all three purposes are present. The opening section focuses on the meal aspect of these sacrifices (vv. 1-21), the offering of the first dough functions as tribute to the King (vv. 22-26), while the remainder of the section on offerings discusses which sins can be atoned for and which cannot (vv. 27-36). The case study of the man gathering wood on the Sabbath is included at this point as an example of a sin that cannot be atoned for, and then the chapter closes with the requirement that the Israelites wear tassels on their garments as a reminder of their covenant God (vv. 37-41). As we will see in our next study, this last section sums up the theme of the whole chapter, describing the obligations that flow from a relationship of grace.

First, the narrator describes the offerings made by fire (vv. 1-13). These sacrifices were not those that were required to atone for specific sins but rather those associated with more general fellowship with God, whether burnt offerings or fellowship offerings.[1] These sacrifices were offered in the fire on the altar, and the smoke from the sacrifice ascended as an aroma pleasing to the Lord, as if the Lord too were participating in the meal. The regulations in Numbers 15 strengthen the picture of table fellowship between God and man by requiring a symbolic balanced meal at these offerings: a large portion of meat must always be accompanied by the appropriate carbohydrates and beverage. A grain offering of two quarts of flour mixed with oil was required with a sheep or a goat, together with a drink offering of a quart of wine (vv. 4, 5). Moreover, a sheep or a goat was only the small-size serving. These sacrifices also come in "regular" portions (a ram; vv. 6, 7) and "super-size" (a bull; vv. 8-10). In each case, the accompanying "side orders" had to be scaled up to match (vv. 11, 12).

Rebuke and Promise

In the context of the surrounding narrative, these laws were both a rebuke and a promise. They were a rebuke to the unbelief that doubted the goodness of the Promised Land: if the future Israelites would be able to offer such substantial meals to their God, then they themselves would hardly go hungry. There would be abundant food for all. Yet alongside the implicit rebuke is a clear promise of grace for the future: in the days ahead, the Lord will enjoy fellowship with his people on a continuing basis. God and man will still eat together at one table.

Aren't you amazed by God's overwhelming grace to sinners? I don't know about you, but if I were the Lord, my patience with Israel would have been long since exhausted by this point in the journey. He had brought them safely all the way from Egypt. Yet at the threshold of entry into the Promised Land, the majority of the scouts fell victim to unbelief and spread a bad report about the nature of the land and the power of its occupants (13:32). For their part, the people chose to believe the bad report of the majority, which left the Lord out of the equation entirely, in spite of the passionate pleas of Joshua and Caleb to trust God. They were ready to stone Joshua and Caleb, elect new leadership, and march right back to Egypt (14:1-4, 10). Even after the people heard the Lord pronounce judgment on their unbelief and send them back toward the wilderness, their next act was a further step of unbelief, trying now to enter the land without the Lord's help (14:40-45). What is the Lord to do with such a people? I know what I would do! After all this ingratitude, if I were the Lord, I would have been ready to wipe out the whole nation on the spot, whatever Moses might say on their behalf.

The Lord's very next word to his people after this renewed act of unbelief was this, however: "When you come into the land you are to inhabit, which I am giving you . . ." (15:2)! Isn't that incredible? God's good plan for this people was not aborted in spite of all of their sin. There was a future for Israel in the land of promise, a future of intimate relationship. What is more, God didn't simply restore Israel while keeping them at a distance. Sometimes we do that. Perhaps we promise a friend that we will take him or her to the airport next week. In between our making the promise and the time for the trip, though, we have a falling out. We may still do what we said we would for our friend because we feel obligated, but the atmosphere on the trip may be like the inside of a freezer. We do what we have promised, but we do not restore the relationship. God is not like us, however. He welcomes Israel back into his presence, to share fellowship. Our God is indeed, as Moses said, "slow to anger and abounding in steadfast love, forgiving iniquity and transgression" (14:18, quoting Exodus 34:6, 7).

Native-Born Israelites

God's grace is also evident in the insistence of the passage that this fellowship with the Lord extends to both native-born Israelites and sojourning aliens alike (vv. 13-16). The rules are to be the same for both. Once again the significance of that ruling in this context goes beyond the obvious. On the one hand, it is certainly true that in this regulation there is a faint foreshadowing of the gospel call to the nations, that one day Jews and Gentiles would be able to stand before God side by side on the same terms. Far from the Gentiles always being enemies to be feared, one day at least some of them will come to worship Israel's God. Aliens and strangers were to be welcomed into the covenant community. However, that is not the only significance of the regulations here. In this context the key significance of this ruling is surely that one day in the future there will be native-born Israelites! There will one day be a generation of children who from birth can call the Promised Land home.

At this point in the book of Numbers, this declaration calls for faith on the part of Israel. The Israelites were still themselves wandering aliens, trekking through the wilderness. In fact, they had just been condemned to wander there for another forty years (14:34). Yet God promised that their children would nonetheless enter the Promised Land and inherit it as their own. This regulation that sojourners and native-born Israelites be treated alike depends on, and reaffirms, that promise. One day there would be native-born Israelites, people with a natural birthright of access to God that mere aliens and sojourners in their midst would envy. The new generation of native-born Israelites, the very ones whom the older generation in their unbelief had asserted would become plunder for the inhabitants of the land (14:3), would actually have profound rights and privileges before God.

First Dough

However, along with privileges also come responsibilities, as we see in the next sequence of laws concerning the first dough (vv. 17-21). Since God is the one who gives the land to his people, they in turn need to make an offering from everything that it produces. That is the principle behind the requirement elsewhere that Israel tithe all of their crops and herds and that every year they offer the firstfruits to the Lord. In the days to come, though, they were also to take the first portion of every batch of dough[2] and present it to the Lord. This law also presupposes that the people will receive the promise of the land, which will provide grain and flour in abundance. What is more, this regulation brings the law of firstfruits home to every household: the firstfruits of both the threshing floor and the vat were already claimed by God (Exodus 22:29; cf. Numbers 18:12, 13), but that would merely have been a single annual obligation, much like we have to file an annual tax return. Now they had to bring the first cake out of every batch of bread that they prepared to the priest as a gift to the Lord. In that way the cooks would constantly be reminded of the one from whom their daily bread came.

The Way to True Freedom

When you look at these laws in their narrative context, they thus show us profound spiritual truths. To begin with, they challenge our instinctive notion that obedience to God's Law is bondage and that doing whatever we want brings freedom. In the previous chapter Israel chose the way of unbelief, which led to disobedience. They were afraid that if they obeyed God and did what he required, it would lead to death for themselves and bondage for their children (14:3). Yet, in reality it was their unbelief that led to their lives being wasted in the wilderness. Disobedience broke their relationship with God and led to death. On the other hand, faith follows the way of obedience to the demands of God's Law, which in turn, as these regulations underscore, leads to life in God's presence and fellowship with him. The goal of God's regulations is not to ruin our lives but to fulfill them.

The same negative dynamic often operates in our own lives. Why is it that we give in to sin and disobedience so often, even though we know what we are doing is wrong? Why is it that we are so ineffective when we try to sanctify ourselves by our own effort, by telling ourselves to work harder? Such an approach rarely brings about lasting change in our lives because the root of our sin lies buried more deeply than our effort can reach. Tackling sin with mere effort is like trying to fight a tank with a water pistol: our weaponry cannot reach the heart of the issue. In fact, our heart is the heart of the issue: the underlying dynamic that drives our sin is our unbelief.[3] Like the Israelites, we have false beliefs about God that we persist in doggedly in spite of all of the evidence to the contrary. Until these deep-rooted core beliefs are challenged, little real change is possible in our lives. That is why even when we recognize that our sinful patterns lead to painful consequences, we often find that we cannot change them.

The fundamental problem that drove Israel's patterns of sin was their failure to believe that God is good and had good purposes for them. Faced with oversized enemies entrenched in fortified cities, Israel concluded that they would certainly die in any attempt to conquer the land (14:3). This is unbelief. In spite of the evidence of the firstfruits of the land in the shape of an enormous bunch of grapes (13:23), Israel chose instead to believe the majority report of the scouts that the land was bad and that it devoured its inhabitants (13:32). This is unbelief. When the Lord condemned them to wander another forty years in the wilderness, they *then* decided they could conquer the giant-infested land after all, with or without God (14:40-45). This is unbelief. Unbelief drove their disobedience.

The Dynamics of Unbelief

We need to clarify something at this point, however. When we speak of unbelief, it sounds very passive. Sometimes people will say, "Oh, it's wonderful that you believe the things you do about God. You are a person of such faith. But I'm afraid I don't have your kind of faith." They make it sound as if Christians have the ability to believe in something, but they, poor souls, do not. Actually, though, unbelief is a position involving just as much faith as belief. Unbelief is as strongly committed to its view of the world as belief is. There is no such thing as a faith-free zone in this world.

This is clear from the example of the Israelites. Their actions were all profoundly irrational, if the Creator God of the universe was committed to them. They only make sense if Israel believed that God was actually their enemy, determined to do them harm. Unbelief is the opposite of faith not in being the absence of faith, but in being faith in the opposite set of propositions about God. Unbelief is the firm faith that, for all practical purposes, God does not exist, God does not care, God is not involved actively in my life.

The same dynamic of unbelief drives our own patterns of sin. Does giving in to sin really work for us? Does it fulfill us and leave us feeling warm and cozy all over? Does not following the path of sin, in most cases, leave us in the wilderness, thirsty and hungry and profoundly empty? So why do we continue to do it? Why are we so easily led astray into temptation and sin? It is because at a deep level we don't really believe that God is good and has good purposes for us. We have a deep-seated practical belief that, on the contrary, God is not really working all things for our good. If we believed profoundly in God's existence, power, and good purpose for us, then studying his laws and following them would become so natural and obvious that our lives would be transformed from the center outward.

The Road to Relationship

That is why Numbers 15 makes a fitting sequel to Numbers 14. Israel's unbelief and disobedience that led to a broken relationship was not the end of the road for God's relationship with his people. Relationship with him is, after all, the good purpose for which God has designed us. The Westminster Shorter Catechism tells us that we were made "to glorify God and to enjoy him forever." Or to put it another way, we were created to enjoy a relationship of close fellowship with God. Why was God going to bring Israel into the Promised Land? Was it simply so they could have a beautiful place in which to live, equipped with all of the ancient conveniences? Far from it: entry into the land was merely the beginning of God's purpose for them. Once they were in the land, Israel would begin to offer these sacrifices, which would then be the means of their experiencing rich fellowship with the living God. Whereas Numbers 14 showed that disobedience leads to death, Numbers 15 shows that the doorway to a life-giving relationship with God is still open. If the older generation had truly believed that was God's enduring purpose for them, as Joshua and Caleb did, then they would have been prepared to take on whatever giants they faced in order to enter the land. They would not even have feared death if they had truly believed in God's good purpose of lasting fellowship with himself.

The nature of God's good purpose for us is an important point to grasp because for some people around us sin does seem to be "working"—at least, if our understanding of the purpose of existence is skewed. If the chief end of man is to have a comfortable life, surrounded by everything our heart desires, then sin is definitely working for some people. That is what troubled the psalmist in Psalm 73. He saw people around him who had no commitment to follow God and pursue his ways, yet whose lives were free from visible trouble and pain, who seemed outwardly to be prospering (vv. 2-12). His faith was jolted, and he wondered if his obedience to God was just so much wasted effort (vv. 13, 14).

Visiting the sanctuary reoriented the psalmist's thinking, however. What he saw there was exactly what Numbers 15 makes provision for: rich fellowship between God and his people that transcends the generations. There in the sanctuary, the psalmist realized what he had that the wicked lacked: God's presence and favor with him now and the prospect of that fellowship continuing on into glory. "Whom have I in heaven but you? And there is nothing on earth that I desire besides you. My flesh and my heart may fail, but God is the strength of my heart and my portion forever" (vv. 25, 26). He grasped afresh the fact that God's good purpose for his people was fellowship with them, both now and forever, and suddenly the position of the wicked didn't seem so enviable after all. Embracing that relationship as his highest desire changed his heart and dealt with his grumbling spirit.

The motivating power of all sin lies in failing to believe God's good purpose for us, which is for us to glorify him and enjoy him forever. Temptation always offers us something: Satan never goes fishing with a bare hook. It doesn't always deliver what it seems to offer, but it always offers something. Yet whatever temptation offers us, it cannot offer us the opportunity to glorify or to enjoy God. Whatever we are pursuing when we sin, it is always something less than God's good purpose for us. It is a functional idolatry of something other than the Lord. In practice, we are believing that something else is better than experiencing joyous fellowship with him forever. Something else has become our chief purpose in life, the desire that is driving us. Perhaps it is comfort or pleasure or pleasing people or succeeding in our career or having the perfect home. Idols come in all shapes and sizes, but until we do what the psalmist did and reorient our thinking at the most basic level, sin will always seem more attractive to us than righteousness as a means to satisfy our idolatry. As long as something other than fellowship with God is our chief purpose in life, we will easily be seduced away from obedience.

The Consequences of Fellowship

Desiring fellowship with God above all else is not only the foundation for our obedience—it will shape our attitude toward giving as well. Numbers 15 makes substantial demands on the resources of God's people. We may well not grasp how substantial they were since we don't typically own working livestock, but an ox was the equivalent of a tractor or a car in the ancient world. Imagine taking your car to church as an offering and watching it go up in flames. That would be quite a commitment! The animal sacrifices laid out in the opening verses were thus not cheap, and even the commitment to give the first of every batch of dough would have meant an offering if not daily, at least weekly. It would be almost like setting another place at your table every mealtime for the Lord. How does your heart respond to such demands from God? Do they seem reasonable and desirable or burdensome and repressive?

Let me suggest that our response to the Scriptural obligations for giving is a good diagnostic test of what we are really thinking about God and about our chief purpose in life. The issue is not how much we give but our heart attitude to giving. Under the new covenant, we are no longer obligated to bring sheep and bulls to offer God, along with loaves of bread and offerings of wine. Nor are we obligated to bring to church the first roll out of every batch of sourdough bread that we bake. As a pastor, I certainly appreciate it when people in my church bring me a cake or a meal they have made, but they are not under any Scriptural duty to do so. How do we respond to that freedom? If we don't really think God has our best interests at heart, and our chief desire is something other than fellowship with him, we will view that freedom as freedom from giving. We may still give something to the Lord, because it would look bad if we let the plate pass us by Sunday by Sunday. We may even give a large amount, if doing that feeds our functional idolatries by making others think well of us. However, we will be giving essentially for our own sake, and not for the Lord.

How will we respond, however, if we are thoroughly convinced that God is good and has the good purpose of fellowship with us, now and forever? We will desire to excel in the grace of giving, to use Paul's terminology (2 Corinthians 8:7). We will seek to cut down our other expenses so we can give more generously to the Lord's work, so that others too—others who are presently aliens and strangers when it comes to God—can know his beauty and enjoy his fellowship as their supreme purpose as well.

Often discussion of our giving revolves around the question "To tithe or not to tithe?" Am I obligated to give 10 percent of my income to the Lord, as Old Testament believers were, or does that requirement no longer apply to me? However, that question is already headed in the wrong direction.[4] Even in the Old Testament, the tithe was merely the first of many obligations and opportunities to give, obligations and opportunities that flowed out of Israel's relationship with God and the grace they had received from him. It is not coincidental that the various offerings that speak of fellowship with God come before the requirement to offer tribute through the first dough offering. Knowledge of God and his grace is foundational to the requirement to give.

Indeed, many of the offerings in Numbers 15 were voluntary, not compulsory, and there was certainly no rule that established how large the cake offered from the first of the dough had to be. If Israel's thinking about God was correct, it would have been constantly evident to them that everything their land produced came to them from the Lord, the one who had given them the land in the first place. If they understood that, then the question on their lips would not be "Do I have to give?" but "How much am I able to give?"

It is the same for us. If we understand that everything we have comes to us from the Lord and that he has a good purpose for us, which is nothing other than fellowship with him, then we are ready to ask ourselves, "How much am I able to give?" In fact, it is even more true for us, for we understand more fully the cost at which our fellowship was bought. For the Old Testament saints, their fellowship meals with God were never vegetarian affairs. An animal had to die for the fellowship between God and man to take place. That is not coincidental. It is a picture of how fellowship between God and man would ultimately be restored through the death of Christ on the cross. Our Savior didn't ask, "How much do I have to give?" He didn't just give the first lump of his dough or even sacrifice a costly bull out of his own resources. For the sake of our fellowship with the Father, he offered himself as a living sacrifice, nailed to the cross. His fellowship with the Father was temporarily broken so our fellowship with the Father could be permanently restored. All of his sufferings were experienced so the vision depicted in the fellowship sacrifices of Israel could become a reality: God and man seated together around a table, enjoying rich fellowship together. As the apostle Peter put it, "you were ransomed . . . not with perishable things such as silver or gold, but with the precious blood of Christ, like that of a lamb without blemish or spot" (1 Peter 1:18, 19).

If we understand the sacrifice of Christ, by which God pays for our forgiveness, then obedience to his law is transformed. No longer is it a burden for us to bear as slaves; now it is an opportunity for us to serve as sons or daughters, a way for us to experience deeper fellowship with him. If we understand that God's goal for us is to redeem us from an empty way of life and give us the fellowship with him that we were created for, then nothing can be too much for him to ask. God's gift of Jesus proves beyond a shadow of a doubt his care for us and the power of his desire for relationship with us. He so wanted us to be with him for eternity that he died for us on the cross.

Why then will we persist in our unbelief? How can we remain skeptical about God, no matter what difficulties face us? Why do we hold back from doing what we know God wants us to do because we fear it may be too costly? His unquenchable purpose for us is that we may know him and enjoy him forever, and his plan for our lives is entirely directed toward that goal. The gospel rescues us from our wilderness of unbelief and brings us into a new relationship with God even now, with all of its privileges and responsibilities. It continues to transform us day by day until we enter his presence, once and for all. How awesome that such grace should be shown to sinners! How incredible that such mercy should be shown to us! Yet in Christ, God who is full of grace has shown rich mercy to us so that we should be called the children of God, heirs of his promise.

19

This Is Your God

NUMBERS 15:22-41

ONE OF THE PROFOUND DIFFICULTIES when you are counseling people about their relationships is to get them to deal with reality. Many times people are willfully blind to the character of the person to whom they are married. They come to you and complain that they want their spouse to be a certain way, though in reality that is not the person they chose to marry. Perhaps a woman wants her husband to be more romantic and sensitive, or a man wants his wife to be more supportive and submissive; yet the spouse just does not have that trait as part of his or her makeup. Facing up to reality is not always easy; yet it is an essential first step in building a true relationship.

In the same way, many people do not want to deal with reality when it comes to God. They prefer to try to relate to a god whom they have created, their projection of what an ideal deity ought to be, instead of seeking to relate to the one true God who really exists. In this case the irony is that the character features that people most often seek to blur about God are not flaws but rather his uncomfortable perfections. It is God's holiness, righteousness, and justice that we find awkward because he is so different from us. These features may leave us desiring what we perceive as a kinder, gentler (though less perfect) god. What happens when we seek to eliminate those awkward aspects of God's character, though, is that any possibility of true relationship is immediately sacrificed. Until we deal with God as he really is, we cannot begin to enter a relationship with him. Paradoxically, the more we deal with God as he really is, the more we find that he is exactly the God whom we need. After all, he is the one who created us in the first place with just such a relationship in mind.

The sacrifices listed in Numbers 15 are designed to show us a full-orbed view of God. In verses 1-16, which we looked at in the last chapter, we saw various sacrifices that underscored God's ongoing desire for a relationship with his people. In spite of their rebellion in the previous chapter, the Lord confirmed the fact that he would still bring their children into the land of promise and show them his favor there. The requirement for the people to pay tribute to the Lord as the one who gave them their land was also highlighted (vv. 17–21). In context, this commitment to follow through on his original promise confirms Moses' description of God as "slow to anger and abounding in steadfast love, forgiving iniquity and transgression" (14:18, quoting Exodus 34:6, 7). Israel's God is indeed a God of grace and mercy.

Yet Moses also confessed that the Lord is a God who "will by no means clear the guilty, visiting the iniquity of the fathers on the children, to the third and the fourth generation" (14:18, quoting Exodus 34:7). Israel's God is a God of justice as well as mercy, and this is the aspect of God's character that comes to the fore in the latter part of Numbers 15. If our God is a God of justice, how shall the needs of that justice be satisfied?

A Remedy for Sin

The answer to that question, of course, lay in the sacrificial system. As well as being a means of enjoying fellowship with God and paying tribute to him, the sacrificial system of the Old Testament provided a remedy for sin. Those who had sinned could bring the appropriate sacrifices, and they would be forgiven. If the whole community sinned, then along with the burnt offering that symbolized the restored relationship they desired, they would offer a male goat as the sin offering (v. 24). If an individual sinned, the sin offering was a less valuable female goat (v. 27). The same rules applied to native-born Israelites and aliens alike: the sins of all people, whether Israelite by birth or by choice, could only be dealt with in one way—through the shedding of blood.

This remains the case for us, which is why the cross was necessary for our salvation. God couldn't simply pretend that our sins didn't exist or didn't really matter. Fellowship with a holy God is only possible if our sins are atoned for, and without the shedding of blood there is no remission of sins (Hebrews 9:22). In order for us to be reconciled to God, therefore, the blood of a perfect sacrifice had to be offered in our place. The sin offerings of the Old Testament were pictures preparing God's people for the cross. All of the blood of bulls and goats shed under the old covenant pointed forward to that final perfect sacrifice by which Jesus atoned once and for all for the sins of all of his people.

Not all sins could be atoned for, however. The sacrificial system only covered "unintentional" or inadvertent sins (vv. 22, 27). In one sense, of course, many of these sins were not exactly unintentional. Sin is rarely completely devoid of intent: at some level, we invariably know that what we are doing is wrong. Yet there was a distinction made in the Old Testament between sins that were inadvertent and sins that were defiant (v. 30). This is much like the difference that we recognize between murder and manslaughter. If you are convicted of manslaughter, you are responsible for the death of another human being. Perhaps you drove your car carelessly or too fast or you tossed a rock off a high building that then killed someone on the ground: you have done wrong, and you are culpable for it, but you didn't set out to kill someone. Your responsibility is not the same as that of a man who deliberately lay in wait in order to run over his enemy or a woman who planned and schemed how to poison her husband. That is murder. In our legal system, we even distinguish between premeditated murder and crimes of passion: in the latter, you may have meant to kill the person in the heat of the moment, but at least you didn't plan to do so ahead of time. You were in the grip of a kind of temporary insanity.

It is the same way with sin. Much of our sin falls either under the category of carelessness or of acts of passion. In most cases we didn't set out with the intent of saying a cruel word or hitting that annoying person or thinking proud and lustful thoughts. In one sense, "it just happened." It was a careless act of thoughtlessness. Other sins could be characterized as "temporary spiritual insanity." These sins flow out of the war that goes on inside us between our sinful natures and our transformed hearts. This is the conflict that Paul describes in Romans 7, where we see that we find ourselves doing what we do not want to do because of the continuing power of the sinful nature (vv. 15-17). As long as we continue to inhabit our earthly bodies we find ourselves repeatedly overpowered by our sinful natures, carried away into sin. Now none of these causes of sin release us from responsibility for our actions. We are responsible for our careless thoughts and our sins of reaction, just as we would be responsible if we drove without due care and attention or in the heat of the moment picked up a baseball bat and hit someone with it. Sin is still sin, whatever its source.

Defiant Sins

Yet there are sins that fall into a different category, that of defiant sins. Defiant sins are literally in the Hebrew "sins with upraised hand." These are premeditated sins that are flaunted in the face of God. In this case persons have not fallen into sin or been overcome by sin; rather, they deliberately dived into sin and embraced it. Such persons could not have their sins forgiven through the sacrificial system because they had no desire for the relationship with God that the system was designed to restore. Until their proud defiance was broken, they could not have fellowship with God. As long as they remained in such a defiant state, they did not belong as part of God's people, and so the Israelites were instructed that such people must be cut off (v. 31). Whether native-born Israelites or aliens, they were to be removed from the people of God.[1]

What follows these regulations is a case study in just such defiant, premeditated sin. A man was found gathering wood on the Sabbath day (v. 32). This was actually a double sin: not only was gathering the wood itself work and therefore forbidden on the Lord's holy day (Exodus 35:2), but the only reason for gathering wood on the Sabbath would be in order to light a fire on the Sabbath, which was explicitly forbidden in Exodus 35:3. Thus the man was committing one sin in order to be able to commit another—a defiant, premeditated flaunting of God's commandments. When Moses sought the Lord's guidance as to what should be done with this man, the answer was definitive: he must die. The whole community had to take him outside the camp, symbolizing his exclusion from the community, and there stone him to death (vv. 35, 36).

Questions Ancient and Modern

This incident raises two questions that we need to address, one modern and one ancient. The concern that this passages raises in the minds of modern readers is this: Isn't stoning a rather harsh punishment for such a trivial offense? This is a question that would probably never have occurred to the ancient audience, so it is something of a digression from the purposes of the passage; but it is a question that is pervasive enough in our context that we need to deal with it. After we've dealt with that modern question, we can return to the real question that this passage raised in the ancient context and continues to raise for us.

First, though, why should a man be stoned to death simply because he gathered a few sticks on the Sabbath? Is that a fair punishment for such an offense? The answer to that question is to recognize the attitude that lay behind the sin. It is not coincidental that this case study immediately follows the legislation on defiant sin. In one sense we could say that the man wasn't put to death for gathering the sticks: he was put to death because of his flagrant defiance of God. He knew the law that forbade working on the Sabbath (Exodus 35:2). He also knew the law that said he shouldn't kindle a fire on the Sabbath (Exodus 35:3). Meanwhile, he was camping in the wilderness in the middle of approximately two million people. Was it likely that no one would have seen the smoke from his fire once he had kindled it? That is hardly plausible. More likely, he brazenly went out in front of everyone and broke God's Law defiantly. Such defiance had to be dealt with or the whole community would be compromised.

Within our legal system the concept of "contempt of court" has a similar function. You won't typically be put in prison for parking in the wrong place. Yet if you repeatedly fail to respond to a citation to appear in court because of that parking ticket, the judge can and will put you in jail. Furthermore, if you continue to defy the system, he has the power to keep you in prison indefinitely. You cannot be put in prison for life for a parking offense, but you can be for ongoing contempt of court related to that initial offense. If the courts failed to respond severely to such contempt, the whole legal system would be endangered.

It is the same way with sin. There is no such thing as a trivial sin. Some sins may seem less severe than others. It may look on the surface as if swearing and coveting are less serious than murder and adultery. But the heart attitude is what counts. All sin is, on one level or another, an expression of cosmic rebellion against our Creator. It is a more or less deliberate turning of our backs on the one who made us for fellowship with him. That is why the wages of all sin is death, as Romans 6:23 reminds us. If we turn our backs on God in sin, it is fitting that he should turn his back on us. That is what we deserve every time we sin, and if he carries out that sentence upon us, it will mean our eternal death. All sin is therefore serious, but defiant sin is especially so. If we willfully and persistently turn our backs on God, how shall the relationship be restored? How can there be anything in store other than the death we have chosen for ourselves?

This highlights the importance of repentance as the pathway to forgiveness. Defiant sin necessarily leads to destruction, whether the sin is murder or self-centeredness. In repentance, on the other hand, we agree with God that our sin is offensive and wrong, and we humbly plead for his forgiveness. A repentant and contrite spirit is the exact opposite of a proud and defiant heart, and therefore when we approach God with such a spirit, we find him more than ready to forgive even the most heinous offense. King David committed adultery and arranged for the murder of Uriah, but when he came before God with a broken and contrite heart, he found forgiveness and acceptance (Psalm 51:17). A gross sinner who repents is welcomed in, while others who have committed apparently much less serious crimes but have hardened their hearts against God and remained defiant are cut off forever. There is no sacrifice possible to atone for such a spirit.

Excommunication and the Cross

This is why the new-covenant equivalent of the penalty of cutting off—excommunication—is only ever truly administered for the sin of defiance. The pattern given by Jesus in Matthew 18 shows this clearly. If there is sin within the church, the first step should be to try to resolve it privately (v. 15). If private attempts to resolve the issue fail, others should be brought in to help find a resolution (v. 16). If that also fails, the matter is to be brought before the leadership of the whole church (v. 17). Ultimately, if the person will not listen to the testimony of the church, then there is no alternative but for him to be excluded from the covenant community and treated as a pagan or a tax collector (v. 17).[2] The occasioning sin that leads to the person being confronted in the first place may be large or small, but if there is true repentance, excommunication is not necessary. The only sin that inevitably leads to excommunication is persistent defiance.

This now brings us back to the real question this passage poses to all readers, ancient and modern, which is this: if defiant sins deserve exclusion from the community and death, how could Israel survive? What could be more defiant and willful than listening to the unbelieving report of the ten-man majority and spurning the faithful report of Joshua and Caleb (14:1-4)? What could constitute a clearer turning of their backs upon God than the community's attempt to conquer the land in their own strength after God had judged them and sent them back to the wilderness (14:39-45)? If God's judgment on the Sabbath-breaker was exclusion and death, how could Israel live? Theirs was not the inadvertent sin of an individual, or even of the whole community, for which the death of a mere goat might atone. What sacrifice could be sufficient to atone for their sin and give them a future in God's plan?

The answer lies in the greater sacrifice that God would offer at the cross, the sacrifice to which all of the other sacrifices pointed, so that through his covenant faithfulness, his original purposes for his people would conquer. The first generation would indeed experience exclusion from the land and death in the wilderness; yet God's irresistible grace could not be overcome by their sin. Ultimately, his purpose of blessing for his people must be accomplished

The Tassels: Signs of Covenant Faithfulness

That covenant faithfulness brings us to the tassels. The Lord instructed Israel through Moses that from now on all Israelites should have tassels on the corner of their garments, tassels that must contain a single blue (literally, "violet") thread (v. 38). At first sight this commandment may seem like a colossal *non sequitur*, entirely unrelated to what has gone before. Yet in fact it is an exposition of the third aspect of God's character to which Moses made reference in his prayer of intercession (14:19): God's covenant love (*ḥesed*). At that time Moses confessed that the Lord is a God of mercy and of justice, and he appealed to the Lord's covenant love as the foundation for his request that God would forgive his people's sin and remain in relationship with them (14:18, 19). So also here, having given the Lord's people laws that demonstrate his mercy (15:1-21) and his justice (vv. 22-36), the final commandment in this section speaks of the Lord's covenant faithfulness. The tassels were designed to remind Israel who they were by God's grace, which in turn was the foundation for their call to obedience.

The key to understanding the tassels lies in the location of the tassels and the single blue thread that each one contained. In the ancient world, the hem of someone's garment was regarded as an extension of the person.[3] We read in 1 Samuel that David crept up on King Saul while he was relieving himself in a cave and cut off the hem of Saul's cloak (24:4). Afterward he was remorseful over what he had done. Why? Was it merely that he had spoiled Saul's clothes? On the contrary, it was a much more symbolic act than that: in cutting the hem of his garment, he had effectively assaulted Saul himself because the hem was part of his identity (v. 6). In some ancient cultures, a man could divorce his wife by cutting off the hem of her robe, symbolically turning her loose, while in others an imprint of the hem served as a personal signature. Putting the tassels on the hem of the robe was thus not merely a matter of decoration. In that location, the tassels expressed something fundamental about the Israelites' identity.

Clothing and Identity

This use of clothing to convey identity is familiar to our experience also. In Britain, football fans identify themselves as devotees of their favorite team in numerous ways, but by far the most common way is by wearing a scarf in the team colors. Scarves form a cheap and readily identifiable marker of football identity. In fact, for that very reason it is not safe to wear certain colors of scarf in rival areas of big cities on game days. The same is true for gangs in the larger cities in the United States. Certain colors are regularly outlawed in some public schools because of their use in identifying people as belonging to one gang or another. In our culture we may not wear tassels, but we still have ways of marking out who we are by what we wear.

The key element within each of these tassels was also a color, a single violet thread. Violet dye was phenomenally expensive in the ancient world since it came from tiny sea snails that had to be harvested by hand, each of which only produced a single drop of dye.[4] The color violet therefore came to symbolize wealth and nobility in society at large. Even more significantly, violet was the most sacred color in the tabernacle (see the discussion on 4:6, 7). The single violet thread in the midst of the tassel thus symbolized Israel's identity as a royal priesthood. Requiring a single thread made it an affordable badge for everyone to wear, even the poorest members of society. All the Israelites would be reminded by their tassels to live according to the sanctity and nobility of their calling.

In particular, the tassels served as a reminder of two things. In the first place, they reminded the Israelites who they were by God's overwhelming grace. They were the people of the Lord, the people he had redeemed from Egypt. He had redeemed them so that they might have an ongoing relationship with him: neither the power of Egypt nor their stubborn, defiant rebellion could compromise that purpose (v. 41). Secondly, though, it reminded the Israelites of the obligations that went with their calling. They were redeemed from Egypt to be a holy nation and a royal priesthood. God brought them out of bondage so that they might obey his commands and be consecrated to their God, instead of going after the lusts of their own hearts and eyes (vv. 39, 40).

In some ways, with this combined emphasis on their privilege and responsibility, the requirement to wear the tassels sums up the thrust of the whole chapter. God redeemed Israel by his grace for relationship with him; yet that did not now leave them free to do whatever they wanted to do. Such "freedom" would actually merely be a different kind of bondage, prostituting themselves to their own lusts (v. 39). A relationship with God by grace does not eliminate the need for obedience but rather forms the foundation for it. The God who commands us is the same God who first delivered us from bondage; so we know that his purposes in commanding us are good. In fact, he delivered us from our former bondage to sin so we could experience the true freedom that comes as we obey his commandments and law. His law turns out to be the path to true liberty.

This is exactly what Israel failed to see in Numbers 13, 14. Instead of following God's commands and trusting his good purposes for them, they chose their own path, which led not to freedom but to death. God's path is the way to life and happiness, even though it may seem circumscribed with all kinds of regulations and limitations. Tassels, sacrifices, and Sabbath-keeping seem, to the natural mind, to be narrow and restrictive; yet they are actually the way to fulfilling the goal for which we were created—fellowship with God.

New-Covenant Obligations

So what are the obligations that God places on us in the new covenant, now that we are no longer under law but under grace? We don't have to bring goats for sin offerings anymore because the definitive sin offering has already been presented. Jesus Christ took his own blood into the heavenly Holy of Holies and presented it there to make atonement for all of the sins of his people (Hebrews 9:24-28). God's irresistible grace has completely accomplished our salvation. Yet that does not mean that we have nothing to give in return. Our response to that sacrifice is to "continually offer up a sacrifice of praise to God, that is, the fruit of lips that acknowledge his name" (Hebrews 13:15). It is "to share what you have, for such sacrifices are pleasing to God" (Hebrews 13:16). It is "to present your bodies as a living sacrifice, holy and acceptable to God" (Romans 12:1). Those are all-embracing demands: hearts that continually worship God, hands that share everything we have with others, and bodies that are pure and holy, completely given over to God's service.

Fulfilling these obligations will take more than Sunday-only religion: to give God these things will fill our Sabbaths so full that one day is not sufficient to contain them, and they will spill over into the rest of our week. To those around us, these demands may seem narrow and restrictive. A life full of worship, generous giving, and holy purity is not most people's idea of fun. To many, it has all the attraction of a smoke-free day to a nicotine addict. Yet if you understand the salvation that God has wrought for you in Christ and know that you were once dead in your transgressions and sins but have now been made alive by grace, you will understand that this is real life. This is what you were made for: a relationship with the holy Creator God of the entire cosmos.

Baptism: A Sign of God's Covenant Faithfulness

How can we remind ourselves of these realities? We don't wear violet tassels on our robes. Some may have fish symbols on the back of their cars or wear crosses around their necks, but neither of these is ordained by God. That doesn't necessarily make them sinful, but it does highlight the difference between such identity tags and the Israelite tassels. What is the required marker that God has placed on each one of his new-covenant people? Surely it is the water of baptism. Although not a visible mark in the way that the tassels were, it nonetheless communicates the same reality. It declares that we were called out of the world by God's irresistible grace and marked out as belonging to him, children of the King. We have been marked with a symbol of purity—clean water—as a sign of our priestly calling. It identifies us as being united to Christ in his death and resurrection and therefore even now enthroned with him in the heavenly realms. The water was poured out upon us as a symbol of God's pouring out the Holy Spirit into our hearts, turning loose his sanctifying power within us, making us saints. Our baptism is thus what identifies us as part of God's new-covenant kingdom of priests (1 Peter 2:9).

I suggest that most of us don't think nearly often enough about our baptism. Typically we view it as a long-past event without much significance in our present lives. Yet it is what marks us in our identity as belonging to the people of God. The old Puritans, who were wiser than us in so many things, spoke often about "improving your baptism." If we would think about our baptism daily, it would remind us to be thankful for the relationship we have with God by his grace and to be careful to live a life worthy of the calling we have received. If we would talk to our children regularly about their baptism, it would open up the door each time to speak to them of their need of Christ and the way in which the gospel meets all of their deepest needs, as well as their obligation to pursue obedient living. Baptism reminds them and us that the way to life is not through following our own wisdom but in submitting ourselves joyfully to the commandments of God, which bring true freedom. It reminds us that real life comes through dying to ourselves and rising to a new, holy life in Christ.

The hymn-writer declared, "Redeemed, how I love to proclaim it!" Perhaps that could also read, "Baptized, how I love to proclaim it!" What could be more incredible than God's persistent grace that takes families of stubborn, defiant sinners like you and me and turns them into holy saints? What could be more amazing than the work of God's Spirit that brings us into a daily relationship with him? Remind yourself daily, therefore, of the reality of your baptism and what it symbolizes. Recall daily the grace you have received and the wisdom of obedience to God's Word. Rejoice daily in the high calling you have received as part of his kingdom of priests. Resolve daily to live a life worthy of that calling, a life of purity and praise.

20

The Southside Rebellion

NUMBERS 16:1-40

DISTRUST OF THOSE WHO ARE IN CHARGE is a widespread phenomenon. It is easy to stir up dissension against those in authority, especially when life is difficult and progress is slow. The fans of professional sports teams with losing records often want the managers fired. Aspiring politicians regularly harp on economic difficulties as they attempt to unseat the incumbent. Sometimes the criticism goes deeper and seeks to overturn the existing order completely and replace it with a new and different authority structure. There are indeed times when a change in personnel or the system is justified. Many such revolts, however, are generated by the wrong motivations and aimed at the wrong targets.

Korah's Complaint

Numbers 16 shows us just such a revolt against the leadership in Israel. It was a revolt that combined together two distinct groups of people. On the one hand there was a group made up of Korah and the Levites, while on the other were Dathan and Abiram, who were Reubenites, along with 250 chiefs of the community (vv. 1, 2). Each of these groups had its own distinct target within the authority structures of Israel. Korah and the Levites challenged the religious leadership of Aaron, while Dathan and Abiram with their followers assaulted the civil leadership of Moses. It is not perhaps coincidental that these two groups rebelled together because the Kohathite Levites, from whom Korah came, camped to the south of the tabernacle, on the same side as the Reubenites (2:10; 3:29). We could therefore call this incident "The Southside Rebellion."

The first volley in the assault came from Korah and the Levites. They

said to Moses and Aaron: "You have gone too far! For all in the congregation are holy, every one of them, and the LORD is among them. Why then do
you exalt yourselves above the assembly of the LORD? (v. 3). They sound
thoroughly modern in their denunciation of the narrowness of Moses' religion. You can almost hear them say, "I like to think of God as a kind and
welcoming God, whom anyone can approach at any time." However, their
argument here is a classic case of a false conclusion constructed on a true
premise. It was certainly true that the whole community of Israel was holy:
God had called them to be "a kingdom of priests" (Exodus 19:6). It was also
true that the Lord was with the Israelites: he had promised to dwell in the
midst of them and be their God (Exodus 29:45). In fact, those were precisely
the points that the Lord himself had underlined in the regulations concerning tassels at the end of the previous chapter. The tassels were designed
to remind each Israelite of their holy status and calling as part of a nation
of priests, consecrated to God (15:40) and of his commitment to be present with them (15:41). Yet that high calling on the life of every Israelite
did not mean religious egalitarianism, in which everyone had precisely the
same status and responsibility before the Lord. There was still an authority
structure set in place by God, in which those he had chosen and called had
leadership positions.

The truth that a common high calling from God does not eliminate dis-
tinctions within society should not have come as a surprise to the wilderness
people of God. They should have remembered the intense care with which
the Lord arranged their stations around the tabernacle in the opening four
chapters of the book of Numbers. There the Lord assigned each tribe and
family to a particular place in his economy. Some were assigned places of
greater honor (and greater responsibility) in his service, while others had
lesser roles. Those places did not necessarily reflect natural precedence or
personal giftedness. In some cases, as we saw, past sin or faithfulness had
an ongoing impact on a family's destiny, and yet the decisive feature in
every case was the Lord's will. The Lord assigned to all their place in his
community, and to rebel against that structure was to rebel against the Lord.

The rebellion in Numbers 16 is exactly that—a frontal assault on the
order established by God at the time of the census. That becomes clear
when you look more closely at those taking part. The ranks of those rebelling are drawn from the first of the Levites to be counted, the Kohathites
(4:1-3), the first of the people to be counted—the Reubenites (1:20, 21),
and those who were doing the counting—the leaders of the community
(nᵉśîê hāēdâ; 4:34). What is particularly striking about this group is that the
rebellion does not come from the lowest rungs of Israelite society but from
the higher rungs. Bearing in mind that status around the tabernacle goes
downward as you travel clockwise, from east to south to west to north, it is

noteworthy that this is not a northside but a southside rebellion. It is not those at the bottom of the heap who rebel against God's order but those who are close to the top and who think they ought themselves to be at the top. This marks an escalation from the earlier grumbling that originated among the marginal riff-raff (11:4): now grumbling has infected the center of the camp.[1]

This fact further highlights the deceptive agenda in Korah's speech. As a southsider, part of the leading clan of the Levites, he didn't really want all social order eliminated: he would actually have had more to lose than most Israelites from such an egalitarian leveling. While declaring all Israelites equally sacred before the Lord, what he really wanted was access for himself to the group that would be above the rest, the priesthood (16:10). Likewise, the Reubenites held a privileged place in the Israelite community; yet that was not enough for them. It still rankled them that their premier place as first-born of Jacob's sons had been stripped away because of Reuben's sins. Like the pigs in George Orwell's novel *Animal Farm*, the southsiders wanted a society in which everyone was equal, with some people (themselves) being "more equal" than others.

Moses' Response

Moses' response to this rebellion was to fall down on his face, a posture of submission before the Lord and of appeal for divine assistance.[2] This is how Moses responded to several of Israel's rebellions in the book of Numbers (14:5; 16:4; 20:6), which itself was a mark of his meekness. Even when he himself was under attack, he didn't immediately lash out at those responsible but instead first took his concerns to the Lord. This is a model for all leaders who find themselves under attack. Such assaults are an almost inevitable part of ministry, as people who are disgruntled with the leadership attack it verbally and in written form. It is easy to respond in similar fashion, but that simply escalates the conflict. It is far better to take the complaints before the Lord and fall down on your face before him. Sometimes there will be sufficient truth behind the allegations, however exaggerated their tone, that repentance on the part of the leaders will be necessary. At other times the allegations will be completely unfounded, but even then it is best to place the matter in the Lord's hands rather than seeking to respond on our own.

When Moses did respond, it was with a challenge to Korah to put his claims to the test and let the Lord demonstrate whom he had chosen to draw near to him as a priest. Korah and his followers were instructed to come before the Lord the next day with incense burners and fire, and then the Lord would show everyone who his chosen priest was (vv. 6, 7). The form of the test should have sobered Korah and his followers, for it should have reminded them of the fate of Nadab and Abihu. Those sons of Aaron were legitimate priests who were allowed to burn incense before the Lord, yet they made the mistake of being careless about where the fire to ignite the incense came from. They used unauthorized fire—fire that was not from the altar—and they paid for their mistake with their lives (Leviticus 10:1-3). If that was God's attitude to those who were authorized to approach him when they were careless, what will happen to those who approach him presumptuously? How will they escape? Their ultimate fate, being consumed by fire from the Lord (16:35), should be no surprise to those who have followed Israel's story carefully thus far.

Moses also uncovered the true nature of the target of their rebellion: it was not Aaron but the Lord himself they were challenging (v. 11). As Levites, the Lord had assigned them a position of honor and responsibility, doing the work of the tabernacle and ministering among the community (v. 9). Yet because they were not content with the place they had been assigned, Korah and his followers were seeking a place they had not been assigned—namely, the priesthood.

The Desire for Leadership

The desire for a leadership position can sometimes be a dangerous thing. The humorist Douglas Adams observed in *The Hitchhiker's Guide to the Galaxy*, "Anyone who is capable of getting themselves made president should on no account be allowed to do the job." In other words, those who desire most intensely the ability to wield power are also the most likely not to wield it well. This can also be true in the church. Some people aspire to positions of authority in order to lord it over others, not so they can serve others. If Korah's and the Levites' desire had simply been to serve the Lord and his people, their present position would have given them plenty of opportunities to do so. They didn't need to be priests to be servants. However, they thought that the position of the priests had more prestige and standing than theirs did (not to mention more income), and so they coveted it. In the process, though, they were rebelling not just against Aaron and the other priests but against the Lord who had assigned Aaron and his family to that position.

The fact that there is an authority structure set in place by God is true in his New Testament people as well as in Old Testament Israel. God promised his people in Jeremiah 3:15 that in the days to come, "I will give you shepherds after my own heart, who will lead you with knowledge and understanding." This promise has been fulfilled in the church in the provision of elders to lead God's people as shepherds. So in 1 Peter 5:2, 3, Peter appealed to the elders of the flock to which he was writing that they should "Be shepherds of God's flock that is under your care . . . not lording it over those entrusted to you, but being examples to the flock" (NIV). Likewise, Paul charged the Ephesian elders, "Pay careful attention to yourselves and to all the flock, in which the Holy Spirit has made you overseers, to care for the church of God, which he obtained with his own blood" (Acts 20:28). God has thus appointed a structure in the church, with leaders and followers; the church is not a democracy. The elders are to be leaders in the church, acting as shepherds of his flock. They are to guide and direct the flock from the front, leading the way rather than lording it over the sheep in their common calling as disciples of Jesus.

If this is true, then we need to be similarly careful about those who desire leadership positions in the church. It is certainly not wrong to aspire to lead God's people. In fact, Paul commends just such a desire in 1 Timothy 3:1. Yet those who desire to lead should be examined and tested, not just so their abilities and gifts can be discerned, but so others can discern as far as possible their hearts and motives. Character is far more crucial than knowledge or gifting, important though those are. Do such persons simply long for the prestige of the title of elder or pastor, or do they have a genuine desire to serve God and his people? Have they demonstrated that servant attitude already, doing the work of ministry without the title? Are they as ready and eager to do the most humble aspects of the work of the church—setting up and taking down chairs, serving refreshments, visiting the sick and elderly—as they are for positions in the public eye? Finally and most profoundly, is the mark of God's call to ministry evident in their lives, so that God's people have been convinced they fit the Biblical qualifications? It is a fearful responsibility to lead God's people, and not one to be taken up lightly.

Dathan and Abiram's Complaint

The second complaint came from Dathan and Abiram and was directed against Moses himself. They refused to meet with Moses and flung his own words back in his face. Moses had said to Korah in essence, "Isn't it enough that God gave you Levites the work of the tabernacle?" (v. 9). Dathan and Abiram said to Moses, "Is it a small thing that you have brought us up out of a land flowing with milk and honey, to kill us in the wilderness?" (v. 13). The heart of their complaint was that Moses had not delivered what he promised. Instead of bringing them into a land flowing with milk and honey, the land of Canaan, they argued, he had brought them into a wilderness that made the land they left, Egypt, seem like a land of milk and honey (vv. 13, 14). They asked, "Will you put out the eyes of these men?" (v. 14), which is an idiomatic way of saying, "Can you make us blind to the realities we see around us?"[3] In other words, "You may have tricked everyone else into blindly following you, but we see clearly what you have done." They were arguing that Moses had deliberately deceived the people for his own ends.

Dathan and Abiram were people who were disappointed in God. Their experience of his way had not lived up to their expectations, and so they took their disappointment out on the leaders of God's people. Once again, even though Moses was their ostensible target, it was the Lord against whom they were really in rebellion. The Lord, not Moses, was the one who brought them out of Egypt. He was the one who made the promise to give them a land flowing with milk and honey, a promise that could have been fulfilled by now were it not for the unbelief of the people. The reason their present circumstances were so dire was the result of their own sin, not the failure of Moses or of the Lord. Nor had Moses himself profited from his position: he had not taken anyone's donkey,[4] nor had he wronged anyone in any other way (v. 15). Their accusation was without foundation.

In fact, even though they rebelled together, the charges leveled by Dathan and Abiram were fundamentally different and more sinister than those brought by Korah and the Levites. Korah's complaint at least presupposed the existence of the Lord and sought higher status within the covenant community. Dathan and Abiram, on the other hand, made no reference to the Lord in their complaint. In fact, they assumed the nonexistence of the Lord, or at least his practical irrelevance.[5] They assumed that Moses was the key figure, a magician who had made startling claims but then was unable to deliver the impressive trick he had promised. While Korah assumed that leadership was all about status and privilege, Dathan and Abiram declared that it was about power and pragmatic effectiveness. None of them understood Biblical leadership, which is about divine calling to service.

The same misunderstandings often rear their heads in the contemporary church. Some want leadership in the church for the prestige it brings, and some are quick to criticize if results seem less impressive than another church down the road. Biblical leaders, however, serve because God has called them to that position and recognize that sometimes even those whom God has called may not see dramatic visible results. The prophet Isaiah had as clear a call to preach from the Lord as possible, yet in the very next breath he was informed that few would respond to his ministry (Isaiah 6:9, 10). Pragmatic thinking will often find godly leadership unimpressive. This should not surprise us or dishearten us, for we follow the way of the cross, in which God's power is made all the more evident by the personal weakness of those whom God has chosen as his leaders (see 2 Corinthians 4:1-11). Our shortcomings make the glory of God's grace shine out all the more clearly.

God's Response

The result of the opposition of the southsiders was to bring the whole assembly of God's people into danger. Korah had claimed that every one of the Israelites was holy and could approach the presence of the Lord. Yet the Lord himself had said that anyone apart from Moses and the priestly tribe of Aaron who approached him would be put to death (3:38). Those who believed Korah's words would inevitably find death instead of the freedom that he claimed to bring. That is always the way it is with sin: it offers freedom to those who are "liberated" from God's Law, but in the end all it delivers is death. At first it seemed that the death penalty would be exacted on the entire assembly, but then Moses and Aaron fell facedown once more before the Lord and interceded for them (v. 22). They asked the Lord, "shall one man sin, and will you be angry with all the congregation?" They asked the Lord for an opportunity for the people to distance themselves and their families from the rebellions of Korah, Dathan, and Abiram.

That is exactly what they received. The Lord instructed the assembly to move away from the southsiders' camp (v. 24). Those who distanced themselves from this rebellious spirit would live, while those who identified themselves with the rebels would die, along with their families. Moses warned the people that the earth would swallow up Dathan, Abiram, and Korah, along with their wives and their children and their little ones (vv. 23-27). That was exactly what transpired (vv. 31-33). The Lord demonstrated graphically that he is neither dead nor irrelevant but is capable of bringing those who show him contempt into judgment (v. 30).

Covenantal Responsibility

This form of judgment also demonstrates the principle of covenantal responsibility, whereby the sins of the family head are charged also to his children. Here the sins of Korah, Dathan, and Abiram had fatal implications not just for themselves but for their whole families, from infants on up (v. 32). There was no "age of accountability" below which the children were spared. All those who were in the families of Korah, Dathan, and Abiram were judged together and died together. They paid the penalty for the defiant sin of their family head. Yet covenantal responsibility flows in a positive direction as well, conveying life as well as death. The infants of the other families camping nearby were not consulted by their parents before being dragged away; yet they were brought to safety through their parents' actions.

The covenantal nature of this separation between life and death is itself a small-scale reenactment of the grand covenantal separation that will take place on the last day. There will be only two family groups in that final judgment—those who are in Adam and those who are in Christ. Those in Adam, who have only been born once, have received his sinful nature and the condemnation that accompanies it (Romans 5:12-14). They are destined for death because of Adam's rebellion, which they have themselves reenacted in their own lives from the moment of birth onward. However, those who have been born a second time by the Spirit of God are in Christ and receive from him his perfect nature and the justification that accompanies it (Romans 5:18, 19).

What is more, the promise of this life-giving Spirit is given covenantally, not just to believers but to believers and their children (Acts 2:39). When we baptize our children, we are, as it were, dragging them away from the rebellion of Korah and his followers onto safer ground. We are signing and sealing to them the covenant of grace, warning them of the danger that hangs over all who are in Adam and pointing them to the precious promises of life in Christ. We are telling them that these promises are made to them and are theirs as they trust Christ and submit their hearts to him.

What is more, in the mercy of God the negative covenantal connection is not unbreakable. Even though Korah and his family were swallowed alive and 250 of his followers were burned up by fire from the Lord, not all of Korah's descendants perished. In Numbers 26, when the second census is taken, it becomes clear that even though Dathan and Abiram were completely cut off and left without descendants, this was not the case for the line of Korah (vv. 9-11). How can this be? The only explanation for this phenomenon is that some of Korah's family broke out of their natural covenant loyalty to their father and crossed over to the other side. They joined the rest of the community in leaving the tents of Korah, and so they lived when the rest of their kinfolk died. It is the same way with you: even if you do not have believing parents or family members, there is no reason why you should die with Adam. The grace of God is extended to you too, summoning you to come out from those who are condemned to eternal death. The doorway to life is open to you too in Christ: come into his family, receive his righteousness, and you too will live.

God's Leaders Confirmed

If the swallowing alive of Dathan and Abiram and their families was visible disproof of their claim that the Lord was either dead or irrelevant, then the fire from the tabernacle that consumed Korah's 250 priestly pretenders was visible disproof of Korah's claim of priestly equality (v. 35). He had said that all Israel was holy and could safely approach the Lord; yet when the claim was tested, it was found false. Only those whom God had chosen could approach him safely; all others would die, just as he had warned them earlier (3:10, 38). The remains of the bronze censers with which they had tried to offer incense were hammered into an overlay for the altar of sacrifice as a permanent reminder of this state of affairs (v. 39). Only the one whom God had chosen could draw near to him. There is no truth in the claim that all roads lead to God. Apart from the one he has chosen, all roads lead to a consuming fire.

The conclusion of the passage shows us clearly the falsehood of the charges against Moses and Aaron. Far from being just like everyone else, Aaron was indeed distinct from the community, called by God to a special role, not so he could lord it over the community but so he could serve. As priest he was the mediator for all, not their master. Far from bringing the community from the land of life to death, Moses was the one who repeatedly saved the community from the judgment of God's wrath. Far from being an ineffective and irrelevant deity, the Lord was the one who could and would carry out his judgments of death on those who showed contempt for him. Yet at the same time he is also a gracious God who spared the undeserving, or the whole community would long since have been terminated. Far from people needing to have their eyes blinded to believe the truth of these things, you would have had to be blind not to recognize them. God's sovereignty was vindicated, and the leaders he chose were affirmed.

A Better Mediator

Yet Israel needed a better leader than Moses and a more powerful mediator than Aaron. Moses was in the end unable to bring his people into the Promised Land because he had sins of his own. Aaron could stand before the Lord and intercede, but he could not bring spiritually defiled people into God's life-giving presence. All the bulls and goats he offered and all the incense he burned could not effect the radical change they needed in their standing before God. The formula that Paul pronounces in 1 Corinthians is not, "As in Adam all die, so in Moses and Aaron all will be made alive" (see 15:22). The leadership of Moses and Aaron points us beyond themselves to the one who was yet to come.

Jesus took upon himself all of the guilt that we inherited from Adam, along with that which flows from our own sins. As Paul put it in Romans 5, through the disobedience of one man, Adam, sin first entered the world, and along with sin came death (v. 12). But now through the obedience of Jesus Christ, the second Adam, God's gracious gift of life has come into the world (Romans 5:15-17). On the cross Jesus, the holy one, experienced the burning fire of God's wrath against all that is unholy. The one who of all people had the most right to draw near to God met the fate of those who are by nature excluded from God's presence. Death swallowed him up as he descended into the grip of the tomb for three days. In fact, we could say that the fate that the rebellious sinners experienced in Numbers 16 was his fate, even though Jesus had not rebelled as they did.

Why should holy Jesus share the fate of the unholy at the cross? The reason is simple. He covenantally identified himself with sinners, sharing their destiny so that they might by grace share the destiny that he had merited through his perfect obedience. His death was the fate I deserved for my rebellious heart. He took on himself my judgment, and he transferred to me the vindication he had earned. He went down to the dead, so that in him I might ultimately ascend to the true promised land of milk and honey, Heaven itself. If it were true that all are equally holy and can approach God in themselves, why would the death of Jesus be necessary? The cross would have been a wasteful tragedy. Yet if his death is absolutely necessary for us to be made holy, how could any of us presume to approach God by any other way than through his blood?

The Answer for Jealousy and Pragmatism

Since God has loved us and gave himself for us, how then can we rebel against the leaders whom God has appointed and thus show contempt for him? Are you jealous of the positions others have in the church? The cross is the answer for our jealousy that others have been given gifts and positions in Christ's church that we have not. At the cross Jesus purchased us to be his servants, giving him the absolute prerogative to assign us our places in his kingdom, be they small or great. As we contemplate the cost of the cross, we recognize that great suffering and responsibility often goes hand in hand with great privilege in God's kingdom. There is therefore reason to thank God if he has given us a less challenging and exalted calling than he has given to others. It is our glory to be found obediently doing what God called us to do, whether that task is small or great.

The cross is also the answer to our doubts about the Lord's presence and effectiveness in our lives. Like Dathan and Abiram, we may sometimes question the circumstances in which we find ourselves. We perhaps expected greater successes or more comfortable circumstances, and so we ask, "What is life doing with me? Why is my situation so much worse than it used to be or than I think it ought to be?"

These questions are not wrong in themselves, but they can easily spill over into an angry resentment toward God and those he has set in authority over us. The reality is that in whatever circumstances we find ourselves, God is neither dead nor absent. Life is not doing anything with us; it is the sovereign God who is doing something with us. The cross reminds us that whatever the difficulties of our present situation, God does care about us. Whatever people may have done to us, God is still in control.

When we seek to discern in the light of the cross what God is doing in and with us in the midst of many challenges and disappointments, our grumbling hearts are reminded that these circumstances too are part of his perfect sanctifying program for us. The Lord knows our strengths, and he knows our weaknesses. He knows the means by which he will ultimately present us to himself as part of his spotless church. In the meantime it is our glory to submit to his direction and leading, through those who in his wisdom he has placed over us, whether the paths he leads us along pass through sunny meadows or steep and winding trails. In the light of the cross we may be confident that in the end he will indeed bring us to the place he has prepared for us, where all of our disappointments will be over, transformed by the joy of his presence.

21

The End of Grumbling

NUMBERS 16:41—17:13

SOME THINGS NEVER SEEM TO END. A Wagnerian opera, for example, seems to go on and on. So does a root canal visit to the dentist, or a losing season for your favorite sports team. To that list of seemingly endless trials, we may add the sin of grumbling. In an earlier study we noticed that grumbling is a contagious sickness that spreads from one person to the next. Here we may add that grumbling is a chronic sickness: it is habit-forming and addictive. Once started, if left to itself, grumbling just goes on and on. In C. S. Lewis's novel *The Great Divorce*, he imagines a group of inhabitants from Hell on a coach trip to visit the outskirts of Heaven. One of the memorable characters he describes is a woman who started out as a grumbler and ended up as a mere grumble. Lewis's guide on the tour, George MacDonald, says of this phenomenon:

> It begins with a grumbling mood, and yourself still distinct from it: perhaps criticizing it. And yourself, in a dark hour may will that mood, embrace it. Ye can repent and come out of it again. But there may come a day when you can do that no longer. Then there will be no more you left to criticise the mood, nor even to enjoy it, but just the grumble itself going on forever like a machine.[1]

We all know that to be true from our own experience, don't we? Grumbling has enormous capacity to capture us in its power. How then can we cure grumbling? How can we finally break its power and emerge from its grip? You might think that simply exposing the truth would do the trick. If so, then you need to think again. In Numbers 16 we saw those who brought a complaint against Moses' and Aaron's leadership incinerated by fire from the

Lord and swallowed alive by the ground. You would imagine that such a visible demonstration of the Lord's power in support of Moses and Aaron would bring the issue to an end. Not so. Even though the ringleaders and their families were consumed by God's judgment, their grumbling spirit lived on after them. Like spores of the anthrax virus, which have the ability to survive fire and flood, lying dormant in the soil for centuries before emerging to do their deadly work, the spores of the grumbling virus survived the dramatic judgment of God.

The Return of Grumbling

It didn't even take long for the virus of grumbling to reappear. The very next day all of the congregation of Israel grumbled against Moses and Aaron, saying, "You have killed the people of the LORD" (16:41). That short sentence incorporates both aspects of the rebellion of the last chapter. Dathan and Abiram's complaint against Moses totally denied the existence and relevance of the Lord, charging Moses personally with bringing Israel out of Egypt in order to kill them in the desert (16:13, 14). Now the whole congregation echoed that charge by blaming Moses and Aaron personally for the deaths of the conspirators (16:41).[2] Even though these deaths were the result of dramatic judgments from God—fire from Heaven and the earth swallowing people alive—the people acted as if the Lord were not really involved and the deaths were solely the result of the actions of Moses and Aaron.

Similarly, Korah's complaint against Aaron was that the whole community was equally holy and that the Lord was with them all (16:3). This claim was visibly disproved by God's removing Korah's associates from his presence once and for all (16:35). They were rejected and destroyed as unfit to burn incense before a holy God. Yet these same rebels who had died under the Lord's judgment were now described by the community as "the people of the LORD." It is as if they were asserting all over again that the whole community (even those who were destroyed for their sin) were really all one holy people. They said to the Lord in effect, "God, you have no business judging sin. Get over your narrow-mindedness and accept all of us just as we are." Doesn't that charge against God have a terribly modern ring to it? The spirit of the southside rebellion lives on in our contemporary context.

Once again, although the complaint is directed against Moses and Aaron, the people are not really grumbling against them so much as they are against the Lord. It is no surprise therefore that the Lord himself appears in the cloud over the tabernacle to answer their charge (16:42). Because it is the same rebellious charge as in the previous incident, the Lord responds in exactly the same way to Moses and Aaron: "Get away from the midst of this congregation, that I may consume them in a moment" (16:45; see 16:20).

Once again Moses and Aaron fell facedown before the Lord, interceding on behalf of the people.

Standing Between the Living and the Dead

It is at this point, however, that the story line diverges from the earlier incident. In this case, apart from Moses and Aaron, there were no innocent bystanders who risked destruction along with the sinners (16:22). The whole assembly had joined in the sin of rebellion, and therefore all had to face the Lord's judgment. There was no separation between guilty and innocent in the plague that ensued, for all were guilty. However, the community's survival was still secured because Aaron, the high priest, was an effective mediator to intercede for the sinners. The incense-offering priestly pretenders of Korah's line had been consumed by the fire of God's wrath the previous day (16:35). Their mediation could not even save themselves, let alone anyone else. Aaron, however, had been called by the Lord to this task of providing a remedy for sin and was granted the necessary access into God's presence. Thus when he intervened, offering incense and interceding on behalf of the people, the plague was restrained (16:48). Aaron took up a position between the living and the dead, and by means of the incense that he offered, he drew a line of separation between the two groups. By his faithful ministry, he prevented those who remained alive from joining those already dead.

Once again we see the covenantal dimension of salvation. The faithful acts of the one man carrying out the task appointed by God had a life-giving impact on the fate of many. All are not equally holy, equally able to approach God, as Korah had claimed. Only God's chosen priestly representative for the community, Aaron, could offer the intercession that turned away God's wrath and halted the spread of the plague (16:48).

There is a challenge here for all of us. Under the new covenant, we have all been given the task of being ambassadors for Christ, bringing the aroma of the gospel to those around us (2 Corinthians 2:14-16). We have all been commissioned to intercede on behalf of our friends and neighbors and to set before them the line between life and death. Aaron could not perform his ministry in the comfortable confines of the tabernacle, however. He had to take the incense offering out to where the people were dying for it to be effective. This was a risky endeavor for a priest, for it carried with it the potential of being contaminated by touching a corpse. Such contact would have rendered Aaron ritually unclean. Yet he took the risk of encountering death for the sake of preserving some alive. Our calling of spreading the aroma of life will similarly require us not to huddle in little circles of believers but to take the risk of going out to where the spiritually dead are. It is our task to release the gospel freely so it can do its work of separating those called to life and those left alone in death. In that way, many may be delivered from God's judgment upon sin and rebellion. We need to have a sense of the urgency of the gospel task, knowing that our friends and neighbors, our workmates and our fellow students, are quite literally dying for want of hearing the gospel.

The End of Grumbling

It is one thing to restrain[3] God's judgment, however, and quite another to bring it completely to an end. The plague may have ceased for now, as a result of Aaron's intercession, but the threat of its return still remains over the people. In fact, before the book of Numbers is over, the Lord's judgment of plague will again return to haunt the people (see 25:8, 9). What Israel needed was someone or something that would bring to an end the grumbling and rebellious spirit of the people once and for all. It is this need that is addressed in Numbers 17. On the one hand, it seems like a simple repetition of the lesson of the previous chapter, underscoring the choice of Aaron and the Levites out of all of God's people to approach and serve him. Yet the goal of this positive sign is more ambitious than simply restricting the effects of the curse. By what this sign signifies, the Lord twice declares that he will bring to an end this constant grumbling by the Israelites (17:5, 10).

The sign itself is simple enough. The leaders of all twelve of the tribes of Israel, plus the tribe of Levi, are to submit their staffs to Moses (17:6).[4] These staffs were symbols of authority and may well have been instantly identifiable by their distinctive shape or markings,[5] though each man is told to write his name on the staff as well (17:2; compare the similar sign in Ezekiel 37:16, 17). Using their staffs was by no means a random choice of personal possession, since the Hebrew word for "staff" (*matteh*) also means "tribe." These staffs thus self-evidently represented the various tribes of God's people. The Lord declared that as these staffs were placed overnight before the Lord in the tabernacle, one of these dead sticks would sprout (17:5). In fact, the fulfillment of the sign was even greater than that: Aaron's staff not only sprouted but budded, blossomed, and produced almonds (17:8). When the staffs were returned to their owners the next day, the evidence was undeniable. The Lord had definitively demonstrated whom he had chosen to serve him and stand in his presence (17:9).[6] After the tribal leaders had each reclaimed his staff, the Lord instructed Moses to keep Aaron's staff as a permanent sign to the rebellious people to put an end to their grumbling, so they would not die (17:10).

Why is God so bothered by grumbling? It seems on the face of it to be a victimless crime: when we grumble, it seems that no one is robbed or hurt. So why is grumbling a sin worthy of death? The answer is because grumbling robs and hurts God. Grumbling assaults God's glory. John Piper has rightly argued that God is most glorified when his people are most satisfied in him.[7] If that is true, though, what happens when his people are most dissatisfied with him? He is robbed of his greatest glory. When God's people grumble, they miss out on their chief end in life: as long as they are grumbling, they are neither glorifying God nor enjoying him. In addition, grumbling believers give non-Christians little reason to want to join them. When we grumble against the order that God has set in place, we are robbing God of the praise and glory that is his due, holding our hearts closed against him, and distracting others from seeing his greatness. That is why grumbling is such a serious sin.

The Staff and the Lampstand

How, though, was this simple sign in Numbers 17 supposed to put an end to their grumbling? To answer that question, we need to look at the sign more closely. It is not simply a sign that God had chosen Aaron and the Levites to serve him—it was a sign of his *purpose* in calling Aaron and the Levites to serve him. If God had wanted simply to indicate that Aaron's staff was the chosen one, he could have had it emerge and stand upright while the other staffs bowed down to it. What actually happened was that the apparently dead staff showed incredible signs of fruitfulness—sprouting, budding, blossoming, and bearing fruit overnight. Moreover, the fruit that this little tree produced was not just any fruit but specifically almonds.

Where else in Scripture do you find a miniature tree with almond flowers and buds? That is exactly what the lampstand in the tabernacle was (Exodus 25:31-40). It was a stylized tree with symbols of fruitfulness on it. This tree with buds, blossoms, and flowers all at the same time was a static picture of the whole cycle of life under God's blessing, nothing less than an image of the tree of life.[8] The symbolic function of the lampstand was to shine God's favor forward onto the Table with the twelve loaves of showbread (see the discussion of Numbers 8:1-4 in Chapter 10 of this book), which symbolized God's favor and blessing resting on all twelve of the tribes of Israel.

The lampstand was not just any fruitful tree—it was specifically an almond tree. The Hebrew word for almond (*šāqēd*) is related to the verb "to watch" (*šāqad*), for the almond tree blossoms early and was thus a marker of the onset of spring. Thus in Jeremiah 1:11 the Lord used an almond branch as a visible symbol of the Lord's watching over his word (in this case of judgment) and bringing it to imminent fulfillment. So too the lampstand as an almond tree was a marker of the certain fulfillment of a greater blessing that was yet to come. The Lord was watching over his people for blessing, both now and in greater measure in the future.

The Budding of Aaron's Staff

With that as background, we can return to the budding of Aaron's staff. The Lord took Aaron's dead stick and turned it into a miniature lampstand in the midst of the other twelve sticks, a sign of life and future blessing in the midst of the community. This blooming almond branch was a symbol of the certainty that the Lord would fulfill his promise of great blessing for his people through the gift of the priesthood. That is why the sign should have put an end to the grumbling of the rebellious (17:10). It should have reminded them that the Aaronic priesthood was God's chosen channel of blessing and life for the community in the present and a sign of an even greater blessing to come.

Ironically, the Israelites responded to this demonstration of beauty and life with the fear of death. They said to Moses, "Behold, we perish, we are undone, we are all undone. Everyone who comes near, who comes near to the tabernacle of the LORD, shall die. Are we all to perish?" (17:12, 13). In one sense they got the message. Their cry was a repudiation of their earlier assertion that all are holy and can safely approach the presence of God. Now they rightly feared approaching God. Yet they failed to see that this holy God whom they could not approach had graciously established a means in the Aaronic priesthood through which sinners could safely approach God and not die (17:10). God's purpose for his people was resolutely good: his goal for their lives was not death but life. They needed to wake up and smell the sweet scent of almond blossoms: in spite of their rebellion, the Lord was watching over them for blessing.

There is a profound lesson for you and me in the blossoming of Aaron's staff. In the first place, like the Israelites we need to see that by ourselves we are unfit to stand in the presence of a holy God. We are nothing more than dead sticks, fit only for the fire. Without God's promise of grace we too would be forced to cry out, "We will die! We are lost, we are all lost! Anyone who even comes near the presence of the Lord will die." We are not by nature holy or naturally part of the Lord's people. We are dead in our transgressions and sins (Ephesians 2:1), without hope and without God in the world (Ephesians 2:12). Yet the Lord is able to take dead sticks and bring them to life and make them fruitful under his blessing.

How did he do that? Ultimately it was not through Aaron and his line. Aaron was a great blessing to his people, an intercessor whose incense offering halted God's judgment in its tracks and made a separation between the living and the dead. Yet Aaron himself was a sinner, ultimately unable to enter the Promised Land. His offspring faithfully served as priests, offering sacrifices on behalf of the people and teaching them God's Law. Yet all of their ministry was provisional, temporary, until the coming of God's new covenant in Jesus Christ. Aaron's blossoming staff pointed beyond himself and his offspring to the Messiah to come. Jesus is the great High Priest who, through his personal holiness and ultimate sacrifice on the cross, enabled the blessing of God's favor to be poured out on all of his chosen ones.

Through Death to Fruitfulness

Yet if Aaron's staff was distinguished as the chosen one of God's blessing through the marks of life and fruitfulness, Jesus was distinguished at the end of his earthly ministry as God's chosen one by the signs of God's curse.

> For he grew up before him like a young plant,
> and like a root out of dry ground;
> he had no form or majesty that we should look at him,
> and no beauty that we should desire him.
> He was despised and rejected by men;
> a man of sorrows, and acquainted with grief;
> and as one from whom men hide their faces
> he was despised, and we esteemed him not.
> Surely he has borne our griefs
> and carried our sorrows;
> yet we esteemed him stricken,
> smitten by God, and afflicted.
> But he was wounded for our transgressions;
> he was crushed for our iniquities;
> upon him was the chastisement that brought us peace,
> and with his stripes we are healed. (Isaiah 53:2-5)

Jesus didn't merely straddle the line between life and death; he himself entered the grip of death to free those who were rightfully death's captives. He took upon himself Aaron's curse, the curse deserved by all the rebels for their grumbling. It was not just *their* curse that he took, however. More importantly, it was *my* curse. I too am a rebel and a grumbler. I too question the Lord's wisdom and his ways in choosing some for particular earthly service or blessing that he has not chosen to give to me. I too grumble about the judgments that he chooses to execute (or not to execute) on others. Yet Christ has taken all of those sins of mine and has borne them on the cross, despising their shame, so that I might ultimately taste the blessing that God has in store for his people. In Christ, God testified to his chosen priest with an absence of glory and a cursed death on the cross, so that through that death his unholy people might be made holy. In so doing, he removed the power and sting of death once and for all.

There at the cross we see the true wideness of God's mercy. He does not admit all into his presence indiscriminately, ignoring their sin. Rather, he welcomes in all kinds of sinners as they trust in Christ and have their sins paid for at the cross. The way of salvation is as wide and as narrow as Christ. There at the cross, fearful rebels find peace with the Lord whom they spurned, in spite of their sin, and are safely drawn into intimate fellowship with him through Christ. Now, clothed in the righteousness of Christ, we are able to do what Old Testament believers could not: we can draw near to God's presence with boldness. However, the self-righteous who stubbornly refuse to come to God through Jesus find no way into his life-giving presence.

What is more, in the resurrection of Jesus we see the almond branch blossom. Spring is in the air in the empty tomb: in Christ's rising, the firstfruits of the harvest of eternal life have appeared, and their scent is unmistakable. Death is clearly defeated, its power broken. It is only a matter of time now before the full harvest of God's blessing is experienced. God is watching over his people to bring them into his presence forever.

Here is the final answer for our grumbling. The Law that says, "Do not grumble" is not ultimately able to transform us and change our hearts. The Law can bring the judgment of death, which can restrain grumbling, but it cannot cure it. It has no power to redeem grumblers and bring their grumbling to a permanent end. Grumbling and rebellion can only be overcome as we contemplate the cross. As we look on the awesome judgment of God that took place there on all unrighteousness, will we still say, "All of God's people are holy and can enter God's presence just as they are"? Surely not. The cross demonstrates the necessity of the cleansing that only Jesus Christ can give.

When we think about the way the Lord dealt with his own Son in order to make us holy, will we murmur and rebel against his ways in our lives that have the same design? If he did not spare his own Son but freely gave him up so that we could receive blessing and life, how will he not along with him give us everything we need? When we see that the Lord's purpose for us is blessing, a purpose that is assured in the resurrection of Jesus, why then do we still doubt his goodness? The Lord will accomplish his purpose to sanctify us, one way or another. Some of those ways are intensely painful, to be sure. Yet as we stand before the cross, are we really able to say to the Father, "No, Lord, this is too painful. I cannot bear this. It is too much"? How can anything be too much when it is compared to the searing loss that the Father endured at the cross to make us holy? As Samuel Rutherford put it, "The weightiest end of the cross of Christ that is laid upon you, lieth upon your strong Saviour."[9]

We are so blessed in this new-covenant era, for we no longer have a mere sign of God's commitment to bless us. We have something better than a flowering staff that sits mutely in front of the symbol of God's presence, the ark of the covenant. That staff spoke eloquently of God's set purpose to bless his people and transform their grumbling hearts. Yet how much more effective and eloquent is the reality to which the staff pointed. The reality that we have been given to ponder is our great High Priest, Jesus Christ, standing in the heavenly Holy of Holies, interceding for you and me day by day. In the death of Christ, God assures us of his settled purpose for our blessing. In the resurrection of Christ, he assures us that the almond is already in bloom: our final salvation is near. In Christ, the Lord has indeed put an end to our grumbling, and in its place he has given us abundant life in all its fullness. Faced with the reality of the cross and the empty tomb, may we let our grumbling die away, lost in an upswell of wonder, love, and praise.

22

The Fear of the Lord

NUMBERS 17:12—18:7

WE LIVE IN AN AGE that suffers from a lack of the fear of God. That statement may surprise some of you at first hearing. How can a lack of fear be something bad? Doesn't the Bible say that "perfect love casts out fear" (1 John 4:18)? In fact, most churches today go to great lengths to assure people that when they come to church there will be absolutely nothing to be afraid of. For example, one evangelical church advertises their services as follows:

> At _____ you're free to enjoy yourself.
> Enjoy God as you experience Him through the timely message, caring people, and inspiring music. And it's okay to laugh at church—in fact we encourage it! We've got a casual atmosphere where you can enjoy your morning with a cup of Starbucks House Blend, a donut and some new friends.

In such churches, worship services increasingly seem to resemble coffee shops more than encounters with a holy God. While I'm sure that the people at this church mean well, their advertisement is certainly not designed to encourage the fear of God. Rather, they suggest that worshiping God is a casual and non-threatening activity, an enjoyable and fulfilling experience for everyone. They make coming into the presence of Almighty God sound like the spiritual equivalent of a visit to a favorite uncle.

The Problem of the Absence of Fear

So what is the problem with an absence of fear in approaching God? Am I just a grumpy old-fashioned preacher, upset because other people seem to be having too much fun? I don't think so. Even while as a culture we flee from all kinds of fear, we need to recognize that proper fear is essential to healthy living. Wise parents know that a large part of raising children is training their fears in the right direction. Some of our children are filled with irrational fears, and we have to teach them not to be afraid. They don't need to be afraid of the dark or of terrible monsters hiding under their bed. They don't need to be afraid of going to the doctor or having a haircut. Other children, however, seem born without fear, and so we spend a great deal of time teaching them to be afraid. Be afraid of touching the stove. Be afraid of climbing forty feet up a tree, especially in your best clothes. Be afraid of strangers who offer you candy or ask for your help looking for a lost puppy. Be afraid of what drugs can do to your brain. In our modern world a child who grows up completely without fear may not live to grow up. Life is not a casual and non-threatening activity, a fun and fulfilling experience for everyone. Some things truly ought to scare us to death. As the popular proverb wisely reminds us, "Fools rush in where angels fear to tread."

For sinners, the prospect of standing in the presence of a holy God should be one of those truly frightening things. As a culture we resist that truth because we have lost our awareness both of God's transcendence and holiness and of our own sinfulness and unworthiness. This trend was noted by J. Gresham Machen more than half a century ago when he observed, "There are those who tell us that fear ought to be banished from religion; we ought, it is said, no more to hold before men's eyes the fear of hell; fear, it is said, is an ignoble thing."[1]

The fruit of that attitude is evident all around us. Somewhere in our church doctrinal statement, we may still confess the desperate danger that faces sinners in the hands of an angry God.[2] But even in Christian circles, this note tends to be a subdued element in the contemporary chord. We should hardly wonder, then, that there is so little fear of God in our culture at large. Why should others be afraid of a God in whom they do not believe when we who confess his name stand so little in awe of him? Our churches have been radically infected by the spirit of the southside rebellion (see Numbers 16) that views everyone as by nature essentially holy and able to enter God's presence without fear.

The Cure for the Absence of Fear

We have seen how God dealt with that spirit in Numbers 16. The Israelites saw with their own eyes the earth open and swallow rebels alive (vv. 32, 33). They saw fire come out from the Lord's presence and incinerate Korah's 250 priestly pretenders (v. 35). They saw nearly 15,000 of their fellow Israelites killed by a plague of judgment from the Lord because they grumbled about the earlier deaths (v. 49). Then they saw the Lord confirm through a dramatic sign that only Aaron and the Levites could approach his presence (17:1-11). Little wonder that the Israelites cried out, "Behold, we perish, we are undone, we are all undone. Everyone who comes near, who comes near to the tabernacle of the LORD, shall die. Are we all to perish?" (17:12, 13).

An absence of fear was no longer Israel's problem at the end of Numbers 17. They had learned through bitter experience to be afraid of the consequences of their sin.

Yet in their panic they missed the gracious aspect of the budding of Aaron's staff, which through the symbol of the almond blossom spoke powerfully of the Lord's purpose to bless them. This is typical of our spiritual experience: when we discover that we have made a mistake in one direction, we overcompensate in the opposite one. Until the Israelites understood God's mercy and grace, they did not fear the Lord properly. The God whom they were called to serve is both the God who "will by no means clear the guilty, visiting the iniquity of the fathers on the children and the children's children, to the third and the fourth generation" and "The LORD, the LORD, a God merciful and gracious, slow to anger, and abounding in steadfast love and faithfulness, keeping steadfast love for thousands, forgiving iniquity and transgression and sin" (Exodus 34:6, 7).

Satan will always try to separate these two aspects of God's character in our thinking. If he can persuade us that the Lord is all love and mercy and will not judge anyone, he will do so. But the moment it becomes clear to us that there is indeed a reckoning for sin, Satan immediately switches tack and tries to push us in the opposite direction, to make us believe that the Lord is hard and judgmental and that there is no forgiveness to be found with him. As the Puritan Thomas Manton put it:

> Satan labors to represent God by halves, only as a consuming fire, as clothed with justice and vengeance. Oh no! It is true he will not suffer his mercy to be abused by contemptuous sinners; he will not clear the guilty, though he waits long on them before he destroys them; but the main of his name is "his mercy and goodness."[3]

The true fear of the Lord flows out of an understanding of the whole character of God as both holy and merciful.

This is what Numbers 18 is about: the Lord in his grace had taught Israel to fear, and now the Lord was able to retrain and relieve those fears. Yet unless we first learn to identify with them in their fear of God, the remedy for that fear will make no sense to us. There is certainly a place for laughter and fun in church, but there must also be a place for being deadly serious. Unless you see with compelling certainty the fact that sinners cannot approach the Lord without being destroyed by his holiness, you will never understand the remedy that God has provided for our sin, which lies at the heart of Numbers 18.

The Ministry of the Priests and Levites

The remedy to which God drew their attention was the Aaronic priesthood, who together with the Levites were given the task of taking care of and guarding the tabernacle so that wrath would not fall on the Israelites again (18:5). As we saw in the last study, this ministry was implied by the sign of Aaron's staff. The priests and the Levites, like the lampstand of the tabernacle, were a sign of the Lord's favor and determination to bless this people. The goal of their ministry was that the people should not die (17:10). So what kind of ministry did the priests and Levites have, and how did it deliver the people from their fear of death?

First, it was a ministry that was ordained by the Lord for the sake of his people. This is a central theme in these chapters of the book of Numbers: the Lord himself chooses those who come close to him and serve him. It was the Lord who chose Aaron and his sons for the priesthood (18:1), and it was the Lord who chose the Levites to assist them (18:6). All roads do not lead safely into God's presence; that much has been made abundantly clear. Even the Levites could not help with the altar ministry and the work inside the veil of the tabernacle. Yet at the same time, one road *does* lead safely into the Lord's presence. The Lord could legitimately have closed off access for Israel into his presence forever, but he chose not to do so. In the Aaronic priesthood, the doorway to Heaven was still open. The ones whom he had chosen could still approach him and serve him safely. The sacrifices they offered would be accepted by the Lord, just as Aaron's incense offering was in Numbers 16:47. Through this means, the Lord would bless his people. The calling of the Aaronic priesthood by the Lord was thus a sign that his plan for his people is life and fellowship with him.

What is more, this ministry of the priesthood was a gift from God to Aaron and his sons (18:7). It was not something they had earned or deserved; on the contrary, what Levi had earned for his descendants was the sentence of being scattered in Israel. Because he slaughtered the inhabitants of Shechem, along with his brother Simeon (Genesis 34:25-29), Levi was cursed rather than blessed by his father Jacob:

> Simeon and Levi are brothers;
> weapons of violence are their swords.
> Let my soul come not into their council;
> O my glory, be not joined to their company.
> For in their anger they killed men,

and in their willfulness they hamstrung oxen.
Cursed be their anger, for it is fierce,
and their wrath, for it is cruel!
I will divide them in Jacob
and scatter them in Israel. (Genesis 49:5-7)

Yet now there was an eternal covenant between the Lord and Aaron, and his descendants after him (18:19),[4] a relationship that involved a number of privileges, most notably that of access into the Lord's presence. The Levites would still be scattered, just as Jacob had prophesied, but their curse was turned into a blessing for the whole people. This transforming grace in the lives of the Levites was a demonstration in sample form of the Lord's plan for his people. Even though the sin of Levi had earned his descendants a just punishment, the Lord's grace was greater than all their sin. So too, the sin of the people did not necessarily mean their death. Even their ultimate scattering among the nations for their sin would be turned by the Lord from a curse into a blessing, as through them the gospel would eventually come to the whole world. God's grace could redeem them also, just as it had the Levites.

The Responsibility of the Priesthood

Yet the ministry of the priesthood was not only a gift to the family of Aaron—it was also a responsibility. This responsibility is the primary focus of the passage here. It was the priests' responsibility to prevent fools from rushing in where angels fear to tread. Their ministry was to be a ministry of exclusion, protecting the sanctity of the most holy things against encroachment by profane people (18:1). Such encroachment in the last two chapters had very nearly led to the destruction of the whole community, but now the Lord charged the priests with the responsibility of ensuring that such problems didn't happen again. If there was a similar encroachment in the future, instead of the whole community being held responsible and liable to death, now only the priests would be held responsible. That is what it means when it says that the priests "shall bear iniquity connected with the sanctuary" (18:1):[5] the buck stopped with them. They were now to carry sole liability for protecting the most sacred things.

Assisting them in this task were the Levites, who were to keep guard over the tabernacle as a whole. The priests were to guard the most sacred items and areas, while the Levites kept watch over the outer environs (18:3). Together they were to take responsibility to guard and protect God's holiness. If they failed in that mission, both they and the one who encroached on the sacred things would be liable to death—but not the entire community. The priests and the Levites were thus assigned a substitutionary ministry, bearing the danger of death for sin on behalf of the people.

This aspect of the job of the priests and Levites is in some ways like the work of Secret Service agents who are charged with protecting the President of the United States. These citizens surround our leader and guard him against anyone who would try to get too close to him. It is a responsibility that must be undertaken with the utmost seriousness, even to the point of being willing to take a bullet in place of their Commander-in-Chief. They are required to bear the danger of death on his behalf. However, unlike the Secret Service men, whose job is to protect an essentially harmless President against potentially dangerous citizens, the purpose of the priestly guard was also to protect the citizens of Israel against a potentially dangerous God. It was not on God's behalf that they risked death, but on behalf of their people. The goal of their ministry was to keep the people at a safe distance from God so "that there may never again be wrath on the people of Israel" (18:5). They freed the people from the fear of death by being willing to substitute for the people in paying the penalty of death should someone sin by trespassing on holy ground.

The Ministry of Exclusion

Who carries a similar responsibility in our situation? We do not have priests in the New Testament church because access into the Lord's presence is now available to all who come through Jesus Christ, our great High Priest. Yet those who are leaders in Christ's church—ministers and elders—are still called to a ministry of exclusion as well as inclusion. They are assigned the keys of the Kingdom of Heaven, welcoming some people into the fellowship of the church and keeping others out. The Heidelberg Catechism (Q. 83) puts it like this:

> What are the keys of the kingdom?
> The preaching of the holy gospel and Christian discipline toward repentance. Both preaching and discipline open the kingdom of heaven to believers and close it to unbelievers.

Ministers and elders are responsible, through preaching and church discipline, for guarding against careless intruders who would encroach on the sanctity of God. That is a serious responsibility, which is why James warns that not many should presume to be teachers because we who teach will be judged more strictly (James 3:1). We need to proclaim clearly the message of God's fearsome holiness and righteousness, as well as his grace, to those who are presently living careless lives. The task of the church is not to suggest to everyone that they are already "in" when it comes to God; rather, we need to show them that by nature they are excluded from his presence. We need to make it clear to people that they cannot simply approach God casually, with a designer coffee in one hand and a donut in the other, and wave a cheery hello. By nature they are God's enemies, objects of his wrath (Ephesians 2:1–3).

Thus, when God summoned Adam and Eve into his presence after the fall, they didn't come eagerly expecting to enjoy a timely message about how to make their marriage better, an inspiring song or two, and great refreshments. They came in fear and trembling, knowing that they had transgressed against the Lord's power and majesty. They could not but come when God called them, but they came knowing that they deserved nothing but death. Until their desperate need for forgiveness was dealt with, nothing else mattered. This somber reality is part of the message that we have to communicate to our culture. The fact that "the wages of sin is death" (Romans 6:23) is perhaps not a popular or appealing part of our message, but until this truth is understood, the gospel itself will make no sense. We need to show people the gulf that exists between them as sinners and a holy God for their own sake, lest they be consumed by his wrath. It is not that there is anything necessarily wrong with preaching on marriage or providing great music and offering refreshments. Yet the atmosphere we foster should be one that matches the serious message that we have to deliver to those around us.

The Centrality of the Cross

The ministry of the Old Testament priesthood was well designed to communicate that serious message because it was built around sacrifice and exclusion. The armed guards who kept the people out of the Lord's presence communicated vividly their separation from God. The constant shedding of blood and burning of flesh kept the reality of the consequences of sin very much in front of the people. You couldn't visit the temple without being visibly confronted with both your exclusion from the Lord's presence and the necessity of death to restore you into a relationship with God.

This is why our ministry must constantly be centered around the cross of Jesus Christ, which is the culmination of all those Old Testament sacrifices. We must be resolved, as the apostle Paul was, to proclaim only "Jesus Christ and him crucified" (1 Corinthians 2:2). The cross of Christ shows us the death that is the Lord's answer to our spiritual exclusion from his presence. There at the cross Jesus Christ himself bore the responsibility for all of our transgressions against God's holiness. It is not pastors or elders who substitute themselves to death for our sake: it is Jesus Christ. God's wrath fell on him so that it might not fall on us and crush us forever. He was put to death so that you and I would not have to be put to death. He was cut off from the Lord's presence so that the door might be opened for us to walk right in.

Does the cross mean no more fear for the believer? Certainly it means no more fear of the wrath of God. Because of the cross there is now no more condemnation for those who are in Christ Jesus (Romans 8:1). As a result, believers in Christ have a peace with God that cannot be challenged. Even the reverses that I may suffer in my ongoing battle with sin cannot cause me to fear the loss of my salvation, for Jesus has undertaken to bear the responsibility for all my offenses. That kind of fear is gone forever. There is now no exclusion for all of us who are in Christ Jesus: precisely because we are in him, we have the right to go where he goes and to stand in God's presence as he does. Now even when I have sinned, I can run to God without fear of judgment and confess my sin, asking for his cleansing.

Fitting Fear

Yet the nature of God has not changed, and there is still a fitting fear in the life of the believer. Indeed, the Lord promises such godly fear to believers in Jeremiah 32:40, where he says, "I will put the fear of me in their hearts, that they may not turn from me." Our God is still a consuming fire, as Hebrews 12:29 reminds us, a God who must be worshiped with reverence and awe (Hebrews 12:28). It is a solemn truth that many will be excluded from the Lord's presence on the last day who are much smarter, better-behaved, and more sincerely religious people than we are: it is only God's grace that allows us to enter in.

What makes the believer's fear of the Lord distinct is that it is a fear that flows not simply from the prospect of God's judgment but from a knowledge of God's mercy. It is one thing to fear the Lord's judgment, as Adam and Eve did when they heard the Lord walking in the garden. It is something else entirely to fear the God who combines judgment with mercy. Psalm 130:4 makes the connection between mercy and the fear of the Lord explicit: "But with you there is forgiveness, that you may be feared." Why should God's forgiveness lead us to godly fear? The answer comes once again as we contemplate the means of our salvation and inclusion. What was the cost of my sin? Nails piercing the hands and feet of my Savior; a sharp spear penetrating his heart; a crown of thorns adorning his head; a back beaten to a bloody pulp; a Son's face turned upward desperately seeking his Father and hearing no answer to his cry. Look at Jesus stretched out in agony, and tell me that our sin doesn't really matter. Contemplate the cross, and sin will never again seem like a light thing to us. Pondering the Lord's mercy will give us a healthy fear of the Lord and an abhorrence of sin.

After we have stood at the foot of the cross, coming into God's presence will never again seem like a casual thing either. The Creator of the universe loved us enough to curse his own Son so that we might enter his presence. Giving him the thanks and praise he deserves is therefore no light matter. Coming to church to worship this God is not something to fit into our schedule whenever it suits us. It is not something to be undertaken casually, as we might meet with a few friends at a coffee shop for a stimulating conversation. What in the world could be more precious, more glorious than this? As we gather with other believers, we proclaim Christ crucified, our means of access to God, our way to life, our hope of glory. Worship is an awesome and fearsome event, yet at the same time deeply joyful and profoundly inspiring. For in Christ we now have an access into the Lord's presence that is even greater than the special access God promised his chosen Aaronic priests. There are no longer any "Keep out" signs, warning us to stay at a safe distance, not even around the Holy of Holies. Dressed in the bloodstained robes of Christ's holiness, we can draw near to the very presence of God himself and sing our praises to him.

The Lord is ready to receive our worship and praise in the assembly of his people Sunday after Sunday. In Christ the doorway is open, and we may go in. By his Spirit, the Lord is there as we offer our sacrifices of praise and lay our lives on his altar. The elements of the Lord's Supper are there to communicate to us afresh the profound realities of the gospel of Christ crucified: the body of Christ was broken for us and his blood poured out to establish a new covenant relationship with us. Church is therefore always a place for doing serious business with God—business that is joyful, to be sure, but also serious and solemn. We must come ready to respond with deep gratitude for his gift of a perfect priest, Jesus Christ, who has stood between us and the judgment of God, bearing the responsibility for all our transgressions and sins. Our hearts must be filled with reverent fear as we contemplate the cost of our redemption. We must be touched with fresh wonder at the new and eternal life in God's presence that was purchased for us. Then we will be prepared to stand in God's presence and worship him.

23

The Reward for
Faithful Service

NUMBERS 18:8-32

AN OLD JOKE RUNS LIKE THIS: "Serve the Lord. The salary is meager, but the fringe benefits are out of this world!" In reality, there is more than a little truth behind both sides of that joke. Many pastors around America and throughout the world live on less than adequate provision from their church;[1] they persist in their ministry, however, because they have a calling from God. It is certainly no easy ride for the lazy these days.[2] Pastoral ministry involves long hours preparing sermons, counseling people, visiting the sick and elderly, sharing the good news with those who have no idea who Jesus is, and so on. Surely only someone called to the task by God would want to take up such a serious responsibility, for one day pastors will have to stand before the Lord and give account for the flock under their care.

By the same token, you might wonder who in ancient Israel would want to be a priest. It was a dirty and smelly job, involving the slaughter and burning of various animals. It was also a highly dangerous job, involving bearing the responsibility for safeguarding the sanctuary (18:1). Failure to carry out this ministry faithfully could result in one's death (v. 3). Did little Levite boys dream of the day when they would grow up to be a priest? Did they play "priest and sacrifice" with their toy animals? It's a little hard to imagine, isn't it? Perhaps that is why the Lord called and designated a particular tribe and family to be his priests rather than leaving the job open to whoever felt called or inclined to the occupation.

Rewards for Priestly Service

There were some rewards for priestly service, though. In return for their labors, the priests and Levites received income from their ministry. This income came in a number of forms. The first means of support came through the sacrificial system. The priests had the privilege of receiving part of the meat from the various animals that were sacrificed as sin offerings, guilt offerings, or fellowship offerings (v. 9). Part of the animal was offered as a sacrifice on the altar to the Lord, and another part was given to the priest. The same was true for the grain offerings and the wave offerings:[3] part was offered to the Lord on the altar and part given to the priest (vv. 9-11). The priests were also to receive all of the firstfruits of the land and the firstborn of the animals (vv. 12-19). If the animals were holy (that is, ceremonially clean animals that were unblemished), their blood and fat would be offered as sacrifices, while the meat would belong to the priests. If the animals did not belong to a class that could be offered as sacrifices, such as donkeys or camels, they were to be redeemed by the owner, who was required to pay the market rate for the animal plus 20 percent (see Leviticus 27:12). The same requirement of redemption was true of firstborn male babies: they were to be redeemed at the set rate of five shekels of silver, and the money in either case was paid to the priests.

The Levites, meanwhile, were also to be supported in their ministry. Their income would come from the annual tithe of agricultural products in Israel. All of the crops that were grown and all of the produce of the herds were to be tithed annually, with that 10 per cent of the agricultural produce going to the Levites (v. 21). This was not to be the least appetizing 10 percent either: the people were to give to the Lord the very best of the oil, the best of the wine, and the best of the grain (vv. 12, 29). The Levites were in turn required to tithe their tithe, giving the very best of it to the Lord through the priests (vv. 28, 29). The rest was then theirs to enjoy as they wished (v. 30). This financial provision for both the priests and the Levites was a recompense for their not being given any land as an inheritance in the Promised Land (vv. 23, 24). They had no land to farm, for the Lord was their inheritance, and the care of his sanctuary was their lasting responsibility. They were not to split their focus between earthly and heavenly responsibilities but to devote themselves wholly to eternal things.

Don't miss the encouragement and hope that these regulations convey implicitly at this particular point in Israel's history. Remember that this chapter is an answer to the cry of the people, "Behold, we perish, we are undone, we are all undone. Everyone who comes near, who comes near to the tabernacle of the LORD, shall die" (17:12, 13). The regulations for the support of the priests and the Levites confirmed the fact that the people as a whole had a future with the Lord. In the first place, the provision that the priests be supported by the sacrifices of the altar confirmed the fact that the priests would be able to draw near to the tabernacle and not die. Meanwhile, the provision of support for the Levites through firstfruits and tithes confirmed the fact that one day Israel would inherit the land of promise and have crops and harvests from which to bring these offerings. The whole chapter thus affirmed the Lord's gracious purpose for his people at a time when they were inclined toward fearful doubt.

Priesthood and Ministry

A number of lasting principles can be drawn from these instructions to God's Old Testament people and applied more broadly to Christian ministry. First, under the new covenant, just as under the old, God desires to have men set aside to serve him on a full-time basis. He calls men to teach his people his Word and shepherd his flock (1 Peter 5:2). The normal practice, now as then, is that these ministers of the gospel should be supported by those to whom they minister. Jesus himself said, "the laborer deserves his food" (Matthew 10:10), while Paul assumes the right of those who labor for the spiritual good of a community to receive material support in return (1 Corinthians 9:4–12). The goal is that they should be able to have a single-minded focus on heavenly things for the sake of the congregation as a whole, instead of having to split their attention between earth and Heaven.

Strikingly, the pattern laid down in the book of Numbers suggests that this material support should be generous. Sometimes congregations seem to think that the best way to keep their minister holy is to keep him poor! The Lord's provision for his servants is not so restricted: he ordained that 10 percent of the national produce be given to support a tribe that comprised about 4 percent of the total population (see Numbers 4 for the figures). Now, of course, the actual income of the priests and Levites depended on the faithfulness of God's people in giving. So it is not surprising that in practice the Levites were often classed among the poor and needy of Israel (see, e.g., Deuteronomy 14:29). If the people did not faithfully tithe, the Levites would certainly have found their means of support very limited. That was not God's design for them, however. God wanted his servants to be more than adequately maintained, and as long as his people were faithfully honoring the Lord, they would also honor his servants and provide abundantly for their financial needs.

Tithes and Firstfruits

The second principle is contained in the means the Lord chose to provide for his servants, through tithes and firstfruits on the one hand and through redemption and sacrifices on the other. The medium itself carries a message.

The offering of sacrifices and the practice of redeeming the firstborn male of both humans and animals reminded the people that every life belonged to the Lord and needed to be redeemed. A price had to be paid by or on behalf of every firstborn. Some of those firstborn animals would pay the price of death for themselves as they were offered as sacrifices. In the case of others, the price was paid for them, and they were redeemed from death. This practice was a vivid and regular reminder of Israel's own redemption out of Egypt: the firstborn of the Egyptians had not been redeemed and had died (Exodus 4:22, 23), while Israel, as God's firstborn, had been redeemed and given life. This sovereign act of the Lord's grace was the foundational motivation for their giving to God: they were to give because he had first given life to them.

The giving of tithes and firstfruits was also designed to remind his people that every area of life belonged to God. It was not just their lives that they owed to the Lord. *Everything* they had came from God, because he was the one who had given them the Promised Land as his gift. They lived as tenants in God's land and therefore had to render to him both the firstfruits and a share of the produce.[4] Since the land belonged to the Lord, part of what it produced belonged to him by rights. The practice of tithing was not unique to Israel.[5] Throughout the ancient Near East, it was a common practice for kings to tax their people in the amount of a tithe of their produce. Often that income went to support royal officials or temples.[6] The tithe in Numbers 18 seems to function somewhat like these royal taxes of the ancient Near East. The Lord was Israel's Great King, and the tithe was an annual obligation to give 10 percent of their produce for the regular support of Levites, who were the servants of the King.[7] The giving of tithes and firstfruits was thus an obligation of the covenant relationship between the Lord and his people.

For the sake of completeness, we should note that there appear to have been two distinct tithes in the Old Testament. The tithe here in Numbers is explicitly collected for the support of the Levites. Another tithe was mandated in Deuteronomy 14:22-29, however:

> You shall tithe all the yield of your seed that comes from the field year by year. And before the LORD your God, in the place that he will choose, to make his name dwell there, you shall eat the tithe of your grain, of your wine, and of your oil, and the firstborn of your herd and flock, that you may learn to fear the LORD your God always. And if the way is too long for you, so that you are not able to carry the tithe, when the LORD your God blesses you, because the place is too far from you, which the LORD your God chooses, to set his name there, then you shall turn it into money and bind up the money in your hand and go to the place that the LORD your God chooses and spend the money for whatever you desire—oxen or sheep or wine or strong drink, whatever your appetite craves. And you shall eat there before the LORD your God and rejoice, you and your household. And you

shall not neglect the Levite who is within your towns, for he has no portion or inheritance with you. At the end of every three years you shall bring out all the tithe of your produce in the same year and lay it up within your towns. And the Levite, because he has no portion or inheritance with you, and the sojourner, the fatherless, and the widow, who are within your towns, shall come and eat and be filled, that the LORD your God may bless you in all the work of your hands that you do.

This tithe was to be brought to the central sanctuary two years out of three, to be consumed as a celebratory meal (Deuteronomy 14:23). If the people lived too far from the sanctuary in Jerusalem to carry the tithe with them, they were to convert it into money and bring the money to the temple. There they were to buy party fare, such as meat and alcoholic beverages, to enable them to feast in style in the presence of the Lord (Deuteronomy 14:26). In the third year, however, the people were to store up the food within their own towns to act as a resource from which to meet the needs not only of the Levites but more generally of the poor of the community (Deuteronomy 14:28, 29). The tithe in Deuteronomy is also an annual offering, but not one that is directly donated to the Levites.[8]

Christians and Old Testament Law

Are we as Christians obligated to tithe? Is it appropriate to call the weekly offerings of Christians their tithes? The answer to these questions is more complicated that a simple yes or no. Calling our offerings tithes certainly underlines the continuity between Old Testament giving and ours; at the same time it tends to obscure the radical differences that are also present. To make the point, simply substitute the word *firstfruits* for *tithes* in the questions. Are we as Christians obligated to bring our firstfruits to give to the church? Are our weekly offerings our firstfruits? I don't know of anyone who would insist that we need to bring in our firstfruits every year to give to the church, and yet we are frequently urged to bring the full tithe to the church. In the Old Testament generally, as here in Numbers 18, the firstfruits and tithes always belong together. This suggests that there are differences between their obligation and ours, as well as similarities.

In order to answer the question of tithing, we need to think about the differences between Old Testament giving and our own, as well as the obvious lines of continuity. That sets the question in a much broader context. How do we find those lines of continuity and discontinuity between Old Testament command and New Testament application? The answer is to consider the three aspects of the Old Testament law: the moral, civil, and ceremonial. To use the language of the Westminster Confession of Faith, the moral laws are those that have enduring significance for all times and all places, the civil laws were intended for Israel while they dwelt in the land and consequently expired with the state of Israel, except for their general equity, and the ceremonial laws pointed forward to Christ and were fulfilled in him.[9]

An example of moral law, binding in all times and places, would be, "You shall not commit adultery" (Exodus 20:14). This is a universally binding commandment, no matter what culture or century you inhabit. Ceremonial law, on the other hand, would include the laws associated with the sacrificial system. We no longer bring a goat to the Lord's house on Yom Kippur (the Day of Atonement), even though the Old Testament commands it, because Christ has made the perfect sacrifice for us. Likewise, because Jesus Christ is our Passover Lamb (1 Corinthians 5:7), we as Christians are no longer obligated to celebrate the Passover. Meanwhile, civil laws are those laws that were particularly designed for Israel during their occupation of the Promised Land. An example of civil law would be the requirement that when the Israelites were harvesting their grain, they were not to cut all the way to the edges of their fields but were to leave some of the grain unharvested for the poor (Deuteronomy 24:19-21). That law doesn't apply to us today (even if we are farmers) because it was intended for national Israel during the period when they occupied the Promised Land as a specific application of more general principles of divine justice.

Nonetheless, the general equity of the civil law still has applications for us. A lawyer or doctor who sets aside a portion of his time for pro bono work for the poor is fulfilling the motivation behind the law of Deuteronomy 24, even though the details have changed. There are also basic principles that are of lasting significance, encouraging our society to make provision for the poor to support themselves through work rather than through handouts.

It is important to note that these divisions are not mutually exclusive, so that if something is moral law, it cannot also be ceremonial law or civil law; rather, these are *aspects* of the Law. For example, on one level the Ten Commandments clearly have a moral-law dimension, applying to all people everywhere. However, they also point forward to Christ as the only one who ever fulfilled them, and they are civil law inasmuch as they were given to Moses on Mount Sinai as part of God's covenant with Israel.[10] Individual laws, then, do not always neatly fall into one category or another: some regulations may have elements of two aspects, or even all three.

Christians and Tithing

Which of these categories of Old Testament law best describes the tithe laws? The first fact to notice is that the annual tithe (along with many other civil institutions, such as firstfruits and the year of Jubilee) belongs distinctively to the era of the Sinai covenant. The patriarchs had no obligation to render 10 percent of their annual income to the Lord. They chose to do so on special occasions, but it was not a regular occurrence or obligation.[11] Indeed, even during the Sinaitic era the tithe was precisely not a 10 percent tax on income. Unlike other ancient Near-Eastern states, Israel's tithe was limited in scope to agricultural products, whether animal or vegetable, and did not encompass non-agricultural products. The reason for this is not hard to discern. Because the Promised Land was distinctively the gift of God to his covenant people, as a mark of God's fundamental ownership a percentage of its fruits belonged to him. Israel was to recognize its vassal status in the land through the payment of tribute to the Lord in the form of the firstfruits of the land and the tithe. Because the tithe was a covenant obligation, blessings and curses were therefore attached to it (Malachi 3:8-12). Obedience to the law of the tithe would lead to fruitfulness; disobedience would lead to the land becoming barren. These kinds of covenantal blessings and curses on the land are often, though not exclusively, associated with civil law.

Nor did the tithe law continue in force into New Testament times. To be sure, Jesus commended the Pharisees for tithing their spices in Matthew 23:23. Some people cite that as evidence of a continuing obligation on Christians to tithe. Yet we have to recognize that Jesus stood in an interim position with respect to the Mosaic covenant. During the days of his earthly ministry, the Mosaic covenant was still in force, though it was about to be superseded. In precisely the same way, Jesus also paid the temple tax (Matthew 17:24-27), though no one would argue that this is a continuing obligation on Christians.

After the death and resurrection of Jesus, the tithe disappeared completely from the vocabulary of the New Testament church. Strikingly, when Paul quotes the Old Testament in support of his argument that ministers of the gospel deserve to be paid, he doesn't appeal to the tithe laws to support his case! Rather, he appeals to the principle, "You shall not muzzle an ox when it is treading out the grain" (Deuteronomy 25:4—itself civil law!), as well as the general practice that priests were fed from the sacrifices offered in their temples.[12]

This limited scope of the tithe law suggests that it was part of the civil law given by the Lord to govern Israel during their occupation of the Promised Land, rather than part of the moral law, which is universal in scope. As a result, the tithe law does not bind us except in its general equity—that is, in the general principles of behavior before God that can legitimately be extracted from it.

General Equity Principles for Giving

General equity principles that come from the tithe include the following:

First, Christianity affirms that God is no man's debtor. While under the old covenant there was a closer connection between covenant obedience and agricultural blessing than there is under the new covenant, it remains true that "Whoever sows sparingly will also reap sparingly, and whoever sows bountifully will also reap bountifully" (2 Corinthians 9:6; see also Mark 10:29, 30). Under the new covenant, we cannot assure people on the basis of Malachi 3:8-12 that if they tithe, their business will grow and their investments will flourish. Yet it nonetheless remains true that you cannot outgive God and that, as a general rule, those who give generously to the Lord will receive bountifully in return, even if the proof of that fact may be less visibly apparent in our era.

Second, Christianity radicalizes the source of the tithe: the Mosaic tithe was an annual obligation to give 10 percent of the produce of the land. For Christians, however, it is not simply our garden produce that is under the lordship of God but the whole of life. Otherwise, for many of us our tithe would be pretty small! For me, Old Testament tithing would simply mean bringing a few oranges and grapefruit to church along with a handful of figs and some persimmons. Since I happen to live at the heart of the avocado capital of the world, agricultural tithing for the support of the pastor would have its attractions, but Christian giving has a much wider scope.

Third, Christianity personalizes the amount of the tithe: Christian giving should be proportional to our income, as the tithe was (1 Corinthians 16:2). Yet it should also be willing and generous (2 Corinthians 9:7), even hyper-generous (2 Corinthians 8:2). The practice of designating a particular percentage of your income to give to the Lord's work is not found in the New Testament. If you look for examples, the widow gave 100 percent of her income (Mark 12:41-44), while Zacchaeus committed 50 percent (Luke 19:8)! This suggests that the discontinuities between Christian giving and tithing are the exact opposite of giving us a soft option. There is certainly no excuse for giving less under grace than those under law were required to give.

Fourth, Christianity affirms the purposes of the tithe. The tithe had three basic objectives in the Old Testament. The first objective, the only one mentioned in Numbers 18, was to provide for the support of those involved in full-time ministry, the priests and Levites (v. 21). The tithe in Deuteronomy 14, however, was intended to provide for the needs of the poor in the community (Deuteronomy 14:28, 29), as well as to provide opportunity for communal celebration as God's people together in God's presence, with feasting and drinking (Deuteronomy 14:23). Even though I have never heard someone who was preaching on the obligations of Christians to tithe urge them to use their tithe to buy steaks and a bottle of wine for the next church potluck, that would seem to be an apt parallel for one of the uses of the Deuteronomy tithe. In other words, an appropriate confession of God's lordship in our lives involves using our money not simply to pay for the pastor and the missionaries and the building fund,[13] but also to meet the needs of the poor in our community and to practice hospitality and mutual fellowship.

Both of these areas are, in my estimation, areas of weakness in the contemporary church. We may be quite happy to pay for a good minister and a fine building, but what proportion of our personal and church budget is specifically directed to ministries of mercy? We often have relatively little concern for the poor in our community, assuming that the government should take care of that need. Yet the tithe provision in the Old Testament challenges us to be mindful of the poor. This could be as simple as sponsoring children in need in another country through an organization like World Vision or as profound and challenging as adopting an orphan or neglected child. That costly commitment is tithing at work. This is not just a matter for individuals though. Each church should constantly be looking to see where the poor are in our community, asking how we can be a blessing to them. To do that will certainly take more than our money, but it will not take less than our money. We need to hear the challenge of the tithe to serve the poor.

Moreover, to what extent do we obey the injunctions of the New Testament to practice hospitality? When I was first planning to plant a church in Oxford, England, I asked an experienced minister there if he had any advice for me. He considered deeply and then responded, "Everything goes better with food!" At first I was disappointed by his answer. I had expected something deep and profound! Yet, as I thought about his response I came to see that he had expressed a foundational Biblical principle: fellowship and food belong together. Community-building starts with consumption. We put this principle into practice in a little church I pastored. From our first prayer meeting to our final Sunday service, we shared fellowship around the table, whether the contents of that table consisted of coffee and brownies for half a dozen or a weekly lunch for the entire church. Out of that table fellowship grew relationships in which lives were touched by the gospel. To misquote the writer of the epistle to the Hebrews, "Brethren, let us not neglect eating together." Such hospitality is costly, both financially and in terms of the work it takes. Yet the tithe laws urge us to expend ourselves in this way as a gift to the Lord, as well as a ministry of service and blessing to our brothers and sisters in Christ.

So why don't we practice this kind of Christian tithing? Why don't we give generously to meet the needs of the poor? Why don't we delight to eat celebratory meals with the Lord's people? I suspect it is because we have forgotten God's graciousness to us. When we forget God's grace to us, we come to view the poor as merely a nuisance, people who are undeserving of our aid. When we forget the Lord's grace, we see the Lord as a hard taskmaster who has failed to grant us what we wanted. We become like the elder brother in the Parable of the Prodigal Son (Luke 15:28-30). We insist on standing outside the party with hard hearts, begrudging the kindness that has been shown to the prodigal, counting all the ways in which we believe the Father has not given us what we deserve. Like the elder brother, the reason we have no generosity in our hearts toward others is because we don't see the great gifts that we ourselves have been given. The reality is that we are all utterly undeserving of God's generous gift of salvation and that everything we have in this world comes as a gift from his hand. The principle of the tithe was given to drive home that truth into the hearts of the Israelites, and we need it driven home to our hearts as well.

The whole earth and everything that it produces is the Lord's (Psalm 24:1). The Lord has freely given eternal life to us at the cost of his Son, Jesus Christ. We are a people who have been redeemed at a far more costly price than five shekels of silver—nothing less than the precious blood of Jesus. What is more, the Lord is not only the inheritance of the priests and Levites but the inheritance of all of the saints as well. The Lord has prepared a heavenly home for us that he gives to us as a free gift of his grace. If we understand and remember these truths, it will be our delight to give generously to support those whom the Lord has called to serve him full-time. We will be overjoyed when we have an opportunity to meet the needs of the poor, and we will make it a priority to show hospitality and celebrate fellowship with the Lord's people in his presence. That is the essence of all true Christian tithing and giving.

24

True Cleanliness

NUMBERS 19

WHEN HIS WIFE WAS AWAY FROM HOME, the novelist Nathaniel Hawthorne once wrote:

> The washing of dishes does seem to me the most absurd and unsatisfactory business that I ever undertook. If, when once washed, they would remain clean for ever and ever (which they ought in all reason to do, considering how much trouble it is), there would be less occasion to grumble; but no sooner is it done, than it requires to be done again. On the whole, I have come to the resolution not to use more than one dish at each meal.[1]

We can all surely identify with that quote. Even in these days of dishwashers, it seems that we are no sooner finished loading it with the dishes of one meal and putting away the clean plates before we start the same cycle all over again. The same is true of laundry and vacuuming. Can we ever say that these jobs are really done? In our experience, cleanliness is not so much next to godliness as it is next to impossible to maintain, at least without an interminable effort. If someone were to invent a plate that once washed remained clean forever and ever or a suit of clothes that self-cleaned while hanging in your closet, his fortune would be assured. The same is true in the spiritual realm. Spiritual dirt—sin—accumulates constantly without any significant effort on our part. Spiritual cleanliness seems impossible for us to maintain.

Dealing with Dirt

How do we deal with that reality in the realm of physical dirt? Well, one way to approach the issue is to redefine the nature of dirt. Does that pair of jeans really need washing, or can it be worn another day? How many dust bunnies does it take to form a quorum sufficiently large to require vacuuming? If we are able to define the acceptable level of dirt upward, then maybe our task in combating it will become manageable. Alternatively, we can try to limit the sources of contamination. Use only one dish per meal, as Hawthorne suggested; tell your children they can only play with one toy car or doll at a time; make everyone take off their shoes before they come into the house. Maybe that will make the impossible job of keeping the house clean and tidy achievable.

Essentially, people tend to adopt the same kinds of strategies when it comes to dealing with spiritual dirt. Many people try to redefine the nature of sin, thereby making obedience more manageable. I know I have to love my neighbor, but if I limit the extent of who my neighbor is, then obedience to the Law seems more achievable. If righteousness is defined merely in terms of external obedience to a set of rules and regulations, then perhaps I can manage to achieve it by carefully writing in enough loophole clauses and exceptions. Alternatively, others try to achieve spiritual cleanliness by limiting the potential sources of contamination. They huddle in their own family and religious group so the world cannot soil them. They don't watch movies—not even *The Sound of Music*—or listen to the radio or read secular books for fear of defilement. They try to separate themselves completely from anything and everything that might be a source of impurity.

Neither of these is a Biblical approach to the problem of the pervasiveness of spiritual dirt in our lives. On the one hand, the Bible works very hard to show the searching nature of God's definition of sin. Just as the Marine Corps drill sergeant performing an inspection is not impressed by attempts to persuade him that a blotch of ketchup does not make your uniform dirty, the Lord is not impressed by our attempts to redefine sin. In fact, the Scriptures are far more searching than any other religious code in their definition of sin. In the Bible, sin is not just failing to keep an external code of rules—it is having a heart that is not right with the Lord. Sometimes I meet people who insist that they keep the Ten Commandments. Immediately I am tempted to ask how they are doing on the first one—"I am the LORD your God. . . . You shall have no other gods besides me" (Exodus 20:2, 3). Are they really loving the Lord, the God of the Bible, with all of their heart and soul and mind and strength? Are they putting him first in their use of time and money? Do they truly wake up each morning with adoration in their heart toward the Lord and go to sleep with his name on their lips? If they are really achieving this, then I'd like to know how they do it, for I know that I'm not like that. However, if they are not loving the Lord wholeheartedly moment by moment, then they are daily breaking the most fundamental part of God's Law.

Equally, though, the solution to the pervasiveness of spiritual dirt is not for individuals to hide themselves away from the world. The Bible reminds us that sin comes not simply from outside human beings but from within. Like the Pharisees, such people are putting all of their attention on external sources of defilement when the reality is that sin comes from within. Figuratively speaking, they are carefully removing every speck of dirt from the dish before filling it with sewage-contaminated food and then wondering why they still become ill (see Matthew 15:1–20). The truth is that even if we were stranded on a desert island, we wouldn't lack for opportunities to sin. The reason is simple: our sinful nature would be right there with us. Sometimes when we are caught in some sin, we blurt out, "I don't know what happened. It's not like me to do that!" The sad reality, though, is that sin is exactly like us. We bear the seeds of every possible sin within our hearts; all it takes is the right external environment to bring it out. As the book of James reminds us, "Each person is tempted when he is lured and enticed by his own desire. Then desire when it has conceived gives birth to sin, and sin when it is fully grown brings forth death" (James 1:14, 15).

In the absence of a suitable external encouragement, the depth of our sinfulness may remain concealed, even to ourselves, but it nonetheless remains present.

The Need for Cleansing

If what the Bible says is true, and we are deeply sinful people at the core level of our existence, then what we need is a comprehensive and regular cleaning. Just as we have a plan for removing physical dirt from our homes on a regular basis, so also we need regular provision for our spiritual dirt to be removed and our hearts cleansed. This is not something we can do for ourselves, any more than Lady Macbeth could cleanse her own hands through repeated washings. It is something that the Lord needs to do for us.

This concept of spiritual dirt and the need for regular cleansing is the principle that underlies Numbers 19. The ritual system of Israel was not an arbitrary set of rules and regulations that would have provided them a means of earning righteousness before God. Rather, it reflected in a profound way the values that the Lord was laying down for Israelite society.[2] It was a simplified model of reality designed to help Israel understand the nature of the world in which she lived and the relationship she was required to have with the Lord. In that model, impurity could be contracted in a number of ways in ancient Israel, as we saw in an earlier study (see Numbers 5, considered in Chapter 6 of this book). Essentially, however, these diverse sources of contamination all reflected one central cause: contact with the realm of death.[3] The purpose of the prohibition of touching a corpse in Numbers 19 was not mere superstition or the fear of contracting disease. Rather, it flowed out of the close connection between death and sin. The Lord is the God of life, and those who would approach him need to reflect that life. The Israelites were being taught that death has no place in his presence, nor does anyone who has had contact with the realm of death. Like matter and antimatter, the Lord and death cannot peaceably coexist: the Lord will ultimately vanquish death (1 Corinthians 15:26), and thus even traces of death adhering to a person made him or her unfit to enter the Lord's presence.

The sharp separation that the Lord imposed between his people and death was designed to impress on the Israelites the defiling power of sin, which similarly contaminates us and makes us unfit for the Lord's presence, even in the least quantities. Yet the commandment to remain separate from death and sin could never be enough by itself. In their present context the entire community had recently come into contact with death because of Korah's rebellion and its aftermath. As a result, no one was free from death's contamination, and all needed to be made clean. Numbers 19 thus fittingly concludes the central portion of the book (11—19), where death has been such a prominent feature.[4] Everyone needed the cleansing that the Lord provided for them in this chapter, which itself was a profound picture of the ultimate cleansing the Lord would provide for the sins of his people. Through the regular application of the water of cleansing, the Lord promised to purify all those who had become contaminated by contact with death.

The Provision of Cleansing

How was this powerful cleansing detergent that would wash away their contamination to be made? First, the priest was to take a perfect, red cow[5] that had never been worked (19:2). The red-brown color highlighted the importance of blood as the key cleansing element. Two of the other key ingredients involved in the sacrifice, cedar and scarlet wool (v. 6), also share a reddish hue with the cow.[6] The answer to the scarlet stain of our sin is thus a blood-colored sacrifice.

Once selected, the cow was to be taken outside the camp and slaughtered (v. 3). Some of its blood was then sprinkled seven times toward the entrance to the tent of meeting (v. 4). This ritual is reminiscent of the normal procedure for a purification offering (often called a sin offering), with the appropriate modifications necessary due to the fact that the slaughter was taking place outside the camp (see Leviticus 4:6). After the sprinkling, the entire animal was burned, including the blood (v. 5). This was the only sacrifice in the Old Testament where the blood was burned rather than poured out at the base of the altar. The reason for this change is simple. Since the cleansing power of this sacrifice resided in the blood, the blood too had to be rendered into ashes. The other ingredient put into the fire, along with the cow, the cedar, and the scarlet wool, was hyssop (v. 6), an herb traditionally used to sprinkle the cleansing blood on objects and people. Everything in this procedure thus focuses our attention on the blood.

After the sacrificial heifer and the other ingredients had been burned completely, the ashes were to be gathered up and stored in a ceremonially clean place outside the camp until they were required (v. 9). The ashes were thus, if you like, a kind of "instant purification offering."[7] Just as we have instant tea or instant soup, to which we simply add water and they are ready to serve, so these ashes were reconstituted by the addition of water to make them ready for cleansing use (v. 17).

In addition to the centrality of blood in this ritual, the other remarkable, even paradoxical feature of this sacrifice was its power to defile the ones preparing and administering it. At the same time as the ashes made the defiled person clean, they also made the ceremonially clean person defiled.[8] From the priest who administered the ritual (v. 7), to the man who burned the animal (v. 8), to the man who gathered the ashes (vv. 9, 10), to the man who sprinkled the water (v. 21), every clean person who touched the ashes was defiled by them. Whoever or whatever they touched in the cleansing process became unclean because of the contagious power of defilement (v. 22). The ashes had to be stored outside the camp so they would not defile the camp by their very presence. It is as if the ashes were a kind of ritual detergent that cleansed the impure person by absorbing their impurity. In the process, though, they themselves became both defiled and defiling.

This is not a hard concept for us to grasp in the modern world. When I worked in the oil industry, we had a number of electrical transformers filled with polychlorinated biphenyls (PCBs). As part of the regular maintenance procedures, we wanted to change the oil in these transformers, but because PCBs are hazardous to the environment, we couldn't simply replace the old oil with new oil. Instead we contracted with a company to fill the transformers with fresh insulating oil, knowing that it would immediately become contaminated itself by the residue of PCBs. Then they removed this newly contaminated oil, along with the PCBs it now contained, leaving a cleansed transformer that could once again be returned to service. The cleansing process required the contamination of the clean as a condition for the cleansing of the contaminated.

Through the sacrifice of the red cow, cleansing was made easily available to all in the community, both native-born and alien alike (v. 10). The cost of the cleansing was kept low to the ones being cleansed. Yet the cost for the ones who made the offering on their behalf was substantial. It was not simply that the community had to bear the financial cost of sacrificing the cow. The one making the offering also had to temporarily sacrifice his own state of ritual cleanliness in order to let those who had become defiled enter in.

Once made, the ashes of cleansing had to be applied. As long as they remained stored away in a jar, they were of no benefit to anyone. The ashes had to be mixed with fresh (literally, "living") water (v. 17). Then hyssop was dipped into the mixture and was sprinkled on anyone and anything that had been contaminated by contact with death. This sprinkling was not an instantaneous cure, however. It was not a magic ritual that removed the need for the normal cleansing process, as if contamination could be simply removed with a wish and a pinch of magic dust. The water and ashes needed to be applied twice, on the third and the seventh day of defilement, and the person also needed to wash himself and his clothes (v. 19). Only then would the purification process be complete. Anyone who failed to follow this procedure remained defiled and would be a cause of defilement to the whole camp. Such a person would necessarily be cut off from the community (v. 20).

Our Modern Need for Cleansing

What does all this have to do with us and our deep need of cleansing? The answer is that this comprehensive ritual shows us both our need of cleansing and God's answer for it. In the first place, the ritual shows us our need of cleansing. Like the ancient Israelites, we are inevitably contaminated in our daily walk through this world. Just as they inevitably came into contact with death in their culture, so too we inevitably come into contact with sin. Some of their contact with death was deliberate, while other encounters were accidental, but it was virtually impossible for them perpetually to avoid such contact. They didn't have mortuaries and funeral directors and all of the means that we have developed in our society to avoid facing the ugly reality of death. Sometimes, therefore, they had no choice but to come into contact with death. At other times their contact with death was the result of carelessness or thoughtlessness. Either way, contact with death defiled them.

So too for us. Some of our sins are deliberate, while others are the result of carelessness and thoughtlessness on our part. Some sin, such as failing to love the Lord our God with all our hearts and all our souls as we should, is virtually inevitable due to our weakness as fallen human beings. We are pervasively contaminated people on every level of our beings. Instead of redefining sin so that it no longer covers the things that we do, or pretending that sin doesn't exist in our carefully sheltered world, it is far better to recognize the inevitable reality of our contact with sin and let that realization drive us back to God and to the cleansing he has provided.

In our society some churches are reluctant even to use the word *sin* anymore. They feel it is a negative word that will keep seekers away from God. Unfortunately, that refusal short-circuits the whole cleansing process: refusing to talk about sin is actually what keeps seekers away from God and not vice versa. Our natural tendency is to try to wash ourselves, substituting our own cleaning fluid for the living water and ashes. Just as ancient Israel insisted repeatedly on drinking from her own cracked and broken cisterns instead of looking to the Lord for living water (Jeremiah 2:13), so too we often substitute moral reformation—turning over a new leaf—for the Lord's cleansing water. We are easily persuaded that going to church, developing healthy relationships, and a good self-image are sufficient to pass muster with God. We will never be cleansed by the waters of cleansing, however, unless we first recognize the depth of our need and name it as what it is, *sin*. Until we recognize the hand of death in our lives in the form of sin, we cannot bring it to the Lord and receive the cleansing that he has provided for us.

Ongoing Cleansing

Moreover, the cleansing that we need is not simply a once-in-a-lifetime experience. Now, there is a once-in-a-lifetime experience of cleansing from sin, symbolized by baptism. That sacrament cannot be repeated, for it represents and communicates the completeness and sufficiency of our cleansing in Christ. What Jesus did on the cross is a once-and-for-all event that cannot be, and does not need to be, repeated. When we come to Christ by faith, at that moment our sins are washed away once and for all. Yet having been baptized does not in and of itself do away with our need for ongoing cleansing. Jesus pointed that out when he washed the disciples' feet. Peter (typically!) wanted not simply his feet washed but his whole body (John 13:9). Yet Jesus responded, "The one who has bathed does not need to wash, except for his feet" (v. 10). In other words, there is a once-and-for-all washing that does not need to be repeated, but there is also an ongoing, repeated washing.[9] As Christians, there are specific sins that we are conscious of having committed, along with the general grime that we acquire in the regular course of living in this fallen world. Both of these things need to be regularly washed away.

This is why the practice of confessing our sins to one another is so important. John reminds his hearers in 1 John 1:8, "If we say we have no sin, we deceive ourselves." To refuse to recognize our sins puts us in the category of the person who refused the cleansing waters in Numbers 19. Such a person must be cut off from the community of faith because he or she has refused the means that the Lord has provided to deal with his or her defilement. Being a Christian doesn't mean never having to talk about sin, any more than being in love means never having to say, "Sorry!" On the contrary, the reality is that it is those who are truly in love who are most likely to be found saying, "Sorry." For the same reason, true Christians are the most likely to be saying, "I have sinned." They don't live in denial, proudly pretending there is nothing amiss in their life. Rather, they recognize that when they sin they have offended someone they love deeply, and they are confident that the Lord will extend his mercy and forgiveness to wash them clean.

In our church we regularly confess our sins to the Lord as part of our worship service precisely as an encouragement to each of us to be honest about who we are and how much we still need the gospel, even as believers in Christ. It is an opportunity to go before Almighty God and recognize publicly that we all individually need the waters of cleansing applied to our hearts and lives. After we confess our sins, the minister then announces afresh to us from the Scriptures the assurance of the gospel, that in Christ there is cleansing and forgiveness for all who come to God by faith in him. We say to God, "Lord, I'm filthy inside and out. I'm sorry. This is who I am by nature." God in turn responds, "Here is the living water of cleansing that flows from the cross. Jesus died to make you acceptable to me just as you are, and I have sent my Holy Spirit to indwell you, to remake you ultimately as a new person."

What stands in the way of confessing our sins to God and to one another? Surely it is our pride. I know that to be the case for myself. It is because I am such a proud and hard-hearted person that I find confession of sin really difficult. It is so much easier for me to excuse my sin or to deny my sin. Yet when I do confess my sin, my pride is placed on the anvil and delivered another shattering blow. My eyes are opened afresh to the depth of my need for the gospel, and I am made thankful afresh for the cleansing waters that flow from the cross.

When we confess our sins weekly in church, we look back to that once-and-for-all event and look forward to anticipate all the more eagerly that final day of cleansing. We come and receive the absolution that Jesus purchased for us through his death in our place. We come asking that his blood be applied to our sins, washing away their stain upon us. We know that because the Lord is faithful and just, he will do it, cleansing us afresh and making us fit to stand in his presence. We come thankful that one day our cleansing will be over and we will be perfectly clean forever.

God's Faithfulness to Forgive Sins

The Apostle John sets out for us exactly that pattern of confession and assurance. Having reminded his hearers that they are indeed sinners, he goes on to say, "If we confess our sins, he is faithful and just to forgive us our sins and to cleanse us from all unrighteousness" (1 John 1:9). The talk of Christ cleansing us from all unrighteousness resonates exactly with the application of the waters of cleansing, doesn't it? It is Christ's blood that washes us clean from our filth. However, the passage also raises the question of how it can be "faithful and just" for God to forgive our sins. We can easily see how it could be "merciful and kind" of God to forgive us, but how can it be "faithful and just" for him to do so?

Once again the sacrificial ritual of the red cow makes it all clear. Remember that this ritual required two things for the cleansing to take place. There had to be a spotless sacrifice who was slaughtered to provide the means necessary for cleansing and a clean person who was willing to give up that state of ritual cleanliness and access to God for the sake of another. Both aspects of the ritual point forward to Jesus, the one who gave us his perfect holiness as our clean substitute and suffered for us as the spotless sacrifice. These two aspects of Jesus taking our place are what theologians call the active and passive obedience of Christ. On the one hand, there is the active obedience of Christ: this is the means by which Jesus became our clean substitute. He is the only human being who has ever been perfectly clean. We could have called a surprise inspection of his life at any moment, but we would never have found a speck of dirt where it didn't belong. He lived his life in perfect alignment with God's Law, in perfect tune with God's harmony. He thus took our place as the law-keeper, the clean one who administers the cleansing sacrifice for us.

But there is more. In addition to his perfect life, there is also his death for you and me—his passive obedience. He has not only taken our place as the law-keeper—he has also taken the place we deserved as law-breakers. He went outside the camp and offered his own blood as the atoning sacrifice: through his death he paid the debt for all of the sins of his people, and he became defiled in the process. As Paul puts it: "[God] made him to be sin who knew no sin, so that in him we might become the righteousness of God" (2 Corinthians 5:21). Just as in the offering of the red cow, the clean one had to become defiled, so the defiled one could be made clean, Jesus took our sins upon himself. If Jesus has died and made full payment for our sins, however, there is no payment left for us to make on them. God can't punish two people for the same offense. If Jesus has taken our defilement into himself, there is no stain left upon us. The foul spot has finally been purged away, transmitted to Christ. Therefore, because God is faithful and just, and the penalty for our sin has been paid in full, he must and will forgive all who are followers of Jesus for all of their sins.

Pleading Jesus

When you stand before God as your judge in the heavenly courtroom, there are therefore only two options as to how you can plead—and *innocent* isn't one of them. Nobody will be able to plead innocent before God because of a lack of contamination. The truth of our defilement will be clear to all. We have all disobeyed God and have gone our own way times without number. We are all thoroughly tainted by sin and death. One option is to plead guilty and pay ourselves for what we have done, refusing the water of cleansing that the Lord has provided. Tragically, many people will do that, and they will be separated from God forever as a result. "The wages of sin is death," says the Bible (Romans 6:23). If we are determined to pay that price ourselves, we will be eternally cut off from God in Hell.

But there is an alternative open to us. We don't have to plead guilty. We can plead Jesus. We can look to the purification offering that the Lord has established for us. We can say to God, "Lord God, I committed all those sins. They are all mine. The death that they deserve is mine. But your only Son Jesus has paid for every one of them. The payment for them all is death, but he paid it all when he died on the cross. He took my defilement on himself, and so now I am clean before you."

Do you feel clean in the Lord's presence today? Some people go through life like Lady Macbeth, scrubbing and scrubbing and scrubbing their hands with their own cleansing fluid, but they are never quite able to get rid of that foul spot. Perhaps there is some sin that clings to us like a neoprene wetsuit, defying our best efforts to dislodge it. Or perhaps there is some great sin in our past for which we are not sure God has ever really forgiven us. The cleansing that Christ provides for us not only makes us definitively clean when we first trust in him but also encourages us to come daily before him and ask for fresh cleansing in his blood. We must not ever get tired of bringing our sin to God; we have his word that he will never get tired of washing it away. In this fallen world, just as we continually wash our clothes and our dishes, we will continue to have to come to Christ regularly for washing. There is no magic cure that will keep us from further defilement. Praise God for the cleansing blood of Christ that purifies us from all unrighteousness. Praise God for the wonderful news that in Christ even our ongoing indwelling sins are presently covered and will ultimately be removed completely. Praise God that the day will come when we will have a spiritual cleanliness that will endure forever, when we enter into the presence of the Lord.

25

Repeating the Mistakes of the Past

NUMBERS 20

AN OLD SAYING TELLS US, "Those who don't remember the mistakes of the past are doomed to repeat them." Along similar lines some define *expert* as someone who recognizes his mistakes when he makes them again. Many of us can relate to this concept: we don't remember the mistakes of our past well enough to avoid making them again, but they certainly begin to look familiar after we have made them for the second or third or umpteenth time. Whether it is failing to measure the materials accurately before we cut them for a hobby project or failing to be consistent in disciplining our children, we all have areas in our lives where we live out the adage, "The only thing we learn from history is that we learn nothing from history" (Hegel). In that experience we have a great deal in common with ancient Israel. They too consistently failed to learn from their experience.

By Numbers 20 we have nearly reached the end of the wilderness wanderings: the events recorded here took place in the fortieth year after the Israelites started out (see 33:38).[1] So what had they learned in the course of those forty years? The sad answer, at least for the older generation, was, virtually nothing. If there had been an exit exam for leaving the wilderness, as there is in California for leaving high school, these people would have been doomed to wander there forever.

Back to the Future

This failure to learn is highlighted by the fact that the primary event recorded in Numbers 20, the miraculous provision of water from the rock, was a mirror image of a similar event that had taken place in the very first year of their wandering (Exodus 17).[2] That previous event is one of several backdrops against which we need to see this passage. At that first occasion in the wilderness of Sin (a similar sounding, yet different location from that in 20:1), the people quarreled with Moses and put the Lord to the test because there was no water for them to drink (Exodus 17:2, 3). They charged Moses with bringing the people out of Egypt simply to make them die of thirst in the wilderness (v. 3). However, on that occasion the Lord instructed Moses to bring the people to the rock at Horeb and to strike the rock there; water would flow from the rock for the people to drink (Exodus 17:6). In that first test Moses did exactly what the Lord told him to do, and the needs of the people were graciously met (Exodus 17:6).

That brief recap enables us to see what was still the same and what was new forty years later. The people's quarrel with Moses was the same on the surface, but now it was amplified by the resuscitation of all of their intervening grumbles. Though the presenting problem for the people was once again the lack of water, their complaint was far more wide-ranging than that. In counseling terminology this is called gunnysacking. Perhaps a husband offends his spouse by failing to pick up his socks, which she has legitimately asked him to do every other week for the past ten years or so. Or perhaps the wife forgot to pick up her husband's favorite suit from the dry cleaners as she had promised. Once the argument ensues, though, instead of focusing on the specific issue under dispute, all kinds of unresolved grievances emerge. One spouse inundates the other with every single one of his or her failings that he or she has carefully been saving up over the last six months, from the time she ran over the neighbor's cat to his habit of failing to put the lid back on the milk. The result is that instead of a limited argument over a minor issue, the couple ends up with a full-scale war because now they are dealing with six months' worth of issues all at once.

In the same way, in this case the Israelites' real problem was that they had nothing to drink, but once the Complaints Department was open for business, everything and anything was fair game. They repeated the complaint they had made when Moses had first brought them and their livestock into the wilderness—that he had led them there to die (Exodus 17:3), but now with an added edge. Now it was directed at Moses and Aaron together: "Why have you brought the assembly of the LORD into this wilderness, that we should die here, both we and our cattle? And why have you made us come up out of Egypt to bring us to this evil place?" (20:4, 5). That complaint has a familiar ring to it because it combines the charge made against Moses and Aaron by Dathan and Abiram in 16:13 ("Is it a small thing that you have brought us up out of a land flowing with milk and honey, to kill us in the wilderness?") with that of the people as a whole in 16:41 ("You have killed the people of the LORD"). In fact, the people now identified themselves explicitly as kindred spirits with Dathan and Abiram and the other rebels when they said, "Would that we had perished when our brothers perished before the LORD!" (20:3).[3] In spite of the Lord's grace to them as seen in the last three chapters, they declared that they would rather have died with those who had rebelled against the Lord.

Nor was it simply the sin of Numbers 16, 17 that was being recapitulated. The people also blamed Moses and Aaron quite unfairly for the consequences of their own choices. In chapter 14 they chose to believe the spies' "bad" or "evil" (*rā'â*) report concerning the Promised Land (v. 37) and so refused to enter it, in spite of the positive evidence that the spies had brought back of its fruitfulness in the shape of grapes, pomegranates, and figs (13:23). Now, however, they charged Moses and Aaron with bringing them out of Egypt to an "evil" (*rā*) place (v. 5), the same word that the spies had used to characterize the Promised Land. They were frustrated because the wilderness had no grain or vines or fig trees or pomegranates—the very fruit the spies brought back with them from Canaan (13:23). In other words, the people were blaming Moses and Aaron because the wilderness was not like the Promised Land that the people themselves had refused to enter!

Two familiar patterns of sin in their complaint are problems for us as well: catastrophizing and blame-shifting. Catastrophizing means that we paint our situation in far darker colors than is really warranted. Was their situation in the wilderness really a fate worse than death by fire (v. 3)? They may have been thirsty and missing some of their favorite foods, but the Lord had supplied those needs before, and he could do it again. They weren't really as bad off as they alleged—and often neither are we. Isn't it amazing how full of woe we can be while we are still healthy, surrounded by a family that loves us, with a roof over our heads? If we lack anything, is it too hard for the Lord to supply what we need? Instead of catastrophizing and anticipating the worst, we need to take our concerns to the Lord and trust in his goodness and power to provide for us in the situation.

The Consequences of Our Choices

Yet if the Lord is able to provide for our need, why doesn't he keep us out of difficulty in the first place? One answer that we often do not want to face up to is that we may be there as a result of our own wrong choices. God is sovereign over all things, even over my sinful choices, and sometimes he chooses to let me suffer the consequences of my sinfulness so that I may learn something of their true impact. When that happens, though, instead of repenting and accepting responsibility for my actions, I often exhibit the fact that my heart has a blame-retardant coating. Never mind what I did, this problem must surely be someone else's fault. I cry, "Lord, how could you let me end up in this terrible situation?" even though "this situation" is exactly where my own decisions and actions have logically brought me.

This is a trend that started all the way back in the Garden of Eden, with the woman blaming the serpent and the man blaming the woman and also God for giving her to him (Genesis 3:12, 13). Instead of blame-shifting, we need to take responsibility for our own actions and recognize that whatever our present situation, the Lord has always been far more gracious and merciful to us than we could possibly deserve. He never allows us to suffer in full measure the fate we truly deserve, and he always has good purposes for us in our trials, whatever our present difficulties may be.

The Response of Moses and Aaron

However, unlike Exodus 17, the main focus of Numbers 20 is not the sin of the people in grumbling against the Lord, serious though that is. The main focus here is the response of Moses and Aaron to that complaint. They started out well enough, falling down before the Lord and receiving his instructions (v. 6), just as they had with the people's previous complaints (16:4, 45). In response to their intercession, the Lord said to them:

> Take the staff, and assemble the congregation, you and Aaron your brother, and tell the rock before their eyes to yield its water. So you shall bring water out of the rock for them and give drink to the congregation and their cattle. (v. 8)

These instructions are clear enough, and the first two steps were carried out correctly: Moses took the staff from before the Lord, and he and Aaron gathered the people together, just as the Lord had commanded him (vv. 9, 10). However, this is where the obedience stops.[4] Instead of bringing water from the rock by the simple expedient of speaking to it, as he had been commanded, Moses launched into an impromptu speech to the people and then struck the rock, not once but twice (vv. 10, 11). Both of these acts were problematic, and together they show us that Moses too had been caught up in the people's sinful mind-set, even while he was ostensibly doing what the Lord told him to do.

First, there was his speech: "Hear now, you rebels: shall we bring water for you out of this rock?" (v. 10). There were two problems in this brief sentence. On the one hand, he termed the people "rebels." You might say, "Well, that is what they were." That is true. However, the problem is that Moses was putting himself in the place of judge to make that declaration though the Lord had not authorized him to do so. The Lord told him to extend his mercy and grace to the people in giving them water in a way that demonstrated unequivocally that the source was God; instead, Moses set himself up as their judge.

Not only did Moses set himself up as the people's judge, he also set himself (and Aaron) up as their deliverers. He said, "shall we bring water for you out of this rock?" (v. 10). Then he struck the rock twice, as if it were his action that brought forth the water. Who provided water from the rock for the people? It was the Lord, of course. In his frustration with the people, Moses was drawn into the same mind-set they had, forgetting the Lord's presence and power and acting as if everything were up to him. Moses presented himself as if he were a pagan magician with the ability to manipulate the gods to do his bidding.

There is more to Moses' sin than mere self-exaltation though. In the first encounter with the rock in Exodus 17, it was clear that the rock represented God himself (compare Genesis 49:24; Deuteronomy 32:4; Psalm 78:35). There the Lord allowed himself to be put on trial, standing before Israel, instead of putting them on trial for their complaining. In that awesome picture of grace, the Lord was willing to be struck himself instead of his rebellious people, so that they might receive life-giving water.[5] It is one thing to strike God when he instructs you to do so; it is quite another to smite him (twice!) on your own authority. Moses' act was thus nothing short of a direct assault on God himself.

In setting himself up as judge and deliverer of the people, Moses was demonstrating that he too had failed to learn from the past. That same self-exalting attitude was exactly what he had demonstrated when he first recognized the plight of his people when he was living as a prince in Pharaoh's court. At that time, Moses saw an Egyptian beating an Israelite, and he intervened and killed the Egyptian (Exodus 2:11, 12). The next day he saw two of his fellow Israelites fighting and tried to rebuke the one who was in the wrong. The man's response was, "Who made you a prince and a judge over us?" (Exodus 2:14). In other words, as a youth in Egypt Moses had been trying to judge and deliver his people in his own strength without a commission from the Lord. That attempt had ended in abject failure. Now, many years later, Moses had reverted once again to that old pattern of self-trust, judging the people in his own wisdom and trying to deliver them through his own acts, with similar results.

Beating the Sheep

Certainly Moses is not the only one who has ever been guilty of judging people or trying to deliver them on his own. It is a common temptation for those in leadership in the church to become frustrated when the sheep don't want to follow their shepherds. It is easy for us to judge them, whether privately in our own hearts or publicly in our sermons, berating them for their lack of vision. Sometimes the problem is that we, the shepherds, are trying to make them jump through the hoops of the latest ministry fashion or leadership fad, which the sheep have far too much sense to be caught up in. At other times we are seeking to lead them in good directions, challenging their comfortable inertia and urging them to move out in fresh obedience, and the sheep are simply being stubborn in their refusal to follow our lead. Either way, though, we can easily end up substituting law for grace and guilt for gratitude as the motivation for their obedience.

We can even do the same thing with ourselves. When we respond to our own sin by beating ourselves and judging ourselves as worthless people, we are acting as if we are our own judges. When we despair of ourselves in our ongoing struggle with sin, we are acting as if we are our own deliverers. What matters, however, is not how we judge ourselves but how God the Father judges us—and he declares us "Not guilty," for Jesus' sake. In spite of our sin, he calls us "saint" and "my child," because he sees us through Jesus and has committed himself to deliver us to himself holy and pure on the last day. It is his verdict that counts, not our own, and he is our gracious judge and faithful deliverer.

It is worth noticing that in Numbers 20, even though the people were clearly at fault in their complaining, the Lord viewed the sin of Moses and Aaron in judging them as a far more serious infraction. In other words, even when the sheep are simply being stubborn and recalcitrant in not following our leadership, we are not called to beat and berate them, even in our own minds. Instead, we are to love them and keep on urging them forward, gently and persistently pointing them to the cross.

In truth, much of our frustration in ministry comes from the fact that we have begun to see ourselves as the functional saviors of ourselves and our people. Remembering that it is the sovereign Lord who is saving and sanctifying us, and not we ourselves, will deliver us from much of our frustration. The Holy Spirit is the one who is responsible for transforming his sheep, and he will do so according to his agenda, not ours. We want ourselves and our people to be "fixed" right now, in part because it would give us a sense of personal satisfaction and achievement. We would then be able to bask in the glory of our renovation, feeding our pride and sense of self-worth. The Holy Spirit, however, is not eager to share his glory. He bears his fruit in the lives of his people in *his* season, not ours, so that it may be clearly seen that the work is entirely of him.

Rebelling against the Lord

The irony is that in judging the people and seeking to deliver them on their own, Moses and Aaron became exactly what they accused the people of being: rebels against the Lord. When it was time for Aaron's death at the end of the chapter, the Lord recalled their actions at Meribah and said, "Both of you rebelled against my command" (v. 24, NIV). The same was true when it came time for Moses to pass on the leadership of Israel to Joshua (27:14). In setting themselves forward as the people's judges and deliverers, Moses and Aaron publicly displayed their own failure to believe in and fear the Lord as a holy God (v. 12). Because of this lack of faith, they too were now excluded from entry into the Promised Land. Like the rest of the first generation, Moses and Aaron would die in the desert, yet more object lessons of the holiness of Israel's God.

The sin of Moses and Aaron was thus itself a recapitulation of the sin of the people in Numbers 13, 14 when they refused to enter the Promised Land. What Joshua had warned the people not to do ("Do not rebel against the LORD," 14:9) was exactly what Moses and Aaron now did (v. 24). The Lord's complaint about the people then would fit Moses and Aaron as well: "How long will this people despise me? And how long will they not believe in me, in spite of all the signs that I have done among them?" (14:11). Little wonder, then, that their punishment was the same as that entire generation: those who rebelled against the Lord through a lack of faith would never enter the land, no matter who they were.[6]

In essence, most of our sins boil down to a functional failure to believe God. In theory, we believe that God is our rock and our refuge; in practice, however, we often act as if God doesn't even exist. Why do we judge people and write them off as hopeless? It is because in practice we do not really believe that God can rescue and redeem them. Why do we get so angry and frustrated when our spouses and our families disappoint us? It is because we don't really believe that God is their judge, and we aren't willing to let their sanctification rest in the Lord's hands. Why are we so fearful for our own future? It is because we don't really believe that the Lord will deliver us at the critical moment. Why are we so angry with God at the way our lives have turned out? It is because we don't believe he has our best interests at heart or that there is more to life than what we see around us in this world. We are condemned by our failure to believe in the Lord as rebels against his goodness, just like Moses and Aaron and an entire generation of the ancient Israelites.

The Encounter with Edom

The parallels between Moses' and Aaron's failure to believe in the Lord and the failure of the people to do the same thing in Numbers 13, 14 help us see the significance of the enigmatic encounter with Edom that follows the events at Meribah (vv. 14-21). Moses sought to travel east from Kadesh, through the territory of the Edomites, but his request for passage was opposed by force and ended up in retreat. What we see here seems to be Moses doing exactly the same thing that the people did when they heard the Lord's judgment upon them: refusing to accept that judgment and attempting to force their way into the land in their own strength (see 14:39-45).[7]

Notice that the Lord did not instruct Moses to take this route, nor is the Lord's name mentioned in the account, except in passing (v. 16). This is in dramatic contrast with the conflict that we will see at the beginning of the next chapter (21:1-3), when the people sought the Lord before going into battle and received victory from the Lord. When Israel's first request was rebuffed by Edom, they sought to resolve the matter through political negotiations rather than through prayer. If the Lord had been with Moses and the people in this endeavor, it would not have mattered that Edom came out against them with a large army; but without the Lord's presence they had no power to prevail over those who opposed them (vv. 20, 21). Like the earlier abortive campaign of the people, Moses' attempt to find a shortcut into blessing ended up in a blind alley.

The Wages of Rebellion

Numbers 20 thus shows us the judgment of the Lord on the wilderness generation reaching its climax in judgment on their leaders. Moses and Aaron joined the rebels in their sin and paid the same price as they did—exclusion from the land. The fact that the wages of rebellion is death for leaders as well as for followers is highlighted by the deaths that bracket the chapter: it began with the death of Miriam at Kadesh (v. 1) and ended with the death of Aaron (vv. 22-29). It was actually unbelief and rebellion that threatened death in the wilderness, not a lack of water.

Aaron's death was announced ahead of time by the Lord: he was to go up Mount Hor with his brother Moses and his son Eleazar, where he would die (vv. 25, 26). There he was to be stripped of his robes of office, which were then to be transferred to his son (v. 26). This was more than a mere rite of transfer from father to son. The language of stripping implies that a measure of degradation was involved. To go along with the judgment of not being allowed to enter the Promised Land, Aaron was being stripped of his office as high priest, which from now on would be his son's responsibility.[8]

This time we are told that Moses did exactly as the Lord commanded him. The earlier disobedience that took place in the sight of the whole community (v. 12) was at last replaced by obedience in the sight of the whole community (v. 27). The high-priestly baton was transferred from one generation to the next, and the whole congregation mourned Aaron's passing (v. 29). The old generation was fading away, their epitaph the words of Psalm 90, the only psalm written by Moses:

You sweep them away as with a flood; they are like a dream,
like grass that is renewed in the morning:
in the morning it flourishes and is renewed;
in the evening it fades and withers.
For we are brought to an end by your anger;
by your wrath we are dismayed.
You have set our iniquities before you,
our secret sins in the light of your presence.
For all our days pass away under your wrath;
we bring our years to an end like a sigh. (vv. 5-9)

Signs of Grace

In the midst of the death and disgrace that so dominate Numbers 20, it would be easy to overlook the positive signs of the Lord's grace that it contains. Even though Moses and Aaron sinned in carrying out the Lord's command and received a curse, the Lord nonetheless granted his rebellious people the flow of water that they needed. Even though Moses would not lead the people into the land, yet the Lord's promise to grant the land to them still stood, and he would raise up Joshua to take Moses' place. Even though Aaron was now dead, the next generation was ready to take up his priestly work through his son, Eleazar. In fact, the deaths of Miriam and Aaron in this chapter in some ways mark the beginning of a generational transition. Even though the definitive turning point of the census of the next generation is still six chapters away, from the beginning of Numbers 21 things started to look up for Israel. The Lord is not only far more gracious than we believe him to be—he is far more gracious than we deserve.

On what is your trust for the present and your hope for the future built? You might think that a leadership team of Moses, Miriam, and Aaron would be a tough combination to improve upon, but by the end of this chapter their story is effectively over: they are dying, dead, and dead. We need a better leader than Moses, someone who will not get frustrated with his people and judge them. We need someone who will show his people grace and effectively deliver them in their hour of need. The good news of the gospel is that a leader who is better than Moses has come in the person of Jesus. The Apostle Paul tells us that Jesus Christ was actually part of this story in Numbers 20: he was the spiritual rock that accompanied his people through the wilderness and from which they drank (1 Corinthians 10:4). In Jesus Christ, God himself took the blows that we deserved for our rebellion. He is the righteous High Priest who was stripped not because of any failure on his part but to enable him to take our place on the cross under God's curse. From him flows the living water that we need to slake our thirsty souls and to transform our lives increasingly into his image.

The wages of sin is death. This chapter demonstrates clearly the fact that this was true for Miriam, for Aaron, and ultimately for Moses as well. This is equally true for us all: we all have our own besetting sins to which we return, which are simply the outward overflow of our inner unbelief. It may be an uncontrolled temper or a sharp tongue or a lustful heart. It may be a complaining attitude or judgmental pride. Whatever it is, such sin marks us out as rebels against God. Like Moses and Aaron, we are all rebels who deserve death. Yet in Christ there is an answer for our rebellion. In Christ we have someone who has taken the death that we deserved and has paid fully for our sins. His perfect obedience is now credited to our account, exactly as if it were our own. In him we are justified freely right now, sinners though we are. In that reality lies our hope, our peace, and our comfort in the weary wilderness.

How long, then, will you and I refuse to believe in this God who has so wonderfully demonstrated his love for us in so many ways? How long will we trust in ourselves and judge others? How long will we become angry and frustrated over our own lack of sanctification and the failures of others? We must look to the Lord and submit our hearts to him, trusting in his goodness and mercy, believing that his timing is perfect, being filled with thankfulness for his death and resurrection. We must ask God to teach us wisdom and patience, grace and gentleness, and, above all, love. The day will come when our earthly struggles and rebellions will be over, and the Lord will welcome us into his presence; then all our frustrations will finally be over. Until then, the good news of his gospel of grace will faithfully sustain our thirsty souls step by step along the way.

26

A New Beginning

NUMBERS 21

WATCHING YOUR CHILDREN GROW UP is an odd experience. In some ways they are so like their parents. Yet, in other ways they couldn't be more different. One of your children looks just like you perhaps, yet has a mellow temperament that is the opposite of yours. Another child has looks that must be a throwback from several generations ago, yet loves the same music that you do. A third shares your sense of humor but leaves you wondering, "Where did her artistic genes come from?" Moreover, however much our children are like us, they all speak a different language and, in some respects at least, inhabit a different culture from the one in which we grew up. The next generation is both like and unlike their parents.

The same was true of Israel in the book of Numbers. We have pointed out several times already that this book is essentially the story of two generations: the first generation who rebelled against the Lord and ended up dead in the desert, and the second generation who will stand on the brink of entry into the Promised Land at the end of the book. In many respects Numbers 20 was the end of the line for the first generation: it shows us the events of the fortieth year of wilderness wandering, bracketed by the deaths of Miriam and Aaron. Now in Numbers 21 we begin to read the story of the second generation.[1] As in real life, such transitions are not hard and fast. The remnant of the first generation is still present until chapter 26, when the complete transfer is marked by a new census. Nevertheless, in some ways the story of the new generation starts here in Numbers 21. What will they be like? How will they be similar to and different from their parents? What this chapter shows us is that in this generation there is something different and something still the same, along with some other things that never change, whatever generation you find yourself living in.

A New Victory

The story begins with something completely different: victory over the Canaanites (vv. 1-3). It is a brief snippet within the overall narrative but one that is full of significance. The Canaanites initiated the conflict, attacking the Israelites and capturing some of them (v. 1). In the past this kind of reverse at the hands of their enemies could easily have been enough to send Israel into a catastrophic tailspin of despair and grumbling, but the new generation took the challenge in their stride. They went to the Lord and vowed that if the Lord gave them success, they would devote to destruction all of the Canaanite cities (v. 2). The Lord gave them the victory, and they obediently fulfilled the terms of their vow, completely destroying the Canaanites and their towns. This victory was a kind of firstfruits of the conquest of the Promised Land, a paradigm example of how to take on and defeat the Lord's enemies through trust in him.[2]

The practice of total destruction of the cities of their enemies (*herem*) was not a regular part of Israel's warfare throughout the ages.[3] On the contrary, it was for the most part a unique and temporary feature particularly associated with the conquest of the land of Canaan. Just as the possession of the land of Canaan by the Lord's people foreshadowed their heavenly inheritance, so too the slaughter of the present inhabitants was a foreshadowing of the final judgment of sinners by God. At the end of all things, there will be a judgment for sin that will encompass all men, women, and children and will result in a final separation of humanity into two groups. According to the Bible, all those who are outside of Christ will be cast into the lake of fire (Revelation 20:11-15), while those who by God's grace are the Lord's people will enter into their heavenly rest (Revelation 21). What happened in the conquest of Canaan was a visual depiction in time of that ultimate reality. The Lord had declared that when the sins of the Amorites were full, they were to be exterminated as a judgment from the Lord (see Genesis 15:16). In that judgment, Israel served as the human equivalent of the fire and brimstone that destroyed Sodom and Gomorrah (Genesis 19:24, 25) or the flood that destroyed the wicked in Noah's time (Gen. 6—8).

This comprehensive judgment also served important purposes in Israel's conquest campaign. In the first place, it marked out the battle as the Lord's by dedicating the spoils of victory to him. Since the Lord won the victory, it was only fitting that he should receive the spoils of the war. Israel was not fighting merely to acquire territory or wealth for themselves. Rather, their battle was for the Lord: they fought for his glory and at his direction. That is why failure to observe the rules of *herem*, as when Achan took some of the spoil from Jericho for himself (Joshua 7:1), was such a serious offense. It was stealing from the Lord, and it resulted in the Lord's fighting *against* Israel instead of *for* them. In addition, the practice of total destruction of the Canaanites also removed the practical tempta-tion for Israel to assimilate the ways of the inhabitants of the land, inter-marrying with them and being drawn into the worship of their gods (see Deuteronomy 7:3, 4). A little later in the book of Numbers we will see just how serious that temptation to assimilate was, when we see the Israelites drawn into sexual immorality and idolatry through their contacts with Moabite women (25). Obviously, *herem* warfare removed that potential temptation at the source.

Israel's victory here in Numbers 21 marked their very first success against the Canaanites, and it was all the sweeter because it occurred at Hormah. Hormah was the site of the first generation's defeat by the Canaanites back in Numbers 14, when they tried to enter the Promised Land in their own strength (v. 45). Now, though, it earned its enduring name of Hormah (derived from *herem*) as the new generation demonstrated their faith in the same location where their forefathers had demonstrated unbelief. As a result, they saw the Lord grant them the firstfruits of the conquest.

More Victories

Nor was this first success a solitary victory. Much of the chapter is taken up with the defeat of Sihon and Og, two kings of the Amorites. Israel at first sought to pass through Sihon's territory peacefully (v. 22), just as they had asked the King of Edom for passage in the previous chapter (20:14-21). Just like the King of Edom, Sihon refused to let them pass and marched out against them with a sizable army. Here, though, the story line diverges from the preceding incident. Unlike the previous generation, the new generation was not so easily intimidated by a show of force. When Sihon fought against them, they put him to the sword and occupied his territory (vv. 23-25).

They then moved on to Jazer, where Moses sent out spies to survey the territory (v. 32). This kind of maneuver makes you nervous, in view of what happened after the last scouting trip (13, 14). Yet this time the story moves straight on from the scouting trip to the capture of Jazer and its surrounding settlements. It is once again clear that this new generation is not like their fathers, and it shows what could have happened earlier, if the people had only had faith in the Lord. Finally, they met Og, King of Bashan, and his mighty army (v. 33). The Lord reminded Moses not to be afraid of him, for the Lord had handed him over to the Israelites (v. 34). Once again, the result was a comprehensive victory for Israel and the total destruction of their enemies (v. 35; see also Deuteronomy 2:26—3:7).[4] Israel then took posses-sion of his land as well. The new generation was clearly *new* in more than just name: they were a generation who by faith were winning the battles that their parents never dared to attempt.

The Same Old Grumbling

Yet in other ways the new generation was not so radically different from their forefathers. We can see that from the incident with the bronze serpent, which took place right after their initial victory over their enemies. Having defeated the Canaanites, the Israelites headed south once again to go around the territory of Edom, back toward the Red Sea (v. 4). Perhaps heading toward the Red Sea at this point felt altogether too much like going back to the starting point of the whole exodus. After forty years, the victory at Hormah notwithstanding, were they still just going in circles? Would they ever see the full harvest of victory over the Canaanites? Whatever the cause, the new generation found themselves in the same cycle of grumbling as their fathers had, over exactly the same things. They grumbled against God and Moses, suggesting they had brought them into the wilderness to die there (v. 5; compare 14:3; 16:13; 20:5). They complained about the lack of food and the monotony of the manna (v. 5; compare 11:6). They even moaned about the lack of water (v. 5), just as the older generation had in the previous chapter (20:5). It seems that the more things change, the more they stay the same.

The aftermath of this grumbling was no different for the new generation than it had been for the old generation. The Lord sent judgment upon his grumbling people in the shape of fiery serpents,[5] whose bite was fatal (v. 6). The wages of sin and unbelief continued to be death for the new generation as it had been for the old. Yet once again Moses was there to intercede for the people when they repented. In response to his intercession, the Lord commanded him to make a bronze serpent and lift it up on a pole, so that anyone who had been bitten could look at the serpent and live (v. 8).

To understand what is going on here, it is important to recognize that neither the judgment nor the remedy was a random phenomenon. It is not as if the Lord saw his people sinning and then said to himself, "Now what shall I afflict them with today? I think I'll send snakes! I haven't tried that punishment before." Nor was the form of the judgment simply due to the fact that snakes were a convenient commodity with which to afflict people in that part of the desert. Rather, it was a sign that was full of meaning for the Israelites, who had only a few years earlier emerged from Egypt and were therefore well-versed in Egyptian symbolism. These serpents were a potent representation of the power of Egypt, to which they were apparently so eager to return. Snakes were well-known symbols of power and sovereignty in ancient Egypt, as the familiar image of a cobra on Pharaoh's crown reminds us.[6] Having once been freed from Pharaoh, did they really want to be subject to the power of the serpent all over again?

Even more profoundly, though, the serpent (*nāḥāš*) is a symbol of the ultimate enemy of mankind, Satan himself. It was in the form of a serpent (*nāḥāš*) that Satan deceived our first ancestors and brought about the sin that caused us to be cast out of the garden into the desert of this fallen world. It was not the Lord who had brought them into the wilderness to die, as they alleged (v. 5). Their death was not due to his power failing to give them that which he had promised. On the contrary, death in the wilderness was the result of their own sin and that of their forefather, Adam. It was their refusal to submit to the Lord that led to bondage to Satan, who is the real hard taskmaster.

Nor was the standard on which the serpent was to be transfixed merely a convenient means of lifting the serpent up where everyone could see it. In Egypt, such a pole or standard was a recognized symbol of the deity's power.[7] Here it served to demonstrate that the Lord's power was present in the midst of the camp, granting life to those whose sins had condemned them to death through the serpent's bite. The transfixed serpent on the standard thus demonstrated in visual terms the defeat of Israel's mortal enemies, Egypt and Satan, overcome by the power of the Lord. When the people felt afresh the bitter pain of their sinful rebellion, they were given a sign to show them the life-giving power of the Lord that was constantly available to heal them.

The serpent on the pole was not a magical cure for snakebite, however. On the contrary, it was a sign that worked by taking the Lord at his word through faith. The people were to look intently at the bronze serpent, putting their trust in the power of the Lord's victory over evil, and then they would be healed. It is not coincidental that the Lord chose this means of healing the people, for faith is the key marker of those who would enter the Promised Land. The unbelieving generation of their parents, including Moses and Aaron, were excluded from the land because of their unbelief (see 14:11; 20:12). The judgment by the fiery serpents would similarly eliminate any from the new generation who were lacking in faith, for those who refused to look to the Lord through the bronze serpent would die. Only those who believed could enter the land, for only those who believed would live.

Camping and Moving On

Grumbling was not the only experience that the new generation shared with their forefathers. They also experienced their fair share of camping and moving on, as verses 10-20 show us. This lengthy travel itinerary may seem at first sight a waste of our time as well as theirs. Who really knows where "Waheb in Suphah" was (v. 14)? The commentators can only guess. More pertinently, why would anyone really care? Yet the travelogue of desert camps heightens our awareness of the experience of the new generation of traveling on and on while apparently going nowhere. That is the precise point of its inclusion. It shows us that the new generation proceeded onward through a succession of nowhere places in the wilderness around Moab just as their fathers had; yet it was precisely in these places that they learned of God's continuing faithfulness. There, in the middle of nowhere, they experienced the Lord's faithfulness in providing a well (vv. 16, 17), contradicting their earlier complaint that there was no water in the wilderness (v. 5). There in the middle of nowhere they also experienced the Lord's faithfulness in giving them victory in battle, as demonstrated in the reference to "the Book of the Wars of the LORD" (v. 14), along with the defeat of Sihon and Og, two of Israel's most archetypal enemies. These victories disproved their earlier claim that the Lord had brought them into the wilderness to die (v. 5).

What is more, it was there in the middle of nowhere that the people started to sing. The first generation had entered the wilderness with a song on their lips (Exodus 15), but that song soon died away, overwhelmed by the harsh realities of life and the growing unbelief of the people. Grumbling is irreconcilable with singing. Grumbling feels sorry for itself, while singing delights in what God has given and what he has promised to give. It is therefore not coincidental that with the rise of the new generation and their healing for their sin, we see a new burst of song, which was the outward expression of their faith.[8] When God's people sing, they confess that life is not merely an endless cycle of one barren campground after another, as it sometimes appears to be. Rather, they proclaim that God is faithful in the present to provide provision along the way and that he can be trusted to give ultimate victory. Singing is always an index marker of faith in the greater realities to come.

Faith Needed and Rewarded

The bronze serpent was itself a sign of a greater reality to come. When Jesus met with the Jewish leader Nicodemus, he said, "And as Moses lifted up the serpent in the wilderness, so must the Son of Man be lifted up, that whoever believes in him may have eternal life" (John 3:14, 15).

In other words, just as the bronze serpent was a sign calling for faith to which people could look and be delivered from death, so Christ's crucifixion would have the same effect. God was going to provide a means of dealing with the wages of sin through Jesus Christ being lifted up on the cross.

Yet, if you think about the symbolism of the original sign, the fulfillment is richer than merely a superficial parallel. For it was precisely on the cross that Jesus won his victory over the ancient serpent, Satan himself, fulfilling the original gospel promise of God: "I will put enmity between you [the serpent] and the woman, and between your offspring and her offspring; he shall bruise your head, and you shall bruise his heel" (Genesis 3:15). At the cross, Jesus broke the serpent's power, just as in the wilderness the serpent was transfixed on the symbol of God's power. Yet in the fulfillment of the sign, Jesus took upon himself the curse when he was lifted up on the cross. At that moment Satan seemed to have triumphed, killing God's chosen one and extinguishing the light of the world. It seemed as if God himself had been transfixed by Satan's power rather than vice versa. Death could not hold Jesus though: the resurrection showed that Satan had, after all, only struck Jesus' heel. God's power had indeed triumphed through that incredible substitution. Jesus bore in his body the covenant curse of God, so that through his death Adam's offspring might be freed from that judgment. By his suffering we were healed. All we have to do to receive the blessing of eternal life in God's presence is to believe in Jesus Christ and look intently to his death on the cross as the source and guarantee of our salvation.

The challenge that this passage presents to each one of us is therefore the question, to which generation do we belong? Are we part of the old, unbelieving generation that perishes in the wilderness, or part of the new, believing generation that is saved from its sin and grumbling by faith in the sign of God's awesome victory over the evil one? If you have not yet placed your faith in Christ, now is the time to do so. The good news of the gospel is that those who were once part of the old, unbelieving generation, under sentence of death for their sin and already experiencing its effects, can become part of the new generation destined for life. Faith is the doorway to a whole new life. Whether you are young or old, all you need to do is look to Jesus Christ and confess him who was crucified for your sins and raised for your justification. In that simple confession of faith is the gift of eternal life. Just as Jesus told Nicodemus, "God so loved the world, that he gave his only Son, that whoever believes in him should not perish but have eternal life" (John 3:16).

Living by Faith: *Simul Cantor et Peccator*

Faith is not merely the first step in our journey with God, however. We do not begin with faith and then move on to trusting in ourselves and our own efforts. Faith is the stuff of life in the wilderness, unleashing the power of God by which Satan is overcome. What, then, are the marks of those who are living by faith?

First, those who live by faith are committed to a life of repentance. Repentance is the reflex of the faith that brought you into the kingdom, for looking to Christ means at the same time turning away from all other means of salvation. You couldn't look intently at the bronze serpent and at something else as well. What is more, repentance continues to be the reflex of faith throughout our earthly pilgrimage. We are constantly being bitten by sin, as it were—feeling the painful effects of failure in our ongoing struggle against our sinful nature. Just as we daily see those bitter fruits of sin, so too we are daily to take those sins and nail them afresh to the cross.

Repentance is not simply a matter of recognizing and bemoaning what great sinners we are. As long as we are doing that, our eyes are still fixed on ourselves. Repentance is turning our heart to Christ in the midst of recognizing our own sin and fixing our eyes once again on the remedy for that sin, offered to us in the gospel. Repentance is catching ourselves when we have grumbled over some challenge to our comfort or our sense of being in control of our lives or our acceptance by the in-crowd and deliberately turning our face afresh toward Jesus. Repentance is picking ourselves up after we have sought comfort in some earthly substitute for God, whether food or lustful thoughts or shopping or gossip or an angry outburst, and saying to ourselves, "This is not my comfort. My only refuge is Jesus." The life of faith is a life of repentance that is constantly turning away from sin and turning toward Jesus.

Second, those who live by faith persevere by faith. The road through life is long and hard, and our progress is often slow and hard to measure. Sometimes it seems in our lives as if we are faced once again toward the Red Sea, going backward rather than forward. In those moments, faith remembers that our arrival at the promised destination depends on God's faithfulness, not ours, and endures the difficulty. With the psalmist we may cry out, "How long, O Lord?"—the spiritual equivalent of the child's "Are we almost there yet?" However, as long as we are gazing at Christ, we need never wonder whether we will get there. The crucified and resurrected Lord is himself the guarantee that all those whom the Father has given him will reach their destination. There are many wars and multiple campsites for us to traverse along the way, but his faithfulness will never leave us or forsake us.

Third, those who live by faith sing songs of praise. The gospel transforms us from sinners to singers. To be sure, that is often a gradual process. Throughout our lives, we will continue to be *simul cantor et peccator* ("at the same time a singer and a sinner," to paraphrase Luther's famous expression). However, as we near our destination, the songs should gradually increase in intensity. Those whose eyes are fixed on Jesus should be increasingly hungry for worship. They love to join the angels in singing praise to the Father, the Son, and the Holy Spirit, reminding themselves of the good news and declaring the gospel to all creation. They love to celebrate the faithfulness of the Lord in the present and the sure expectation of final deliverance from the Lord in the future.

Fourth, those who live by faith partake joyfully in the sign of the Lord's victory over Satan. Israel was given a visible symbol to look at: a bronze serpent. We have been given a visible and tangible sign of God's victory in the Lord's Supper. As we eat the bread and drink the cup, we are pointed afresh to the Lord's victory: we look backward and proclaim his death on the cross, and we look forward and proclaim his certain return. The Lord's Supper too is a sign that works by faith, feeding and spiritually strengthening and healing those who discern the Lord's body and blood, while those who partake without faith receive no benefits from it. It is spiritual food that sustains us in the wilderness and assures us of the reality of Heaven and the certainty of God's faithfulness to us personally.

Faith gazes steadfastly and intently at the cross of Jesus Christ. The cross is the place where our salvation was accomplished. The cross is the guarantee of God's present love for us, which is so great that he sent his only begotten Son to die so that we might live. The cross is the surety of the eternal rest that awaits us when our traveling and warring days are done. What could be sweeter, then, than to sing of the cross? In the words of the classic hymn by Isaac Watts:

> When I survey the wondrous cross
> On which the Prince of glory died,
> My richest gain I count but loss,
> And pour contempt on all my pride.
>
> Forbid it, Lord, that I should boast,
> Save in the death of Christ, my God:
> All the vain things that charm me most,
> I sacrifice them to His blood.
>
> See, from His head, His hands, His feet,
> Sorrow and love flow mingled down;
> Did e'er such love and sorrow meet,
> Or thorns compose so rich a crown?
>
> Were the whole realm of nature mine,
> That were a present far too small;
> Love so amazing, so divine,
> Demands my soul, my life, my all.

27

The Politician and
the Donkey

NUMBERS 22

LISTENING TO THE 2004 DEBATES between the candidates for President of the United States of America was a fascinating experience. In each debate there were questions from the moderator to each candidate in turn, and each candidate had a chance to rebut the answers of the other man. In order to understand the positions of the presidential hopefuls, though, it was never enough simply to listen to what they said. You always had to be careful to notice what they didn't say as well. In some cases the answer given by the candidate bore little or no relationship to the question he had been asked. In other cases the candidates answered part of the question but left another key aspect deliberately unmentioned. The casual listener might be moved by impressive sound bites or by the outward demeanor of the candidates, but the person wishing to understand their respective political platforms fully had to listen very carefully to the silences as well as to the words.

Numbers 22 has a lot in common with these political debates. The superficial reader, whose attention is focused on sound bites and the surprising appearance of a talking donkey, may easily miss the point and end up confused by this narrative. Is Balaam the hero or villain in this story? Is he a sinner or a saint?[1] Why did God tell Balaam to go with Balak's envoys (v. 20) and then get angry with him when he did just that (v. 22)? Did God suddenly and inexplicably change his mind?[2] Or were there valid reasons for his anger? The key to understanding this story is to recognize that Balaam was a politician as well as a prophet, a man who made a living from his words. Such people do not always say what they mean or mean what they say.[3] The speeches of people like Balaam need to be analyzed closely to hear what they do not say as well as what they do say. When you do that, the narrative springs to life with a whole new level of clarity.

In Search of a Weapon of Mass Destruction

The story begins with Balak, King of Moab, looking across his border in terror at the reality of the Israelites as new neighbors (vv. 2, 3).[4] Given what the Israelites had done in the previous chapter to Sihon and Og, the kings of the Amorites and Bashan respectively, this was perhaps not a surprising response. The idea of a conventional war against the Israelites seemed to have little prospect of success because of their vast numbers, and the thought of seeking a peaceful settlement with this new political reality apparently didn't arise.[5] What Balak and the Moabites wanted was a nonconventional war involving a weapon of mass destruction that would debilitate the Israelites, enabling the Moabites to be victorious over them. In the ancient world there was only one such weapon of mass destruction: a curse from the gods that would decisively tip the balance of power against your enemies.

It was in search of just such a curse that Balak sought out Balaam, a man with an international reputation for dealing in such weaponry.[6] Balak sent messengers to summon Balaam to curse Israel, so Balak could defeat them in battle and drive them away, saying, "I know that he whom you bless is blessed, and he whom you curse is cursed" (vv. 5, 6). At this point, the battle lines were clearly drawn, for in Genesis 12:2, 3 the Lord had already declared to Abram:

> I will make of you a great nation, and I will bless you and make your name great, so that you will be a blessing. I will bless those who bless you, and him who dishonors you I will curse, and in you all the families of the earth shall be blessed.

By summoning Balaam to curse Israel, Balak had set himself against the Lord and the Lord's people, and therefore he was under a curse of his own. Which curse would win out—the pagan prophet's or the Lord's?

Listening to the Sounds of Silence

The elders of Moab, along with their allies from Midian, went to Balaam carrying Balak's message and the down payment on the proposed divination contract (v. 7). Balaam responded by asking them to spend the night with him while he sought the direction of "the LORD" on the matter (v. 8). Now this is certainly a striking and surprising twist in the story: Balaam used the personal name of Israel's God (Yahweh) as the one from whom he would seek direction. It raises the concern that if Balaam were able to consult the Lord, perhaps he could change the Lord's mind from blessing to curse. Perhaps he had enough standing with his master to receive what he requested. Yet one shouldn't jump too quickly from Balaam's words to the conclusion that Balaam was an orthodox follower of the Lord. Like all politicians, Balaam was quite capable of playing the "God" card when and how it suited him to do so. He obviously knew who the Lord was and apparently received messages from him, but exactly what his relationship to the Lord was has yet to be made clear. In a narrative in which a donkey also sees the Lord and speaks his words, the ability to prophesy truthfully in the Lord's name should not by itself be rated too highly.

Sure enough, the Lord appeared to Balaam in the night and asked him, "Who are these men with you?" (v. 9). On the face of it, that is a simple question, but why did God ask it? He certainly didn't need the information from Balaam since he already knows all things. In the Bible God typically asks questions not for his own benefit but for the benefit of his hearers. When God said to Adam, "Who told you that you were naked? Have you eaten of the tree of which I commanded you not to eat?" (Genesis 3:11), he was giving Adam an opportunity to confess his sins. When the Lord asked Isaiah, "Whom shall I send, and who will go for us?" (Isaiah 6:8), he wasn't expressing personal uncertainty; he was giving Isaiah the opportunity to volunteer for the mission. So too when the Lord said to Balaam, "Who are these men?" he wanted Balaam to reflect on who would be giving him his orders if he accepted their commission. What authority did they have to summon him, and what power did they have to reward him? These were not gods who had come to him—they were mere men.

Balaam responded to the Lord's inquiry with a carefully edited version of Balak's message (compare v. 11 with vv. 5, 6). What he left out in his presentation to the Lord was profoundly significant. Balaam omitted the fact that Israel had settled next to Balak but had not attacked him and that Balak's action therefore could not be construed as justified self-defense. He also left out Balak's flattering assertion that Balaam had the power to bless and to curse effectively. In contrast to this dissimulation on Balaam's part, the Lord's answer was definitive and clear: "You shall not go with them. You shall not curse the people, for they are blessed" (v. 12). The promise of Genesis 12 was explicitly still in force. The Lord had declared his will clearly and unequivocally to Balaam.

Confusing Signals

In the morning Balaam took this message from the Lord and conveyed it to the envoys of Balak—once again in carefully edited form. What he said to them was simply, "Go to your own land, for the LORD has refused to let me go with you" (v. 13). There was no mention of the fact that he was unable to curse Israel because the Lord had decreed definitively that they were blessed, nor was there evidence of any reluctance on his own part to do their bidding. In fact, if they listened carefully, they would hear quite the contrary. When my son tells one of his playmates that his dad says he can't come out to play until his homework is finished, he makes it evident that he would very much like to go with them but is presently being detained against his will. So too when Balaam said that the Lord had refused to let him come with them, he clearly implied that he personally would have loved to be able to oblige Balak if only the circumstances had been different.

By the time the envoys returned home to tell Balak the news, the process was beginning to resemble a game of Telephone, in which children whisper a message from one to the next down a line. In that game, the message that emerges at the far end is often quite different from the message that started out. So too here the message that Balak received was quite different from the one that the Lord sent. Far from being told that Balaam could not curse this people because the Lord had declared them to be blessed, he heard from his envoys only that Balaam had refused to come (v. 14). Not unnaturally, Balak read this as a mere negotiating ploy on Balaam's part and responded by sweetening the pot. Balak promised to honor him greatly (i.e., reward him substantially) if he would only come and curse this people (vv. 16, 17). Nothing (and no one) should therefore prevent him from coming. Balak backed up his improved offer by sending a higher-ranking delegation of envoys to convey it to Balaam (v. 15).

When the more distinguished entourage of Moabites and Midianites arrived at Balaam's home with this message, the prophet had to choose where his priorities lay. On the one hand, there was Balak, offering him honor and financial reward, while on the other there was the clear decree of the Lord: "You shall not curse the people, for they are blessed" (v. 12). Which path would he choose?[7]

On the face of it, Balaam's response to the messengers of Balak sounds wonderfully spiritual: "Though Balak were to give me his house full of silver and gold, I could not go beyond the command of the LORD my God to do less or more" (v. 18). What a noble and self-sacrificial position he adopted! However, you mustn't forget that Balaam was a politician, and words are cheap. Balaam promptly exposed the true feelings of his heart with the rest of the words that he spoke to the delegation: "So you, too, please stay here tonight, that I may know *what more* the LORD will say to me" (v. 19, emphasis added). If Balaam really meant the fine words he had just said about not doing anything great or small beyond the command of the Lord, there was no reason for him to invite Balak's princes to stay. What part of "You shall not go with them" didn't he understand? What did the Lord need to add to "You shall not curse the people, for they are blessed"? Inviting the men to stay the night showed that Balaam still hoped the Lord would change his mind or that he might yet find some other way to claim the bounty offered by Balak. For all his wonderful words, Balaam couldn't let the prospect of Balak's gold escape without a fight.

What was the Lord's response to Balaam's request? "If the men have come to call you, rise, go with them; but only do what I tell you" (v. 20). Many commentators fail to notice that this is not a direct command to go to Moab. And it is not the exact opposite of the previous command to remain at home. Rather, it is a conditional sentence: "If the men have come to call you . . . go."[8] Clearly the condition in the clause has been met: the men have, in fact, come to summon him. So what is the point of including the condition here? The answer is that by putting the focus on the men, it brings to the foreground the same issue as was posed by the Lord's original question: "Who are these men?" That is, what authority did they have to summon him? In other words, the Lord was saying to Balaam, "If the summons of men and the glory (reward) that they offer is really so important to you that it outweighs the expressed command of God, then you may go with them." This is the equivalent of Joshua's challenge to Israel to choose whom they would serve, whether the gods of their fathers or the gods of the Amorites or the Lord (Joshua 24:15). Balaam had to make a decision whether to go with the men and follow his idolatry or stay home and follow the Lord. Yet even his freedom to follow his own gods was limited. He was only free until he reached the end of a short leash, for even if he went with Balak's men, he could do nothing other than what the Lord told him.

Another Key Silence

At this point there was another crucial omission on Balaam's part. In verse 13, after the Lord had spoken to him the first time, we read, "So Balaam rose in the morning and said to the princes of Balak . . ." He then recounted the substance of the Lord's words to him. On this second occasion, in verse 21, the scene opens in exactly the same way: "So Balaam rose in the morning . . ." But from there onward the events diverged. What Balaam did *not* do this time was to get up in the morning and tell the princes of Balak what the Lord had said. He didn't say to them, "Look, I can come with you if you want, but I can only say what the Lord says—and he has already made it clear that Israel is blessed and not cursed." Instead, Balaam went with them in haste and without any explicit clarification of what had transpired overnight, presumably giving the envoys the impression that he had straightened out the difficulties with the Lord and was now all set to earn his substantial fees by cursing Israel.

Once that key omission is observed, it is simple to explain why, having given Balaam permission to go to Moab in verse 20, the Lord was so angry with him in verse 22. The Lord was angry not simply because Balaam had gone with Balak's messengers but rather because he had gone in a way that evidenced a lack of submission to the Lord. He acted as if he were a free agent, able to control his own destiny as well as that of other nations. The Lord therefore determined that it was necessary to teach Balaam a lesson about who was in control of his life, whether he liked it or not. He needed to learn that though man may propose, God is still the one who disposes.

Divided Hearts

We have much in common with Balaam. One challenge that the story clearly faces us with is the question of who is pulling our strings. Faced with a choice between obeying the clear command of God and pursuing Balak's house full of silver and gold, the silver and gold triumphed in Balaam's heart, for all his protestations to the contrary. His besetting sin was greed, as Peter rightly diagnosed it (see 2 Peter 2:15). As a result, he went to Moab with the envoys of Balak instead of sending them on their way with the clear word of the Lord. The Lord gave him over, up to a point, to his sinful choices. Are we so very different from Balaam though? To what extent do the very same things that Balak offered Balaam—money and prestige—have a grip on our hearts? Are we ourselves free from the love of money, which Paul describes as the root of all evils (1 Timothy 6:10)? If these precise things do not hold our hearts captive, perhaps other idols drive our thinking just as surely: acceptance, physical beauty, intellectual accomplishment, or the like.

In seeking to understand what drives us, it is important to recognize that the answer is often more evident in our actions than in our words. Just as Balaam's attempt to extract a different response from the Lord exposed his divided heart and betrayed the emptiness of his words, so too our words and actions are often at odds. Like Balaam, we may piously commit ourselves to the Lord wholeheartedly on Sundays, while from Monday to Saturday our lives are driven by the summons of different masters. We may say, "We love the Lord, not money," but our spending patterns in our checkbooks tell a different story. We declare, "We fear the Lord and not people," yet our cowardly refusal to stand up for Christ in the office or the classroom reveals a different truth. The essence of integrity is someone whose words and thoughts and actions are thoroughly integrated: they are all aligned in the same direction. Are we such persons of integrity? Do our words and our actions line up with each other?

If not, then it is almost invariably the case that our actions expose the real truth about our hearts. Our actions make plain what else we must have apart from the Lord to make our lives meaningful and significant. It may be money or power or acceptance or comfort or a myriad of other things, but whenever obedience to the Lord's Word means that our idol is challenged, we find ourselves drawn away from obedience in pursuit of our "what else." No matter how orthodox and impressive our words are, they are not worth the breath expended in uttering them if there is no congruence between them and our deeds.

Balaam and the Donkey

Balaam's lesson in humility took the form of the famous incident with his donkey. The angel of the Lord took up a position on the road in front of Balaam to oppose him, with drawn sword in hand (v. 23). It was a menacing sight, the import of which the donkey clearly understood. Three times the angel of the Lord stood in the way; three times the donkey refused to pass, in spite of Balaam's increasingly insistent urgings. The first time, the donkey turned off the road, and Balaam beat her to get her back on track (v. 23). The second time, the angel barred the way on a narrow path between two walls. In order to avoid the angel, the donkey pressed up against the wall, crushing Balaam's foot, causing him to beat her again (v. 25). On the third occasion, there was no way past the angel; so the donkey simply lay down in the road, refusing to stir even when he beat her with a stick (vv. 26, 27).

At this point the Lord opened the long-suffering animal's mouth, enabling it to confront Balaam. She said, "What have I done to you, that you have struck me these three times?" (v. 28). Balaam responded, "Because you have made a fool of me. I wish I had a sword in my hand, for then I would kill you." Then the donkey replied, "Am I not your donkey, on which you have ridden all your life long to this day? Is it my habit to treat you this way?"

Let's pause at this point and consider what is remarkable about this scene. It is not so much the fact that a donkey speaks: God created all of the animals, and he can cause any of them to do his bidding in any way he chooses. What is remarkable about this scene is Balaam's blindness and impotence. Here is a man who is a professional seer, the kind of person who makes a living discerning messages from God in places where other people see only random tea leaves and miscellaneous flights of birds; yet he cannot see the angel of the Lord when he stands there in plain sight in front of him! His donkey can see the Lord's messenger, but Balaam cannot. Moreover, here is a man who has been hired to travel some distance in order to harm an entire nation—Israel—with the mere power of his spoken word; yet when a simple donkey makes a fool out of him, he is reduced to beating her with a stick and uttering empty threats. He has no power to curse her by turning her into a frog or a pumpkin! The world famous super-prophet is both spiritually blind and unable to inflict harm, while a mere donkey whose mouth has been opened by the Lord is able to see the truth clearly and speak it out in a way that delivers from death. The scene forms a wonderfully humorous picture.

It was at this point that the Lord finally opened Balaam's eyes to see the angel of the Lord standing in front of him with drawn sword (v. 31). The angel rebuked him for beating his donkey, whose actions had actually saved his life. Balaam's reckless path in pursuing Balak's gold instead of telling him the truth about the Lord's purposes for Israel had put his own life in danger. Ironically, at the very same time that Balaam was threatening his donkey with death if he only had a sword in his hand, his own master had been standing over him with a drawn sword. Only the donkey's faithfulness had saved him from death.

Now Balaam's eyes were opened to see the folly of his ways. If he thought that his hitherto faithful donkey deserved death for its apparent perverseness in disregarding his commands, how much more must he himself deserve death for his own perverse pursuit of profit? After all, the donkey disobeyed him out of obedience to a higher authority, while his own disobedience was in pursuit of mere money. He stood condemned out of his own mouth. Balaam then confessed that he had sinned by going with the envoys of Balak, for he did not realize that the Lord was standing in the road to block his path. More precisely, the Hebrew says, "I did not realize you had taken a stand to summon me on the way" (v. 34). The verb used (qr') is different from that used to describe the Lord's purpose in verses 22 and 32, but it is the same verb that the Lord used in verse 20: "If the men have come to call you . . ." In other words, Balaam recognized at last that the issue here was precisely that of whose bidding Balaam was to do. In going to Moab, he had thought to obey the summons of Balak, but through the incident with the donkey, the Lord confronted him afresh with the reality of whose summons he had to obey. Like a mere donkey, Balaam's part was not to be creative and pioneer his own path: rather, he was simply required to be an obedient medium for the Lord's message.

Having made that point comprehensively to Balaam, there was now no need to turn him around and send him home. He could safely be sent on with his companions to Moab, with the injunction of the night vision once again ringing in his ears: "speak only the word that I tell you" (v. 35; see v. 20). It is striking that it was at this point in the story, after he arrived in Moab humbled after the incident with the donkey and reminded that he was not an independent agent, Balaam finally said the words to Balak that he earlier failed to say to his envoys. When Balak asked him why he did not come when the king summoned him (v. 37; the same Hebrew word as before) and said, "Am I not able to honor you?" Balaam replied, "Behold, I have come to you! Have I now any power of my own to speak anything? The word that God puts in my mouth, that must I speak" (v. 38). By this point

Balaam had, however reluctantly, learned his lesson. Balak had neither the authority to summon him nor the ability to reward him sufficiently to achieve what he wanted. Balaam may not have been happy about this turn of events, as the terseness of his reply to Balak perhaps makes evident, but he recognized that he was not a free agent in this matter. He could only say the words the Lord commanded him to say.

The Lord's Determination to Bless

The central lesson behind the story of Balaam is the Lord's determination to bless his people. No hotshot prophet will be permitted to curse God's people, no matter how much he wants to, because the Lord has declared them blessed. Instead, his very attempt to curse Israel will itself be turned into another blessing. Israel was most likely unaware of this whole episode at the time when it happened. This is probably just as well, since the news that an international wizard was on his way to place them under a curse might well have sent them into yet another frenzy of worry and grumbling. Yet even had they been aware of it, they need not have worried. The Lord would turn the curse that they feared into a blessing.

Isn't that a lesson we need to internalize as well? There are many dangers in life of which we are not even aware because the Lord extracts their sting before they even reach us. In other cases, though, we become aware of the rise of threatening thunderclouds, triggering panic in our hearts. Something or someone seems poised to ruin our lives once and for all. We need not be so easily afraid. As William Cowper put it in his great hymn "God Moves in a Mysterious Way":

> Ye fearful saints, fresh courage take;
> The clouds ye so much dread
> Are big with mercy, and shall break
> In blessings on your head.

If the Lord has decreed our blessing, then nothing and no one can turn our blessing into a curse.

This reality is the answer to our sinful worries. Why do we fret about so many of life's problems? As Jesus said in the Sermon on the Mount, the reason we worry is because we have given in to the belief that God loves us less than he loves the birds of the air or the lilies of the field. They do not fret, yet they are constantly fed and clothed by the Lord (Matthew 6:26, 28)! Since we have far greater assurances of God's care for us than any flower or bird ever received, why should we be so concerned about these things? Our worry reveals the fact that we are believing a lie about God, and the answer to our worry is therefore to remind ourselves afresh of the truth about his care for us.

This reality is also the answer to the various idols of our hearts that are continually pulling our strings. Why is it that we are driven by money or the prospect of power and fame? It is because we have begun to seek our blessing in these things. Why is it that we fear people and are so desperately afraid of being excluded from the in-crowd? It is because we are afraid of the curse with which they threaten us. Why is it that the desire for physical attractiveness or intellectual achievement or the need to have a perfect family holds us in its spell? It is because we have come to believe these idols hold sway over our destiny. We have started to believe that real meaning and significance in life is in the hand of our idol to give or to withhold. That is why we are so fearful and depressed, as well as why we are so driven and anxious. If you and I could learn to look to the Lord alone for our blessing and to find our confidence in his settled purpose to bless us, that would cut the strings that bind us under the power of all manner of other things. What peace and assurance would then be ours! If we could only be convinced of the Lord's power and his purpose to bless us, the engine of our idolatry that drives us constantly into a variety of actual sins would be starved of its fuel.

An Anchor for Your Soul

How can we know for sure that the Lord is determined to bless us and not to curse us? Like Balaam, we too have gone astray perversely, wandering after all kinds of other gods. Why shouldn't the angel of the Lord be standing in front of us even now with drawn sword in hand, waiting to cut us down? It would certainly be nothing more than we deserve. After all, even our best deeds—our most unselfish actions and kindly words—are often simply offerings to our idols, not acts of obedience to the living God. What shall I say then of my darkest thoughts and deeds? How shall I escape judgment for them? The answer is that if we are Christians, Jesus Christ has taken the curse that was aimed at us for our sin. The angel's sword has already been plunged into his heart instead of ours. Our perversity earned us death, but Jesus died in our place. Our idolatry earned us permanent separation from God, but Jesus was cut off from the Father for us on the cross. Our sins placed us justly under the Lord's judgment and curse, but in Christ we receive the blessing that the Lord has promised to all of the spiritual descendants of Abraham. The cross is the surety of the Lord's unshakable will to bless his people. As Paul put it, "He who did not spare his own Son but gave him up for us all, how will he not also with him graciously give us all things?" (Romans 8:32). For Jesus' sake, the Lord is determined to bless us, and no one and nothing can ever turn that blessing into a curse.

Sadly, Balaam remained blind to the truth of the Lord's goodness and grace. Even after his eyes were opened to see the angel of the Lord and he confessed with his lips, "I have sinned" (v. 34), Balaam's heart was still a long way from true repentance, as his future behavior demonstrated. His words and his actions did not ultimately agree. He had chosen whom he would serve: Balak's silver and gold, not the Lord. His heart was still captive to his idolatry, and even a face-to-face encounter with the Angel of the Lord did not free him from its chains. At the end of the day his donkey saw the Lord more clearly than he did; the brute beast understood more of God than the professional theologian. As a result, even though the Lord used him to deliver a blessing to his people Israel, Balaam's own destiny was not ultimately changed from curse to blessing. All that happened was that his appointment with the sword of the Lord's judgment was delayed. In the end he was killed by the Israelites when they took vengeance on the Midianites for leading them into sin (31:8).

It is still often the case that the Lord reveals himself to the weak and foolish, while remaining hidden from those who possess the wisdom of this world. Those who were blind receive sight, while those who claim to see are left in the dark. As an Old Testament scholar, I regularly meet and listen to men and women whose knowledge of the Bible and the Hebrew language is far in excess of anything I could ever attain. In academic terms they are racehorses, while I am merely a plodding donkey. When I hear their lectures and read their books, I learn many true and insightful things about the Bible; yet when it comes to the gospel they are utterly blind. They cannot see on the pages of Scripture the simplest truths about God. Many five-year-olds have more true Biblical insight into the gospel than they do, because spiritual truths are spiritually discerned, and for all their "wisdom" these people do not have the Holy Spirit to open up their stubborn hearts and blind eyes so they can see the truth that is right in front of them (see 1 Corinthians 2:14).

Could anything more clearly display God's sovereignty than that? The supreme blessing in this world is coming to recognize who God is and how to find salvation in his Son. It comes as a free gift to those whose eyes he opens and whose hearts he touches with his grace. The work of his Spirit brings one to faith while another is left in unbelief, not because the one has greater merit than the other, but simply out of unconditional sovereign grace. The Lord chose Israel to be his people and left Balaam to his preferred darkness, though neither had any claim on him. Donkeys like us get to see and know the Lord, while professional prophets remain blind.

What is more, the future of those whom the Lord calls to himself is sure, settled by the unchangeable One and sealed in his blood. God cannot lie, and he cannot change his mind, as Balaam himself would declare (23:19). God has settled his inheritance on us with an oath, so that we may have the certainty of an irrevocable inheritance (Hebrews 6:17-19). Nothing and no one can separate us from that blessing, either now or in the age to come. Such a hope is a sure anchor for our souls and spiritual food for our hearts.

How then shall we respond? Surely we must burst forth with praise and adoration. Let us give thanks to the Lord for this inexpressible hope! May we rejoice in his favor shown to us! Let us rest in his love and bask in his settled attitude of blessing toward us, for as the psalmist repeatedly reminds us, "His steadfast love endures forever" (for example, Psalm 136).

28

Settled Blessings

NUMBERS 23, 24

PREDICTING THE FUTURE IS A TRICKY BUSINESS AT BEST, as history demonstrates. In 1929 Irving Fisher, Professor of Economics at Yale University, carved out a niche for himself in history when he said, "Stocks have reached what looks like a permanently high plateau," mere months before Wall Street crashed. Decca Records turned down the opportunity to sign the Beatles in 1962 with the words, "We don't like their sound, and guitar music is on the way out." Ken Olson, founder and president of Digital Equipment Corporation, declared in 1977, "There is no reason anyone would want a computer in their home." Trying to track the trends of the future gives you a wonderful opportunity to fall flat on your face. The things that seem certain bets often backfire, while the most unlikely prospects may end up as runaway successes.

If *predicting* the future is hard, then how about *controlling* the future? What if you don't like the apparently inevitable prospect that your future holds for you—is there anything you can do about it? How do you face and defeat problems that are far beyond your ability to control? Perhaps you have received a diagnosis of an incurable disease, either for yourself or for a loved one. Or perhaps you find yourself in a situation where life seems to have locked you in a box and thrown away the key. You see no way out through your own resources. Is it possible to find help and hope outside yourself when the only light that you see at the end of the tunnel is an onrushing express train that seems certain to crush you?

The Folly of Spiritual Counterfeits

That was the situation in which Balak, King of Moab, found himself. An enormous threatening force, the Israelites, was massing on his border. They had already defeated and destroyed Og, King of Bashan, and Sihon, King of the Amorites. He thought his territory might very well be next on their list (22:2, 3). Conventional warfare held out little prospect of success. So where was he to turn? His solution was to summon the internationally renowned prophet and diviner Balaam, in the hopes that through him he could acquire a weapon of mass destruction, a curse from the gods that would change Israel's future and thereby also his own.

At first sight that solution to Balak's problem may not seem very relevant to our modern situation. Even if the root of the problems in our lives can be identified as a person, we are not normally greatly tempted to call down a literal curse on him. In contemporary society when there is an archrival outperforming us at work or at school, we don't typically pull out a voodoo doll and stick pins in it, hoping through sympathetic magic to debilitate him or her. Yet the broader temptation to pursue spiritual counterfeits as a means to relieve our pain and pursue increased success remains tremendously attractive to our culture as the rising levels of interest in psychics and horoscopes demonstrates. What is more, even if we don't seek out the modern equivalent of pagan divination to seek the solution to our problems, we may still look to created things and people as the ones from whom our blessings will come. Yet this passage demonstrates clearly that the Lord alone has power to bless and curse.

Pursuing this theme, the passage underlines for us the folly of all spiritual counterfeits. Balak's assertion when he first sent envoys to hire Balaam ("I know that he whom you bless is blessed, and he whom you curse is cursed," 22:6) is shown to be mere wishful thinking. Far from Balaam being able to exert a measure of control over the deity, as a pagan prophet was paid to do, extracting whatever outcome he sought from his encounter, the Lord controlled Balaam. The Lord told him where and when to go and required him to say only what the Lord instructed him to say, reducing Balaam to a mere messenger boy. If the Lord could do that to an internationally acclaimed prophet like Balaam, no one would ever be able to stand against him. Balak's plan to curse Israel was doomed from the outset.

Costly and Uncertain Rituals

One aspect of the folly of pursuing spiritual counterfeits that emerges is the vast expense that they require. Three times, in three different locations, Balaam made Balak go through costly rituals. Each time he had to build seven altars, and on each one he had to sacrifice a bull and a ram, the most expensive of the various sacrificial animals (23:1, 14, 29). That was in addition to the cost of sending the envoys (twice) to persuade Balaam to come (22:7, 15), the cost of the feast on his arrival (22:40), and the promised payment of a handsome reward on completion of the contract (22:17). Balaam's services were certainly far from cheap, a fact that is equally true of his modern counterparts.

We also see clearly here the uncertainty of spiritual counterfeits. Even after all this expense, there was no guarantee of Balak receiving any message from beyond, let alone one that would be favorable to him. Whereas in Israel only one altar was ever necessary for sacrifice, since Israel served only the one true God, here seven altars were required for each attempt to contact the deity. Presumably this was an attempt to cover all of the spiritual bases.[1] Yet even with all of that effort, Balaam said to Balak after the first set of offerings, "Perhaps the LORD will come to meet me" (23:3). Balaam could not guarantee results from the process. The second time Balaam expressed similar uncertainty when he said, "Stay here beside your offerings, while I seek a manifestation yonder" (23:15, NJPS). There was no sure access to the Lord through this procedure: it was filled with "perhaps" and "maybe." This uncertainty of approach for Balaam forms a striking contrast with the access that the Lord had promised to Moses. Whereas prophets—even true prophets—were dependent on dreams and visions, Moses had been granted the constant and assured right to meet with the Lord and speak to him face to face (12:7).

Balak might still have thought that all of his money had been well spent if it had finally accomplished his goals of cursing Israel. However, in the end all of his expense went for nothing. Balaam first tried to curse the whole camp of Israel from Bamoth-baal (22:41). From there he could see the whole camp of Israel spread out before him.[2] Yet the only words he found he could utter were words of blessing (23:7-10). His second attempt was more limited in scope, seeking only to curse part of Israel. If he couldn't manage to curse the whole people, perhaps he could at least manage to curse a small part of them. This attempt too was an abject failure: once again, he could only *bless* Israel (23:18-24). Nor was a third attempt from a different location any more successful (24:3-9). In each place, Balaam's best efforts to curse Israel accomplished nothing.

In fact, as a weapon of mass destruction, Balaam proved to be not only impotent but actually counterproductive. Not only was Balaam not able to curse Israel, he repeatedly blessed them at Balak's expense! What is more, when Balak finally ran out of patience with Balaam after three failed attempts and tried to send him packing, Balaam proceeded to deliver yet another oracle free of charge, which contained yet another blessing on Israel (24:15-24)!

That is always the way it is with spiritual counterfeits: they make grandiose claims for themselves and promise to give us substantial rewards, yet in the end they turn out to be expensive, uncertain, and ultimately impotent. There is neither blessing nor curse to be found in psychics or mediums, in astrology or horoscopes, or in any other source than the one true living God. These spiritual counterfeits have no power to affect either the present or the future.

In fact, the same is true of all of the many created things to which we offer allegiance as our idols. They are all ultimately equally impotent to bless or to curse. Some seek their value in money and possessions, but wealth cannot make us genuinely worthwhile as persons, and its absence cannot rob us of our dignity. Others look to power for their validation, but power cannot fulfill us, and its loss cannot make our lives meaningless. Still others invest the approval of people with ultimate significance, but gaining the love of a particular person is not where our value lies, nor will we be destroyed if they are taken from us, however painful that loss may be. None of these created things can make or break us, even though we continually act as if they can.

The power that we ascribe to these idols that we have set up for ourselves is evident in the way we pour ourselves so devotedly into pursuing their demands and are so wrapped up in fears of their loss. We would willingly go to the ends of the earth to do their bidding, and we regularly sacrifice on their altars whatever they demand. They fill our dreams and our nightmares, and they shape our expenditures and our relationships. They are profoundly expensive masters, both in financial terms and in terms of the turmoil that they create in our souls. Yet in the end, like all idols, they are impotent to deliver what they promise or threaten.

The Certainty of Blessing

In dramatic contrast to the expensive, uncertain, and ultimately impotent search for blessing and curse through spiritual counterfeits and the idols of our hearts, there is the free, certain, and effective way to blessing through Israel's God. Israel did not have to pay Balaam or offer special sacrifices to receive a word of blessing from the Lord through him. On the contrary, the Lord had already freely committed himself in advance to bless Abraham and his descendants (Genesis 12:2, 3). The Lord had already told the Aaronic priests to pronounce his blessing regularly on the people, without any fee changing hands (Numbers 6:24-27). Balaam's words of blessing were simply a reflection of the Lord's settled attitude toward his people. As Balaam himself put it, "God is not man, that he should lie, or a son of man, that he should change his mind. Has he said, and will he not do it? Or has he spoken, and will he not fulfill it? Behold, I received a command to bless: he has blessed, and I cannot revoke it" (23:19, 20). Human beings are fickle and changeable creatures, but when the Lord declared a people blessed, they were indeed blessed.

The oracles of Balaam not only declared that the Lord's blessing rested on Israel, however. They also unfold for us different aspects of that settled blessing—past, present, and future.

First, Balaam declared that the Lord has blessed Israel in the past. The Lord had multiplied their numbers to uncountable proportions, like the dust of the earth, just as he had promised Abraham: "Who can count the dust of Jacob or number the fourth part of Israel?" (23:10; see Genesis 13:16). He had brought them out of Egypt (23:22; 24:8), and he gave them the strength to defeat hostile nations resembling a wild ox (23:22; 24:8) or a lion (23:24; 24:9). The Lord made them a people distinct from all other nations, separated for a relationship with him (23:9).[3] All of these predictions must have seemed far-fetched when originally given; yet the Lord had fulfilled each one.

Second, Balaam declared the Lord's blessing upon Israel in the present. The Lord protected them from natural disasters: "He has not beheld misfortune in Jacob, nor has he seen trouble in Israel" (23:21). He guarded them from supernatural dangers: "For there is no enchantment against Jacob, no divination against Israel" (23:23). What made them distinct from every other nation was the unique fact that God dwelt in their midst: "The LORD their God is with them, and the shout of a king is among them" (23:21). They alone out of all the nations of the earth had a special relationship with the Lord, acclaiming him as their King and belonging to him as his people.

Future Blessings

What is more, the Lord would continue to be with Israel in the future, promising them fruitfulness and abundant water (24:6, 7) and victory for their king over Agag, the king of the Amalekites (24:7). This last promise is particularly striking since at this point in their history Israel did not yet have a king, even though God had already promised them that they would have one at some point in the future (Genesis 17:6). This promised monarch of the future would experience the Lord's blessing, resulting in triumph over all of his enemies, who were personified as the king of their primary enemy, Amalek (see 24:20). Ultimately, all of Israel's enemies would be destroyed: Moab would be defeated, Edom conquered, and even the great empire of Assyria[4] would be brought low in the end (24:17, 18, 24).

These oracles of Balaam, which declare not merely positive present realities but a glorious future yet to come, are most certainly true because the Lord's sovereign power extends beyond the present into the future. What man cannot predict—what the future holds—the Lord is able to declare, because he himself holds the future in his hands. Even sickness, disease, and the schemes of evil men are not exempt from his sovereign will to bless his people. For that reason, when Jesus and his disciples encountered a man who had been born blind, Jesus explained that this personal tragedy had happened precisely so that the work of God might be displayed in his life

(John 9:3). That man's disability was not an accident of fate: it was part of God's plan to display his glory. In fact, even the most wicked act of history, the crucifixion of Jesus, was the result of God's set purpose and foreknowledge (Acts 2:23). God's sovereignty does not free human beings from their responsibility for their acts, but it does assure us of the certainty that his purposes of blessing and curse will assuredly come about. Who but the Lord has the power to foretell what the distant future holds? Who but the Lord holds that future in his hands?

This truth is a great comfort when life seems out of control, whether outwardly or inwardly. Outwardly life seems out of control whenever our circumstances threaten to swamp us through one calamity or another. Inwardly life seems out of control whenever our emotions threaten to drown us in a morass of anxiety or sorrow, of fear or depression. Precisely in those times of unsettled circumstances and tumultuous emotions, the Lord's settled purpose to bless his people is a wonderful assurance. As the hymn-writer put it:

> Though Satan should buffet, though trials should come,
> Let this blest assurance control,
> That Christ hath regarded my helpless estate,
> And hath shed His own blood for my soul.

If God is for us, who can be against us? The settled assurance of the Lord's purpose to bless us in Christ enables us in the midst of life's chaos to sing,

> Whatever my lot, thou hast taught me to say,
> "It is well, it is well with my soul."[5]

A Star from Jacob

The greatest declaration of Israel's future blessing, though, was left for the distant future. In Balaam's final oracle he announced that a star would come out of Jacob and a scepter out of Israel, a great king who would definitively crush all of her enemies (24:17-19). In that day, pride of place would not be sufficient to keep Israel's adversaries safe: the Amalekites, who were "first among the nations," would come to ruin (24:20). A secure location would be no defense either: the Kenites would be flushed out of their rocky lair (24:21). Even those whom God used to destroy those nations would themselves ultimately go down in defeat at the hands of others—the Assyrians who would overcome and enslave the Kenites would themselves be subdued in due time by a warlike power from across the sea (24:24).[6] Meanwhile, those who brought low the Assyrians would themselves come to ruin in the end (24:24). Who can endure this great day of the Lord's wrath (24:23)?

This final oracle thus spans the entire sweep of human history. Nation after nation will rise to world domination and then fall to defeat. But when the messianic King arrives on the scene, no people other than Israel, the nation set apart, will survive the final day of destruction. At the end of all things, when all of human history has played out its course of changing fortunes, the Lord's people will be the only ones left standing.

If it is true that Israel as God's people has a unique relationship with the Lord that means both their present blessing and final security, then they are indeed to be envied. If the Lord has chosen Israel to be his own and has promised to be with them in the past, the present, and the future, then Balaam's wish is understandable: "Let me die the death of the upright, and let my end be like his!" (23:10). When you even out the merely temporary fluctuations in the fortunes of people and nations, there are ultimately only two fates offered in this world. There is the Lord's blessing leading to a flourishing life and an enviable death or the Lord's curse leading to defeat and ultimate destruction.

Yet the coming of the star that Balaam foresaw wasn't entirely what you might have predicted. At the birth of Jesus, a heavenly star indeed rose over Israel to mark where the infant King lay. Yet the baby King lay in a manger, not in a palace, and those drawn by the star were not Israelites but foreign Magi, students of signs and portents as was Balaam, who came from the east, Balaam's former home (Matthew 2:1-12).[7] King Herod, an Edomite by descent, was not instantly crushed by the coming of this new King but continued his rule, slaughtering scores of innocent children in Bethlehem. The rising of this star in Christ's first coming did not yet bring about the total destruction of the nations, for Jesus had come first to be "a light for revelation to the Gentiles and for glory to . . . Israel" (Luke 2:32). Yet in another way, his coming was exactly what Balaam anticipated: those who, like the Magi, blessed the new Israel, Jesus, and submitted to him found a blessing for themselves. Meanwhile, those who cursed this new Israel found themselves under a curse, just as the Lord had promised Abraham (24:9; see Genesis 12:3). What is more, the day is yet coming when God's final judgment will be delivered on Herod and on all those who stand against him and his anointed.

Israel's Blessings Fulfilled in Christ

What that means, then, is that these oracles for Israel are precious promises for us. Some Christians believe that Old Testament promises that speak of "Israel" are only intended for ethnic Israel and not for the church. For them, Balaam's prophecies speak of a glorious future for the physical descendants of Israel, but they would call any attempt to apply these promises to the church "replacement theology." I would suggest that this is a misunderstanding of what the Scriptures teach about Israel. It is not that the church has replaced Israel in the New Testament so much as that Old Testament Israel—ethnic Israel—finds its true goal and fulfillment in the person of Jesus Christ. Jesus is himself the star of Jacob, the Israel of God.

In the person of Jesus, therefore, the true Israel has arrived, and all those who come to God by faith in him—Jews and Gentiles alike—become God's children and are thereby incorporated into this new people of God (John 1:11, 12). In Christ, Jews and Gentiles together become the true heirs of the promise given to Abraham, his spiritual descendants (Galatians 3:29). Outside of Christ, on the other hand, there is no longer any true Israel. It is those who are in Christ who are the true chosen people: a royal priesthood, a holy nation, a people belonging to God (1 Peter 2:9). We have been chosen by God for exactly the same special relationship that he had with his Old Testament people. In his incredible grace and mercy, God chose us before the foundation of the world, so that we might be blessed in Christ with every spiritual blessing (Ephesians 1:3, 4). He has rescued us from the final judgment that awaits all those who remain outside his people and has given us the glorious inheritance of a relationship with himself. In Jesus, the star of Jacob has risen for us and for our salvation.

If this is so, then we may have the assurance of the Lord's settled purpose to bless us in Jesus Christ. No one can rob us of that blessing, and nothing can prevent us from inheriting its promises. All those who trust in Christ and are united to him by faith will die the death of the righteous, for Christ's righteousness is credited to them, exactly as if it were their own. Whatever life throws at each of us, it must therefore always be "well with my soul," for Christ has died in our place and is now risen from the dead. If we keep our eyes on that reality, then none of the traumatic rises and falls in our temporal fortunes that are an inevitable part of life in this fallen world can ever completely shake us. We will be settled on a solid rock, established on a firm foundation. People may come and go: some will let us down and hurt us, while others, no matter how faithful, will ultimately die and leave us on our own. But God will still be there. Fortunes may be made and lost, houses may burn, stock markets may crash, and cars will inevitably rust. Yet in Christ, we have an inheritance that no misfortune can touch. At the end of the day, only God remains, and those upon whom his blessing rests.

Balaam's Curse

Ironically, though, Balaam never found that blessing. Even though he declared that he wanted to "die the death of the righteous" (23:10, NIV), once again his life didn't match up to his words. If Balaam truly wanted to die the death of the righteous, the way to do so was to join the righteous during his lifetime. The Magi of Jesus' day showed the way: he should have come to Israel's God and laid his treasures at his feet. Had Balaam been willing to say good-bye to Balak and (more pertinently) to abandon his passion for Balak's silver and gold, he could have received what he desired. The doors in Israel were open to aliens and strangers who wanted to abandon their old religions and join themselves to Israel and to her God. Sadly, though, money was more important to Balaam than achieving the death of the righteous. As a result, he stayed among the Midianites who opposed Israel and Israel's God, and he died by the sword in their midst (31:8).

It is a sobering reality to think that many people say they want to die at peace with God but are not willing to pursue peace with God while they live. Being reconciled to the Lord is not something we can put off until a more convenient time, for in all probability such a time will never come and we will die still in our sins, rebels against the Lord of Heaven and earth. A day is coming when the Star of Jacob will come to crush all such rebels and enemies. When Jesus returns to this earth, it will be as a warrior riding out for the final battle in which he will crush all of his enemies (Revelation 19:11). If we want to spend eternity under God's blessing as part of his people, today is the day to enter into his favor. Come to Christ now, as the Magi did at his incarnation, and submit your life to his lordship. Ask for his forgiveness to cover your sins; receive his righteousness to clothe your spiritual nakedness. The door is open today for everyone who will come in and bow the knee willingly to the Lord to receive his blessing. So come, enter into his people. As you do so, you will receive his blessing, find peace in the midst of a tumultuous world, and be able look forward with joy to the day when his final victory will be accomplished.

29

From the Heights to the Depths

NUMBERS 25

THE HOLIDAY BROCHURE described it as "a magical place that time has forgotten." It went on, "there can't be many places left in the world quite like San Andres . . . if your dream is of a sophisticated island where you can relax, leave the cares of the world behind and enjoy the simple things of life, we have a holiday to make it come true . . . it will give you a taste of something completely different and make your holiday truly memorable." The reality that the vacationers discovered when they arrived on the island of San Andres, however, was not at all what they anticipated. They had no hot water for the two weeks they were there, the air-conditioning didn't work in the hotel rooms, and there was mold and mildew on the walls. There were rats, cockroaches, and scorpions in the bedrooms and fleas in the beds. The hotel beach was littered with dog excrement and hypodermic needles, while raw sewage was being discharged six feet from the restaurants and kitchens. They saw maids wiping the drinking glasses with a cloth they had just used to clean the toilet bowl. Not surprisingly, the guests returned with nine different diseases, including cholera, salmonella, and dysentery.[1] A "truly memorable" vacation? Perhaps, but not exactly for the reasons they had hoped. The reality didn't match up to the idyllic picture in the brochure.

The Ideal and the Reality

The reader may easily have a similar reaction to Numbers 25. For several chapters we have been on the mountain heights with Balaam, surveying

Israel from a distance and hearing about how blessed they are. In Balaam's oracle they are "a people dwelling alone, and not counting itself among the nations" (23:9). They see neither misfortune nor misery, for the Lord their God is with them (23:21). No sorcery or divination could succeed against Israel, for the Lord had blessed them, and he would not change his mind (23:20, 23). These people are "the upright," among whom it would be a privilege to die (23:10). Out of this chosen nation, the glorious messianic King would rise to bring salvation for his people and judgment on all of God's enemies (24:17-24). This is the glorious, ideal picture of Israel, the view from the holiday brochure, if you like.

In Numbers 25, however, we descend from the lofty heights of Balaam's prophecy to the harsh reality of the defiled people of God in the valley below. Far from being "the upright" who remain separate from the nations, the men of Israel engaged in sexual immorality with Moabite women (v. 1). This initial sin led naturally to the further step of joining in the Moabites' sacrifices and entering into a covenant with the god of Moab, Baal of Peor (vv. 2, 3).[2] What is more, this incident involved more than a little compromise on the part of one or two individuals. It was "the people" as a whole who went after Moabite women; it was "the people" who partook of the sacrifices and worshiped their gods; all "Israel" joined themselves to Baal of Peor (vv. 1-3). In other words, this was nothing less than the Israelites' total abandonment of their status as the covenant people of God, separated to the Lord and devoted to him alone. The sexual immorality that preceded the idolatry provided a graphic picture of the underlying spiritual reality. In offering sacrifices to Baal, Israel was abandoning her true husband, the Lord, and was taking up with a foreign lover. God might never be unfaithful to his promises or change his mind about his love for his people, but Israel was certainly capable of unfaithfulness.

The irony of these events coming immediately after Balaam's oracles is staggering. Balaam had visited each of Baal of Peor's sacred sites, from Bamoth-baal (22:41) to the heights of Peor (23:28); yet he had been utterly unable to change the Lord's blessing on his people into a curse. Through their apostasy from the Lord, however, Israel managed it easily enough. In formally abandoning the Lord as their God, they renounced his blessing and exposed themselves to his judgment. The Lord therefore told Moses to take and kill all of the leaders of the people and expose their bodies before the Lord (25:4). Those who were in charge of the people were to bear the covenantal responsibility for the people's sin, so that the people as a whole might be spared. The death of the leaders and the dishonorable exposure of their corpses would not only demonstrate to the people the seriousness of their sin but would atone for it, turning away the Lord's fierce anger against his rebellious people.

A Failure to Discipline

At this point, however, things went from bad to worse. Moses did not do what the Lord commanded him. Instead of a covenantal punishment, in which the family heads were held responsible for the rebellion of those under their care, he advocated a policy of individual punishment, instructing the judges to put to death only those individuals who had actually participated in the worship of Baal Peor (v. 5).[3] What is more, there is no report of even this more limited punishment being carried out: the next scene shows us Israel weeping before the Lord instead of acting to carry out his judgment (v. 6). The leadership of the people, including Moses, seems to have been totally paralyzed by the situation. The result of their inaction was even greater loss of life. While Moses and the leadership dragged their feet, the Lord's judgment descended on all of the people in the form of a plague (v. 8). No one seemed prepared to take the kind of decisive action necessary to bring it to an end.

This is, of course, not the first time that things on the mountaintop have looked different from the realities in the valley below. This is not even the first time that the leadership of God's people has been paralyzed in inaction while the people pursued idolatry. At Mount Sinai, at the very beginning of Israel's wilderness wanderings, a similar scenario played itself out. While Moses was on the mountaintop receiving the Ten Commandments from the Lord, ratifying the covenant between the Lord and his people, Israel was busily making a golden calf and bowing down to it, while Aaron passively did the people's bidding (Exodus 32:1-24). Forty years later, at the end of the wilderness wanderings, it seems that nothing had changed. The beginning and end of the story for this first generation in the wilderness was an idolatrous abandonment of the Lord. At least on that former occasion, though, Moses took charge and led the Levites in the difficult action of bringing the Lord's judgment to bear on the people (Exodus 32:25-29). This time no one appeared willing to step up and exercise discipline.

As so often happens when there is no discipline among God's people, sin became more and more flagrant. In front of the eyes of everyone, an Israelite man—the son of a leader of the Simeonites (25:14)—brought a Midianite woman to his family to consummate their marital relationship (v. 6). Clearly he had discerned that there was no willingness among the leadership to enforce the death penalty that had been announced for those who linked themselves with the Midianites and their gods; so he flaunted his sin in front of everyone. He thought he could sin boldly and there would be no consequences for his actions.

The Faithfulness of Phinehas

In that assessment he was wrong. The first generation might have been unwilling to do what they should have done, but the next generation was ready to step forward and demonstrate leadership. Phinehas,[4] the grandson of Aaron, took action to deal with this flagrant sin, killing both the Israelite and the Midianite with a single spear thrust, thus bringing to an end the plague of the Lord's judgment against his people (v. 8). Since the Israelite was the son of a leader of the Simeonites, his death was an attempt to put into effect the Lord's original sentence. This demonstration of wholehearted commitment to the Lord was all it took to bring the plague to an end. Yet 24,000 people died in the plague while they waited for the leadership to do what God had commanded (v. 9), and had Phinehas not stepped in at the crucial moment to make atonement for them, the whole people might have been eliminated (v. 11). His faithfulness made all the difference.

In the rest of this chapter we see the consequences for those involved. Phinehas received the Lord's blessing because of his action. His zeal for the Lord's honor was rewarded with a "covenant of peace" (v. 12), a lasting commitment by the Lord that his sons would share in his priestly ministry and that the high priesthood would descend through his line. The Midianites, meanwhile, were condemned to be the enemies of Israel from then on for their part in the affair. This is because the Israelites' apostasy was the result of the pursuit of a deliberate policy of seduction on the part of the Moabites and Midianites in accordance with Balaam's counsel (31:16). Those who lead God's people into sin face serious consequences for being the agents of temptation.

Finally, there were apparently also serious consequences for the Simeonites, from whose ranks the Israelite man had come. These became apparent when the second census was taken in Numbers 26. In that census they were the only tribe whose numbers had dramatically decreased over the forty-year period. The other tribes showed minor increases and decreases over the wilderness period from the numbers recorded at the beginning of the book, but the Simeonites had decreased from 59,300 to a mere 22,200. Perhaps because of their leadership in this sin, they suffered most of all of the tribes of Israel in the final plague.

Lessons from Baal-Peor: The Primacy of Idolatry

What can we learn from this sorry episode in Israel's history? In the first place, it shows us that sin is never a private thing. In our society we have elevated privacy into a fundamental human right, and most people regard consenting sexual relationships between otherwise uncommitted adults either as normal and appropriate or at least as no one's business except those personally involved. Yet, in this case the sins of these particular individuals had ramifications for their whole families, and indeed for the whole covenant community. Sin is never a private matter: our sin affects other people, directly and indirectly.

Having said that, though, we also need to be clear that the primary issue in this story is not sex but idolatry. The sex may lead to the idolatry, which is why intermarriage with the nations around them was forbidden to Israelites. However, the sin that resulted in the death penalty for so many people in Israel was not sexual immorality—it was idolatry. Israel's abandonment of the true and living God was the crime that merited their death.

This too is countercultural in our society. Surveys repeatedly show that when asked to rate the Ten Commandments in order of importance, people invariably rank "Thou shalt not kill" as the most important commandment, and "Thou shalt have no other gods before me" as the least important.[5] Our culture clearly regards the things that I do that offend or hurt people as far more important than anything I may choose to believe or not to believe about God. The Bible, on the other hand, knew what it was doing when it put the first commandment first. It thereby asserted that the ban on idolatry was the *most* important, not the least important, of the Ten Commandments.

The reason for this insistence on the primacy of our relationship to God is that all of our duties to our fellowman flow out of our obligation to the Lord. As a character in Dostoyevsky's *The Brothers Karamazov* argued, if God does not exist, then everything is permissible. If there is no transcendent being to define for us what is right and what is wrong, then there can be no absolute right and wrong, only personal preferences. If there is no one with the authority to command us, then "Thou shalt not kill" becomes a mere opinion, a suggestion rather than a commandment. However, if there is a transcendent being who has commanded what our behavior should be, then it is perfectly logical that his first commandment should restrict us from worshiping any pretenders to his throne.

This is exactly what we find in the New Testament as well as in the Old. In Romans 1:18 the Apostle Paul declares that the primary reason for the wrath of God being revealed is the godlessness of mankind that leads us to suppress the truth about God. That godless suppression of truth leads to all manner of sinful behavior, to be sure, as Romans 1:24-31 attests, but the root sin from which all other sin flows is the refusal to worship the Lord as God.

This surely means that much of our repentance is far too shallow. We frequently repent of our actions that get us into trouble, and sometimes even of the wrong attitudes in our hearts toward others. However, when did we last truly repent for our practical unbelief—our failure to set apart the Lord as God in every area of our lives? When were we last crushed by the reality that most of our lives are lived as if the Lord were not the God of Heaven and earth, the sovereign ruler of the universe? Our wrong actions are simply the fruits of our false theology that sets created things on the throne of our hearts. Until we repent of our unbelief, as well as the actions that flow from it, we have not reached the heart of our sins.

The Wages of Idolatry

The second thing that this chapter reminds us is, as we have seen so many times in the book of Numbers, that the wages of sin is death. In Israel's experience this fact was literally true for the Simeonite and the Midianite woman. Their sin resulted in their death, just as the wider sin of the people resulted in the deaths of 24,000 people. Those who failed to believe in the wrath of God had its reality graphically demonstrated in front of their eyes. Their personal experience should also serve as a graphic picture to impress upon us this same spiritual truth.

Why do we need this truth repeated so often and so vividly? The answer is because the doctrine of the judgment of God is one of the fundamental targets of the devil's assault. He began to question it right away in the Garden of Eden when he said to Eve, "You will not surely die" (Genesis 3:4). He painted sin as the way to life and fulfillment rather than death and destruction. He adopted the same strategy when dealing with the Israelites in Numbers 25. What did the Israelites think they would gain through their unions with Midianite and Moabite women? Surely they thought to find enhanced peace and prosperity. Politically, intermarriage held out the prospect of peace and a place in the land without the painful necessity of warfare; spiritually, the sexual and sacrificial rituals with Baal of Peor were designed to ensure fertility and prosperity for the community.[6] The results of their idolatry were, however, exactly the opposite of what they sought: they ended in a permanent enmity between Israel and Midian, and death for thousands of people.

This is always the way it is with Satan's snares. They seem to offer comfort but in reality deliver emptiness; they seem to offer peace but in reality deliver turmoil; they seem to offer a fuller life but in reality deliver death. Time and time again we are deceived by Satan's promises because we have not learned that he is a liar and a cheat. The outcome of choosing his way is always death.

The Importance of Discipline

Third, this passage reminds us that discipline pursued out of a passionate zeal for God's honor is vital to the spiritual health of the community. When Moses and the other leaders in the community failed to act, the judgment on the people of God was profound. Only when one young man stood up and acted to do what the Lord had said and to remove the blight from the community was there a change in the people's fortunes. It is important to note that Phinehas was not acting as a private citizen in executing God's judgment. There is no support here for independent action against anyone we may believe to have offended God. There is no warrant in this passage for bombing abortion clinics or shooting evil men. As the son of Eleazar, Phinehas was in charge of the Levites who were responsible for guarding the sanctuary against defilement (1 Chronicles 9:20; Numbers 3:32). Taking action to defend the sanctity of the camp was thus part of his job description, and he fulfilled his duties faithfully as an officer of the people of God in dealing with this particular abomination.

Once again, this truth is intensely countercultural. The idea of discipline is unfashionable, even when carried out by the properly appointed officers of the church. Immediately it evokes cries of "Abuse!" Indeed, it is sadly true that some have used the label of church discipline to oppress and beat the sheep, but it is also true that in many cases the leaders of churches have tolerated sin in their midst that should have spurred them to action. The Reformers rightly argued that proper church discipline is one of the essential marks of the true church and that where it is significantly absent, one can hardly expect the Spirit's blessing.

Such discipline will not necessarily make us popular with those around us, but then pastors and church leaders are not to seek their reward in that way anyway. In Numbers 25 we are not told what Moses himself thought of Phinehas' action: did he secretly cheer him on, grateful that someone was doing what he did not have the nerve to do? Or was he privately ready to flay alive this young upstart who thought he knew better than his elders what should be done to deal with this sin? Whatever Moses may have thought, both of these reactions are possible when we stand up today for the Lord's honor. Faithfulness to God may or may not win us friends among men. However, what we are told clearly is that the Lord saw Phinehas' actions and rewarded him for it. If our hearts are set on serving the Lord and he is pleased with us, we will not worry too much about what people think.

Will the Real Israel Please Stand Up?

The most profound question that the passage poses for us, however, is this: which is the real Israel—the righteous and securely blessed people of God or the defiled and judged community of sinners? Is the image of Israel described from the mountaintop just a fantasy of wishful thinking, and the foul mess in the valley the true reality? To put the question another way, if Israel must be righteous and separate from the nations to enjoy the Lord's settled blessing, can Israel ever be righteous enough to receive it? The answer to that question must be no if we are speaking of historical Israel. An individual Phinehas here and there cannot atone permanently for a people whose entire history was a long series of compromises. Throughout the Old Testament we see this same truth over and over: the people who were chosen by God for blessing repeatedly turned that blessing into a curse through their rebellion and idolatry.

In one sense this is good news for us. Suppose a new ruler took over the island of San Andres, the disaster holiday resort, and transformed it into a beautiful paradise that greatly exceeded the wildest and most wonderful expectations of all who traveled there. Would we not say, "If he can do it in a place like San Andres, he can do it anywhere"? Reading Numbers 25 in the light of the whole Bible should have the same hope-filled impact on us. The Israel that the Lord had declared he would save and bless was a horrible mess at that time, and yet at the end of the long saga of their history, he will present his people to himself pure and holy, without spot or blemish (Ephesians 5:27).

This is a wonderful word of hope for anyone who has been disappointed by the church. Many people have been troubled by the disjunction between the glorious picture that the Bible paints of the church in comparison with the inglorious reality that they experience Sunday by Sunday. They sought a committed company of believers like that described in Acts 2 and found a compromised community instead. Nor is this simply an isolated problem: even the best of churches is very far from being perfect! How then do we reconcile these realities? The answer is that the church is God's work in progress: it is not yet what it one day will be, but at the same time by the Lord's grace it is not what it used to be. If he is able to make such glorious promises to the compromised people of Numbers 25, surely he can be trusted with the future of my local branch of his people, warts and all.

Hope for the Deeply Flawed

The same is true also of myself and of other believers around me. I am often troubled by my own lack of spiritual progress, and sometimes downcast over the lives of others as well. What have I really learned in all my years as a Christian? How much do I truly live by the truths that I regularly proclaim? Yet if the Lord is able to promise ultimate transformation to the Israel of Numbers 25, surely he can remake me, with all my faults and sins. If that people could be saved, then so surely can I—and so can you!

However, for this people to be saved, they needed something more than a little touching up around the margins of their lives. They needed something better than moral instruction: this people had by now already had God's Law for forty years, and they were no better off than the day when they first received it. Clearly, the Law is unable to transform us. What they and we both need is a covenantal substitute, a new Israel, who completely fits the description of the brochure and thereby earns God's blessing on behalf of his people. We need someone who is always righteous, always faithful, always true.

That new Israel, according to the New Testament, is Jesus Christ, the one who came and lived the only life that has ever truly been free from spiritual adultery. His zeal for the Lord's house certainly sometimes made him an uncomfortable companion. In John 2 he made a whip of cords in order to drive out those who had turned the temple into a marketplace (v. 17). His disciples immediately thought of Psalm 69:9: "Zeal for your house has consumed me." Yet it was that same zeal for God's glory that would ultimately take him all the way to the cross in the ultimate judgment on sin. There, instead of piercing the guilty sinners and putting them to a deserved death, God pierced his own innocent Son in our place. Through his death, Jesus made atonement for all of his people. By pouring out his anger on his own Son, God turned his anger away from us, enabling us to live under his blessing. Our sin was put to death in Jesus, and his zeal for God's glory was credited to us, making us acceptable in God's sight.

Jesus is himself the new, true Israel, the perfect people of God. That is why his death could be accepted in our place as a covenantal offering. We are ingrafted by faith into him: he becomes our covenant Lord, and we are thereby brought under the settled blessing of God. Now God's attitude toward us does not rest on our faithfulness or lack of it. Even though we continue to be idolaters daily, listening to Satan's whispers and enthroning other things in the Lord's place, the Lord now views us through Jesus, in whom we are permanently blessed. That is why there is now no condemnation for us (Romans 8:1). That is why we now have peace with God (Romans 5:1). What is more, this new people of God includes both Jews and Gentiles, even Simeonites (Revelation 7:7) and Moabites such as Ruth, the ancestress of the Lord (Matthew 1:5). The aliens, strangers, and outlaws are invited in and made welcome in the name of Jesus, while those who trust in their own goodness remain outsiders to God.

Where is our hope placed? On what are our hearts set? Even the very best that this world has to offer never quite lives up to the brochure. The best holiday is not quite perfect; the best job is not quite as fulfilling as we anticipated; the best marriage and the most wonderful family are somewhere short of ideal; the best church is not yet Heaven. In this world we are always let down by our hopes and expectations, left looking for something more. In Christ, however, there is a blessing to be found that far exceeds anything we will ever find here, and it is all ours to receive freely through simple faith in Christ, by his grace alone. In Christ we receive peace with God now, along with the prospect of a final transformation of all things, including us. Set your hearts, therefore, on the things that are above, where Christ dwells even now, the things that are true and lasting. Set your minds on these things and feed on them by faith.

30

The Next Generation

NUMBERS 26, 27

THERE IS AN OLD TRADITION that a bride should wear "something old, something new, something borrowed and something blue" at her wedding. Did you ever wonder what the tradition means? As a result of extensive research conducted in the innermost recesses of dusty libraries, I can now reveal to you the significance of these practices. "Something old" represents the link with the past and with the bride's family of origin, while "something new" is a reminder of the new life she will share with her husband. The "borrowed" item is supposed to come from a happily married woman and thereby to convey something of her happiness to the new union, while "something blue" has represented faithfulness at least back to Geoffrey Chaucer's *Canterbury Tales*, written in 1390. Together these four items tell us something about the character of the bride and her hopes for the future as she stands on the threshold of a whole new life.

Numbers 26, 27 is about a new beginning: a whole generation was standing on the threshold of a new life. The previous generation of Israelites who refused to enter the land in chapters 13, 14 and were condemned to die in the wilderness were now all dead, and the transfer to the new generation that began in Numbers 21 was now complete. The completion of the transfer was marked by a second census (Numbers 26), which duplicated the original census in the opening chapters of the book (1—4). Following the census, several events are recorded that highlight key aspects of the nature of the new generation (Numbers 27). For the sake of convenience, we can classify what is described in this passage as "something old, something new, something borrowed, and something blue" (or, more precisely, something purple, as we shall explain when we get there).

Something Old

The first thing we see in these chapters is something old. In fact, several things link this new generation with their forefathers. The first link is the consistent promise of God. The new generation was not an entirely different nation, separate from anything God had ever done before. At various times God threatened to wipe out the people and start afresh with a whole new nation, but such was his faithfulness to his promise to Abraham that he never turned his back on Abraham's offspring, in spite of their sin and unfaithfulness. This new generation is identified as "the congregation of the people of Israel" (26:2), the descendants of those who came out of Egypt (26:4). They are thereby linked by a shared history back to the patriarchs and are thus the true heirs of all of the promises made to Abraham, Isaac, and Jacob. What is more, they are linked by descent to the exodus from Egypt and share in the memory of God's great act of redeeming his people from bondage. God's promises are now theirs to inherit.

This continuity of the new generation with what has gone before is further underlined by the overall total in the new census, which is virtually identical to that of the first census. At this point, near the end of the wilderness wanderings, there were a total of 601,730 fighting men compared with the earlier total of 603,550 (26:51 and 1:46). In other words, in spite of the sin of the previous generation, which had left more than half a million bodies scattered throughout the wilderness, the Lord's faithfulness to his promises to Abraham meant that his people were still a mighty army, equipped with all of the resources necessary to inherit the land of promise.

God's faithfulness to carry through to completion the things that he has promised in spite of our sin is good news for us too. We too repeatedly let God down in one way or another, both through our deliberate sin and through our accidental blunders. If God were to treat us the way that we treat others, he would have given up on us long ago. Our faithfulness to do what we have promised is quickly withdrawn from others when people let us down. In fact, even when I have the best intentions, my commitment to persevere with people often falls short. God never fails to do what he says, however. As a result, we can count on his promise to sanctify us through and through. As Paul reminds the Philippians, "he who began a good work in you will bring it to completion at the day of Jesus Christ" (Philippians 1:6). There are many uncertainties in this life, but our ultimate sanctification is not one of them.

God's purpose for his people Israel was that they should inherit the land. The first generation had forfeited that promise through their unbelief, but the Lord told Moses that the purpose of this second census was specifically to prepare the people for the allotment of the Promised Land (26:53). What an encouragement it must have been to this younger generation to hear that God declared them ready to receive their inheritance! The previous census may have counted the people as a fighting force, but because of their lack of faith they never really had the opportunity to demonstrate that force in action. This new generation, however, would not merely be engaged in a fight for the land—they were the ones who would inherit the land and distribute it among the tribes. The land was theirs to possess: all they had to do was step out in faith and see the Lord win the victory on their behalf.

As believers in Christ, our heavenly inheritance is equally sure. It is kept for us by the promise of God and is guaranteed for us by the cross. If God gave his Son to win that inheritance for us, what can keep us from receiving it? We too can therefore step out in faith, with confidence in God's promise, knowing that our destiny is assured. Nothing can separate us from what God has committed himself to give us.

Yet along with encouragements to have faith, the passage also returns to the familiar warning theme that unbelief leads to death. Unlike the first census, the second census contains a number of historical snippets interspersed with the list of names. Several of these historical reminiscences underline the theme that unbelief leads to death. The passage reminds us about Dathan's and Abiram's fate of being swallowed by the earth along with their families when they rebelled along with Korah (26:9-11). It remembers Er and Onan, the two sons of Judah, who died childless in Canaan, put to death by the Lord for their wickedness (26:19; Genesis 38:6-10). When the families of the Levites are listed, there is a special mention for Nadab and Abihu, the two sons of Aaron who died without offspring when they offered unauthorized fire before the Lord (26:61; Leviticus 10:1, 2). Do you discern the pattern here in recording these deaths that took place at diverse moments in Israel's history? It is the familiar theme that "the wages of sin is death."

The theme of the sin of unbelief leading to death emerges also in chapter 27, where Moses was reminded that he would not enter the Promised Land but instead, like his brother Aaron, would die in the wilderness (vv. 13, 14). The reason for that death was reiterated: he and Aaron failed to honor the Lord as holy before the people when the people grumbled at the waters of Meribah (20:12). Moses and Aaron had behaved as if they could judge the people for their sin and themselves provide the remedy for it by bringing water from the rock, instead of carefully following the Lord's commandments to them. Their unbelief and self-glorification led to the sentence of death outside the land being passed on them both by God. The execution of that sentence on Moses would not be carried through until the end of the book of Deuteronomy, but he was being reminded here that his sentence had only been deferred, not lifted. Every single one of the former generation, with the sole exceptions of the two faithful spies—Joshua and Caleb, would die outside the land for their unbelief.

This reinforces the message that we have seen repeatedly in Numbers of just how crucial faith is to the people of God. When people draw up a list of "great sins" and "little sins," unbelief doesn't typically come at the top of the list of great sins. Adultery and murder come near the top, followed perhaps by lying and stealing, but why is unbelief such a dangerous sin? The answer is that, as was the case for Moses, our unbelief draws the focus away from God and onto ourselves. When faced with trials, unbelief doubts that God can really fulfill his promises and draws away the glory that is his due by leaving us in a state of frantic worry and despair. When we fear the future, God's glory is not on our lips and in our hearts. Likewise, when we encounter success, unbelief thinks that our triumphs are the result of our own gifts and efforts, not God's work. Once again, unbelief siphons off glory that ought to go to God alone. Unbelief is thus a great sin because it is robbing God of some of the glory that is due his name. God takes the honoring of his name very seriously indeed, and unbelief dishonors it.

Something New

Yet these old, old themes that we have seen so many times already in the book of Numbers here serve primarily to highlight, in contrast, what is new. Another generation is rising, a new generation that by God's grace will enter and inherit the land that God promised to the patriarchs. Central to the passage, therefore, is the truth that God's grace can and will transcend his judgment. This theme emerges from another of these historical snippets. Although Dathan and Abiram were left without offspring, and Er and Onan had no one to carry on their name, and Nadab and Abihu were a dead end in the priestly line, we read that Korah's descendants were apparently not completely wiped out (26:11). Why were they not exterminated? Reading Numbers 16, you might have thought that Korah's offspring were all dead, just like Dathan's and Abiram's families. Yet some of the sons of Korah survived. What is more, not only did they live, but some of these same "sons of Korah" were responsible for writing a number of psalms (Psalms 42—49; 84, 85; 87, 88). God's grace took a family that was under a deserved sentence of death and redeemed their offspring, giving them life and a place of honor in the covenant community. What a beautiful picture of God's grace at work in the lives of the next generation!

A similar theme runs through the story of a man named Zelophehad, which is the focus of the first portion of Numbers 27. Zelophehad died as a consequence of his sin during the wilderness era. He wasn't involved in Korah's rebellion, but somewhere else along the way he sinned against the Lord, and it cost him his life (27:3). We don't know where or when. Perhaps he grumbled about the lack of variety in the food and died with a quail sandwich between his teeth (11:33). Perhaps he complained later about the lack of food and water and was bitten by one of the fiery serpents (21:6). Perhaps he sinned with the Moabite women and was killed by the plague (25:9). Any number of possibilities exist for his demise, but the key fact is that he died through his own unbelief with no sons, leaving only daughters. Even if they married, they would not normally inherit. They would be absorbed into another clan, and so would their father's land, which would go to brothers or uncles. As a result, Zelophehad's name would disappear. Normally in the ancient world, sons inherited the father's property, while the daughters inherited through their husbands. Dying without sons, it seemed as if Zelophehad's line would die out and his name would be forgotten, erased by the judgment of God. In ancient terms, this was a tragic story of a wasted life.

His daughters, however, went to Moses and appealed their case (27:1-4). In this instance, where there were no sons, they asked if daughters could still inherit a portion in the land of promise. Moses then took their case to the Lord, who responded with the verdict that the daughters could indeed inherit their father's property if there were no sons (27:5-11). In order to maintain the name of the one who had died, the property could be inherited by daughters or brothers or even uncles.

Do you see the significance of this ruling? There is much more at stake here than ancient civil rights for women. Here the Lord was declaring once again that the effects of his grace are wider than the judgment of death caused by man's sin. The theme that we saw in the future given to the sons of Korah in spite of their father's sin emerges again in the future given to the name of Zelophehad through his daughters in spite of his death for sin. Even if the parents were judged for their sins, the children might still have a future in the Lord, through his grace and mercy.

This is indeed good news for the next generation, and for us too. Some of us may have similar personal testimonies. Our parents, perhaps, did not walk with the Lord or have faith in Christ. As a result, we grew up with no knowledge of the gospel and no expectation of a relationship with God. We were strangers and aliens to the people of God, outsiders to his promises. Yet here we are, the next generation, trophies of God's grace that has rescued us and given us lives that were different. Do we ever stop to marvel at what God has done for us? Now we have the opportunity to pass on to our children something we never received from our parents.

This is not the only "new" theme in Numbers 27 either. We also see a new attitude exemplified in what we might call Zelophehad's feisty females of faith. Notice what these women are asking Moses for: they don't want the right to vote or a say in the running of the country (though neither of those things are necessarily bad). Rather, what they want is an inheritance in a land that was promised by God but not yet possessed. They are indeed

young women of faith, quite different from their parents. In the ancient
world you would expect leadership to come from the older generation, especially from the men; yet these young women had far more faith than their
fathers.[1] Unlike the men of the former generation, who had lacked the faith
to enter the land when it lay at their feet, their female children declared in
essence, "The land is ours, and we want our share!" They believed God's
word of promise and acted accordingly, and so they fittingly received what
they asked from the Lord. No Israelite would ever have a stronger claim to
their land than these daughters of Zelophehad.

There is a challenge here for Christians of all ages. Mature men should
certainly be leading the people of God, modeling the life of faith for the
next generation, instead of abdicating that leadership role. Mature women
should provide examples for their spiritual daughters to follow (Titus 2:3-5).
Yet when the older generation has failed to provide the proper lead, there
is a challenge here to the younger generation to learn from Zelophehad's
daughters to step forward in faith to fill in the failings of those who have
gone before.

Something Borrowed

In addition to something old and something new, there is also something
borrowed in this chapter—namely, the authority of Joshua, which was "borrowed" from Moses. When the Lord reminded Moses of his coming fate,
Moses pleaded with the Lord to appoint a man to lead his people into the
Promised Land. More specifically, Moses asked for someone to lead them
out and bring them in and be their shepherd (27:16, 17).

In some ways Moses' request was answered in the person of Joshua,
who along with Caleb had argued in favor of entering the land so many years
ago and who had been Moses' assistant for many years now. Moses was
instructed to take Joshua and lay hands on him (27:18), transferring some of
his own authority to him so the Israelites would obey him. God was faithful
in providing leaders for his people.

At the same time, however, even though Joshua would become a great
leader, he was not another Moses. His authority was not his own—it was
borrowed from Moses (27:20). Moses was the one who uniquely received
the Law from God and delivered it to the people. Joshua's role as a leader
was simply to obey that Law given through Moses (Joshua 1:7). Moses spoke
with the Lord face to face (12:8), while Joshua received guidance from the
Lord through Eleazar the priest, who would use the Urim and Thummim to
discern the Lord's will (27:21).[2] To be sure, Joshua was commissioned to lead
the people out to battle and back in afterward, a role that he filled admirably
in the conquest of the land, and he was the one who assigned the land to the
people after its conquest. The people were not left leaderless after the death

of Moses; yet there wasn't ever another leader in Israel quite like Moses (Deuteronomy 34:10-12).

Something Blue (or Purple)

In fact, Moses' request itself asked the Lord for something more than Joshua. That brings us to the "something blue" or, in this case, "something purple," because purple is often a symbol of royalty. When Moses asked the Lord for someone to lead his people on their military campaigns and to be their shepherd, he was really asking the Lord to provide a king for his people. The only other place in the Bible where these two idioms come together is 2 Samuel 5:2, where all Israel came to David to anoint him as their king at Hebron.[3] There they asked David to rule them because he was the one who had led them out in their battles, and he was the one of whom the Lord had said, "You shall be shepherd of my people Israel." In other words, Joshua was part of the answer to Moses' prayer, but he was not the full answer.

David was also a part of the answer to the prayer of Moses, but he too was not yet the full answer. That is because once David became settled into the kingship, he forgot what he had been called to do as Israel's king. Instead of leading the people out to war, as he had done in the days of Goliath, David stayed at home in Jerusalem while his army went out to fight against the Ammonites (2 Samuel 11:1, 2). That led to his sin with Bathsheba, when he committed adultery with another man's wife (2 Samuel 11:4). Moreover, it is not coincidental that when Nathan the prophet came to confront David over that sin, he told him a parable about a rich man stealing a poor man's sheep to feed his own appetites (2 Samuel 12:1-4). Nathan was showing David that in taking Bathsheba for himself, he had failed to be a good shepherd to his people. Instead, he had abused his position of leadership and power, and the consequences of his sin haunted him (and his people) for the rest of his reign.

Throughout the Old Testament we are constantly left looking for something more than that. Israel kept searching for someone to lead them out to war and then safely home again and for someone to shepherd the Lord's people. Everyone who filled those roles fell short in one way or another. In one sense, that is not really surprising because both of these roles are ultimately God's. In the wilderness it was the ark of the covenant that led the people out from their camp, ready for whatever conflict the journey would bring, and then returned them safely home to camp at the end of the day (see 10:35, 36). The Lord was the warrior who led Israel into their wars, and the Lord was also the shepherd of his people, their true King (see Psalm 23).

Yet in spite of that long history of failure on the part of their human shepherds, the Lord promised through the prophet Ezekiel that in the days to come he would send a good shepherd who would replace these former worthless shepherds (Ezekiel 34). He declared that he would send a new and better David to care for his flock (Ezekiel 34:23, 24). The fulfillment of that promise came in the person of Jesus, who was both the Good Shepherd (John 10) and the divine warrior (Revelation 19:11-16). As God in human form, Jesus is able to be our perfect King, succeeding where all those before him failed. As the Good Shepherd, he laid down his life for the sheep (John 10:11). Far from using the people to feed his own interests, he gave himself for the sake of his people, for us. As divine warrior, he went out to war on our behalf, confronting the power of Satan and triumphing over him through his death on the cross. As a result, he can now call us, weary and heavy-laden as we are, to enter into his rest, the inheritance that he has won for us through his victory on the cross.

This is not just *good* news for us—this is the very *best* news. For the reality is that most of us are not Joshuas and Calebs, nor even spiritual daughters of Zelophehad. We have little faith and no strength, and if securing our spiritual inheritance were left up to us, even in part, we would be condemned to a perpetual wilderness life. Our new beginnings simply end up marred with the same old failings. For us, life is just like our experience in elementary school, where the wonderful opportunity of being given a brand-new exercise book in which to write very soon simply led to the same old frustration of copious mistakes and blotted lines, overwritten in an abundance of red ink. A new book wasn't enough for us then: what we needed was a new heart and a new brain! So too now in life, a new beginning would not be enough for us. Instead, we need Jesus to complete our lessons for us in his perfect script, without flaw and blemish.

This is what it means for us to say, "The Lord is my shepherd." It not only means that we can trust God to supply our daily needs for us—it also means we can trust that God has provided our greatest need for us. He has given a substitute to go out for us and be our champion in the fight against sin. His righteousness and his victory are credited to our account as if they were our own, and the Promised Land of Heaven, which he earned through his faithfulness, has become our inheritance. Because that victory has been won for us, we can now live by faith in that victory, just as Zelophehad's daughters did, trusting that the inheritance is ours in Christ. We can live confident that nothing can separate us from our final reward, not even death. We can live confident that the Lord will not abandon us to ourselves but will be our shepherd throughout our wilderness wanderings, our guide until the end, and our God forever.

31

Communion with God

NUMBERS 28, 29

WE LIVE IN AN AGE that is increasingly spiritual in ways we might not expect. In fact, a recent study concluded that more than one in five people in America, and more than half of those who never go to church, identify themselves as "spiritual but not religious."[1] What this means is that while many of our neighbors and friends do not wish to attend a church or other religious service, many of them are seeking the kind of spiritual meaning and significance that comes from having a relationship with God. People don't want religion, but they do desire to have communion with God.

The search for communion with God is not a new phenomenon. It is as old as mankind, for we were created to have just such a relationship with God. As a result, we are spiritually empty when we lack communion with God, and at a deep level we long for the fulfillment that it alone can bring. The subject of communion with God is, of course, a central theme in the Bible, which explains how, having been made for such fellowship, mankind lost it through the fall. It goes on to unfold the long story of God's provision of a new way of fellowship with himself. In a sense, therefore, every chapter in the Bible addresses this topic, but these chapters in the book of Numbers actually address that basic search for communion with God in a profound way. A section that may seem at first sight simply to be a boring list of sacrifices—religion at its worst—actually helps us see the only way in which such an intimate relationship with God may be found and maintained.

Fellowship with God

The first point to notice in our passage is that the reason the Lord commands these various sacrifices to be offered is precisely for the purpose of fellowship with him. Sacrifices had a number of symbolic functions within Old Testament religion, as we have seen in our earlier studies, but several elements in this context highlight the symbolism of a shared meal between the Lord and his people. The sacrifices are explicitly called "the food for my offerings made by fire" (28:2, NIV), and the point is repeatedly stressed that the scent of these offerings ascended to the Lord as an aroma pleasing to him (28:2, 6, 8, 13, 24, 27; 29:2, 6, 8, 13, 36). What is more, these burnt offerings were always to be accompanied by the appropriate grain and drink offerings, which emphasized the fact that the sacrifice was to be a symbolic balanced meal. These sacrifices were thus a kind of communal meal shared with the Lord, a celebration of fellowship between the people of Israel and their heavenly Father. The daily burnt offerings represented daily fellowship between the Lord and his people, while the weekly and monthly offerings provided times of richer fellowship. Meanwhile, the three annual festivals were to be celebrated together as special occasions of feasting and celebration, family gatherings for the people of God.

It is important to notice at the outset that the Lord is the one who initiates communion with man, and he is the one who sets the terms for it. We may live in a society of seekers, but many of them are still seeking because they refuse to be found on the only terms offered by the Lord. They insist on searching for a deity who suits their desires and preferences, one who will let them live according to their own lifestyle choices. What they want from God is communion without commitment and relationship without responsibility.

In fact, there are striking parallels between the search for communion without commitment in the spiritual realm and in the realm of human relationships. Many people today are searching for meaningful relationships with people of the opposite sex, yet are not willing to make the commitment of lifelong faithfulness and self-sacrifice that marriage entails. They simply want someone with whom they can hook up. On a human level, however, the result of the search for connection without commitment is emptiness, for men and women were meant to commit to one another in a permanent marital bond. By the same token, the search for spiritual communion without commitment is equally fruitless. If we want to find God, he is there to be found. However, he will only be found by those who come to him without demands and ultimatums, ready to bow down and worship at his feet, submitting themselves gladly to his laws and ordinances. On the human level, those who commit themselves devotedly in marriage find that the restrictions that it places upon them are themselves the source of true freedom. In the same way, on the spiritual level those who come and submit to the Lord find that through that submission they experience true freedom and meaning for their lives. Communion with the Lord is only to be found through commitment.

The Cost of Communion

Like marriage, communion with the true God is certainly not cheap. In Numbers 28, 29, the Lord makes great demands on his people, and these demands are required, not optional. The offerings listed here are cumulative; so the weekly sacrifices on the Sabbath were to be offered in addition to the daily offerings, while the festival offerings were in addition to both the daily and weekly sacrifices.[2] If you do the math, the total comes out to an annual obligation for Israel to provide approximately 1,093 lambs, thirty-seven rams, 113 bulls, and thirty goats, along with all of the associated grain offerings and drink offerings. That doesn't include any of the freewill offerings or the purification and sin offerings that were also required to atone for particular offenses. Communion with the true and living God is thus a costly affair.

This, of course, is part of the message that the daily, weekly, monthly, and seasonal offerings were designed to teach Israel. The vast bulk of the sacrifices were to be offered as whole burnt offerings, a type of offering that served a variety of symbolic functions.[3] In its wholeness, it served as a symbol of total commitment. When Paul told the Christians in Rome to offer their bodies to God as living sacrifices (Romans 12:1), he was using the imagery of the whole burnt offering: the sacrifices served as symbols of complete consecration to God. Communion with God will cost us everything we have and everything we are.

This truth is not news to anyone who has studied the history of the church. Many Christians have paid dearly for their faith, not just with their possessions but with their lives. Early believers were thrown to wild animals in the Coliseum of Rome, and contemporary martyrs in Sudan and the Middle East are shot or beaten to death for proclaiming the good news of Jesus Christ. True faith always occurs in the context of a response to what God has done for us, a response that may be enormously costly for us. The Christian faith is a free gift that demands everything you have.

In fact, it is the costliness of the free gift of Christianity that keeps many seekers from becoming disciples. You may remember the story of the rich young ruler who came to Jesus and said, "Good Teacher, what must I do to inherit eternal life?" (Mark 10:17). The Lord's response was that the young man needed to sell everything he owned and give it to the poor, then come and follow him (Mark 10:21). The young man went away sad because the cost of communion with God was too high for him. He remained a spiritual seeker instead of becoming a devoted disciple because he found the price tag of commitment too expensive. Following Jesus may not cost us the same things as it did the rich young ruler, but communion with God is never cheap. It demands everything we have and everything we are.

An Atoning Sacrifice

Yet however costly the burnt offering was for the person offering it, it was far more costly for the animal that was being offered! The cost for the animal was death, a death that was necessary to make the offerer acceptable to God. This is the primary symbolic function of burnt offerings in the Old Testament.[4] The whole burnt offering had to be a perfect animal, without spot or blemish, whose death expiated sin by providing a perfect substitute to take the place of the offerer. The animal's blood atoned for his offenses. How many people in Israel understood that truth? How many people stood there as the temple lamb went past, morning and evening, and said to themselves, "That could have been me"?

The reason such atonement was necessary is because in the Bible, as in real life, sin never just goes away. Transgression always has to be paid for, either by the sinner or by someone else. When an uninsured motorist slams into your car and totals it, their saying, "Sorry" doesn't deal with the cost. Your saying to them, "I forgive you" doesn't deal with the cost either. Someone has to pay—either the guilty party has to pay for the damage done to your car, or you, the offended party, have to pick up the tab.

It is exactly the same way with sin against God. Someone has to pay the cost of sin, which is death. Either you, the guilty party, have to pay by your own death, or God, the offended party, has to foot the bill on your behalf. In the burnt offering, God allowed a perfect substitute to take Israel's place and pay for their sin: the blood of these repeated offerings was the only way for Israel to have fellowship and communion with a holy God.

Thus, at the same time that God makes great demands on his people in these sacrifices, he also promises in them a gracious response on his part. Numbers 28, 29 follow Numbers 26, 27, chapters that emphasized both Israel's guilt and God's grace. The second census, and the events that followed, highlighted the themes of God's judgment on the first generation for their sin, leading to their death in the wilderness, and God's grace to the next generation that was leading them to life and an inheritance in the Promised Land. The Lord who offered the new generation communion with him through these sacrifices was the same God who had brought their fathers out of slavery in Egypt and promised to give them the land of Canaan. Everything they had came from the Lord and was a result of his gracious gift to them. As a result, he certainly had every right to demand that they should give a portion of that bounty back to him—or even all of it, if he asked it from them.

A Response to Grace

This is an important perspective for us to maintain when the cost of communion with God presses in upon us. God sometimes makes great demands of us, taking away from us things and people that have become very precious. For one person, it may be a business that he has labored for years to build up that is rapidly destroyed by changing markets or corrupt business partners. For another, God may take away a devoted spouse or a treasured child through an apparently senseless accident or illness. For yet another, it may be the dreams he had for his life that have gradually crumbled into dust as one door after another closed in his face. Communion with God can be costly, and at those times we need to remind ourselves that everything we have comes from him. He gave us those people and those opportunities in the first place, and he has the right to take them away from us if he sees fit.

Not only does God have the right to take away the things he has given us—he has also himself fully borne the cost of our sin through the death of his Son. All of the burnt offerings that Israel sacrificed merely symbolized a perfect substitute taking away the sins of God's people, but ultimately the blood of bulls and goats, even in vast numbers, could not actually atone for sin. That would require a far greater offering—the sacrifice of the perfect Son of God as the substitute for our sin. As you look at the cross, do you ever say to yourself, "That could have been—and should have been—me"? God has borne the cost of our sin for us.

A Pattern for Communion

There is more to Numbers 28, 29, though, than the Israelites' offering themselves to God through a large number of symbolic sacrifices and receiving in return a gracious daily invitation to commune with God. There is also a distinct pattern in the way the various sacrifices were to be offered that forms a pattern for our own communion with God, a pattern that was intended to remind Israel constantly to orient their lives according to God's calendar.

The pattern in the sacrifices is straightforward enough: the various sections were ordered by increasing periods of time, starting with the daily and the weekly offerings. After them, we hear about the monthly offerings and the offerings for the three great annual festivals: Passover, Weeks, and Tabernacles. The further up the time scale, the more substantial the offerings become. For example, the daily offering is two lambs, while on the Sabbath that offering is doubled, as the Sabbath offerings were added to the daily requirement. On the first of the month, the new moon, the offering was two bulls, a ram, and seven lambs, along with a male goat as a sin offering. At Passover and the Feast of Weeks, the first two annual festivals, the same sacrifices were offered as were required at the monthly new moon.

Once the seventh month arrived, however, the offerings moved up to a whole new level, as Israel prepared for and celebrated the Feast of Tabernacles. This was the most important festival in the Israelite calendar, a place that is underlined both by the offerings that were required at this feast and by the literary attention it receives in the passage. The feasts of Passover and Weeks are dealt with in nine verses and five verses respectively, but the Feast of Tabernacles receives no fewer than thirty-eight verses. It was a three-part festival that began with the blowing of the trumpets on the first day of the seventh month and continued with the Day of Atonement on the tenth day of the seventh month. After these preliminaries, the eight days of the feast itself were observed from the fifteenth to the twenty-second day of the seventh month. The offerings for the preparatory events, the Feast of Trumpets and the Day of Atonement, were slightly less than those required for Passover and Weeks—one bull, a ram, and seven lambs, along with a male goat as a sin offering. However, the offerings for the Feast of Tabernacles proper were much larger than those required at any other time in the year. Substantive offerings were to be made on each day of the feast, gradually decreasing from thirteen bulls, two rams, and fourteen lambs on the first day down to seven bulls, two rams, and fourteen lambs on the seventh day, along with a male goat as a sin offering each day.

The Ordering of Sacred Time: Daily, Weekly, Monthly

What we have here is, in effect, nothing less than an ordering of sacred time, to match the ordering of sacred space in the camp of Israel in Numbers 1—4. Through these sacrifices, God was teaching Israel how to view time and how to order their lives in accordance with God's calendar. What lessons are we to learn from this ordering of time?

The first lesson to learn is the importance of daily fellowship with God. The daily sacrifices each morning and evening are foundational to the whole calendar. Israel was to begin their day by symbolically offering themselves to the Lord and sharing communion with him, and they were to end it in the same way. The same is true for us as well. If our whole days are to be given to God, then we should begin them by committing them to the Lord in prayer. When you get out of bed in the morning, take a moment to ask the Lord to be at work in your life in the day ahead. Give into his care the tasks and trials that you already know will face you, along with the ones you cannot predict. Ask God to use the day to develop your holiness and your trust in him. As you have time, read his Word, and ask him to teach you more about himself through it. When the end of the day arrives, thank the Lord for his goodness to you. Ask for his forgiveness for your failures and sins, and pray for the concerns that remain in front of you. Thank him for the gift of Jesus Christ, the atoning sacrifice for our sins.

This daily fellowship with God is so foundational, and yet it is so easy to forget, or to allow it to be squeezed out by the busyness of life. Even as a pastor, I confess to my shame, I can be busy doing all kinds of good things, yet fail in this most basic area. What I find in my own life, though, is that the result of failing to begin and end the day in fellowship with God is that the remainder of the day often gets lived as if God were not there either. I begin to live my life like an unbeliever, even while outwardly serving God, because I have failed to seek God at the outset and ending of each day.

The next level of ordering our time that this passage teaches is the importance of weekly celebration of fellowship with God Sabbath by Sabbath. Monday through Saturday may be, and often are, frantic and fraught with activity and busyness. That is why God has given us a day to draw breath, a day to step aside from the regular duties of life, a day to be given over to him. Sundays are a precious gift, a gift of time to be with the Lord and with the Lord's people. They are opportunities to have our attention refocused corporately on the things that are truly important. Writing to discouraged Christians, the writer to the Hebrews urged his hearers to "not neglect to meet together, as is the habit of some, but encouraging one another, and all the more as you see the Day drawing near" (Hebrews 10:25). Our weekly fellowship and communion with God and with our fellow believers is a great source of encouragement and challenge that will keep us persevering, even when the way is hard. Just as the Israelites celebrated the new moon monthly, so too churches can observe special ways of celebrating the rest that is ours in Christ each month, perhaps as we celebrate the Lord's Supper and eat together as the family of God.

The Ordering of Sacred Time: The Annual Festivals

The annual cycle of festivals was also far from being a random series of unconnected events. The first celebration, Passover (along with its partner, the Feast of Unleavened Bread), was a time to celebrate Israel's redemption out of Egypt and their call to be God's special people. As they remembered the Angel of Death passing over their houses, which were marked with the blood of the Passover lamb, and visiting death on the firstborn of the Egyptians, Israel was reminded afresh of God's grace in sparing their firstborn and bringing them into freedom (Exodus 12:24-27). As they ate the unleavened bread, untouched by yeast, which symbolized change and decay, the Israelites were to be reminded of their need to be pure and holy, separate to the Lord.

The Feast of Weeks, which took place seven weeks later at the end of the barley harvest, was a time to celebrate God's providence. As the Israelites brought the firstfruits of the harvest to the Lord's house, they confessed that everything their land produced belonged to God (Deuteronomy 26:2-11). Later on this festival was also associated with the giving of the Law on Mount Sinai, which took place at this same time of year, at the beginning of the third month (Exodus 19:1). It thus became a day to thank God for the gift of his perfect Law, which showed Israel the way to live a wise life that would be pleasing to God.

The third and climactic feast, the Feast of Tabernacles, began with the Feast of Trumpets on the first day of the seventh month. It was a time to acclaim the Lord as Israel's King, with fanfares and shouts of praise (see 10:10). Later on in the same month, it was followed by the Day of Atonement, a national day of repentance and purification, when the priest would enter the Holy of Holies and sprinkle the blood of the atonement offering on the mercy seat on top of the ark of the covenant to remove the accumulated sins of the people (Leviticus 16). Finally, there was the Feast of Tabernacles proper, a week in which the people would reenact the wilderness wanderings by living in shelters. This formed a perpetual and joyous reminder to Israel that even after they possessed the Promised Land, they were not to settle down entirely as if that were their final destination. The Feast of Tabernacles was designed to keep Israel constantly looking forward to the final consummation of all things, the day when the heavenly trumpet will sound to bring in the fullness of God's reign upon earth.

Each of Israel's festivals thus had a redemptive-historical connection that transcended the agricultural reasons to hold a festival at that time of year. Like our Christmas and Easter, however, these Old Testament festivals often tended to lose their connection with their redemptive-historical roots and became mere festivals of consumption, celebrating the joys of getting and eating. Their distinctive meaning could easily be lost in a haze of consumer-driven excess, and it was that meaning of which Numbers 28, 29 was designed to remind them.

The Festivals and Christ

For us as the New Testament people of God, the religious calendar of the Old Testament, with its repeated cycles of Sabbaths, new moons, and festivals, does not bind us as law. Paul specifically states in Colossians 2:16, 17 that these things were merely a shadow of what was to come; the reality, however, is found in Christ. So how do these shadows point us to the reality that is to be found in Christ?

First, it is in Christ that we find our rest. Each of these shadows provided a day of rest for Israel from their labors and relief from the drudgery of life in a fallen world. Christ is the substance of that rest, which he invites the weary and heavy-laden to find in him (Matthew 11:28, 29).[5] Jesus is our rest because he himself has accomplished everything that the Law demands from us, giving us the perfect righteousness that we need to stand in God's presence. His perfect record is imputed, or reckoned, to those who trust in him, exactly as if it were their own record. Our salvation therefore rests on his obedience, not our own, which enables us to find assurance and rest in him. This rest is unique to Christianity. In most religions, communion with God is the reward given to those who achieve a high enough grade in pursuing the daily round of religious activities. There is no true rest to be found in that eternal round of activity, but in Christ we are set free from that burden and thus enabled to find true peace with God. Jesus Christ is also our rest in that he himself is the goal of our salvation. The heartbeat of Heaven is nothing other than knowing Christ and being perfectly known by him (Philippians 3:10, 11). The essence of our communion with the Father is knowing Jesus Christ, the one whom he sent to us.

Second, Jesus Christ is himself "our Passover lamb" (1 Corinthians 5:7). He is "the firstborn over all creation" (Colossians 1:15, NIV) through whose blood, shed on the cross, peace is made between us and God, reconciling us to him (Colossians 1:20). He is the only begotten of God, whom God did not redeem but gave him up out of his great love for the world (John 3:16). On the cross his legs were not broken as were those of the two criminals crucified alongside him (John 19:33), so that the symbolism of the Passover Lamb could be fulfilled. Seeing Jesus as our Passover Lamb brings out the significance of Jesus' statement in the institution of the Lord's Supper: "Take, eat; this is my body" (Matthew 26:26). In the normal Passover meal, the Israelites feasted on the body of a lamb, whose death protected them from the wrath of God and established communion among the family unit and between them and God. Here Jesus was inviting them to recognize him as the Passover Lamb of the new covenant, the one whose death atones for the sins of the covenant people of God and establishes communion with one another and with God. Now, however, the figure under which the communion is celebrated shifts from a lamb to the associated image of unleavened bread. This image symbolizes the purity that must be ours as Christians, the sanctification that must accompany justification. Thus Paul, having called Christ "our Passover lamb," goes on to say, "Let us therefore celebrate the festival, not with the old leaven, the leaven of malice and evil, but with the unleavened bread of sincerity and truth" (1 Corinthians 5:8).

Third, Christ is our lawgiver and our law-keeper. In the Sermon on the Mount, Jesus delivered the manifesto for his covenant community. This is the New Testament equivalent of the giving of the Law at Mount Sinai. Unlike Moses, however, who simply received the Law from God, Jesus gave the Law on the basis of his own authority. He said, "You have heard that it was said . . . But I say to you . . ." (Matthew 5:21, 22). The problem with the Law throughout Israel's history was that they were unable to keep it and therefore were constantly experiencing its curses rather than its blessings. The Law was perfect and good, but they were sinful and defiled, as are we. As a result, the Law inevitably condemns us because all of us repeatedly fall short of its standards. Only in Jesus can we truly celebrate the gift of the Law, because he is not only the lawgiver but also the law-keeper. As our covenant head, he has kept its demands in our place. Now, therefore, the Law can once again serve as our guide to godly living, something to be revered and loved rather than feared.

Fourth, Jesus is both the King toward whose enthronement we look and also our atonement offering. The Feast of Trumpets was a hosanna moment—a time to acclaim the coming King and to celebrate the prospect of his coming, just as the crowds did for Jesus on the first Palm Sunday. Yet the Feast of Trumpets was followed each year by the Day of Atonement. On that day two goats were selected. One was slaughtered and its blood sprinkled on the mercy seat over the ark of the covenant, while the other, the scapegoat, was driven out into the wilderness, exiled from the community into the place of barrenness and death (Leviticus 16). Together the two goats formed a complementary pair of images for God's judgment. God's judgment on sin entailed, on the one hand, total separation from God and, on the other, violent death. These two images came together in the cross of Jesus Christ. There on the cross the Son was isolated from the Father, excluded from his presence, and sent out into the outer darkness. For the first time ever, the intimate fellowship between the Father and the Son was shattered, their communion severed by the weight of our sin that Jesus bore in our place. The supernatural darkness around the cross symbolized a yet deeper darkness that engulfed the soul of Jesus. In addition to the separation from God, there on the cross Jesus also bore the penalty of violent death that our sin deserved, atoning by his blood for our iniquity. Only in such a way could our communion with God be restored.

Looking Forward to the Feast

Yet the Feast of Tabernacles that followed the Day of Atonement was a joyful, forward-looking affair. The Day of Atonement was a solemn celebration indeed, but it was followed by riotous rejoicing that looked forward to the consummation of God's relationship with his people. The temporary shelters that the Israelites built reminded them of the transitory nature of their present experience and pointed them on to the day when God would fulfill everything he had promised to give them. As Christians, we too need to be reminded regularly of the transitory and passing nature of life on earth and to look onward to the fulfillment of all of God's promises to us in Christ. Having accomplished our salvation, Jesus has now gone from us into Heaven to prepare our eternal inheritance. With all creation, we therefore wait on tiptoes, as it were, to see the consummation of our salvation when Jesus returns (Romans 8:19-23).

All of these things were there in shadows and pictures in the festivals of the Old Testament. God wanted the Israelites to learn from the festival calendar to number their days aright, and so gain wisdom (Psalm 90:12). We need to learn the same lessons they did. We need to be constant in our daily devotion and regular in our weekly fellowship with God's people. We need to be faithful in all of the passing seasons of life to give thanks for our redemption accomplished in Christ and for his ongoing care for us day by day. Above all, we are to be forward-looking believers, neither overly elated nor unduly cast down by the twists and turns of life's fortunes, instead keeping our eyes constantly fixed on Christ, who is our heavenly inheritance.

Are we seeking communion with God today? It is not to be found in a spiritual experience on a mountaintop nor in an obscure religious discipline. It is to be found in a committed relationship to the one true God—Father, Son, and Holy Spirit. The door is open for us to enjoy an ongoing relationship with the Father as we come to him through the work of the Son and receive from him the gift of the Holy Spirit. Rest in Christ, and in his finished work on the cross, and delight in the communion that comes from knowing Christ and being fully known by him.

32

Cross My Heart, Hope to Die

NUMBERS 30

WHEN IS A PROMISE NOT A PROMISE? As children, we could argue the case like skilled lawyers. A promise was not really a promise if we crossed our fingers when we said it. But if we said, "Cross my heart, hope to die," we were bound to follow through on our commitment. As adults, it becomes more complicated. A promise is certainly not a promise if it is extracted under duress, but it seems that it is also not really a promise if it simply becomes inconvenient and less than fulfilling for me to do what I committed myself to do. People stand in the presence of God and their friends and say, "I do," only to change that statement a few years later to "I don't anymore." They say, "We grew apart and became different people" or "We're no longer in love," as if those are self-evidently legitimate reasons for breaking sacred vows. However, our lack of faithfulness to our wedding vows is simply the most dramatic example of a more general unreliability in our society. We live in a culture in which faithfulness to fulfill what we have promised is in short supply.

God's people are not to be like that: they are to be people of their word, even when it is costly for them. Specifically, when they make a vow, they are to fulfill their promise and keep the commitment that they made before God. Numbers 30:2 states: "If a man vows a vow to the LORD, or swears an oath to bind himself by a pledge, he shall not break his word. He shall do according to all that proceeds out of his mouth."

No ifs or buts or finger-crossing equivocation: whatever you commit yourself to do before the Lord, you are to do.

The Importance of Faithfulness

Why is faithfulness to fulfill what we have vowed so important to God? Why is it important to God that his people be truth-tellers who are faithful to do what they have promised? The answer is that we are his covenant people who are called to bear his likeness. Satan is a liar and the father of lies, as Adam and Eve discovered in the Garden of Eden. God, however, is the Author of Truth and the Father of Light. God's yes means yes, and his no means no. He will surely do whatever he has said he will do. He is a faithful God.

This attribute of God is crucial to our understanding of who God is. The Lord is a God who has made a covenant with his people, which by definition is a promissory oath. He promised Adam eternal life in his presence in exchange for perfect obedience. Had Adam been obedient and not eaten of the tree of the knowledge of good and evil, he could have counted on God's giving to him and to his posterity what he had promised. Yet even when Adam failed to keep the conditions of the first covenant, the covenant of works, the Lord promised a new covenant, a covenant of grace, in which he himself would fulfill all of the conditions. God was so determined to do what he had promised originally and create a people to worship and enjoy him forever that even Adam's sin could not prevent it from coming about. We serve a faithful God. Indeed, in the New Testament we read that the Lord has sworn by himself to accomplish our salvation, because there is nothing greater he can swear by (Hebrews 6:13-20). The faithful God, whose word by itself is utterly reliable, actually swore an oath to accomplish our salvation, and so we may be sure that he will do it. Our hope for eternity is anchored on the truthfulness of the Lord and his faithfulness to keep his Word.

That is why God is so concerned about our faithfulness to do what we have promised. We are children of our heavenly Father, called to be perfect just as he is perfect (Matthew 5:48). What is more, we are the means by which the world around us gathers much of its information about God. How are your neighbors supposed to know who God is and what he is like? They could read the Bible, but many of them won't. What they will do is to read you and draw conclusions from your character about the God whom you serve. This is exactly as it should be: we are to be salt and light for the world (Matthew 5:13-16), images that highlight the impact we are intended to have on our surroundings. People are intended to look at us and glorify God as they see his character increasingly reflected in us.

One key aspect of that reflection of the Lord's character is to be shown in our faithfulness to do what we have promised, no matter what the cost. When we fail to keep our vows, we undermine people's confidence not only in our own faithfulness but also in the faithfulness of the God whose name we bear. That is why it is so crucial that our yes be yes and our no no, as Jesus told us in Matthew 5:37. People should be able to count on us to fulfill whatever we have committed ourselves to do.

Oaths and Vows

There were a number of different kinds of oaths and vows that people would take in the Old Testament.[1] A promissory oath, usually involving self-denial, was a commitment to do something or to give up something, normally for a particular period of time. The temporary Nazirite commitment was an example of this: someone might commit himself not to cut his hair or drink alcoholic beverages or come in contact with dead bodies for a particular period of time (see Numbers 6:1-8). An oath of abstinence was usually a temporary commitment in the Old Testament, as an expression of personal or corporate repentance, for example, or as an outward sign of inner personal devotion to the Lord who had shown such grace to his people.

A vow, meanwhile, was a conditional oath: the person making the vow promised to dedicate a particular object at the temple or to offer particular sacrifices if the Lord answered his or her petition. An essential element of Old Testament vows was the vow of praise, which would be fulfilled by delivering a personal and public testimony to what the Lord had done, along with the requisite thanksgiving sacrifice.[2] The psalms of acknowledgement, in which the psalmist gave thanks publicly for the Lord's deliverance from a particular situation of need, were composed for such situations.

The third category covered dedications, which were the immediate and unconditional transfer of ownership of an object to the Lord, such as when the Israelites brought their tithes and offerings to the Lord's presence and dedicated them in his service (Leviticus 27:30-33). Sometimes more than one aspect would be combined. Hannah, for example, vowed that if the Lord would give her a son, she would dedicate him to serve the Lord at the temple in Shiloh all the days of his life (1 Samuel 1:11). When the Lord answered her prayer, she not only took Samuel to Shiloh, she also brought the requisite sacrifices to accompany her public act of thanksgiving to the Lord for his favor.

Monastic Vows

Biblical vows and oaths were thus commitments to express thankfulness for the Lord's favor publicly, not attempts to win that favor. Within the medieval Catholic system, however, vows replaced the commitment to praise with promises to do something for God.[3] The primary assumption was that God would not be favorable toward you without some kind of *quid pro quo*, a religious act that would repay your debt to God. Thus when a young Martin

Luther was caught in the open during a terrific thunderstorm at Stotternheim, he cried out in terror, "Help, holy St. Anna, and I will become a monk." He thought that a vow made to a saint would engage God's help and thus preserve his life.

Indeed, the monastic movement itself centered around the vows of poverty, celibacy, and obedience. Through these acts of asceticism, monks and nuns hoped to reach a higher spiritual life than could be accomplished by those who didn't take such vows. Inner devotion was replaced by outward renunciation of the world as the mark of true spirituality. As such, it involved an anti-Christian rejection of the physical world as inherently sinful and defiling, rather than seeing the created order as God's good gift that is to be received with thanksgiving. This view of the world was precisely the attitude that Paul warned Timothy about, condemning false teachers who

> forbid marriage and require abstinence from foods that God created to be received with thanksgiving by those who believe and know the truth. For everything created by God is good, and nothing is to be rejected if it is received with thanksgiving, for it is made holy by the word of God and prayer. (1 Timothy 4:3-5)

That is why the Old Testament oaths of abstinence were usually temporary. Oaths of abstinence were not made because abstinence was a better, higher way of life. It was simply an expression of the present absence of joy in one's life for the purpose of repentance or consecration for a particular task. After that period was over, the person who had made the oath would return to normal life.

There are still people within the church who assume that the ascetic approach to life is the way to true holiness. They think that Christianity is about what you don't do and that the more you give up, the closer you are to God. This is not the Biblical approach, which in contrast regards everything God created as being fundamentally good, to be received with thanksgiving. There may be times to give things up for the sake of the gospel and for the sake of ministry to others, but that is not a path to higher spirituality. The Biblical goal is not abstention but discernment and wisdom in what we do and do not commit ourselves to partake in, and faithfulness to fulfill whatever legitimate vows we have made.

The Vows of Women

Yet the bulk of the chapter is not taken up with vows in general. It is assumed that you understand when and why people may make vows, and the passage simply asserts that when such vows and oaths are undertaken, they are to be kept. The majority of the chapter describes a variety of situations in which women might find themselves, in which their vows and oaths were not binding without the ratification of a man.

First, if a woman made a vow or an oath who was a minor, still residing in her father's house, it was not binding unless her father ratified it (30:3-5). More precisely, if her father did not object to the vow on the day he first heard about it, then she was bound by it. However, if he contested it, she was absolved from her vow or oath.

Second, if she made a vow or oath while she was still single and then subsequently was married, her new husband had a right to veto her vow, if he objected on the first day he heard about it. Even though her father had not objected when the vow was originally formulated, her husband had the right to object and so dissolve the vow.

Third, if a married woman made a vow or an oath, her vow was subject to review by her husband. If he did not object at the time he first heard of it, then her vow was valid. However, if he did object, her vow was not effective. If, having failed to object initially, he subsequently prevented her from carrying out her vow, he would personally bear the punishment for her broken oath. If she were a widow or a divorced woman, however, she was bound by whatever oaths or vows she might make, just as a man would be (v. 9).

To sum up, then, men were bound to fulfill their oaths without exception, as were widows and divorcées. However, girls still living with their parents, engaged women, and married women were only bound by their vows if their husbands or fathers did not object when they first heard about them.

Why Treat Women's Vows Separately?

Why was there this difference in the way young women and married women were treated from the rest of the population? To begin with, we need to clear up some possible misconceptions. First, their vows were not less binding because the Bible views women as being inferior to men, less rational and therefore needing more protection from making rash vows. Our society sometimes views women in these terms. For example, one California radio station has a segment every Friday morning called "The PMS Patrol." In it, women call in and confess to a variety of misdeeds, ranging from ill-tempered outbursts to full-scale felonies, which they committed while supposedly under the influence of PMS (premenstrual syndrome). The woman with the "best" story each week receives a prize for her antisocial behavior, presumably on the theory that she was not fully responsible for her actions: PMS made her do it. In our society, in some circles at least, it is apparently considered acceptable and normal for women to behave in such irresponsible ways.

Certainly that is not the reason why certain women's vows required the affirmation of their husbands or fathers in Numbers 30. Women were free to make oaths and vows, just as men were. If they were widows or divorcées, their oaths were immediately binding, just as men's oaths were. There is nothing inherent in women as the "weaker" sex that required them necessarily to have their vows reviewed by a man.

Nor is the reasoning simply that the vows made by married women and girls who are still at home could have a negative impact on their fathers and husbands. It is certainly true that many vows would have had a financial impact on the family unit and that a wife's vow of abstinence might negatively impact her husband. Hannah's vow to dedicate Samuel, along with the sacrifices that had to be offered at that point, would certainly have been an economic drain on the family of Elkanah. However, it is also true that a husband's vows might equally easily impact his wife's financial and emotional well-being, and the rash oaths and vows of a male child could be just as damaging to his family as those of a female child. The principle of mutual submission and consideration in vows of abstinence that Paul lays down in 1 Corinthians 7:4, 5 held just as true in the Old Testament context as in the New.

So why then does this chapter single out girls and married women as a special case whose vows must be ratified by their husbands and fathers before they are effective? The first answer is surely that the husbands and fathers were the covenant heads for their families. Scripture is eager to ensure that the fundamental principle of male headship was not undermined, even in the name of serving God. Claiming to dedicate something to God can never be an excuse for evading the responsibilities that God himself has placed upon us (see Mark 7:8-12). God is the God of order, not disorder. As a result, greater dedication to his service must mean greater devotion to the structures that he himself has set up, including male headship in the home. Pursuing God can never be an excuse for subverting God's order.

Yet that explanation still doesn't account for the omission of the vows of male children from the list. They too were under the covenant headship of their fathers while still living at home, and young men are surely at least equally prone to make rash vows as young women are, if not more so. So why is the spotlight so exclusively on the women in this chapter?

Israel's Vows

The answer is to think back to Numbers 5, which had an equally unbalanced focus in the case of the suspected adulteress, with no corresponding ritual for wives who harbored doubts about their husbands' faithfulness. As we noted there, the reason for the omission is that the Law served the larger narrative purpose of illustrating the relationship between the Lord and his adulterous wife, Israel. [4] The Lord would never be unfaithful to his promise as Israel had been.

Applying the same approach here, we may observe that the Lord has perfectly fulfilled the demand of Numbers 30:2 to carry out every promise or oath he has made and to do everything that proceeds out of his mouth. Here is an anchor for Israel's soul: the Lord is faithful to do everything he has promised. Meanwhile, the language of "in her youth" (v. 3) when applied to Israel refers to her origins in Egypt (see the identical language in Hosea 2:15; Ezekiel. 23:8, 19), since which time she had continually gone astray. She foolishly bound herself to other gods in marriage and vowed to follow them instead of her true husband and maker, God himself. Yet like the wife and daughter of Numbers 30, she was not free to make such oaths and rashly bind herself to them. Unless the Lord were to ignore her oaths or to divorce her or were himself to die—all equally unthinkable alternatives—her foolish oaths could never stand. Israel might seek to become like the nations all around her and worship gods of wood and stone, but her desire could never be achieved (see Ezekiel 20:32). As long as the Lord was her covenant head, he would step in and nullify her oath, freeing her from her folly.

The Lord's Faithfulness

Do you see how comforting this truth is for us too? In relationship to the Lord, none of us are completely free agents, able on our own authority to choose whom we will serve, perhaps today choosing the Lord and tomorrow making a different choice. Our hearts are certainly fickle enough that, were we left to ourselves, we just might do that. Like Israel, we are constantly prone to wander away from the Lord. Yet we are not left to ourselves, and we are not left free to roam. As Paul reminded Timothy, "God's firm foundation stands, bearing this seal: 'The Lord knows those who are his'" (2 Timothy 2:19).

Our salvation is secure precisely because it does not rest on our ability to keep our vows to serve God. It is not our decision to follow Jesus that is decisive but the covenant that was made between God the Father and Jesus Christ in eternity past to choose us as his own, a covenant the benefits of which we receive through union with Christ. Before the foundation of the world we were chosen by God to be part of Christ's people and to have him as our covenant head (Ephesians 1:4). Joined to Christ by faith, we have become part of God's family, heirs in Christ to all of the promises of God. Our inheritance rests on his faithfulness, not our own. God is the Promise Keeper to whom we look.

What is more, our faithful husband, Jesus Christ, has even paid the penalty for our broken vows. We are all promise-breakers, people who have repeatedly failed to live up to our commitments. Our "Yes" has often turned out to be "Actually, I meant no." On the cross Jesus bore the punishment for all of our broken promises. That is going far above and beyond the terms of Numbers 30. There a husband was only responsible for the penalty of his wife's broken vow if he had prevented her from fulfilling a vow to which he earlier did not object. Christ, however, has borne the curse for all of our idolatry and failures, even though he never approved of our wandering desires, nor did he in any way cause our sin. The punishment for our sin was nonetheless laid on his shoulders as our covenant head, so that through his suffering we might find peace. We were the ones who said, "Cross my heart, hope to die" as we committed ourselves to one foolishness after another, but he was the one who had to die to atone for our failures. This is how God keeps his promise to have a people for himself, even though we have been utterly unfaithful. He paid the full price necessary to redeem our souls.

Numbers 30 is thus not a charter for wives and young women to utter rash oaths, trusting in their husbands and fathers to bail them out of their folly. On the contrary, every one of us—male or female, married or single, adult or child—is to be a person of his or her word, whose yes means yes and whose no means no. We are to be people who are faithful to do what we have promised, just as our God is faithful to carry out all of his commitments. We are to respect the structures that he has set in place, whether the principle of male headship in the family and the church or the governmental authorities he has set over us or other aspects of his order. Most of all, however, we are to be truly thankful for the faithfulness of our divine husband and father, whose enduring commitment to his people in life and in death is the solid anchor for our hope of Heaven and our peace in the midst of a wilderness world. His yes triumphs over all of our noes and results in life and peace with him forever. Thanks be to God, therefore, for his enduring faithfulness!

33

Judgment and Atonement

NUMBERS 31

WAR IS HELL. There is nothing glorious about war, nor should we have any romantic illusions about it. The Roman poet Horace penned the line, *Dulce et decorum est pro patria mori* ("It is sweet and fitting to die for one's country"), but his own experience of war was quite different. He fought on the side of Brutus at the Battle of Philippi in 42 B.C., and far from dying a glorious death for his country in battle, he fled with the routed army, throwing away his shield as he ran.[1] He discovered that it is one thing to write noble poetry about war and quite another to go through the horrors of war yourself.

And war has not improved through the centuries. Over the past hundred years we have seen some of the most horrific wars in the history of mankind, ranging from full-scale global conflicts to bloody local skirmishes between one ethnic community and another. War is surely never something to be desired or sought; nonetheless there are times in human history when war is necessary, either in self-defense or in pursuit of greater justice. We live in a world where evil regularly rears its ugly head and must sometimes be combated directly by force. Even more profoundly, though, we live in a world in which all evil will one day be brought to an end through a cosmic act of judgment, when God finally goes out to war against all of his enemies. Indeed, whenever we pray, "Thy kingdom come, thy will be done in earth, as it is in heaven," we are seeking the day when that final war will come to earth, the true war to end all wars.

The Larger War Against Evil

That final war to end all wars is the backdrop against which we need to read Numbers 31. This conflict between Israel and Midian is no ordinary human war. Nor is it an act of ethnic cleansing on Israel's part, with the Israelites seeking to wipe out every trace of a rival ethnic group, the Midianites. There is, in fact, nothing ethnic about this conflict, for this war is part of God's larger war on sin and evil. It is simply the continuation and completion of God's judgment on those who were involved in the sins of Numbers 25. At that time the Midianites and the Moabites led Israel astray into the worship of Baal through the strategy of sexual seduction. It was a deliberate policy maneuver on their part, following the advice of Balaam who apparently recognized that the only way to bring the Lord's curse on Israel was to incite them to sin against him (31:16). Having failed to curse Israel directly, Balaam nonetheless found a way to bring the Lord's curse on his people indirectly—by luring God's people into idolatry. In that strategy, the Midianites were willing collaborators.

The first stage of God's judgment on that sin occurred at the time of its occurrence. In Numbers 25 the Lord's wrath burned against Israel in the form of a plague because of their enthusiastic participation in this abomination and the failure of their leaders to confront and deal with those who were involved. That plague was only brought to an end at last when Phinehas, the son of the high priest, executed an Israelite man and a Midianite princess named Cozbi (25:15), who had flaunted their sin in front of the whole community (25:6-9). At that same time, having judged his own people, the Lord also declared war on Midian for their part in this sin (25:16-18). Those who lead God's people astray will be held accountable for their actions, as will those who are themselves led astray. As Jesus said:

> Temptations to sin are sure to come, but woe to the one through whom they come! It would be better for him if a millstone were hung around his neck and he were cast into the sea than that he should cause one of these little ones to sin. (Luke 17:1, 2)

God is angry with those who incite others to sin, as well as with those who yield to that temptation. The declaration of war that the Lord made at that time had not yet been carried through, however. Now it was time for action to complete God's judgment on those involved in the sin of Numbers 25 by waging holy war against Midian (31:2).

Holy War

This kind of holy war was a war of terminal judgment on the enemies of God. In it, Israel's opponents were put to death, along with their families, and their cities were burned. This destruction was not by any means a routine feature of Israelite military practice. Rather, it was restricted to conflicts directly associated with the exodus out of Egypt and the entry into the Promised

Land.[2] In that context, as we said earlier, such wars had a symbolic function: just as entry into the Promised Land formed a picture of receiving the blessings of Heaven, so too the comprehensive death of those opposed to God formed a graphic picture of the final judgment. It was designed to demonstrate to the Israelites (and to their neighbors) that the Lord is implacably opposed to evil. All those who set themselves against the Lord are doomed to destruction, especially those who lead his people into sin. Rebellious mankind cannot reasonably expect to persist in their attitude of cosmic treason forever. There will come a day when God declares the list of their sins "complete" or "full" (NIV) and brings down the curtain on them in judgment (see Genesis 15:16). For this branch of the Midianites, that day had simply come a little earlier than it would for the rest of mankind.

Several features in this conflict mark it out as just such a holy war. In the first place, the conflict was initiated by God to execute his vengeance (31:3). It was not Israel's idea to start this war but the Lord's. In addition, the force sent into battle was not the entire Israelite army but one thousand from every tribe, 12,000 in all.[3] Each tribe thus had an equal part to play in this war, and each contributed its choicest soldiers to the conflict. The army was led into battle by Phinehas, the son of the high priest, who brought with him the holy objects (presumably including the ark of the covenant) and the priestly trumpets with which to invoke the Lord's aid (see 10:9). These objects served as constant reminders to the warriors of the necessity and promise of the Lord's presence in their midst if they were to triumph. In this case it was also fitting that Phinehas should lead the army to complete the work of judgment since he was the one who had faithfully intervened in the initial aspect of the conflict in Numbers 25. He was the one who executed the Israelite and the Midianite princess by driving a spear through both of them (25:7, 8).

The war itself proceeded smoothly because the people did precisely what the Lord had commanded them to do (v. 7). They slaughtered the Midianites and their five kings, including Zur, the father of Cozbi, the Midianite princess at the heart of the trouble in Numbers 25 (see v. 15 of that chapter). They killed Balaam as well, executing judgment on him for his plan to lead God's people astray (31:8). They took the Midianite women and their children captive and plundered their property, taking their cattle and possessions as the spoils of war (v. 9). It is worth noting that this new generation, acting in obedience to the Lord's command, gained a victory that clearly highlighted the folly of the first generation's unbelief in Numbers 13, 14. Their parents had refused to enter the land because they feared fighting against its inhabitants: they were sure that if they went forward, their wives and children would become plunder for their enemies (14:3). In fact, as Numbers 31 demonstrates, when Israel was obedient, it was not their wives and children who were at risk of becoming plunder but the enemies of God.

The Anger of Moses

However, when they returned home with their plunder, Moses was angry with them because they had not put the adult Midianite women to death (vv. 14, 15). At issue here was the exact nature of this holy war. In Deuteronomy 20 the rules for holy war described two distinct kinds of conflict. The first kind involved nations that were "far" from Israel—in other words, peoples whose homes were not within the boundaries of the Promised Land itself. In the case of these nations, the Israelites were to kill all of the males but might take as captives the women and children of their cities and absorb them into their community (vv. 13-15). However, in the case of the nations that inhabited the Promised Land—the Hittites, Amorites, Canaanites, Perizzites, Hivites, and Jebusites—they were to exterminate the entire community, so that those pagan peoples would not remain in the land to be a snare for Israel, leading them astray into idolatry (vv. 16-18).

This conflict in Numbers 31 fell between these two categories. On the one hand their opponents were Midianites, and the conflict took place in the Transjordan, outside the boundaries of Canaan. Thus it would normally have fallen under the more lenient category of warfare against distant nations. That was presumably why the soldiers initially allowed the Midianite women to live. However, Moses was angry because he rightly pointed out that these women were precisely those who had already led Israel into idolatry, and therefore in this case an approach closer to the more stringent measures normally reserved for the inhabitants of the Promised Land needed to be applied. The adult women and the boys were also to be executed (31:17). Yet there was still a measure of mercy shown to the Midianites in distinction from the practice with the inhabitants of the land of Canaan: the younger girls were to be allowed to live (v. 18).

Stringent measures of ritual cleansing were also required for the returning troops and their booty. Even though they had taken part in a war that had been commanded by God, the soldiers were still defiled by their contact with dead bodies in that conflict. Both they and their spoil had to follow the purification procedures that the Lord had ordained in Numbers 19, being washed by the waters of cleansing before they could return to the camp of the Lord's people (31:19-24). Only in that way, with the stain of death washed away, could they reenter the camp of the living God.

Distributing the Spoils

What is more, since the Lord had commanded the war and provided the victory, he also directed the distribution of the spoils of war. Strikingly, he did not demand that all of it should be destroyed as an offering devoted to God, as was the case in the conflict with Jericho (Joshua 6:17). Nor did it all go to the soldiers who had fought in the battle. Instead, it was to be shared three ways: those who had fought in the battle received 49.8 percent of the spoils, those who had remained at home received 48 percent, while the Lord reserved the remaining 2.2 percent for himself as a tribute, to be given to the Levites (31:27-30). In this way, both those who had actively participated and those who had not qualified for front-line service shared in the booty; yet at the same time those who fought received a larger share,[4] reflecting the greater risks they had undertaken. Meanwhile, the share the Lord required for himself was remarkably small, a mere token of appreciation of his role in assuring the victory for his people.

Yet another sign of the different nature of this new generation from their parents, however, is that they gave to the Lord far above and beyond what he required of them. It would have been easy for them simply to have given to the Lord what he had required of them and then to move on to enjoy the plunder, but they did not do so. As the leaders of the troops counted their people, they realized that not one of their soldiers had been lost in the conflict, and their hearts were moved to respond to God's overwhelming grace. Out of the booty that the Lord had assigned to them, they freely brought the gold objects they had plundered and gave them to the Lord, rendering the very best of the booty back to him (v. 50).

Making Atonement for Their Lives

It is interesting to note how they described this offering: it was "to make atonement for ourselves before the LORD" (v. 50). In other words, they recognized that their lives were not their own but belonged to the Lord. As they fought against and exterminated a people who had transgressed against the Lord, perhaps they recognized that they too were natural-born rebels against God, by nature children of his wrath. The Midianites had sinned and had died as a result of their rebellion against the Lord, just as the first generation of the Israelites had sinned and died in the wilderness. That much was fitting and right. Yet as the new generation purified themselves externally from the uncleanness of battle, they were confronted with the reality of their own internal need for cleansing. If God had dealt with Israel as they deserved, they themselves could easily have been completely wiped out, just as the Midianites were. In his grace the Lord had not dealt with them according to their just deserts. On the contrary, not one of their soldiers was missing: the Lord's wrath upon sin had been poured out on his enemies, and they, by his grace, were all still standing.

That, I think, was what touched their hearts to give so generously to the Lord. The Israelite soldiers recognized that as unclean sinners, their own lives were forfeit before a holy God, yet they had been spared. In appreciation of God's goodness and mercy, therefore, they responded with a freewill offering to "make atonement" for their lives. They reacted to the Lord's grace with generous offerings.

Our Atonement

This surely is where the passage intersects directly with our own experience. Numbers 31 shows us clearly the wrath of God against sin, a wrath that leads to a sure judgment that we dare not take lightly. God judges sinners and those who lead others into sin, and we are all guilty before him on both of those counts. We have all sinned and fallen short of God's glory, and we have all encouraged others to commit a variety of transgressions. The very best lawyer in the universe could not convincingly plead our innocence of these charges. To be sure, the execution of that judgment has been delayed in our case, just as it was for a time for the Midianites, but we would be foolish to presume that judgment delayed is the same thing as judgment abrogated. The day of the Lord's final war on sin is drawing ever closer, the day when he will settle accounts with all of his creatures. It is an inevitable reality, far more certain than even death and taxes. After all, some people manage to escape the net of the Internal Revenue Service, and those who remain alive on the day of Christ's return will not experience physical death. No one will escape without facing a date in God's heavenly courtroom, however.

As objects of God's wrath, then, our lives are naturally forfeit in the presence of a holy God. What we need is an offering that will make atonement for our souls and enable us to remain alive in the midst of that final holy war on sin. In God's mercy and grace he has provided the ultimate atonement offering for our sin in the person of Jesus Christ. It is not silver or gold that makes atonement for our lives, but the precious blood of the Lamb of God, slain in our place. The holy war of God against our sin has not by any means been abandoned: the charges are real, and someone must answer for them. However, Jesus has been our substitute, bearing in his body on the cross the full penalty of that warfare. There at the cross the Lord executed total warfare against sin in the person of Jesus, so that we might be spared the consequences of our unbelief, disobedience, and sin. Through his death, our lives are spared.

To pick up another image from this passage, through his self-offering Jesus provided the water of cleansing that removes the stain of death from our lives. Remember that the water of cleansing required the person making it to become ritually unclean, so that all those whom it touched could be brought from the realm of death into life (see Numbers 19). At the cross God's water of cleansing flowed from the body of Jesus, making all those who come to God by faith in Christ clean in God's sight. Jesus took upon himself our defilement, so that we might receive in him his perfect unblemished holiness. Now when we stand before God in the heavenly courtroom and Satan reads out the charges against us, the Father answers each charge with the ruling, "This one's sin has all been paid for at the cross! There is no possible charge against him for which he can be condemned." The cross thus stands as our memorial before God, the testimony that constantly reminds both the Lord and our guilty consciences of our right of access into his presence through Christ.

Responding to Grace

If you understand the cleansing that you have received, the atonement that God has provided for you in Christ, then you too will delight to respond with an offering of your own. It is a fresh appreciation of God's grace that moves our hearts to worship. It is not coincidental that the writer to the Hebrews follows up his reminder that "Jesus also suffered outside the gate in order to sanctify the people through his own blood" (Hebrews 13:12) with the exhortation, "Through him then let us continually offer up a sacrifice of praise to God, that is, the fruit of lips that acknowledge his name" (v. 15). Do you sometimes find your heart cold toward God when you come to worship? I know that I often do. I need a fresh glimpse of the reality of the gospel to warm my icy heart and to stir me to joyful praise. How can we not delight to confess his name, though, when our eyes are filled afresh with his sacrifice for us?

The fruit of our lips is just the beginning of our response, however. The writer to the Hebrews goes on to remind his hearers, "And do not forget to do good and to share with others, for with such sacrifices God is pleased" (v. 16, NIV). That is a striking phrase, isn't it: "do not forget to do good"? That suggests that we are constantly in danger of forgetting what we should do for others because we have forgotten what God has done for us. Once again I find myself convicted by this point. I easily become focused on myself and my desires and needs, as if the whole world revolves around me. As a result, I resent it when people place demands on me or when they fail to see and meet my needs. How am I to refocus outward on the needs of others? That happens when I refocus my attention on the cross, the permanent memorial of the atonement that God has provided for me. As I look at Jesus' self-offering, how can I hold onto my selfish desires and demands any longer? As I see the forgiveness I have received from God, how can I resent the far lesser injuries that others have done to me?

Third, contemplating the cross is what motivates us to the mortification of sin. Considering the death of Christ is the means by which we are to put to death the misdeeds of the body (see Romans 6:1-14). Christ died to deliver us from these acts that lead to death: how then shall we live in them any longer? How shall we spare even our most cherished sins when we see clearly what these sins deserve and what paying for them cost our Lord? If God did not spare his Son, how shall we spare these sins? What is more, now that Christ has died and has been raised from the dead, sin no longer has any power even to tempt him. Since we are united to Christ by faith, we must therefore reckon ourselves just as dead to sin. Its power to command us is fundamentally broken at the cross. Even though we are not yet what we shall be, we are already not what we once were: we are no longer sin's slaves but are set free to pursue righteousness with the same passion with which we once pursued sin (see Romans 6:15-23).

When we look at the cross, therefore, our response will not simply be lips that praise the Lord and hands that serve others. The cross is a gift from God that demands in response the gift of everything we have and everything we are: our whole lives presented as living sacrifices, wholly devoted—or, rather, holy and devoted—to the service of the God who has loved us this much.

34

The Problem of
Having Too Much

NUMBERS 32

WHEN DID YOU LAST HEAR SOMEONE COMPLAIN about having too much money or too many possessions? If you are like me, that is not a thought that has occurred to you recently—unless, perhaps, you were moving and lamenting the vast mounds of possessions that had to be sorted, boxed, and transported. In general we are conditioned by our society to think that there is no such thing as having too much. When it comes to material things, we live in a culture in which more is most definitely not less but indeed more. It is also true that our "more" is a good deal more than that of any other culture or time. Most people throughout history have lived in tiny houses with only a few basic clothes and prized objects; most people around the world continue to do so. Yet we continue to add more and more to our catalog of possessions, so that we require more and more space simply to store all the clothes that we are not wearing. If there is such a thing as the problem of having too much, our generation most certainly suffers from it.

In this chapter of the book of Numbers, we will see an ancient version of the problem of having too much. The Reubenites and Gadites had accumulated a very large number of livestock (v. 1). They had acquired it perfectly legitimately, through diligence and hard work and, most recently, through their share of the spoils that came from the holy war against the Midianites in Numbers 31. There was no sin per se in their having all of this stuff. However, having too much stuff placed a temptation in their path, as we shall see in this chapter—a temptation to which we are every bit as prone as they were.

Home Is Where Your Possessions Are

The temptation that faced the Reubenites and the Gadites was to settle in a place dictated by their possessions, not by the Lord's promise. In this chapter these tribes came to Moses and asked for permission to settle down in the Transjordan region, outside the land promised to Abraham by the Lord. What motivated their request? They saw that the area of Gilead was cattle country, and that made it a desirable home in their sight because they had abundant cattle (v. 4). If they'd had only a few cattle, there would have been nothing to hold them there, a few miles short of the Promised Land proper. Their possessions chose their inheritance for them, not the word of the Lord.

The key word in the first verse is the verb, "They saw." Seeing in the Bible is definitely not believing. On the contrary, sight is often the exact opposite of faith. Seeing is frequently the prelude to bad decisions because our eyes tend to make superficial judgments. Eve "saw" that the fruit of the tree of knowledge was good for food and pleasing to the eye, and so she ate the forbidden fruit instead of believing God's Word that this fruit was not good (Genesis 3:6). The result was disaster for humanity. Later, when Lot "saw" that the plain of the Jordan was well watered, like the Garden of the Lord or like the land of Egypt, he chose to separate from Abraham and settle in the unpromised land to the east of the Jordan (Genesis 13:10).[1] Before long he found himself living in Sodom and in danger of sharing in the judgment that was coming on that place (see Genesis 19). Choosing with our eyes often leads us into spiritually dangerous places—places that may then be hard to leave because our possessions weigh us down and hold us there. Wherever our possessions are, there our heart is also.

This was exactly what happened with the Reubenites and Gadites. Their wealth of cattle combined with the grazing potential of the Transjordanian plain prompted them to ask if they might receive the area of the Transjordan that they were then occupying as their inheritance, rather than crossing the Jordan with the remainder of the people into the Promised Land proper (32:5). To be sure, they made their request sound spiritual by arguing that the Lord was the one who had subdued this territory before his people (v. 4), but it was ultimately economics that was driving their request, not theology. In effect they were asking to settle down somewhere other than where God had called them to live because it was more suitable for their lifestyle.

The temptation to choose with our eyes rather than by faith is one that we also face. We are tempted to choose spouses based on looks rather than Christian character, or careers based on their income potential rather than the opportunity to use our gifts to serve our community. We are tempted to spend vast amounts of money on clothing, cars, and the accessories of an affluent lifestyle instead of investing our treasure in heavenly causes. Our affluence constantly poses a temptation to us to settle down here and invest ourselves in this world instead of setting our hearts on the things that are above.

The Sins of Affluence

Moses responded to the request of the Reubenites and Gadites with an uncompromising challenge. He called them a "brood of sinful men" (v. 14) and diagnosed the sinful motivations that lay concealed behind their plea. In the first place he challenged their selfish desire for comfort. Why should they sit comfortably in a place that had been conquered by the people as a whole while their brothers went on to fight for the Promised Land (v. 6)? This is surely a prime temptation of affluence: the more we have, the more comfortable we become with what we have, and the harder it is to give it up for the sake of others. We become inwardly focused on maintaining our own personal standard of living, and we easily lose sight of the needs of our brothers and sisters. We become self-sufficient and isolated from others.

Isn't this true in the church around the world? Those who have little are often extremely generous with the little that they have. I think of visiting tiny villages in Liberia where the people would sacrifice a great deal simply to serve you a can of mackerel with your "soup" or to give you a pineapple. Meanwhile, we who have so much can sometimes be very possessive in our abundance, finding it hard to share with others. The Reubenites and Gadites were ready to sit thoughtlessly in their already-won territory, watching from the sidelines while their brothers slogged their way through a lengthy campaign. Moses, however, uncovered their selfishness and challenged it.

Second, Moses pointed out the likely impact of their desire to settle down outside the land on the rest of the Israelites. He reminded the Reubenites and the Gadites that their decision might well turn the hearts of the remainder of the Israelites away from the Promised Land (v. 7). After all, why should the rest of Israel battle the inhabitants of the land of Canaan for a foothold there if the Transjordan was just as good a place for them to settle? The halfheartedness of the Reubenites and Gadites might become contagious and lead to Israel's failing to follow through with the conquest. Such an outcome would inevitably have resulted in the Lord's judgment descending on the whole people, just as it did in Numbers 14 (see 32:15).

It is the same way with our self-centered affluence. The decision to settle down comfortably to enjoy what we have, without any thought of God's call on our lives, never simply affects ourselves. It affects our brothers and sisters in the church as well. Each of us has a part to play in setting the spiritual temperature of our own congregation. If I am cool toward God, comfortably satisfied with what I already have, then that coolness will dampen my neighbor's enthusiasm for God. Equally, if I am on fire for the Lord, passionately pursuing a life of holiness and service, then something of that heat will radiate out to those around me. We never live our lives in a vacuum. Our commitment, or lack of commitment, affects the body as a whole.

Third, though, by comparing the Reubenites and Gadites to the reluctant scouts in Numbers 13, Moses identified the root sin that lay behind their proposal: unbelief. What seemed to them to be a perfectly reasonable request was in fact turning their backs on what God had set before them in preference for something else. They would rather settle for comfort in the Transjordan than keep pressing on by faith into the difficulties of the Promised Land. It is worth observing that this temptation confronts us particularly strongly in times of affluence. None of the Israelites wanted to settle down and make their home in the howling wilderness: it was only when their earthly surroundings seemed conducive to comfort that they were tempted to put down roots. It is the same way for us. When we find ourselves buffeted by the storms of life, we have little desire to settle down here on earth and live as if this were all there was. However, when life is good and earth's blessings are all around us, it is easy to fall prey to that temptation.

The root of our desire to settle down and live for the blessings of the here and now is unbelief, however. Whenever we say in our hearts that life cannot get any better than this, we are despising and rejecting God's promise of a life that is indeed better than the very best that this world has to offer. We have abandoned God's promise in favor of a second-rate alternative because we have stopped believing in the ultimate goodness of what God has offered us. As C. S. Lewis put it:

> We are half-hearted creatures, fooling about with drink and sex and ambition when infinite joy is offered us, like an ignorant child who wants to go on making mud pies in a slum because he cannot understand what is meant by the offer of a holiday at the sea. We are far too easily pleased.[2]

Sight is content with the best that this world has to offer. To put it in Lewis's terms, sight is happy with a better bucket of inner-city mud than the one that our neighbors have been given. Faith, however, looks beyond the mud and grime of this world to the far greater glory that God has promised us. Faith is therefore marked by a holy discontentment with this world, not merely when life is going badly but even when life is at its very best. Faith's eyes are always set onward, always looking beyond this world, always straining for a glimpse of the land of promise.

Reoriented Thinking

Moses' statement that the attitude of the Reubenites and Gadites was the same as that of their fathers in Numbers 13, 14 is ominous. Was Israel indeed to be plunged back into the wilderness for yet another forty years? Fortunately, the answer was no. This new generation was not like their fathers. The Reubenites and Gadites responded to Moses' rebuke with a fresh initiative that met the desires of both sides. The Reubenites and Gadites would build pens for their livestock and places for their women and children to live in the Transjordan, so they were not left exposed, but they would then send their best troops to go as the vanguard of the assault on the Promised Land, leading Israel into the action from the front lines (vv. 16, 17).[3]

It is important to hear the different tone of voice that was present in their response. This was not merely a grudging acquiescence to Moses' rebuke on their part but rather a complete change of heart. The Reubenites and Gadites promised to hasten to equip themselves to lead Israel into the conflict (v. 17) and to remain on the field of combat until every single one of the Israelites received their inheritance (v. 18). They thus took up the challenge to provide leadership for the community of faith in the ongoing struggle and to persevere in that struggle until every one of their brothers and sisters had received what God promised. Like the U.S. military, they committed themselves to a "No man left behind" policy. That in itself was an expression of their faith, for if the Lord did not grant his people the land he had promised them, the Reubenites and Gadites would be permanently committed to a life of war.

A Compromise Accepted

This is why Moses was able to accept the counteroffer of the Reubenites and the Gadites. In committing themselves to the solidarity of God's people and the certainty of the Lord's inheritance, they had shown an underlying faith in the Lord that could survive living on the other side of the Jordan. Yet Moses also made the Reubenites and Gadites swear formally that they would indeed fulfill their promise to go with the Israelites, warning them of the sure consequences of failure on their part. Failure to do what they had said would be sin against the Lord, and they could be sure that such sin would find them out (v. 23). It is easy to make a commitment to do the right thing after hearing a stirring challenge to obedience. It is quite another thing, however, to maintain that commitment through a long and hard campaign. The Reubenites and Gadites needed not only to begin well but also to finish well.

Once again we can easily relate to this temptation. On Sunday morning, after a particularly powerful sermon, we may be ready to devote our whole lives to serving God, whenever and wherever he calls us to do so. By Thursday morning, however, the attractions and comforts that this world offers its servants may well seem to be far more appealing. Have you ever promised the Lord you would do something for him and then slipped back from following through in full obedience? We need to remember the strictures of Numbers 30 about faithfully fulfilling our vows to the Lord and follow through on the commitments we have made.

Life East of the Jordan

The Reubenites and Gadites thus committed themselves publicly to do what they had offered to do, leading Israel into the conquest of Canaan and fighting alongside their brothers throughout the campaign. As a result Moses granted them an inheritance on the east side of the Jordan river, in the former territory of Sihon, King of the Amorites and Og, the King of Bashan (v. 33). They established their own cities there, marking their devotion to the Lord by renaming the existing cities that had pagan names and thus claiming this territory too for the Lord (vv. 34-38). Part of the tribe of Manasseh joined the Reubenites and the Gadites there, conquering additional territory to add to Israel's inheritance (vv. 39-42). A request that began in unbelief was, in the providence of God, used by him to expand the borders of Israel.

In due time the Reubenites and Gadites did exactly what they had promised to do, leading Israel on its assault into the Promised Land (see Joshua 4:12). They followed through faithfully on their commitment to stay with Israel throughout that struggle to the very end and were finally sent home with Joshua's blessing in Joshua 22. They thus received their desired home as an inheritance from the Lord, where they were able to live with a clear conscience.

Yet at the same time, the dangers of which Moses warned in this chapter continued to haunt the Transjordanian tribes. Immediately after they returned home in Joshua 22, they set up an altar near the Jordan River, at the border between their territory and that of the Israelites. That simple act almost caused a war to break out between the two halves of Israel, until the Reubenites and Gadites clarified the fact that it was not a sacrificial altar but rather an altar to act as a witness to their share in the Lord (Joshua 22:28). They had built it because they were afraid future generations would not remember that the tribes who lived east of the Jordan were part of Israel too. The risk of misunderstanding and miscommunication was constantly present because of the land they had chosen to be their inheritance. There was always the threat that there would be a division within God's people due to the geographic divide provided by the Jordan River. That was the ongoing cost of the cattle-friendly land they had chosen for themselves.

Keeping Our Eyes on the Goal

As those who are easily tempted in our prosperity to settle for the good things of this world, how do we keep our eyes fixed on the goal of Heaven and our hearts longing with a holy discontent for the things that are above? The answer is to fix our eyes on Jesus, whose own mission is the true antidote to the problem of having too much. Here was someone who truly had everything—not just the very best that earth had to offer, but the riches of Heaven itself belonged to him by right. Yet far from settling down comfortably with what he had, ignoring the needs of his brothers, as we are so prone to do, Jesus made himself one with those who were not by rights his brothers. He became one of us, humbling himself as a servant, choosing to live with the barest necessities of this world, hardly more than the clothes he stood up in. Jesus traveled around for much of his life, unencumbered by possessions, simply seeking to do his Father's will.

What is more, his Father's will was that Jesus should lead the fight for our inheritance, taking the vanguard position in the assault on our spiritual enemy. That position would cost Jesus not only his comfort but life itself as he was nailed to the cross. But the result of his self-sacrifice is that our heavenly inheritance is sure, won for us by his death. He has fought the good fight in our place, so that we merely need to believe in him and follow in his footsteps and trust in his goodness in order to enter in. His obedience is what earned our inheritance; his suffering paid for our sins.

The passage also reminds us of a fundamental certainty of the universe when it says, "Be sure your sin will find you out" (v. 23). Sin is a tireless pursuer when it comes to seek its just payment: like a shark that smells blood, it will never leave a wounded swimmer alone. It comes on relentlessly, seeking its wages, which are nothing less than eternal, spiritual death. Yet the fact is that for all of us who are in Christ, our sins will never find us out. On the cross every one of those sins found Christ, and they tore him apart physically, emotionally, spiritually. That is why he hung there alone, abandoned, empty. All of our unbelief, all of our self-centeredness, all of our self-serving, all of our lust and gossip and lies, all of our pride and our grumbling—all of our sin descended on him and assaulted him on the cross, extracting the due penalty from him for our failures.

Because Jesus emptied himself to the point of death on a cross for us, God has exalted him and has given him the name that is above every name (Philippians 2:9-11). This is the reality that needs to fill our thoughts daily. The antidote to our fascination with this world's glories is simply to lift up our heads and see the glories of Jesus. We must look above to see our risen, exalted, enthroned King! How can we be enthralled with material things when we have contemplated the risen Jesus? How can we be tempted to think that houses or cars or clothes or possessions are any more than useful trinkets when we have gazed upon the crucified Lamb of God, seated on his heavenly throne? The cure for our unbelieving eyes is to look above and see the King of kings and then to bow down and lay ourselves in worship at his feet.

35

Pilgrim People

NUMBERS 33, 34

THE FAMILY IN WHICH I GREW UP had a strange tradition whenever we went on vacation. At least my wife thinks it was a strange tradition, though it seemed perfectly normal to me at the time. Every year we drove up to Scotland from our home in the south of England, and each time my father would produce a log sheet to accompany our trip. The log sheet contained a list of place names that we would pass, along with the mileage and antici- pated trip time to reach them. As children, it was our job to fill in the actual mileage and trip time and then to calculate our speed, along with adding comments on exceptional circumstances like road work or weather condi- tions that affected our progress. At the end of each holiday, my father would file these sheets away with the rest of his documents.

Growing up, we never discussed why we kept such records. Perhaps it was an engineer's love of order and record-keeping, or perhaps it was simply a practical means of keeping children busy on a long day's drive. However, the result was that we had an ongoing record of our travels that served subse- quently as a vivid reminder of individual journeys that might otherwise have been lost in the mists of our collective imaginations. Thanks to those lists, we have a record of which year the accelerator cable snapped on our Mini and where exactly it happened. We can recall each and every trip, down to where we stopped for a coffee break and how many minutes elapsed between driving off and arriving at our destination. Even today, viewing those lists brings back a flood of memories of past travels for those who lived through the adventures they record, even though their detailed observations might seem enigmatic, or even obsessive, to people outside of our family.

In a similar way, the list of place names in Numbers 33 may seem to us at first sight to be a rather barren and unprofitable wilderness in which to search for meaning and guidance. To those who had lived through the adventures that took place along the way, however, the list would have evoked many memories. This is not just a random collection of place names but is a list designed to shape Israel's perspective on her wilderness wanderings as a whole. As such, it had a message also for future generations who, like ancient Israel, are pilgrims and strangers on a journey through the wilderness of this world. Our journey through life toward our heavenly place of rest holds many parallels to their journey through the wilderness, and so, rightly understood, this list of place names still speaks to us today.

When we look closely at the itinerary in Numbers 33, we quickly discover that there are three different kinds of places listed here. Some of the places where they stayed call to mind the Lord's faithfulness to Israel in providing for their needs in the desert. Other places call to mind Israel's sinful rebellion against the Lord at a variety of points through their wandering. Still others are places where, as far as we know, nothing particular of note happened. Each of these categories has a lesson to teach us.

Perspective on the Lord's Faithfulness

The first group of place names recalls the Lord's faithfulness to his people. Often these are the place names in the list that have an explicit commentary attached to them. We are told that Israel started out from Rameses, where the Lord had brought judgment on the gods of the Egyptians, such that his people could leave Egypt unharmed, in broad daylight. The firstborn of the Egyptians were struck down, while the Israelites were spared, and God's people were thus delivered from bondage (33:3, 4). Later we are reminded that the Israelites passed through the Red Sea at Hahiroth (33:8) and that they found twelve springs and seventy palm trees at Elim, an oasis in the thirsty desert (33:9). We are introduced again to the King of Arad, the Canaanite over whom the victory in Numbers 21 represented the firstfruits of the conquest of the land (33:40). Each of these places stood as eloquent testimony to God's faithfulness to provide for his people along the way.

Do you see how this point addresses us as well as the original hearers? We too need to be reminded regularly of God's faithfulness to us along the way. We need to take time to reflect on all the ways in which that faithfulness has been evidenced in our lives. In 1 Samuel 7, after a battle against the Philistines, the Israelites set up a stone that they named Ebenezer (*eben hāezer*), "stone of help," saying, "Till now the LORD has helped us" (1 Samuel 7:12). It was to be a permanent reminder to them of God's faithfulness every time they walked past it. So also we need regularly to be raising and revisiting our own Ebenezers, the mental markers of the Lord's past faithfulness in our life. For some, keeping a journal is a good way to keep track of God's faithfulness: as they reread the pages they have written, they are reminded of God's persistent goodness. Others have different ways of recording God's goodness. However we personally choose to keep track of God's faithfulness, the goal is that our hearts are stirred afresh to thankfulness and faith as we revisit our own personal Rameses and Elims. At regular times, perhaps at the beginning of each month and the beginning of each year, we should take the time to think back and remember the prayers we have seen answered and the needs we have seen filled by the Lord.

Nor is this simply an individual matter. By including this list of place names in Scripture, the Lord was ensuring that it would be read publicly in the community of believers. In that way they could stir one another up to gratitude and renewed faith. So, too, we need to remind one another of the Lord's faithfulness. When you meet with other believers, ask them, "How have you seen the Lord's faithfulness over the past few weeks and months?" When we come to God in prayer together, we should begin by reminding ourselves of some of the specific ways in which the Lord has been faithful to us in the past. Like a string tied around our finger, these remembrances of the Lord's faithfulness will serve as stimuli to our praise and encouragements to our prayers and petitions. To build up our faith for the trials of the journey, we need to remember step by step where we have come from and who has brought us safely through the toils and dangers thus far.

Perspective on the Lord's Forgetfulness

The second category of place names in the list of Numbers 33 is made up of the places where the Israelites grumbled and rebelled against the Lord. This group includes Marah (Exodus 15:23, 24), the Desert of Sin (Exodus 16:1, 2), Rephidim (Exodus 17:1, 2), Kibroth-hattaavah (Numbers 11:34), and Kadesh in the desert of Zin (Numbers 20:1-3). Each of these names identifies a place where the Israelites turned their backs on the Lord. Yet strangely enough, if you didn't already know Israel's history of rebellion, you wouldn't have known from this account that any of these negative things happened. Whereas the itinerary lists specific reminders of the acts of God's faithfulness, it passes in complete and total silence over Israel's unfaithfulness. It mentions the places cited above but not the spiritual rebellions that happened there. Even Aaron's death, which came as a result of his sin of rebellion in Numbers 20, is here presented as a simple act of obedience to the Lord's command (33:38).[1]

This fact shows us that we need to be reminded of God's forgetfulness as well as his faithfulness. It is significant that in the Lord's inspired summary of Israel's wilderness wanderings, he chose to pass over their sin in silence. Isn't that a precious truth? Sometimes we are afraid to look over our past for fear of being overwhelmed by the reality of our sin. It seems too painful for us to remember all of the ways in which we have failed God. Indeed, it is impossible for us to recall accurately our own travels without remembering our moments—and longer periods—of unbelief and rebellion. Yet this list reminds us that when the Lord looks back over our lives, he passes over our sins. He doesn't keep a record of our wrongs filed away, ready to use against us at an opportune moment. If that were the case, none of us would ever make it to the end of the journey. On the contrary, the Lord shows mercy to those whom he calls his people (Psalm 130:3, 4). If anyone is in Christ, he is a new creation: the old is gone, to be remembered no more, and the new has come (2 Corinthians 5:17). In Christ, our sin is done away with: it is nailed to the cross, buried in the tomb with Christ, and forgotten by God forever. As the psalmist put it, "As far as the east is from the west, so far does he remove our transgressions from us" (Psalm 103:12).

What matters to the Lord is not the foul sinners that we once were, but what we are now in Christ and what we will be ultimately when we stand in his presence as his washed, justified, and sanctified people (see 1 Corinthians 6:11). What a wonderful truth is the Lord's forgetfulness!

We need to duplicate the Lord's forgetfulness in our dealings with one another. Often we hold grudges against one another, allowing a root of bitterness to spring up in our attitude toward a brother or sister who wronged us in the past. There are people in my life whom I would find it hard to meet today because of perceived wrongs that they have done to me years ago, of which they have never repented. I need to learn from the Lord how to show a holy forgetfulness, letting go of the offenses of others, both real and imagined, and instead remembering to show them the same grace that I have received from God.

Perspective on "Tuesdays"

The third category of place name on this itinerary, though, encompasses many locations where nothing particularly significant happened. In fact, there are far more names in this group than in either of the first two. Some of these locations are mentioned in passing elsewhere in the Biblical account of the wilderness wanderings, such as Succoth and Etham (Exodus 13:20), while others are otherwise totally unknown, such as Dophkah and Alush (33:12, 13). Yet even though at the time it seemed that nothing much was happening there, these places had their own part to play in the overall journey. Their inclusion in the list is a reminder that life is more than simply a collection of high points and low points: it is also what happens in between.

This too is relevant to us. Much of our lives—perhaps even most of our lives—is made up neither of dramatic moments of deliverance nor of striking moments of moral failure but of a whole succession of what we could call "Tuesdays."[2] These are the apparently insignificant days in which we simply do the ordinary things that make up the stuff of life: taking care of a child, doing the laundry, fixing the car, or filing routine paperwork at our job. We are often tempted to ignore these days as we look back, as if they didn't really count; yet each of them has its own part to play in God's grand scheme of redemption. God's faithfulness is shown to us in the little things of life and in the ordinary days just as much as it is in the defining moments.

Let me underscore that point with an illustration. If you are driving home and a drunk driver swings across the dividing line in the road and almost hits you head-on but at the last minute swerves back to his side of the road, you immediately thank God for his amazing providence in delivering you. Yet why do you not thank God just as much for all of the hundreds of times you have driven down that same road without any incident whatever? The daily work of God's providence in keeping us safe in boring ways is just as real as the moments when his intervention is dramatic and visible. So too each and every one of our undramatic days—our "Tuesdays"—is another step on our journey to our heavenly home. We should rightly give thanks daily, even on the unexciting days, that because of the Lord's faithfulness we are one day closer to Heaven and to his promise of eternal life.

On the Brink of Rest

It is also worth noticing that there are exactly forty-two stages listed on the journey.[3] This is surely not a coincidental number since the list of camp-grounds is neither concise nor complete. On the one hand it is hardly a brief summary of their journey, mentioning only the most important stopping places. As we have seen, many of the places mentioned here are not particularly significant, and in some cases these places are mentioned nowhere else in the Old Testament. On the other hand, though, the list is not exhaustive: there are campsites mentioned in the rest of the narrative of the wilderness wanderings that are not listed here (see, e.g., 21:10-20). That suggests, therefore, that the number forty-two was a number deliberately chosen for its symbolic significance.[4]

Why were there forty-two stages? Most plausibly in this context, forty-two represents six sets of seven: having endured six complete periods of wandering, Israel now stood on the brink of the seventh seven, the sabbath of rest, as they entered the Promised Land.[5] If that understanding is correct, then the number of way stations on this list stands as a profound encouragement to the people as they were about to enter the land. Their six periods of labor were done, and the sabbath of rest was about to begin. As they would step out in faith and take possession of the land, God would give them the rest that he had promised.

We too may find comfort in the knowledge that our days are numbered by the Lord and that their end is his sabbath-rest. We may not know the number of our days, nor what proportions of trials and blessings and plain vanilla "Tuesdays" the future holds for us. We may not yet have reached our forty-second campground. Nonetheless, our days are numbered, and when that full number has been completed, the Lord will bring us safely into our heavenly dwelling place, where he has prepared a place of rest for all of his people.

A People with a Purpose

In the meantime, however, we have work to do for the Lord. Reaching the end of the six sevens of the itinerary left Israel on the brink of the task of entering the land of Canaan and possessing it, and it is to this task that the passage now turns. This final battle had to be completed before their rest was won. When Israel crossed over the Jordan, they were to drive out the inhabitants of the land, destroy their carved images and their idols, and then distribute the land equally among the tribes (33:52-54). There was no room for compromise or for peaceful coexistence with the Canaanites, for that would inevitably lead to a life of pain for Israel. The Canaanites would be "barbs in [their] eyes and thorns in [their] sides" (33:55), causing ongoing trouble for them. If left alone, the Canaanites would inevitably lead Israel astray because of the seductive power of their false worship, and the end result would be that Israel would face the same fate that the Canaanites faced for their sin—expulsion from the land (33:56). They therefore had to complete the battle with intense commitment to secure their future in the land.

A People with a Problem

Sadly, Israel never lived up to their calling to persevere in holy war. By the end of the book of Judges, they had become completely like the peoples of the land in which they lived. Even in the book of Joshua, while the conquest of the land was still in progress, we find hints of their failure to clear the Canaanites out. Consider the following verses:

> But the Jebusites, the inhabitants of Jerusalem, the people of Judah *could not* drive out, so the Jebusites dwell with the people of Judah at Jerusalem to this day. (15:63, emphasis added)

> However, they *did not* drive out the Canaanites who lived in Gezer, so the Canaanites have lived in the midst of Ephraim to this day but have been made to do forced labor. (16:10, emphasis added)

> Yet the people of Manasseh *could not* take possession of those cities, but the Canaanites persisted in dwelling in that land. Now when the people of Israel grew strong, they put the Canaanites to forced labor, but did not utterly drive them out. (17:12, 13, emphasis added)

"Could not," "did not"—these terms do not sit comfortably in the Word of God. They do not belong as part of Israel's vocabulary of holy war. But more striking still is the phrase in the last reference: "the Canaanites persisted in dwelling in that land." The Canaanites were apparently more determined to live there than the Israelites were. The heathens had more determination to cling to their turf than the believers had to dispossess them. Even when the Israelites became stronger, they still did not obey fully the Lord's command and drive the Canaanites out but instead merely subjected the Canaanites to forced labor. It was certainly convenient to have someone do the dirty work for Israel, but the result was that the Canaanites remained as a continual source of temptation to the Israelites. The confrontation demanded by the Lord degenerated into unholy cohabitation.

The same failure is evident when the boundaries assigned to Israel in Numbers 34 are considered. The area promised to Israel as their inheritance stretched from desert in the south to Lebo Hamath in the north and from the Mediterranean Sea in the west to the Jordan River in the east. This broad swath of land was never fully possessed by Israel. Even at the height of the Solomonic empire, they never succeeded in capturing the entire area assigned to them by God. The unbelief that had kept the previous generation outside the land for forty years continued to dog Israel, leading them to settle for the status quo of the land they had already won instead of constantly pressing forward toward the full possession of the promise. Eventually their compromises with the nations around them and among them caught up with Israel: they were exiled from the land because of the idolatrous practices they had learned from the surviving Canaanites. The threat of Numbers 33:56 was not an empty one: like the Canaanites, Israel too would discover that there were consequences to their sin.

Like them, we have the Lord's command not to compromise with the world around us. We are to be a "peculiar" people, as the old King James Version rendered Titus 2:14 and 1 Peter 2:9, different from our friends and coworkers, separate from the society in which we find ourselves. As Jesus put it:

> If you were of the world, the world would love you as its own; but because you are not of the world, but I chose you out of the world, therefore the world hates you. (John 15:19)

We are constantly tempted to make concessions and allowances for the world's way of doing things instead of fully obeying God. As a result we often live compartmentalized lives in which what we say and do on Sunday has very little impact on what we say and do during the rest of the week. Monday through Friday, at school, at home, or in the workplace, we live just like the modern-day Canaanites, bowing down to the idolatries of our culture, while on Sundays we put on our Christian faces and pretend that we are single-mindedly following the Lord. At school we may talk like everyone else, using foul language or cruel gossip or suggestive speech to fit in with those around us. At home we may idolize our own comforts and pleasures, pursuing with a passion things that can be consumed or worn out or dented instead of serving others with a whole heart. At work we may pursue our own reputation and career, building an ephemeral house on a foundation of sand instead of constructing a lasting legacy on the solid rock. We are constantly tempted toward unholy compromise with the world.

We don't only fail by our concessions and unrighteous peaceful compromises, however. Like Israel, we also fail by not pressing on to the full extent of God's promises. They heard God delineate the boundaries of the land he had promised them, but they lacked faith, and so they never achieved the full scope of their inheritance. So too, we have been given great promises by God. He promises to give us the power to speak to our neighbors about him; yet we remain sinfully silent, not believing that our words will really make any difference. He promises to give us peace in our hearts that transcends anything this world can give; yet we sinfully worry about tomorrow—about our bills, our jobs, our churches. He promises to bear much fruit in our lives by his Holy Spirit; yet we are satisfied with small progress in sanctification, not pressing forward in faith and new obedience. Our faith in God is so small, and our service of God is often correspondingly limited.

The Faithful Redeemer

If Israel's failure, unbelief, and compromise were so certain to lead to their exile, even before they had begun the conquest (33:56), what hope was there of ever entering their rest? More pointedly, if our unbelief robs us of so much peace and joy that might be ours, what hope is there for us? I am constantly amazed at the boundless optimism people demonstrate about the possibility of contributing something to their own salvation. If there is one thing we ought to learn from the Old Testament, it is that if our ultimate destiny really rested in our own hands, we would rightly despair. Fortunately for Israel and for us, in Jesus the Lord has sent a redeemer to win our inheritance for us through his faithfulness. There was no unholy compromise in his life. He went into the temple in Jerusalem and drove out the merchants and money-changers who had transformed that place from a house of God into a marketplace in service of Mammon (John 2:14-16). He had a passionate zeal for God's holy reputation that could not peacefully coexist with those who would profane it.

Yet Jesus' total war against sin didn't simply take the form of an external assault on those who worshiped idols; otherwise no one on earth would have survived. We are all idolaters in our hearts, bowing down to graven images of our own imagination. Our actions, both good and bad, are often driven by other masters than the Lord. Yet in his incarnation Jesus came not to condemn sinners but to redeem them. In his zeal for God's holiness and his love for us, he took upon himself the "barbs in [his] eyes and the thorns in [his] sides" that our idolatries merited. In his case, these were not merely metaphorical pains but literal pains: a crown of thorns adorned his head on the cross, and a spear pierced his side. He was driven out of the Father's presence for our sins, into the darkness of total abandonment, where he endured the agony of death in our place. The covenant curse that we deserve for our unbelief and compromise was laid on his shoulders.

Yet that was precisely how Jesus won our inheritance for us. Because of his sin, Moses could not lead his people into the Promised Land. Joshua could lead Israel into the Promised Land and divide it among this next generation, but even he could not give them the rest they needed (Hebrews 4:8). Jesus, however, satisfied the demands of God's holiness by his faithful life and the demands of his perfect justice by his substitutionary death. As a result, he is now able to say to us, "Come to me, all who labor and are heavy laden, and I will give you rest" (Matthew 11:28). The sabbath-rest to which Israel was looking forward was to be found in Jesus alone. What the world can never give you, and what you can never find within yourself, is offered to you freely by God through Jesus Christ.

His inheritance is far greater than a small piece of the Middle East: it is a vast kingdom of people from all four corners of the world, from every tribe and nation and period of history. Jews and Gentiles alike are now brought together as one people in him, all gathered around the throne of God for that final, enduring celebration of God's kindness and mercy. There we shall sing forever of the grace of the God who does not keep a list of all of the places where we sinned and failed him but instead nailed that itinerary once and for all to the cross.

So take the time to look back on your journey and to give thanks for the Lord's faithfulness to you thus far. Be alert to the compromises that the world presses in on you, and resist its insistence that you live at peace with its standards. Be "peculiar," different from those around you who do not serve the Lord. Yet above all else, look forward to the end of the journey, the seventh seven of rest that God has prepared for you in Christ. Ask God to strengthen your faith and to help you combat your unbelief, so that you may live a fruitful life for him along the way and may enjoy his peace that passes earthly comprehension. Give thanks that your inheritance is won for you by Christ's goodness and not your own, and rejoice in the reality and certainty of that rest.

36

Cities of Grace

NUMBERS 35

WHEN I WAS A SMALL CHILD, we had a standard formula we would recite in our family before we ate: "For what we are about to receive, may the Lord make us truly thankful. Amen." We called it "saying grace." It was a reminder, albeit in a somewhat rote fashion, that everything that was set on the table before us came to us as a gift from the Lord. Our meat and potatoes were not simply the fruit of our father's labors but were the Lord's good provision for us—a gift of his grace. I'm not sure how much we understood that concept as children, but it is nonetheless true. Everything that we receive in life comes to us from God, not as something that we have merited but as an undeserved act of his favor.

What this means is that even when I work my hardest and do my very best, I cannot earn God's favor. None of us can ever merit godly spouses or loving and obedient children; if God gives us such, they are gifts of his grace. None of us merit rewarding and fulfilling jobs or the favor of our peers; if God sees fit to give us those things, he has been more than kind. Even if we have behaved wisely and responsibly in pursuing these things, we still don't merit them, for who gave us the gifts, the wisdom, and the diligence to seek after good things? God did. So there is no merit per se in our obedience. Everything we have comes from God's grace.

Demerited Favor

Some of God's gifts, though, are not simply *un*merited—they are positively *de*merited. Perhaps we diligently pursued ungodly spouses, but God preserved us from our desires. Certainly we have often been less than adequate parents to our children; yet God has guarded them from many of the

355

effects of our sin. Sometimes we have been irresponsible and foolish in our actions; yet God has taken us through the valley of our sin and brought us safely through to the other side. Looking back on what we have received (and on what we have not received), we surely have reason to be truly thankful.

A country song underlines this point. In it, singer Garth Brooks finds himself face to face with an old high school flame at a football game. With the benefit of maturity, he now recognizes how little they have in common, and how foolish he was when he used to pray night after night that she would be his bride. Looking at his own wife and children, he concludes, "Some of God's greatest gifts are unanswered prayers." God's grace doesn't simply mean not getting what you deserve, but receiving something that is exactly the opposite of what you deserve.

Getting the opposite of what you deserve, or grace, is the central point of Numbers 35. It begins with the Levites being given cities in which to live, scattered throughout the Promised Land (vv. 1-8). Whereas the other tribes were assigned whole portions of the land, the Levites were only given a few cities, forty-eight to be precise, scattered among the inheritance of the other tribes. In comparison to the land granted to the other tribes, that might have seemed to be a poor provision for their faithful labor around the tabernacle during the wilderness wanderings. If you were a Levite, you might have thought you were not getting what you deserved. Why should everyone else get so much more than you?

A Curse Reversed

The answer was that, in truth, the Levites were not getting what they deserved. To understand that, though, we need to review a little ancient history. Back in Genesis 34, Jacob's daughter, Dinah, was raped by a man named Shechem. To gain their revenge, Simeon and Levi massacred the inhabitants of Shechem, first using the covenant sign of circumcision to debilitate the men of the city (Genesis 34:13-26). It was a reprehensible act, and in his final "blessings" their father Jacob pronounced the Lord's curse upon them:

> Simeon and Levi are brothers;
> weapons of violence are their swords.
> Let my soul come not into their council;
> O my glory, be not joined to their company.
> For in their anger they killed men,
> and in their willfulness they hamstrung oxen.
> Cursed be their anger, for it is fierce,
> and their wrath, for it is cruel!
> I will divide them in Jacob
> and scatter them in Israel. (Genesis 49:5-7)

This curse was indeed effective: both the tribes of Simeon and of Levi were scattered in Israel. Yet whereas the tribe of Simeon was scattered and ultimately largely absorbed into Judah, the tribe of Levi retained its integrity as a tribe, even while being scattered. They remained a distinct group with distinct tasks. Even after their work of carrying and guarding the tabernacle through the wilderness was complete, they still remained a tribe especially devoted to the Lord: they were assigned the new tasks of helping the people understand the Law, and when Solomon's temple was built, they were responsible for guarding it and for leading the people in the praise of God. Compared to the fate of the tribe of Simeon, their scattering throughout the land was indeed a blessing.[1]

What is more, their very lack was a means by which they would be a blessing also to the people as a whole. The Levites' absence of an earthly inheritance was always intended to force them to recognize that the Lord himself was their inheritance. They had houses to live in and enough land to graze their livestock (v. 3), but they never had enough to settle down and become altogether comfortable. In this, the Levites were a sign to Israel: they were to be a group within Israel whose eyes were to be firmly fixed on the heavenly inheritance, pointing others in the same direction.

A People of Grace

These realities speak to us as well. For we all, as descendants of Adam, enter this world under a curse. If God were to give us what we deserved as heirs of that curse, our lives would be nasty, brutish, and short. Yet God, in his grace, has given us much more than that. Even the worst men experience a measure of good things in life, through God's common grace. The sun shines on them as well as on us, and they too receive rainfall in its due season (Matthew 5:45). Yet we who are believers in Christ have received so much more than God's common grace. We have received God's uncommon grace, in which he adopted us as his sons and heirs in Christ and has prepared for us a glorious inheritance in Heaven along with all the saints. What that means is that whatever our earthly circumstances, we should be truly thankful every day that we do not receive what we deserve in this world and that God has stored up for us in Heaven a glorious inheritance.

Is that our attitude regarding what God has given us in this world? Are we constantly rejoicing in his grace? Or do we find ourselves grumbling because of what he has chosen not to give us? Do we murmur in our hearts because our earthly inheritance doesn't include something we really wanted? I know that I often do. Perhaps we wanted a husband or a wife—or perhaps we wanted a better husband or wife than the one God gave us. We wanted children or a better career or a more exciting church or more of this world's toys, and God chose not to give us those things.

We need to remember first of all that some of God's greatest gifts are indeed prayers that go unanswered. If we actually received many of the things for which we long, they might actually be to our hurt, not our blessing. Sometimes in our folly we ask God for bad things. He knows better than to give his child a snake or a scorpion. At other times we ask for good things, but we ask for them because we want to make idols out of them. God in his fatherly grace knows how to give good gifts to his children and when those good gifts are better withheld.

If we understand this truth, it should create in us both a holy contentment and a holy discontent. On the one hand, remembering that everything we have comes from God's fatherly grace gives us a holy contentment, for it reminds us to let go of the things he has chosen not to give us, trusting that his wisdom is greater than ours. We can trust that he has given us what is best for us. On the other hand, the knowledge of his grace also creates in us a holy discontent. While we are on this earth, our present possession of God's grace is always partial, always incomplete, a mere token of the glorious inheritance that is yet to come. So we are to long with a holy passion for what is yet to come. If God were to give us everything we wanted here and now, we would be easily tempted to think that here and now is Heaven instead of merely a way-station along the heavenly road, a lodging place for a brief sojourn. Here we do not yet see the full glory that God has prepared for his saints, but then we shall see it in all of its fullness. In the meantime, the awareness of what we lack should sharpen our hunger for our heavenly home.

Cities of Refuge

Yet the primary focus in this chapter is not the undeserved blessing that these cities will be to the Levites but the blessing that particular cities will be to the people as a whole. These were the cities of refuge, six of the Levitical cities that were designated as places of sanctuary for those who had committed manslaughter (v. 6). Three of these cities were to be east of the Jordan River, while three were to be to the west, so that no one would ever have to travel too far to reach one of these cities.

The essence of the legislation about cities of refuge was as follows: anyone who killed someone else could flee to a city of refuge. The reason he needed to flee was simple. In the ancient world, before the advent of police forces or judicial systems, the family was the prime unit of justice. If one of your family members was killed, then the family "avenger" was responsible to go after him and even the score (see v. 12). "Avenger" is not perhaps the perfect translation, since the same word is elsewhere translated "kinsman-redeemer" (gō'ēl).[2] In other words, this person wasn't simply a Mafia enforcer, whom the Godfather would send to rub out the responsible party.

He was also the person who had a duty to buy family members back if they became so poor that they had to sell themselves into slavery (Leviticus 25:48) or to marry the widow of a kinsman who had died without an heir so his name would not be extinguished from the clan records (Ruth 3:13). In other words, the *gō'ēl* was the person in the family responsible to look out for his kinsman's interests, at whatever personal cost. In this case, family blood had been spilt, and an accounting for that blood was necessary. Only another death could atone for that shed blood.

The establishment of cities of refuge did not negate the ancient principle that a death was necessary to atone for another death. On the contrary, it upheld that principle. Unatoned blood would defile the land, making it unfit for divine habitation (v. 33). What the cities of refuge did, though, was to provide a distinction between the crimes of murder and manslaughter and to appoint the *gō'ēl* as the agent of the state in executing the murderer.[3] For murder, only the death of the murderer could suffice. The murderer must pay for the life he took with his own life. However, for manslaughter the death of another person—namely, the high priest—could atone for the unintentional shedding of blood. The person convicted of manslaughter was required to live in exile in the city of refuge until the death of the current high priest (v. 25). When the high priest died, then the manslayer's sentence would be completed, and he could safely return to his home.

Within that broad outline, the details of the chapter fall into place. The Lord gave guidelines for determining the difference between murder and manslaughter. Premeditation and intent make a death murder, whatever the kind of implement that actually causes the death (vv. 16-21). If the death is accidental, however, or the result of carelessness, then the crime is manslaughter, and the city of refuge is to provide a shelter for the person against the avenger (vv. 22-24). A proper trial must always be carried out to determine the exact circumstances of the death (v. 24), with more than one witness required before the death penalty could be imposed (v. 30). The death penalty could not be avoided by the mere payment of a monetary ransom, nor could the period of exile be eliminated in that way (vv. 31, 32). Only a commensurate death could pay for the death, either the deliberate judicial death of the killer for a deliberate murder or the "accidental" death of the high priest for an accidental death by manslaughter.[4]

Once again, don't miss the irony of the fact that these cities of refuge were Levitical cities. Remember what it was that had caused Levi to be placed under a curse: it was an act of murder! Had God carried through on Levi the sentence he mandated here, there would have been no Levites at all. Every time his descendants witnessed a trial that resulted in death for the murderer and internal exile for the manslayer, they would be reminded of the grace they had received. As they were required to provide hospitality for the manslayer, they had the opportunity to show to others the outworking of that same grace.

Consistently Pro-Life

What does all this ancient jurisprudence have to do with us? After all, we don't have cities of refuge in our country, nor does anyone argue from this passage that we should institute them. It is generally recognized that the provision of the Levitical cities of refuge was part of the civil law of the Old Testament.[5] As such, it was a specific application of the principles of God's justice to the situation in which God's people found themselves during that period of the history of redemption. However, like other civil laws in the Old Testament, it is appropriate for us to discern general principles of conduct from it that should guide us as well, even though the specifics are not intended for our day.

The first of those general principles is the absolute importance of life and the desperate seriousness of murder. In many respects this principle is far more countercultural in our era than it was in the ancient world. Many people in the West are uncomfortable in principle with the idea of the state executing murderers, and as a result many countries have completely abandoned the death penalty. Now, to be sure, there may be legitimate concerns about the way in which the death penalty actually functions in our legal system. For example, it may be questioned whether people of all races receive equal treatment or whether particular forms of execution are acceptable or what level of proof may be required for the administration of the death penalty. The application of the principle is complex and frequently messy. Yet the principle of a life for a life—that someone who commits murder deserves to die in return—is clearly Biblical.[6] It is enshrined not merely in the civil laws of the Mosaic era but in the globally applicable statement of Genesis 9:6: "Whoever sheds the blood of man, by man shall his blood be shed; for God made man in his own image."

To be consistently pro-life, therefore, recognizing the supreme value of every person made in the image of God, means demanding a reckoning for the shedding of innocent blood. The death penalty is the only reckoning that takes account of the irreplaceable value of a human life. The state has been equipped by God with the sword (Romans 13:4), so that it may serve as our corporate kinsman-redeemer, avenging the blood of our brother or sister. In contrast, the fact that in our society murderers often serve a punishment that is more in line with the Biblical standard for manslaughter than for murder is a shame on our nation. It is a sign of how lightly we value the life that they took.

In contrast to the first principle, the second general principle that we can draw from this passage is the need to protect those who are merely guilty of manslaughter from the lynch mob and to ensure the right to a fair trial. These principles were far more countercultural in the ancient world than they are for us now, and so we may be tempted to dismiss them as self-evident. Yet it is not so very long since lynch mobs and rigged trials were part of our national culture as well. Insofar as we are presently free from them in this country, we should give thanks to God for his mercy and grace to us: it is certainly not because we modern people are somehow intrinsically more righteous and humane than those who have gone before us. It is God's grace that enables us to take a system of justice for granted.

Surviving Divine Justice

The third principle, however, flows more out of the searching standards of divine righteousness than of human standards. If, on the human level, justice demands fitting payment for deliberate bloodshed, how much more will that be true on the divine level? Yet in the Sermon on the Mount Jesus raised the bar in terms of the obedience that is required of us. He said:

> You have heard that it was said to those of old, "You shall not murder; and whoever murders will be liable to judgment." But I say to you that everyone who is angry with his brother will be liable to judgment; whoever insults his brother will be liable to the council; and whoever says, "You fool!" will be liable to the hell of fire. (Matthew 5:21, 22)

That is a searching standard. If there were a tape running in our houses, many of us would be in trouble. What is more, if the tape was running in our hearts, we would all stand condemned. According to that standard, none of us could find a refuge anywhere from the wrath of God. In the legislation of Numbers 35 there is no city of refuge available to us, for we are all murderers in our hearts and minds, even if not with our lips and hands. No ransom can deliver us: all of our silver and gold cannot save us. There is no good deed that we can do to atone for our sin: our righteousness cannot rescue us. If all of us are murderers and we all face this punishment, then it appears that we have nothing to expect but the certain coming of the Avenger, demanding the just punishment for our sin, which is our death.

Yet at the very moment when it appears that we are most without hope, we see that the provision of the gospel far exceeds the grace available under the Law. In the gospel, the heavenly Avenger has become our Redeemer. These two offices are fused in one, just as they were in the book of Numbers. In Jesus Christ, God himself took on human flesh and became our kinsman, not to pursue us and condemn us but to deliver us. The Avenger comes after us, and we flee from him in fear; yet when he catches us, instead of killing us, he throws his arms around us and says, "Come on home—your sin has been atoned for." The one we expected to be our judge and executioner was himself judged and executed in our place.

To be sure, a death must be paid for our sin: however, a death *has* been paid for our sin in Jesus Christ. Our great High Priest has shed his blood for us in a sacrifice that is effective not merely to purge away our accidental sins but our deliberate, cold-blooded sins as well. His death has paid a far greater ransom than gold and silver, accomplishing the transformation of our destiny from the curse we deserved into blessing. The lips that once cursed our brothers and sisters may now be devoted to singing the praises of our God, for he has taken away our filthiness and has made us fit to stand in his presence forever.

Responding to Grace

How, then, shall we respond to the incredible grace that we have received? Surely the fitting response is to make our churches cities of refuge, places of grace where others encounter the same mercy that we have received. The church is a community of forgiven sinners and should therefore provide a warm welcome for all who come seeking a refuge from their sins. It should be a community of *forgiven* sinners who are also a community of *forgiving* sinners. It is significant that in Matthew 5, having shown us the depth of our sin, Jesus then says:

> So if you are offering your gift at the altar and there remember that your brother has something against you, leave your gift there before the altar and go. First be reconciled to your brother, and then come and offer your gift. (vv. 23, 24)

That is the practical outworking of the grace that we have received: it makes us want to show that same grace to others around us. It makes us forgiving to others when they do sin against us. No matter who we are or what we have done, the church should be a place of forgiveness and fellowship, where we can come in just as we are and be pointed to Christ, the one sure refuge for sinners. His death is a big enough sacrifice for any sin we may have committed in the past or any sin we will ever commit in the future. His mercy is wide enough to welcome us in, to wash us clean and keep us safe throughout our earthly pilgrimage. His grace is all we will ever need to receive, and it is the most important thing we have to share with our family, friends, and others who are as yet outsiders to the grace we have received.

37

Walking the Ridgeline

NUMBERS 36

AS WE COME TO THE END OF OUR STUDY in the book of Numbers, it may seem at first sight that the end of the story is rather anticlimactic.1 We are used to stories that end with a rousing episode involving a great battle between good and evil, preferably involving a cast of thousands. Alternatively, we would settle for the triumphant conclusion to a noble quest in which the hero accomplishes the goal he has been pursuing throughout the story. If that is our expectation, then we will certainly conclude that the book of Numbers ends not so much with a bang as with a whimper.

However, a book that began with a list of names and numbers, followed by a detailed description of the arrangement of a campsite, is not exactly the kind of story to which we have become accustomed. It is not surprising, therefore, that it ends in a different key. What is more, the end of the book of Numbers is certainly not a whimper but rather a quiet and confident affirmation of faith in God as the people of God look forward to the future. To use a hill-walking metaphor, coming to the end of the book of Numbers is not arriving at the main peak, the ultimate destination of the trek. It is much more like arriving at the top of a ridge. The ridgeline provides a convenient point to stop for a breather and survey the view in both directions. It affords a view backward over the ground we have already covered and a prospect forward over the trail that lies ahead of us. The legislation concerning the inheritance of Zelophehad's daughters accomplishes the same two purposes: it concludes what precedes, while inviting us at the same time to look ahead to what is yet to come.

The Inheritance of Zelophehad's Daughters

The content of this chapter is simple enough. Back in Numbers 27, we were introduced to Zelophehad's daughters, those feisty young women of faith who went to Moses to ask for a share in the inheritance in the Promised Land for themselves since their father had died and they had no brothers (vv. 3, 4). Although women did not normally inherit property in the ancient Near- Eastern culture, their request provided a means by which their father's name would not disappear from the community. As a reward for their faith, which was emblematic of the nature of the new generation, they received what they sought from the Lord: they (and other women in their situation) could now inherit land, so that the inheritance would be preserved for the family.

In Numbers 27 this issue was a purely theoretical question since no land had yet been won. However, since Zelophehad's daughters were part of the group from the tribe of Manasseh who captured Gilead in the Transjordan and settled there (32:39-42), the theoretical question now became practical. In the process a new problem was identified. If Zelophehad's daughters were to marry outside the tribe of Manasseh, their land would become part of the inheritance of the other tribe and be lost to Manasseh. You could end up with a situation in which the land became a patchwork of holdings belonging to different tribes jumbled up together instead of a coherent and organized division with different areas belonging to the different tribes.[2] Even the provision of the Jubilee year, which required that every fifty years all land that had been bought and sold would revert to the original family, would not help the situation because this land had been inherited rather than sold.

In response to this difficulty, the tribal heads did exactly what they should have done. They came to Moses and sought additional directions (36:1, 2). In return, the Lord commanded that Zelophehad's daughters were only free to marry within the clan of their father, so that the inheritance would remain not merely within the tribe but within the clan as well (v. 6). No inheritance was to pass from tribe to tribe: on the contrary, each tribe was to retain the land it had been assigned by God (v. 9). Continuing the theme of obedience, Zelophehad's daughters then did exactly as God had commanded through Moses: they married cousins within their clan to retain the inheritance within the clan unit (vv. 10-12). To put the conclusion into our language we might then add, "And they all lived happily ever after."

Numbers 36 as a Conclusion

So how does this story invite us to look backward and forward? In the first place, Numbers 36 acts as the conclusion to several different stories. To begin with, it forms an inclusio with the story about Zelophehad's daughters in Numbers 27: together these episodes bracket the story of the new generation, those who were counted in the census of Numbers 26. This second generation is thereby marked out as a generation of faith and obedience, like the daughters of Zelophehad. They are a generation that trusts that the Lord will fulfill his promises and solves problems when they arise by going to the Lord through Moses. They even obey the Lord's word when they receive it. In this section of the book, therefore, there are no rebellions against the Lord or the leaders he has chosen—only the receiving and obeying of laws for the inheritance that they will receive in the Promised Land. They are, if you like, Israel's "Greatest Generation."[3]

This theme also marks out Numbers 36 as a suitable ending for the story that began in Numbers 1. In the opening chapters of the book, we likewise saw a people being ordered by God according to their tribes, peacefully arranged together around the central feature of the Lord dwelling in their midst (1—4). The end is thus a return to the beginning, a return to order and structure, with each tribe's inheritance being preserved intact in the place assigned to it by the Lord (36).[4] The land had to be kept free from defilement so the Lord could dwell in the midst of his people, another theme from the opening chapters (see 35:34 and 5:3). These similarities between the beginning and the ending of the book also highlight what is different by the end, for the scope of Numbers 27—36 has expanded from a wilderness camp to include the whole land once Israel receives her promised inheritance. There is significant forward progress as well as common concerns.

These themes of land and people also invite us to look further back. We think back to the promise God made to Abraham in the book of Genesis, to make him into an innumerable people and give him a land in which to dwell (15:5-7). The promise of innumerable people was largely fulfilled by the beginning of the book of Numbers: the community of Israel was unthinkably vast, though they could still be counted. In spite of the loss of an entire generation through their sin, the community of Israel remains equally substantial at the end of the book. What is more, the promise of the land is on the brink of being fulfilled by the end of the book of Numbers as Israel camps across the Jordan River from Jericho, waiting for the word from the Lord to enter. Further, this new generation seems not simply to be descended physically from Abraham but also in a profound sense to be Abraham's spiritual daughters and sons, ready to live by faith in the word of God. As an ending to all of these stories, Numbers 36 fills us with hope and expectation of a bright future for Israel as they receive the fullness of God's promise.

Numbers 36 as a Beginning

Yet Numbers 36 is not simply an ending to these various story lines—it is also the beginning point to a new series of stories. Like the ridgeline in our hill-walking analogy, it is not an end in itself but is a stopping point on a longer journey. The land that God has promised to give to his people remains yet to be possessed. In the way stand the major obstacles of the Jordan River and the fortified city of Jericho (v. 13). The old leadership team of Moses and Aaron has been broken up by Aaron's death, and he is soon to be followed by Moses. Joshua has been appointed to follow in Moses' giant footsteps (27:12-23), but he has not yet had the opportunity to demonstrate his leadership gifts.

Those themes point us forward to think about how the story of the book of Numbers continues on into the books of Deuteronomy and Joshua. Deuteronomy is, as it were, the last will and testament of Moses. It embodies God's final instructions to his people through his primary Old Testament servant before they enter the land. The book of Joshua shows Joshua faithfully following in the statutes and footsteps of Moses. He conquers the land and assigns to each tribe its own inheritance, just as Numbers 36 anticipated. God is certainly faithful to fulfill his promises. As the new generation stepped out in faith, they saw the Lord part the obstacle of the Jordan River in front of them and bring the mighty walls of Jericho tumbling down at their feet.

Yet at the same time we are mindful of the fact that there were two different generations in the book of Numbers. There was a generation who grumbled and disobeyed the Lord out of unbelief, and there was a generation that trusted and persevered in faith. As the continuing history of Israel unfolded, the story did not end with the book of Joshua, which largely recounted the lifetime of the greatest generation, the generation of faith. As generation followed generation, however, the predominant feature of Israel's history was not so much faith as unbelief. The continuing story line that began in Genesis 2 with the creation of Adam and Eve and continued through the book of Numbers ended up with the people of God in exile at the end of the book of Kings. The inheritance that God promised Abraham in Genesis and that the people of Joshua's day fought for and largely gained was ultimately lost through the continuing unbelief of subsequent generations. At this point the legislation of Numbers 36 became an entirely moot issue for Zelophehad's great-great-great-great granddaughters: there was now no longer any inheritance for them to receive or to pass on. All of the tribes of Israel had forfeited their inheritance because of successive generations of unbelief and disobedience.

Looking Forward to the Jubilee

For the generations of the exile, the grounds of hope in this passage rested in the passing mention of the Year of Jubilee in verse 4. The Jubilee year, when the land would be returned to those who had been forced to sell it through poverty, may not have helped Zelophehad's daughters, but it did provide a glimmer of hope for his great-great-great-great granddaughters. It reminded them that the Law provided a means for folly, incompetence, and sin to be redeemed. The Lord had promised his people an inheritance, and even their sin could not prevent that promise from being fulfilled. In fact, on a wider level the book of Numbers demonstrated that the fate of one generation did not dictate the future for the next generation. The fathers might sin and die in the wilderness of exile as a fitting punishment for their unbelief, just as the first wilderness generation had done, but their children could still follow the path of Zelophehad's daughters and their generation and experience God's favor and blessing. As they stepped out in faith, they would see the Lord fulfill everything that he had promised.

In measure, there was a limited jubilee for the people in the return from the exile. At least some of the tribes returned home to the land that the Lord had promised to their forefathers. There was a remnant in whom the Israel of God was reborn, a key theme in the book of Chronicles, a remnant who could obey the Lord and experience his promised blessing.[5] Yet they were always a small group, living in a "day of small things" (Zechariah 4:10), still waiting for the fullness of the inheritance God had promised.

That fullness has arrived in the person of Jesus Christ, who is himself our Jubilee, the one in whom our lost inheritance is restored to us. As our "kinsman redeemer" (gōʾēl), Jesus has taken the responsibility on himself to pay the price for our forfeited inheritance. What we lost through our own sin and the sin that we inherited from Adam—a living relationship with the Lord—Jesus has now restored for us through his death on the cross. In him our victory is already accomplished: it is certain, for the Lord has both promised it to us and achieved it at the cross.

At the same time, our inheritance too has a now and a not yet aspect to it. Like Zelophehad's daughters, we find ourselves poised on the ridgeline looking back and looking forward. We look back to the cross, where our salvation was accomplished. We look back to the resurrection, the event that guarantees our salvation. When Christ was raised from the dead, God stamped his work of atonement "Approved," and nothing and no one can separate us from that victory. Because of that fact, our salvation is secure: it doesn't rest on anything that we contribute. At the same time, we still look forward to the day when the final Jubilee trumpet will sound and Christ will return to set up his final kingdom (1 Thessalonians 4:16). We look forward to the day when his purposes will be done on earth as they are in Heaven and to the day when we ourselves will be done with our lifelong battle with sin and unbelief.

The Temptations of Life on the Ridgeline

In the meantime we find ourselves where Zelophehad's daughters and their whole generation stood—on the ridgeline between the past and the future. We are still located in the heart of the battle. Like them and their generation, therefore, we need to step out in faith, confidently believing in what God has promised us. We too face the constant struggle really to believe what we say we believe. Like them, we need to seek the Lord's guidance in all things in the word of the Lord. We are constantly tempted to grant authority to other means of guidance, apart from God's Word. Like them, we need to obey the will of the Lord as it is revealed to us in the Scriptures. We too face the constant challenge to live in accord with the faith we profess to believe.

For Zelophehad's daughters, the specific questions to be addressed were marriage and inheritance. Their obedience to the Lord stood in sharp contrast with their fathers who wrongly united themselves to Moabite women because they failed to believe in the reality and the importance of the Lord's inheritance (25). Their fathers chose present satisfaction and pleasure along with perceived political and economic advantages over the promises of God, while their children chose the way of faith and obedience. The questions that we face may be different, but the fundamental issue of faith versus sight is still the same.

What questions address us with this same challenge? They are different for every person. For one it may be the same issue of marriage that faced Zelophehad's daughters. Whom will you marry? The Bible has only one simple restriction: you must marry in the Lord (see 2 Corinthians 6:14). You are not bound to marry someone from your own clan and tribe: issues of culture, race, social and educational background, interests, and tastes are all secondary to marrying in Christ. To be sure, they may be issues to consider, but they are not necessarily impediments to a strong and healthy Christian marriage. Yet as a Christian, you must marry another Christian. This only makes sense, for how could you unite yourself at the deepest level to someone whose fundamental allegiance is to another master? You would be making two commitments that are at war with one another.

That principle is simple and clear; yet many young people face the temptation to date and ultimately to marry people who do not fit that single Biblical criterion. Why is that? Thinking back on my own experiences, it is because something other than faith in the reality and importance of the heavenly inheritance is driving our choices. We are being drawn to others by their physical or emotional attractiveness or by social and family pressures to find someone with whom to have a relationship. Heaven seems incredibly distant, especially when we are young, while the attractions of the present seem incredibly powerful. Yet if the heavenly inheritance that Christ died to win for us is truly all-important, then other motivations will be put in their proper place. If your eyes are fixed on your future inheritance, present obedience will make much more sense.

For others of us at different stages of life, the questions are rather different. Perhaps you are struggling with peer pressure at school or at work. Perhaps materialism has a grip on your heart, and your life revolves around what you own. Perhaps you find yourself overwhelmed with lust or romantic fantasies. The common thread in all of these temptations is that they offer immediate satisfaction and pleasure in exchange for disobedience to the Lord and turning your back on your heavenly inheritance.

Encouragement in the Ridgeline

As we face these temptations that come with living on the ridgeline, where are we to find strength and encouragement? Who will help us fix our eyes on our heavenly inheritance and so obey the will of the Lord for our lives? The passage's concern for order in the inheritance of Israel, keeping families and clans together in the people of God, can be a helpful reminder. As we said earlier, this focus is a return to issues that were addressed in the opening section of the book, where the people were arranged by tribe and family and clan around the tabernacle (2—4). Why is it so important to God that the system of families, clans, and tribes within Israel remain strong? The answer lies in the need that we have for belonging to a community of faith and to a particular family within that larger community of faith.

There is no place for lone rangers on the ridgeline, striking out on their own with confidence in their ability to reach Heaven unaccompanied. On the contrary, we need one another. Specifically, we need to encourage one another to keep our eyes fixed on our final destination and on Jesus who waits for us there. It is not coincidental that the charge to "Fix your thoughts on Jesus" comes to us in the Epistle to the Hebrews (3:1, NIV), the New Testament book that reflects most strongly on the similarity of our situation to that of those wandering in the wilderness (see 3:7—4:11). Nor is it coincidental that it is in this same book that we are urged not to neglect meeting together but rather to encourage one another to love and do good deeds, and all the more as we see the day approaching (10:24, 25). This is what we need to do for one another as a fellowship of God's people. We need to encourage one another to fix our eyes on the risen Jesus and thus to stir each other up toward love and good deeds.

How do we do that? In a variety of ways. As the preaching of the Word of God enables us to see afresh the glories of the gospel, we are encouraged to fix our eyes on Jesus. As we are fed by the Lord's Supper, we are reminded of his death and resurrection and the banquet he has prepared for us. Yet we are also to encourage one another personally to fix our eyes on Jesus. You can ask someone, "How is the gospel making a difference in your life this week?" You can say to a friend or a neighbor, "How can I pray for you this week? What are the areas in your life where you are struggling to keep your eyes fixed on your eternal inheritance?"

For some of us, this kind of relationship is desperately hard. Asking others to be open with us will require us in turn to be open with them. For me, as someone who is by nature closed and sinfully self-protective, such openness is enormously difficult; yet it is necessary if we are indeed to encourage one another in the way Scripture asks of us. This too is an area where we need faith in the reality of the heavenly inheritance: as the anticipation of crossing the final river becomes sweeter, so our pride and self-protectiveness will gradually be overcome.

The Final Word

The final challenge of the book of Numbers to people like us, people living on the ridgeline, is the challenge to live by faith. If we trust in the Lord and in his Word, we will not be abandoned or put to shame. That does not mean that life on the ridgeline will ever be easy. Jesus Christ came and lived a life of full obedience to God's Word, and yet his life was as difficult and challenging as any human existence ever was. But as we step out in faith, staking our lives on Jesus Christ as our only hope in life and death, looking onward and upward to our final destination, the inheritance that God has prepared for us, we will find that the Lord is indeed faithful to his promises. The wilderness is not the end of the story. The trials and difficulties of our earthly existence are not all there is. The future belongs to the Lord and to his Christ and to all whom he has called to be his. It is promised to all those who persevere by faith in Christ, and it will assuredly be given to them on the last day. The Lord is faithful, and he will do it.

Soli Deo gloria!

Notes

Chapter One: In the Wilderness

1. See also Luke 24:44; 1 Corinthians 10:1-6; Acts 26:22, 23. For further explanation of this principle, see Edmund P. Clowney, *Preaching Christ in All of Scripture* (Wheaton, IL: Crossway Books, 2003), pp. 11-44; Bryan Chapell, *Christ-Centered Preaching: Redeeming the Expository Sermon* (Grand Rapids, MI: Baker, 1996), p. 272; Sidney Greidanus, *The Modern Preacher and the Ancient Text. Interpreting and Preaching Biblical Literature* (Grand Rapids, MI: Eerdmans, 1988), pp. 118-120.

2. See Dennis T. Olson, *The Death of the Old and the Birth of the New: The Framework of the Book of Numbers and the Pentateuch*, Brown Judaic Studies 71 (Chico, CA: Scholars, 1985).

3. The exact point at which we move from one generation to the next is disputed. Won Lee has argued that the victory against the Canaanites at the beginning of Numbers 21 marks the beginning of the experience of the new generation, not the second census (*Punishment and Forgiveness in Israel's Migratory Campaign* [Grand Rapids, MI: 2003], pp. 266-268).

4. In a stimulating book, Mary Douglas has suggested that the whole book of Numbers is arranged structurally around the tabernacle (*In the Wilderness. The Doctrine of Defilement in the Book of Numbers* [Oxford: Oxford University Press, 2001], pp. 135-138). Not all of the structural parallels that she adduces are equally convincing, but the "tabernacle-centered" principle of construction is attractive.

Chapter Two: Stand Up and Be Counted

1. The official census materials stress the latter reason, of course, since they want to encourage you to participate. Yet historically the former was the principal reason for counting people, and it remains an important goal.

2. Since the total numbers counted are exactly the same (603,550), it is possible that the same census data was used for both. However, since the result of the first census was to provide the materials out of which the tabernacle was constructed and the tabernacle was complete by the beginning of the first month of the second year (Exodus 40:1), the data would have been several months out of date by the beginning of the second month of the second year. This may explain, though, why the census could be completed so rapidly: the earlier data simply had to be updated and, by a statistical quirk, the final total was exactly the same.

3. See Jacob Milgrom, *Numbers*, JPS Torah (Philadelphia, JPS, 1989), p. 5. The Levites did have a mandatory retirement age from certain aspects of their work (8:25), but there was no retirement from military service.

4. In fact, the numbers are so large that it has been questioned whether they could possibly be literal: how could so many people survive in the wilderness, or even fit in the Promised Land, given the level of ancient agricultural productivity? For a straightforward survey of the real difficulties, and of attempts to reduce the numbers down to a more plausible size, see Gordon Wenham, *Numbers*, Tyndale Old Testament Commentary (Downers Grove, IL: InterVarsity Press, 1981), pp. 60-66. However, it seems to me that the explanations why 600,000 really means a more "reasonable" number somewhere between 5,000 and 70,000 flounder on two fronts. First, the text clearly understands these to be real

numbers that can be added together and multiplied by one half shekel to make a real amount of money (see Exodus 38:21-38). The second point on which attempts to scale down the numbers fails is that they end up removing the very point that the text is trying to make, which is the enormous blessing of God that has multiplied a single family into such a huge force. It is perhaps plausible that these numbers are hyperbolic, in accord with ancient Near Eastern literary conventions (see David M. Fouts, "A Defense of the Hyperbolic Interpretation of Large Numbers in the Old Testament," *JETS* 40 [1997], pp. 377-388). However, whether literal or hyperbolic, the main point remains the same: the vastness of God's blessing on his people.

5. It is tantalizing to wonder if the very numbers themselves subtly convey that same message. When Israel went down into Egypt, they were seventy—a small yet complete number in Biblical terms. When they came out of Egypt, we are repeatedly told that they were around 600,000 (see Exodus 12:37; 38:26; Numbers 11:21)—a vastly increased number, yet one that begins with the number of incompleteness, six. They had multiplied greatly, but they had not yet arrived at completeness.

Chapter Three: A Place for Everyone and Everyone in His Place

1. See Kenneth Kitchen, "Some Egyptian Background to the Old Testament," *Tyndale Bulletin* 5-6 (1960), p. 11.
2. Edmund P. Clowney, *The Unfolding Mystery* (Colorado Springs: NavPress, 1988), p. 112.
3. Thus in Hebrew one of the ways of indicating south is "right" and west is "behind." These assume an east-facing orientation.
4. The same order of priority will be visible in the arrangement of the Levites in chapter 3.

Chapter Four: Do or Die!

1. See Timothy R. Ashley, *Numbers*, NICOT (Grand Rapids, MI: Eerdmans, 1993), p. 78.
2. See Jacob Milgrom, *Numbers,* JPS Torah (Philadelphia, JPS, 1989), pp. 8-16.
3. See Rebecca Jones, *Does Christianity Squash Woman? A Christian Looks at Womanhood* (Nashville: Broadman & Holman, 2005).

Chapter Five: Danger! Levites at Work

1. This is a more likely translation of the obscure term *taḥaš* rather than "the hides of sea cows," as the NIV renders it. On this, see Jacob Milgrom, *Numbers,* JPS Torah (Philadelphia, JPS, 1989), p. 25.
2. See Philip P. Jenson, *Graded Holiness: A Key to the Priestly Conception of the World*, JSOT Supplements, 106 (Sheffield: JSOT Press, 1992).

Chapter Six: Dealing with Disorder

1. See Jacob Milgrom, *Numbers,* JPS Torah (Philadelphia, JPS, 1989), p. 346.
2. Compare also 2 Kings 2:21, where Elisha heals the cursed water of Jericho because of the repentant attitude of the men of the city.

Chapter Seven: All for Jesus

1. Jacob Milgrom, *Numbers,* JPS Torah (Philadelphia, JPS, 1989), p. 356.

Chapter Eight: I Am So Blessed!

1. Dennis T. Olson, *Numbers*, Interpretation (Louisville: John Knox, 1996), p. 41.
2. Timothy R. Ashley, *Numbers*, NICOT (Grand Rapids, MI: Eerdmans, 1993), p. 152.

Chapter Nine: "And a Partridge in a Pear Tree . . ."

1. In *The Twelve Days of Christmas* (New York: St. Martin's Press, 1998), John Julius Norwich amusingly contemplates the correspondence from the recipient of the gifts to

the donor, culminating in an injunction from her lawyer on the twelfth day to prevent any further unsolicited gift giving!

2. Gordon Wenham, *Numbers*, Tyndale Old Testament Commentary (Downers Grove, IL: InterVarsity Press, 1981), pp. 57-59.

3. See Jacob Milgrom, *Numbers,* JPS Torah (Philadelphia, JPS, 1989) for the translation of "initiation" rather than "dedication" in verses 10, 11 (p. 54).

Chapter Ten: The Light of the World

1. See Jan Michl, "Form Follows WHAT? The Modernist Notion of Function as a Carte Blanche," *1:50—Magazine of the Faculty of Architecture & Town Planning* (Technion, Israel Institute of Technology, Haifa, Israel) 10, Winter 1995. The article is online at http://www.geocities.com/Athens/2360/jm-eng.fff-hai.html (accessed April 22, 2004).

2. Woody Allen, "If the Impressionists Had Been Dentists: A Fantasy Exploring the Transposition of Temperament," *Without Feathers* (New York: Ballantine, 1983), pp. 199-204.

3. Bede, *On the Tabernacle*, trans. A.G. Holder (Liverpool: Liverpool University Press, 1994), p. 21.

Chapter Eleven: The Substitute

1. Gordon Wenham, *Numbers*, Tyndale Old Testament Commentary (Downers Grove, IL: InterVarsity Press, 1981), p. 63.

2. Jacob Milgrom, *Leviticus 1—16*, Anchor Bible (New York: Doubleday, 1991), p. 152.

3. The language of "wave offering" comes from the Rabbinic notion that the *tenupa* was distinguished from the related *teruma* (KJV: "heave offering") by a symbolic gesture carried out by the priest showing that this part of the sacrifice too belongs to the Lord. The "wave offering" was thought to be presented with a horizontal motion "extending and bringing back," while the "heave offering" was presented with a vertical motion of raising and lowering. However, that interpretation does not seem to fit with this text in particular: one is presumably not to imagine them being moved from side to side. It would therefore perhaps be better to understand the "wave offering" as a dedication ritual. See Milgrom, *Leviticus 1—16*, pp. 461, 462.

4. See Timothy R. Ashley, *Numbers*, NICOT (Grand Rapids, MI: Eerdmans, 1993), p. 170.

5. The significance of this complete shaving is not immediately clear. A similar process occurs in some other cleansing rituals, such as Leviticus 14:8. Perhaps the shaving of all bodily hair implies a kind of symbolic new birth into this new role.

6. For a detailed treatment of the significance of these sacrifices, see Milgrom, *Leviticus 1—16*, Anchor Bible, pp. 172-177, 254-258.

Chapter Twelve: The God of the Second Chance

1. See the Westminster Confession of Faith, XXI.

2. For one stimulating attempt to work out the regulative principle of worship in practice, see John M. Frame, *Worship in Spirit and Truth. A Refreshing Study of the Principles and Practice of Biblical Worship* (Phillipsburg, NJ: P&R, 1996).

3. It is important to note that the category of irregular is necessarily a temporary one. If the irregular way of doing things persists longer than absolutely necessary, it starts to become wrong.

Chapter Thirteen: Setting Out

1. Milgrom notes that the word "tabernacle" (*miškān*) also occurs seven times in this chapter and that this is "the linguistic cement that unifies the passage" (*Numbers*, JPS Torah Commentary [Philadelphia: Jewish Publication Society, 1990], p. 71). This may well be correct, although the word "cloud" (*'ānān*) occurs no fewer than ten times, which suggests that it has equal or greater importance to the writer.

Chapter Fourteen: A Good Beginning

1. Baruch A. Levine, *Numbers 1-20*, Anchor Bible (New York: Doubleday, 1993), p. 318.
2. Jacob Milgrom, *Numbers*, JPS Torah Commentary (Philadelphia: Jewish Publication Society, 1990), p. 81. Compare 2 Kings 2:12, where Elijah sees "the chariots of Israel and its horsemen."
3. The classic biography of her life is W.P. Livingstone, *Mary Slessor of Calabar: Pioneer Missionary* (London: Hodder & Stoughton, 1915).
4. So Mary Douglas, *In the Wilderness* (Oxford: Oxford University Press, 2001), p. 58; Stephen K. Sherwood, *Leviticus, Numbers, Deuteronomy*, Berit Olam (Collegeville, MN: Liturgical Press, 2002), p. 151.
5. Milgrom identifies these two apparently paradoxical themes as evidence that the narrative has conflated two traditions concerning Israel's guidance in the wilderness, one natural, the other supernatural. He then goes on to document the fact that this "double causality" is repeatedly present throughout Genesis and the wilderness/conquest narratives (*Numbers*, p. 79). This fact seems to me to undermine his thesis of conflation. Is it more likely that a narrator of the literary skill that we see in the Pentateuch would regularly have conflated contradictory sources without noticing the conflict, or that he would develop his narrative in a way that juxtaposes complementary ideas? The combination of natural and supernatural is not due to a clumsy redactor but to a profound understanding of the nature of reality.
6. Judges 4 shows us that some of the Kenites descended from Hobab were dwelling in the Promised Land in the days of Deborah and Barak (Judges 4:11). Their relationship to the wider Israelite community was certainly tenuous at this time, however, which is why Sisera expected to find refuge there (Judges 4:17).
7. For this translation, see F. F. Bruce, *The Epistle to the Hebrews*, NICNT (Grand Rapids, MI: Eerdmans, 1964), p. 351.
8. According to some early manuscripts of Jude 5, Jesus was the one who brought his people out of Egypt. Compare the similar idea in 1 Corinthians 10:4.

Chapter Fifteen: Surprised by Grumbling

1. According to military historian Eliot Cohen, "American troops have a God-given right and tradition of grumbling" (quoted in Bradley Graham and Dana Milbank, "Many Troops Dissatisfied, Iraq Poll Finds," *Washington Post*, October 16, 2003; http://www.washingtonpost.com/ac2/wp-dyn/A32521-2003Oct15?language=printer (October 21, 2004).
2. In the itinerary in Numbers 33, Taberah does not merit a separate mention, leading scholars to conclude that the two sites were adjacent to one another.
3. Won Lee comments: "The text [11:1-3] functions as a general example of Israel's distrust of Yahweh's ability to fulfil Yahweh's promise of the land to the Israelites' ancestors" (*Punishment and Forgiveness* [Grand Rapids, MI: Eerdmans, 2003], p. 126, n. 92). This structure of a brief paradigm example that may then be compared and contrasted with what follows is also found in the book of Judges, where Othniel is a paradigm judge against whom the later judges never quite measure up.
4. The term *riff-raff* is from Jacob Milgrom, *Numbers*, JPS Torah Commentary (Philadelphia: Jewish Publication Society, 1990), p. 83.
5. The word is the same as the description of the people's complaint in Numbers 11:1 and the opposite of the "good" Moses had so confidently proclaimed to Hobab in verse 29 of the previous chapter. Compare Numbers 11:10: literal translation, "it was evil in the eyes of Moses."
6. It is striking that unlike the manna that fell inside the camp, in the realm of the clean, the quail collected outside the camp, in the realm of the unclean.
7. They didn't continue prophesying because the purpose of this Spirit-induced prophesying was simply to place God's stamp of approval upon them. Once that stamp of approval had been given, it did not need to be repeated continually.

Chapter Sixteen: Grumbling and Envy

1. See C. F. Keil and F. Delitzsch, *The Pentateuch*, trans. J. Martin (Grand Rapids, MI: Eerdmans, 1988 reprint), 3:76.
2. See Westminster Confession of Faith, XX.2.
3. See, e.g. Charles Ryrie, *Dispensationalism Today* (Chicago: Moody Press, 1986), p. 86.
4. For a fuller discussion of this issue, see "Interpreting the Prophets," in Iain M. Duguid, *Ezekiel*, NIVAC (Grand Rapids, MI: Zondervan, 1999), pp. 26-35.
5. See Keil and Delitzsch, *Numbers*, pp. 81, 82.
6. The description of her half-eaten flesh (12:12) is another connection with the judgment of the last chapter, which fell on the Israelites while they had half-eaten flesh still in their mouths (see Mary Douglas, *In the Wilderness* [Oxford: Oxford University Press, 2001], p. 209).

Chapter Seventeen: Snatching Defeat from the Jaws of Victory

1. Jacob Milgrom, *Numbers*, JPS Torah Commentary (Philadelphia: Jewish Publication Society, 1990), p. 100.
2. *Ibid.*, p. 105.
3. *Ibid.*, p. 107.
4. My translation; the words "definitely" and "certainly" reflect strongly emphatic Hebrew forms.
5. See Edward T. Welch, *When People Are Big and God Is Small: Overcoming Peer Pressure, Codependency, and the Fear of Man* (Phillipsburg, NJ: P&R, 1997).
6. So Milgrom, *Numbers*, p. 109.

Chapter Eighteen: Demanding Grace

1. "Sacrifice" (*zebaḥ*) here is shorthand for "fellowship offerings" (*zebaḥ šᵉlāmîm*). See Timothy R. Ashley, *Numbers*, NICOT (Grand Rapids, MI: Eerdmans, 1993), p. 278. The main difference between burnt offerings and fellowship offerings is how much of the sacrifice is consumed by the fire. For burnt offerings, the whole sacrifice was burned in the fire, while in the fellowship offering, part of the sacrifice was consumed by the offerer.
2. Rather than "the first of your ground meal" (so NIV). See *ibid.*, p. 282; Jacob Milgrom, *Numbers*, JPS Torah Commentary (Philadelphia: Jewish Publication Society, 1990), p. 121.
3. David Powlison, "Idols of the Heart and 'Vanity Fair,'" *Journal of Biblical Counseling* 13 (1995), p. 49.
4. For more on the question of tithing, see the discussion of Numbers 18 (Chapter 23 of this book).

Chapter Nineteen: This Is Your God

1. Scholars debate whether the penalty of *karet* ("cutting off") meant excommunication or execution, and whether the penalty was expected to be carried out by God or man. The distinction is not easy to draw since execution may well normally have been preceded by excommunication, while excommunication itself meant being cast out of the realm of life, the covenant community. Normally the punishment was applied directly by God, either by immediate death or delayed retribution that wiped out the offender's progeny, but in certain cases the community was called upon to apply the death penalty. See Jacob Milgrom, *Numbers*, JPS Torah Commentary (Philadelphia: Jewish Publication Society, 1990), pp. 405-408.
2. Excommunication is not the same as shunning. Rather, it is such persons' being treated in accordance with their behavior: since they are living like non-Christians, the church resolves to treat them as such. This involves exclusion from access to the Lord's Table (from which non-Christians have no right to eat), but not from relationships with Christians. After all, our goal for the excommunicated person, as for other "pagans and

tax collectors," is that they should repent and trust in Christ. Thus we will seek to bring the gospel to bear on their situation in all of our relationships with them, and we will pray for their repentance and ultimate restoration.

3. See Milgrom, *Numbers*, p. 410.

4. *Ibid.*, p. 127.

Chapter Twenty: The Southside Rebellion

1. John Sailhamer, *The Pentateuch as Narrative* (Grand Rapids, MI: Zondervan, 1992), p. 392.

2. Baruch A. Levine, *Numbers 1-20*, Anchor Bible (New York: Doubleday, 1993), p. 412.

3. Timothy R. Ashley, *Numbers*, NICOT (Grand Rapids, MI: Eerdmans, 1993), p. 311.

4. This seems to be a standard formula for declaring honesty. See ibid., p. 312.

5. That is why Moses asked the Lord to reject any tribute offerings from Dathan and Abiram. It would be monstrous to receive such offerings of submission when there was such blatant evidence that their hearts were hardened against the Lord.

Chapter Twenty-one: The End of Grumbling

1. C. S. Lewis, *The Great Divorce* (New York: Macmillan, 1946), p. 75.

2. The "you" in "you have killed" is emphatic (Dennis T. Olson, *Numbers*, Interpretation [Louisville: John Knox, 1996], p. 106).

3. The Hebrew word used for "stopped" (*āṣar*) is also used in 1 Kings 18:44 for the rain that blocked King Ahab's way down the mountain. The plague is thus shut up rather than eliminated.

4. This assumes that the method of counting the tribes identifies Ephraim and Manasseh as separate tribes, as consistently elsewhere in the book of Numbers. See Timothy R. Ashley, *Numbers*, NICOT (Grand Rapids, MI: Eerdmans, 1993), p. 332.

5. See Jacob Milgrom, *Numbers*, JPS Torah Commentary (Philadelphia: Jewish Publication Society, 1990), p. 143.

6. This sign thus forms a parallel to, and reaffirms, the opening arrangement in Numbers 1—4, where the twelve tribes were arranged around the tabernacle, with Aaron given pride of place. See Mary Douglas, *In the Wilderness* [Oxford: Oxford University Press, 2001], pp. 132, 133.

7. John Piper, *Desiring God: Meditations of a Christian Hedonist* (Sisters, OR: Multnomah, 1996 expanded edition), p. 9.

8. See Vern Poythress, *The Shadow of Christ in the Law of Moses* (Brentwood, TN: Wolgemuth & Hyatt, 1991), p. 19.

9. *Letters of Samuel Rutherford* (Edinburgh: Banner of Truth, 1973 reprint), p. 13.

Chapter Twenty-two: The Fear of the Lord

1. J. Gresham Machen, *God Transcendent and Other Selected Sermons* (Grand Rapids, MI: Eerdmans, 1949), p. 31.

2. As does the above-mentioned church, whose doctrinal statement confesses in orthodox fashion: "Man was originally created in the image and likeness of God: he fell through disobedience, incurring thereby both physical and spiritual death. All men are born with a sinful nature, are separated from the life of God, and can be saved only through the atoning work of the Lord Jesus Christ. The portion of the unrepentant and unbelieving is existence forever in conscious torment; and that of the believer, in everlasting joy and bliss." One wonders, though, how it is possible to communicate such a searching truth in a casual atmosphere where the emphasis is so strongly on providing everyone with an enjoyable experience.

3. Thomas Manton, "Sermons on Matthew XXV," *Works*, Vol. 9 (London: James Nisbet & Company, 1872), p. 469.

4. Literally, it was "a covenant of salt," as in the ESV. Salt is a regular symbol for enduring relationship in the Scripture, in contrast to leaven, the symbol of change and decay. For

that reason, grain offerings were invariably unleavened but included salt (Leviticus 2:11-13). See Jacob Milgrom, *Leviticus 1—16*, Anchor Bible (New York: Doubleday, 1991), p. 191.

5. On this phrase, see Jacob Milgrom, *Cult and Conscience* (Leiden: E.J. Brill, 1976), pp. 3-11.

Chapter Twenty-three: The Reward for Faithful Service

1. See Becky R. McMillan and Matthew J. Price, "How Much Should We Pay the Pastor? A Fresh Look at Clergy Salaries in the 21st Century," http://www.pulpitandpew.duke.edu/salary.html (accessed October 7, 2004).

2. Pastoral ministry hasn't always been viewed in that way. Prior to his conversion, the Scottish pastor and theologian Thomas Chalmers once wrote, "after the satisfactory discharge of his parish duties, a minister may enjoy five days in the week of uninterrupted leisure for the prosecution of any science in which his taste may dispose him to engage" (William Hanna, *Memoirs of the Life and Writings of Thomas Chalmers, D.D. LL.D.* [Edinburgh: Constable, 1852], 1:93).

3. These are more accurately called "dedication offerings": the distinctive feature of these offerings was not that they were "waved" back and forth in front of the Lord but that they were presented in a dedication ritual at the sanctuary (see footnote 3 in the study on Numbers 8:5-26 [Chapter 11 of this book]).

4. See J.G. McConville, *Law and Theology in Deuteronomy* (Sheffield, UK: JSOT Press, 1984), p. 78. This theme is also prominent in the Jubilee law (Leviticus 25:8-55).

5. The ancient Near Eastern evidence, see Moshe Weinfeld, "Tithe," *Encyclopedia Judaica* (Jerusalem: McMillan, 1971), pp. 1156-1159.

6. In addition, people sometimes voluntarily promised to give a tithe to their god. Both kinds of tithes are seen in the Old Testament. Abraham gave a tithe of the spoils of war to Melchizedek (Genesis 14:20), while Jacob committed himself to give a tithe to the Lord should he return safely from Paddan-aram (Genesis 28:20-22). In both cases these are voluntary tithes, unique responses to particular providences of God rather than a regular, ongoing requirement to give a set portion of their income to God's work. A similar situation may exist in Leviticus 27:30ff., where mention is made of dedicating a tithe of the crops and herds to the Lord. This is covered under a section that explicitly deals with the redemption of votive offerings, of which "the tithe" is mentioned simply as one type of vow that can be made. Once the tithe had been vowed to the Lord, it belonged to him and could only be redeemed by the payment of an additional 20 percent.

7. Jacob Milgrom, *Numbers*, JPS Torah Commentary (Philadelphia: Jewish Publication Society, 1990), p. 432.

8. It is not exactly clear how these two distinct tithes were related. Traditional Jewish (and some Christian) exegesis has identified the tithe of Deuteronomy as a second tithe, so that on top of the basic 10 percent for the Levites, an additional 10 percent would be taken to the temple (in years 1 and 2) or given to the poor (in year 3). This cycle would be repeated twice, followed by the sabbatical year. This indeed seems to have been the practice during the intertestamental period (see Tobit 1:7, 8), though by that time the priests consumed the larger part of the tithe (Moshe Weinfeld, "Tithe," *Encyclopedia Judaica* [Jerusalem: McMillan, 1971], p. 1162). This discrepancy was usually justified as being a punishment on the Levites for their unwillingness to return to Judah with Ezra. The burdensome nature of this level of taxation in a subsistence economy must have contributed to the difficulties of getting the people to tithe in the post-exilic period.

9. Westminster Confession of Faith, XIX. Many contemporary theologians are critical of this classical distinction of the Law into three categories and would like to do away with it. Yet their "solutions" inevitably end up re-creating the same categories under different names, since everyone agrees that some Old Testament laws express timeless principles directly (moral law), others express timeless principles in culturally bound forms that are non-binding (civil law), and still others are intended to point forward to Christ and were fulfilled with his arrival (ceremonial law). See John Calvin, *The Institutes of the*

Christian Religion, trans. F. L. Battles (Philadelphia: Westminster, 1960), IV.15. The threefold classification itself goes back at least to Thomas Aquinas's *Summa Theologica*.

10. The historical debate about whether the Fourth Commandment, the Sabbath law, is properly moral law (and thus of continuing significance) or ceremonial law (and thus abrogated) is a classic example of the failure to comprehend this. In fact, the Sabbath actually has aspects of all three dimensions of the Law. As a creation ordinance dating back to the foundation of the world, it has a universal dimension that makes it part of the moral law. It is also civil law, inasmuch as it was part of the Law given to Moses at Mount Sinai, intended to bind everyone living in the state of Israel, and subject to the sanction of death for disobedience (Exodus 35:2). Failure to keep the Sabbath is one of the sins that caused Israel to be sent into captivity, so the land could enjoy its sabbaths (2 Chronicles 36:21). At the same time, the Sabbath also has ceremonial aspects to it, since it is part of the ceremonial calendar of Israel, along with new moons and the three annual festivals, which itself is a shadow of the rest that was to come in Christ (Colossians 2:16, 17). What we as Christians are called to celebrate, therefore, is the "Christian Sabbath" (see Westminster Confession of Faith, XXI.7), an ordinance that is both similar to and distinct from the Old Testament institution.

11. See note 6 above.

12. It is not coincidental that as the early church expanded its role in society after the conversion of Constantine, tithes reappeared as a means of financing operations. According to *The Catholic Encyclopedia*, legislation for tithes is first found in a letter from the bishops assembled at Tours in 567 and in the canons of the Council of Macon in 585. They persisted beyond the time of the Reformation as a means of supporting the state church but as a mandatory requirement have now largely disappeared once again.

13. Strictly speaking, the costs of the building are not part of the purpose of the Old Testament tithe but of other taxes in Israel, such as the temple tax (Exodus 30:11-16). Synagogue buildings, where such existed, would also have been maintained by separate collections.

Chapter Twenty-four: True Cleanliness

1. Quoted at http://www.foodreference.com/html/qwashingdishes.html (accessed October 11, 2004).

2. See Jacob Milgrom, *Leviticus 1—16*, Anchor Bible (New York: Doubleday, 1991), p. 721.

3. Mary Douglas, *In the Wilderness* [Oxford: Oxford University Press, 2001, p. 24.

4. Timothy R. Ashley, *Numbers*, NICOT (Grand Rapids, MI: Eerdmans, 1993), p. 362.

5. Many translations render the word "heifer," but that is not strictly accurate. A heifer, by definition, has not borne a calf. This cow may or may not have had a calf, though since it had not worked, it was most probably still quite young. The red cow was to be perfect in the sense of without blemish (see Leviticus 22:20), rather than being perfectly red, as Jewish exegesis has sometimes understood it (see *Sifre Numbers* 123).

6. Jacob Milgrom, *Numbers*, JPS Torah Commentary (Philadelphia: Jewish Publication Society, 1990), p. 440.

7. Gordon Wenham, *Numbers*, Tyndale Old Testament Commentary (Downers Grove, IL: InterVarsity Press, 1981), p. 147.

8. See J. Milgrom, "The Paradox of the Red Cow," *Vetus Testamentum* 31 (1981), pp. 62-72.

9. D. A. Carson, *The Gospel According to John*, Pillar NT Commentary (Grand Rapids, MI: Eerdmans, 1991), p. 465.

Chapter Twenty-five: Repeating the Mistakes of the Past

1. Jacob Milgrom, *Numbers*, JPS Torah Commentary (Philadelphia: Jewish Publication Society, 1990), p. 164.

2. The similarity does not mean that these two events are identical (see Timothy R. Ashley, *Numbers*, NICOT [Grand Rapids, MI: Eerdmans, 1993], p. 378). Rather, these comparable events invite the reader to set them side by side and discern their similarities and differences. The placement at the beginning and end of the wanderings fittingly characterizes

the whole period in between as complaining against the Lord. See Peter Enns, *Exodus*, NIVAC (Grand Rapids, MI: Zondervan, 2000), p. 329.

3. The unusual word for "perished" (*gava*) confirms the link back to Numbers 16—17 (see 17:12, 13).
4. Milgrom, *Numbers*, p. 165.
5. See Edmund P. Clowney, *The Unfolding Mystery* (Colorado Springs: NavPress, 1988), pp. 124-126.
6. John Sailhamer, *The Pentateuch as Narrative* (Grand Rapids, MI: Zondervan, 1992), p. 397.
7. Won Lee, *Punishment and Forgiveness* (Grand Rapids, MI: Eerdmans, 2003), pp. 264, 265.
8. Ashley, *Numbers*, p. 396.

Chapter Twenty-six: A New Beginning

1. Won Lee, *Punishment and Forgiveness* (Grand Rapids, MI: Eerdmans, 2003), pp. 266-268.
2. Dennis T. Olson, *Numbers*, Interpretation (Louisville: John Knox, 1996), pp. 134, 135.
3. For a fuller account of the significance of this kind of warfare, see Tremper Longman III, "Spiritual Continuity," in Stanley N. Gundry, ed., *Show Them No Mercy: Four Views on God and Canaanite Genocide* (Grand Rapids, MI: Zondervan, 2003), pp. 159-187.
4. The account in Deuteronomy makes it clear that they also practiced *herem* warfare against Sihon and Og and their people.
5. Commentators argue about whether the "fiery" (*śārāp*) nature of these snakes reflects their color or the burning effect of their bite.
6. See John Currid, *Ancient Egypt and the Old Testament* (Grand Rapids, MI: Baker, 1997), pp. 146-149.
7. *Ibid.,* pp. 149-154.
8. According to Timothy R. Ashley, "As the goal of the land of Canaan came nearer the songs increased, and the people began to anticipate the conquest" (*Numbers*, NICOT [Grand Rapids, MI: Eerdmans, 1993], p. 408).

Chapter Twenty-seven: The Politician and the Donkey

1. See Jacob Milgrom, *Numbers*, JPS Torah Commentary (Philadelphia: Jewish Publication Society, 1990), pp. 469-471.
2. Even the commentators are surprised by this. Olson calls this a "sudden and inexplicable turnabout" (*Numbers*, Interpretation [Louisville: John Knox, 1996], pp. 144); Timothy R. Ashley speaks of "God's seemingly unmotivated wrath" (*Numbers*, NICOT [Grand Rapids, MI: Eerdmans, 1993], p. 455, n. 16).
3. On the fact that, just as in real life, characters in Biblical narratives do not always tell the truth, see J. P. Fokkelman, *Reading Biblical Narrative* (Louisville: Westminster John Knox, 1999), pp. 65-67.
4. It is not coincidental that early in the story we find the verb "to see," which is central throughout these chapters.
5. Even though the Israelites had no territorial ambitions in Moab at this stage, according to Deuteronomy 2:9, the Moabites apparently still considered them too great a threat to be ignored.
6. Extra-Biblical texts from Deir Allā from the mid-eighth century B.C. have now revealed the fact that Balaam was a well-known prophetic figure in the Transjordanian region. See Ashley, *Numbers*, pp. 437-440.
7. The contrast is heightened by the form of the message from Balak, which on this occasion (unlike verse 5) begins with the messenger formula, "Thus says Balak . . ." This formula was used not only by kings to convey their wishes but also by God to declare his will through his prophets, emphasizing the choice that lay before Balaam as to whose mouthpiece he would be.

8. The NIV translation of *'im* as introducing a causal clause—"Since these men have come to call you"—is not supported by any of the standard grammars or lexicons (see, for example, Bruce Waltke and M. O'Connor, *An Introduction to Biblical Hebrew Syntax* [Winona Lake, IN: Eisenbrauns, 1990], 38.4). Most translations, including KJV, NASB, ESV, and NJPS, rightly render it as conditional.

Chapter Twenty-eight: Settled Blessings

1. Jacob Milgrom, *Numbers*, JPS Torah Commentary (Philadelphia: Jewish Publication Society, 1990), p. 194.
2. The Hebrew literally says, "he saw the end [or the extremity; *qaṣeh*] of the people," which could mean either that he only saw a small portion of the camp (so, e.g., NIV) or that he saw all of them. It all depends on whether the extremity in question is the near edge or far edge of the camp. Since the location of the second oracle is explicitly a place where Balaam could only see a part of the people and not all of them (23:13), it seems more likely that for this first oracle he had the whole camp in view.
3. The contrast between a "people" (*am*) and "nations" (*goyim*) is deliberate and significant (Milgrom, *Numbers*, p. 197).
4. Many commentators identify *aššûr* with a little known nomadic tribe rather than the empire of Assyria, on the grounds that Assyria "did not enter the horizon of the Israelites until the eighth century B.C.E." (Milgrom, *Numbers*, p. 209; similarly, Martin Noth, *Numbers: A Commentary*, trans. J. D. Martin, OTL (Philadelphia: Westminster, 1968). However, the result of this substitution is that the prophecy then merely speaks "of the oppression of one small tribal group by another" (Timothy R. Ashley, *Numbers*, NICOT [Grand Rapids, MI: Eerdmans, 1993], p. 508), which makes it a highly anticlimactic ending to what began as a dramatic prophecy of ultimate Israelite victory over the nations. In fact, the Assyrian empire was already in existence as early as the second millennium B.C., and Balaam's prophecy itself claims to be speaking of the distant future (24:17). In such a context, only a great empire fits the bill.
5. Horatio G. Spafford, "It Is Well with My Soul." Spafford knew intimately the experience of which he wrote, since the hymn was written in response to the loss of his wife and children in a shipwreck.
6. Commentators disagree about the identity of Kittim. Some favor the literal designation "Crete"; however, in later times this term expanded to describe any western maritime power, including ultimately the Greeks and the Romans. The assault by Alexander the Great on the Persian Empire, the successors of Assyria, is one plausible fulfillment of the prophecy. See Ashley, *Numbers*, p. 509.
7. I am assuming that "the River" in Numbers 22:5 is the Euphrates, and Balaam was thus summoned from Mesopotamia.

Chapter Twenty-nine: From the Heights to the Depths

1. See Brenda Wall, "Wall and Others v. First Choice: a David and Goliath Story," http://www.holidaytravelwatch.com/Default.aspx?PageId=45 (accessed January 4, 2005).
2. The commitment to Baal of Peor is a more formal step than the NIV ("Israel joined in worshiping the Baal of Peor") suggests. See Timothy R. Ashley, *Numbers*, NICOT (Grand Rapids, MI: Eerdmans, 1993), p. 517.
3. The Targums already sense the tension between verses 4 and 5 and resolve it by changing the Lord's command to match Moses' instruction to the judges. Recent commentators generally recognize that Moses does not, in fact, do what God told him to do. See, e.g., Jacob Milgrom, *Numbers*, JPS Torah Commentary (Philadelphia: Jewish Publication Society, 1990), p. 477; Gordon Wenham, *Numbers*, Tyndale Old Testament Commentary (Downers Grove, IL: InterVarsity Press, 1981), p. 186.
4. The task belonged to Phinehas, not Eleazar, Aaron's son, since by this time Eleazar had taken over from Aaron as High Priest and therefore was not permitted contact with

corpses. In a similar way, Eleazar had acted for Aaron in Numbers 16:39 and 19:2-7. See Milgrom, *Numbers*, p. 215.

5. See, for example, the recent British YouGov survey, which reported that over half of those surveyed rated "Thou shalt not kill" as the most relevant commandment to current circumstances, while "I am the Lord your God; you shall have no other gods before me" was rated least relevant. (Stephen Bates, "O Little Town of . . . Where," *The Guardian*, December 15, 2004; http://www.guardian.co.uk/uk_news/story/0,,1373813,00.html [accessed January 5, 2005]). Similar results were obtained in a 1999 German survey by *Der Spiegel* magazine ("German Survey Shows Few of Ten Commandments Seen as Important," Adventist News Network, February 9, 1999; http://news.adventist.ods.org: 8080/issues/data/918536400/> [accessed January 5, 2005]).

6. Scholars continue to debate the exact nature of the rituals in question, but it seems clear that their goal was in some manner to enhance the life and fertility of those participating in the rituals and of their community. See Milgrom, *Numbers*, pp. 479, 480.

Chapter Thirty: The Next Generation

1. See John Calvin, *Harmony of the Last Four Books of the Pentateuch*, trans. C. W. Bingham (Grand Rapids, MI: Baker, 2003 reprint), 4:256.

2. There is no agreement on exactly what the Urim (which normally appears together with the Thummim) were or how they functioned to indicate the Lord's will. The most popular idea is that they were small objects, perhaps little stones, sticks, or arrows. These could provide a yes or no answer to a particular question, or even a neutral "no answer," depending on the combination in which they were drawn. An alternative speculation is that the Urim and Thummim comprised the twenty-two letters of the Hebrew alphabet, written on little tiles. Any three letters could provide the basis for a meaningful word since Hebrew is built on a series of tri-literal roots, though some combinations would be inherently indecipherable. This would seem to better fit those cases where the answer to their question seems to be something other than yes or no (e.g., 2 Samuel 2:1, where the answer is "Hebron"). On this interpretation the names Urim ("light") and Thummim ("perfect") would stand for the first and last letters of the alphabet: they were the means of determining the A to Z of God's will, the means of receiving "perfect light" (see Jacob Milgrom, *Numbers*, JPS Torah Commentary [Philadelphia: Jewish Publication Society, 1990], p. 486). A third alternative argues that the Urim and Thummim were actually a single gem, the means by which the high priest received "perfect light." Exactly how it functioned is obscure, but it is proposed that it presented a miraculous authenticating light confirming an oracle (see Cornelius Van Dam, *The Urim and Thummim: A Means of Revelation in Ancient Israel* [Winona Lake, IN: Eisenbrauns, 1997]). All of these are speculations, however; all we know for sure is that they provided a means by which the priest could receive guidance from the Lord.

3. Milgrom, *Numbers*, p. 235.

Chapter Thirty-one: Communion with God

1. Robert C. Fuller, *Spiritual, but Not Religious: Understanding Unchurched America* (Oxford: Oxford University Press, 2001).

2. Jacob Milgrom, *Numbers*, JPS Torah Commentary (Philadelphia: Jewish Publication Society, 1990), p. 237.

3. Jacob Milgrom, *Leviticus 1—16*, Anchor Bible (New York: Doubleday, 1991), p. 176.

4. Gordon Wenham, *Leviticus*, NICOT (Grand Rapids: Eerdmans, 1979), p. 63.

5. It is no coincidence that this declaration is immediately followed in Matthew's Gospel by a dispute over the Sabbath.

Chapter Thirty-two: Cross My Heart, Hope to Die

1. On these, see Jacob Milgrom, *Numbers*, JPS Torah Commentary (Philadelphia: Jewish Publication Society, 1990), pp. 488, 489.

2. Claus Westermann, *Praise and Lament in the Psalms*, trans. K. R. Crim and R. N. Soulen (Atlanta: John Knox, 1981), p. 77.
3. See ibid., p. 79.
4. Mary Douglas, *In the Wilderness* (Oxford: Oxford University Press, 2001), pp. 160, 161.

Chapter Thirty-three: Judgment and Atonement

1. See Gian B. Conte, *Latin Literature: A History*, trans. J. B. Solodow (Baltimore: Johns Hopkins, 1994), p. 292.
2. This applies even to cases such as 1 Samuel 15. Although that war was several generations after the conquest, the rationale for it was "what Amalek did to Israel in opposing them on the way when they came up out of Egypt" (v. 2). In a similar way, the holy war of the Jews against their enemies in Esther 9 has its roots in the same ancient enmity since Haman is himself an Agagite (3:1), a descendant of the Amalekite King Agag in 1 Samuel 15.
3. Many commentators think God was testing his people's faith by requiring a small force to be sent into battle (e.g. John Calvin, *Harmony of the Last Four Books of the Pentateuch*, trans. C. W. Bingham [Grand Rapids, MI: Baker, 2003 reprint], 4:265, 266). It is certainly true that less resources were committed than usual, but 12,000 is still a very substantial force in the ancient world, significantly more than the 3,000 that Joshua sent against Ai (Joshua 7:4), or Gideon's 300 men (Judges 7:6). In fact, it is larger than the army that God deemed too large for Gideon to take into battle (Judges 7:3) and the same size as the full-scale army that was sent against the inhabitants of Jabesh-gilead (Judges 21:10; compare also 2 Samuel 17:1). The focus seems not so much on the small size of the army but on its select nature, with equal numbers from each tribe (Jacob Milgrom, *Numbers*, JPS Torah Commentary [Philadelphia: Jewish Publication Society, 1990], p. 256).
4. This is especially true when the spoil is considered on a per capita basis, since the 49.8 percent is divided among only 12,000 men, whereas the 48 percent is divided among the much larger remaining community. In terms of the sheep and goats, for example, the soldiers might expect twenty-eight animals each, whereas the remaining members of the community would average roughly 0.56 animals per adult male. In comparison, the Levites, on behalf of the Lord, would receive 0.32 sheep and goats per male (one month old and upward).

Chapter Thirty-four: The Problem of Having Too Much

1. In fact, the parallels between this narrative and Abram and Lot's experience in Genesis 13 are profound. There too, the initial cause of separation between Abraham and Lot was the abundance of the cattle with which God had blessed them (Genesis 13:2). This led to contention between Abram and Lot's herdsmen, and, ultimately, a separation between them. Given first choice, Lot chose with his eyes, selecting essentially the same area that would later attract the Reubenites and Gadites, the Transjordanian plain east of the Jordan, to the east and south of Bethel (see Genesis 13:10, 11). The area Lot saw east from Bethel, extending south to Zoar at the southern end of the Dead Sea, certainly encompassed the area of Heshbon and Dibon, along with the other less well-known cities mentioned in Numbers 32:3.
2. C. S. Lewis, *The Weight of Glory and Other Addresses* (Grand Rapids, MI: Eerdmans, 1965), pp. 1, 2.
3. Jacob Milgrom, *Numbers*, JPS Torah Commentary (Philadelphia: Jewish Publication Society, 1990), p. 270.

Chapter Thirty-five: Pilgrim People

1. John Sailhamer, *The Pentateuch as Narrative* (Grand Rapids, MI: Zondervan, 1992), p. 419.
2. I am indebted to my intern, Joel Treick, for this description.
3. Jacob Milgrom, *Numbers*, JPS Torah Commentary (Philadelphia: Jewish Publication Society, 1990), p. 277.

4. Timothy R. Ashley notes the comparison with the forty-two generations in the genealogy of Jesus, which are ordered as three sets of fourteen, from Abraham to David, from David to the exile, and from the exile to the coming of Christ (*Numbers*, NICOT [Grand Rapids, MI: Eerdmans, 1993], p. 624).

5. Gordon J. Keddie, *According to Promise* (Darlington, UK: Evangelical Press, 1992), p. 206. Gordon Wenham has a much more complicated analysis of the numerical patterns here; yet it seems difficult to sustain his analysis consistently through the entire list (*Numbers*, Tyndale Old Testament Commentary [Downers Grove, IL: InterVarsity Press, 1981], pp. 217, 218). It seems better to limit speculation to the more obvious pattern.

Chapter Thirty-six: Cities of Grace

1. For the suggestion that Jacob's prophecies are being worked out in the book of Numbers, see Mary Douglas, *In the Wilderness* (Oxford: Oxford University Press, 2001), pp. 185-195, although she takes the idea in a different direction.

2. Jacob Milgrom, *Numbers*, JPS Torah Commentary (Philadelphia: Jewish Publication Society, 1990), p. 291.

3. *Ibid.*

4. *Ibid.*, p. 510.

5. On the division into moral, civil, and ceremonial laws, see my comments on Numbers 18:8-32 (Chapter 23 of this book).

6. See John Murray, *Principles of Conduct* (Grand Rapids, MI: Eerdmans, 1957), pp. 109-113.

Chapter Thirty-seven: Walking the Ridgeline

1. James Philip says, "One almost finds oneself wishing that the final chapter of the Book of Numbers had been more in the nature of a climax to the book" (*Numbers*, Mastering the Old Testament [Dallas: Word, 1987], p. 356).

2. Timothy R. Ashley, *Numbers*, NICOT (Grand Rapids, MI: Eerdmans, 1993), p. 659.

3. The phrase comes from Tom Brokaw's description of the generation of American citizens who came of age during the Great Depression and the Second World War and went on to build modern America (see *The Greatest Generation* [New York: Random House, 1998]).

4. Mary Douglas, *In the Wilderness* (Oxford: Oxford University Press, 2001), p. 246.

5. On this theme, see H.G.M. Williamson, *Israel in the Books of Chronicles* (Cambridge: Cambridge University Press, 1977).

Scripture Index

General Index

Index of
Sermon Illustrations

The Bible

Like sports and literature, Scripture is multi-layered and complex, 15-16

Most find accounting dull, and we react similarly to the censuses and lists of numbers in the Bible, though they're spiritually profitable, 25

Numbers are more important to most of us than we realize (in sports, the Dow Jones Index, computer capabilities, etc.), and especially the numbers in the Bible, 26

Commitment

Edmund Clowney quotation on our wanting to keep God at a distance—if he gets too close, that might be inconvenient in our business deals, entertainment, etc., 39

Both 1960s hippies and Old-Testament era Nazirites abstained from wine and let their hair grow long, but for very different reasons, 77

Pioneer missionaries who gave up much and Christian martyrs contrast sharply with our self-protective attitudes, 84

The trouble with living sacrifices is, they keep crawling off the altar, 104

Mary Slessor took the gospel to cannibalistic tribes unafraid because she knew God was with her, 140

Isaac Watts hymn: "Love so amazing, so divine, demands my soul, my life, my all," 267

William Cowper in "God Moves in a Mysterious Way": "Ye fearful saints, fresh courage take," 277

Just as in human relationships many seek communion without commitment, many want God on their terms, not his, 310

Children cross their fingers so they don't have to keep their promise, and we live in a culture where faithfulness is in short supply, 321

Community

Fellowship and food are useful tools in building spiritual community, 237

Divine Provision

Martina McBride song "I Am So Blessed" reminds us of God's blessings, 87

Three children adopted from other countries become part of God's covenant, illustrating God's grace extended to outsiders, 126

John Newton's tombstone: "once an infidel . . . by the rich mercy of our Lord . . . pardoned," 161-162

Hymn: "Christ . . . hath shed His own blood for my soul," 286

Giving thanks for a meal is sometimes called "saying grace," and indeed all we have is due to God's grace, 355

Giving

Christmas song "The Twelve Days of Christmas" illustrates our giving many gifts to God, 97

God

Edmund Clowney quotation on our wanting to keep God at a distance—if he gets too close, that might be inconvenient in our business deals, entertainment, etc., 39

Just as counselees often do not see things as they really are, many do not see God as he really is, 189

A modern church allows people to enjoy God in a casual atmosphere, going light on the fear of God, 219

Thomas Manton: Satan only gives half of the truth about God—yes, he is a consuming fire, but also a God of mercy, 221

God's Presence

A kindergartner begging, "Mom, please come with me" reminds us how much we need the Lord to be with us, 129

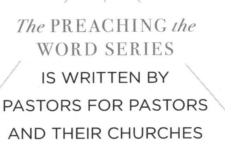